A GAME TAKEN SERIOUSLY

THE FOUNDATIONS OF YORKSHIRE'S CRICKETING POWER

Jeremy Lonsdale

CONTENTS

FOREWORD

The county of Yorkshire is one of the most successful sporting regions in the world. It has produced many great footballers, cricketers, rugby players (of two codes), cyclists, athletes and swimmers, amongst others. During the 2012 Olympics, it did not go unnoticed in Yorkshire that, had the county competed on its own, it would have been high up in the overall medals table.[1] Many of Yorkshire's finest sporting heroes have been seen as 'larger than life' characters, none more so than its cricketers. It is, therefore, not surprising that some have argued that these men and the club they represented, have played a major role in promoting the identity of the county of Yorkshire, as well as shaping perceptions held of it by others. Thus, cricketing success and the way it was achieved have led followers of the game in the county to see 'in their team much of what they wanted to believe about themselves', as well as find confirmation 'that Yorkshire played the game 'properly', seriously.'[2]

For those like the author – born since the start of the 1960s – it can sometimes be hard to grasp the scale of Yorkshire County Cricket Club's domination of English cricket in the first half of the 20th century, given that until recently so much of the last four decades has been characterised by, at best, patchy performances. Changes in the make-up of the county's population, the dominance of football in the media, the precedence given to international cricket, and the absence of the county game from terrestrial television have all helped to alter the place and significance of cricket in contemporary life in Yorkshire.

Nevertheless, a look at the record books will confirm that Yorkshire County Cricket Club is the most successful club in English cricket, and this book examines the foundations of that success back when it started in the 19th century. During that time, I have focused specifically on the period between 1822 and 1893, two turning points in the game's history in the county. The year 1822 saw the opening of the first purpose-built commercial cricket ground in Yorkshire – at Darnall in Sheffield. In 1893, a newly reorganised Yorkshire County Cricket Club won the county championship and began a period of success which went on (with some gaps) until the late 1960s.

My argument is that it is during this period of 70 years that the foundations for later success were laid, and that these foundations were complex, wide-ranging and had their roots off the field, as much as on it. Success for Yorkshire County Cricket Club in 1893 was not just down to the men who made it to the first team. Many others had appeared for the county over several decades beforehand to get them to that position. A larger group just missed out on selection, either not being chosen after appearing in trials, or being unable to take the risk of leaving more secure employment. Many more played club cricket in an increasingly competitive programme of games, and were either not noticed, or were simply not considered talented enough for the first-class level. Thousands more turned out for clubs representing towns and villages, schools and workplaces, churches and mechanics' institutes, and in ad hoc matches for teams which disappeared quickly, often without ever achieving any success.

The Yorkshire side was thus at the summit of a pyramid of cricket across the county which had a very wide human base and which needs to be examined in order to understand how cricket developed in the region. In his history of 18th century cricket in southern England, Underdown argued that 'Aristocratic cricket was merely the tip of an iceberg, and if we are to understand the game we need to swim deeper and discover what was going on in Sussex villages such as Hurstpierpoint and East Hoathly in the fifty years or so before Hambledon reached its pinnacle of glory.'[3] Similarly, we need to scrutinise developments in the local game in Yorkshire in order to understand the forces that shaped the elite county game. For this reason, this book takes a very broad look at what I have called the foundations of Yorkshire's cricketing power. The story culminates in the establishment for the first time of a truly broad-based county club in the early 1890s, but before that, it considers the pieces that had to fall into place for such an organisation to emerge, and examines how the obstacles to success were overcome.

It is also broad in that I have deliberately taken a three-Ridings perspective of developments. Most considerations of Yorkshire cricket inevitably tend to focus on the West Riding, the most populous area, where the majority of the county cricket club's games have been played, and from where the bulk of the players have been drawn. However, as we will see, particularly in Chapters 3 and 10, stepping back and considering how the game developed differently in the individual Ridings sheds light on the growth of Yorkshire cricket as a whole, and helps to explain why it took until the 1890s for a more representative county club to take shape. I have also tried to highlight the continuity between local and county cricket, rather than see the former, especially the highly competitive league cricket that grew up from the 1890s, as 'a popular alternative to the elite county or "first-class" game', as some have depicted it.[4] In the period under consideration, players slipped between the different levels of the game too easily for them to be seen as distinct or antagonistic cultures.

This book has drawn on a number of sources. Crucial has been the ability to search thousands of newspapers from the entire period, initially at the British Newspaper Library in Colindale, but more recently through the excellent British Newspapers Archive at www.britishnewspaperarchive.co.uk. Without this on-line resource, numerous small references to cricket in 19th century Yorkshire would never have been spotted. As is increasingly clear, the digitisation of such material is of huge significance for those wanting to examine the early days of grass-roots sport.[5] What the newspapers provide is a sense of the importance of cricket in Victorian society, a place it is unlikely ever to reclaim. The early minute books of Yorkshire County Cricket Club were particularly helpful for understanding developments in the 1860s and the 1870s, and I also made use of the many books and articles listed in the bibliography.

This is not a history of Yorkshire County Cricket Club and no single volume can ever capture the full story of Yorkshire cricket. Instead, the purpose of this book is to show how in the 19th century the people of all parts of the county of Yorkshire embraced cricket and in many different ways – some small, some more significant – provided the energy, drive and talent which together contributed to the creation of a powerful sporting force. They did so against a background of considerable social, economic and political turmoil. Rapid industrialisation, urbanisation and fluctuating economic performance created miserable living and working conditions for many across the county. At the same time, it expanded the horizons of a considerable number of the same people, and led to improved communications, education and opportunities. It also produced the economic and cultural environment in which people came together to pursue a wider range of leisure interests, and to create many of the foundations of our modern society. The kind of cricket that developed in this dynamic setting took on particular characteristics which are discussed in this book. They are neatly summarised in the advice given to the young Wilfred Rhodes after two seasons as a professional in Galashiels in Scotland. Thanked for his contribution, the great all-rounder was advised that there was nothing more for a player of his calibre in the town. Instead, he has told, 'Go back to Yorkshire, where they take the game seriously.'[6]

Jeremy Lonsdale

October 2016

CHAPTER ONE

A NEW BEGINNING

Just after midday on 23 August 1893, the Yorkshire batsman J.T.Brown cut Fred Martin to the boundary to score the runs needed for an eight-wicket victory over Kent. This led to 'rare enthusiasm' as the outcome meant that, even if Yorkshire lost their final game and other matches went in Lancashire's favour, their rivals could only equal Yorkshire's position in the county cricket championship. By 4.30pm, however, the rain that had prevented play at Lord's ceased and Lancashire went on to lose by seven wickets, with ten minutes' play left. Yorkshire were now in an unassailable position in the table.[7] This triumph was topped off a few days later against Sussex with what the *Sheffield Daily Telegraph* called, 'perhaps their most brilliant performance of the season.' Elated, the paper announced 'Yorkshire have become rejuvenated.'[8]

The season was an undoubted triumph for the county side which the basic facts only start to demonstrate. In total, Yorkshire played 16 championship matches, won 12, drew one and lost three. They started with five straight wins – against Gloucestershire, Sussex, Middlesex, Surrey (when 31 wickets fell in five hours for 280 runs) and Somerset. This generated praise from the Yorkshire press, and in June the *Leeds Mercury* commented optimistically that it looked likely that the side 'will earn more distinction in county cricket this summer than has fallen to their lot for a considerable time.'[9] The team then suffered heavy defeats by Lancashire and Surrey at the end of June (and lost by nine wickets against a 'second-class' county, Warwickshire), before drawing the following game with Nottinghamshire. They then returned to form with four further victories. A final defeat came against Lancashire in early August, but was followed by the necessary wins against Middlesex and Kent. Looking back, *Lillywhite's Cricketers' Annual* was full of praise, concluding that the team's cricket 'was just of the kind to please the public, bright, vigorous, and with plenty of go in it. Hence their success was, and deservedly, popular.'[10]

In his biography of the great Yorkshire captain, Lord Hawke, Coldham suggested that for the first time in years Yorkshire approached the season of 1893 with 'genuine optimism.' In fact, the county's success was particularly satisfying, not only because it had been long awaited, but also because it had been unexpected. The 1892 season had been disappointing, as J.B.Wostinholm (club Secretary between 1864 and 1902) admitted at the first annual meeting of the recently reorganised county club in March 1893.[11] Although an improvement on 1891, there was reportedly 'a great falling off in the play' in the second half of the season, and but for the weather at Nottingham and Taunton the side would probably not have ended with an equal number of wins and losses.[12] Much of the county's press was also fairly gloomy in 1893. Despite early successes, the *Leeds Mercury* suggested that there was 'hardly the material in the eleven to make the first or even the second place in the county competition a probability, but we see no reason why the side should not play a creditable part.'[13] As a result, looking back 10 years later, the county historian, Rev.R.S.Holmes, observed that no one had been prepared for 'the wonderful transformation in 1893 in the fortunes of Yorkshire cricket.'[14]

At the beginning of the summer, there had in fact seemed to be several obstacles to success. Before the cricket had started, the club announced that Lord Hawke would not be available due an extended stay in India, where he had taken a side of amateurs over the winter of 1892/93. Although his performances on the field were often unimpressive, his leadership since 1883 was widely regarded as essential to the club's effectiveness. As it turned out, however, his stay in India was shortened by illness and he eventually played regularly from the start of July, batting 15 times but scoring just 206 runs.[15] There were other glaring weaknesses in the side, which few at the start of the season expected could be overcome. A report read out at the meeting of the county club in March 1893 stated that the bowling attack urgently needed strengthening.[16] The *Leeds Mercury* agreed, suggesting that winning the championship was a 'remarkable refutation' of the view of some Yorkshire officials that there was a dearth of good players in the county.[17] No new men had been added to the side that came sixth in 1892, and in an interview in September 1893, Arthur Sellers commented that, at the start of the season, there had even been rumours of players leaving.[18] The question of how to handle amateurs also remained an issue. Sellers again told 'Old Ebor' (the journalist, A.W.Pullin) he was unsure how often he would get a game since the County Committee had indicated that they did not want players making occasional appearances.[19] Other amateurs, F.S.Jackson (playing for Cambridge University), E.Smith (teaching at Elstree School) and R.W.Frank were also not expected to be available very often.

A third factor was that, off the field, over the winter, the long-running dispute between representatives of clubs in different parts of the county, which had so hampered the creation of a unified county club since the 1860s, did not appear to have ended, despite the reorganisation that had been agreed. At the end of January 1893, meetings of members in the districts of Yorkshire County Cricket Club took place to elect representatives on the new county committee. At a meeting of Skipton and Keighley members, there was controversy when several men turned up who had not joined the club by the cut-off date for being eligible to vote, and some who had voted previously in Bradford district. At the Leeds meeting 'considerable dissatisfaction was expressed at the meagreness of the notice convening the meeting, some of those present having only heard of it casually and quite unofficially.' The absence of J.B.Wostinholm was also seen as an affront – as a paid official, many thought he ought to have attended – and the meeting was adjourned so that he could be present.[20] At Dewsbury, there were complaints that the town had been overlooked in respect of first-class fixtures for the coming year, while at the second Leeds meeting there was criticism of the decision to pay over £700 to the Sheffield club, rather than share it out.[21]

Despite these obstacles, Yorkshire did become the champion county of 1893 and was widely seen to have deserved it. Contemporaries put this success down to a number of factors. The *Sheffield Daily Telegraph* saw it as the culmination of years of effort and not a task accomplished in a single season. It was also considered 'testimony to the sterner discipline, the more habitual self-control, of the professional of to-day as compared with his immediate predecessor.'[22] And *James Lillywhite's Cricketers' Annual* for 1894 commented that no-one could argue that Yorkshire's success was a fluke, remarking that, on the contrary:

> the position they gained was the out-come of really good and consistent allround cricket....Of run-getters there was no lack, with batsmen capable of getting runs to the last man. The out cricket too was decidedly above the average. There was infinite variety in the bowling, and the bowlers moreover could most of them bat.[23]

A number of other observers noted that everyone had chipped in and success had not been dependent on a few stars. Amongst the batsmen, no-one averaged over 30 in all matches. Brown scored the most runs – 1,141 – and Wainwright took the most wickets – 143 – but there was little high scoring. Of 43 centuries completed in the English season, only four were made by Yorkshire batsmen. In total, Yorkshire scored around 4,600 runs in the season while Middlesex, Sussex and Nottinghamshire – below them in the table – all made over 6,000. The team's average per wicket was just over 19, while Nottinghamshire's was 24. Instead, it was on the bowling front that the success was secured. Six bowlers averaged under 17, and against Yorkshire, teams scored just 14 runs per wicket, compared with 27 against Sussex.[24]

The Daily News argued that Yorkshire's allround strength had been the secret and, except for F.S.Jackson who did not appear often, there was no-one 'of quite the first rank' as a batsman. It added that the bowling had been 'excellent' and the fielding 'altogether exceptional in its smartness and accuracy.'[25] Lord Hawke, interviewed in early September in the splendour of the Grand Hotel, Scarborough, took a similar view, emphasising that matches had been won by bowling and fielding.[26] Together, the whole team was considered greater than the sum of the parts, and the experienced George Hearne of Kent commented that he could not remember a stronger Yorkshire side.[27] Others thought it was a matter of attitude. *Lillywhite's* noted an 'evident *esprit de corps*, a cohesion which was certainly not noticeable in some of the county elevens even of older standing.' There was, it added, a 'feeling of self-reliance' which had led to a good team performance.[28] Hawke too considered the players were 'young and steady, and very keen', as well as 'pleasant to play with.'[29] The fact that all were Yorkshire-born was also commented upon favourably by many within the county.

Despite all this team spirit, some commentators nevertheless picked out specific individuals and put the county's success down to the recent introduction of certain young players, which had had a 'wonderfully reviving effect.'[30] Looking back, Coldham too suggested that, during the course of the season, George Hirst, who had played first in 1889 but had not established himself until 1892, became one of 'the most feared bowlers in the land.'[31] In fact, he proved a great success with both bat and ball, and was also very popular despite being described by one older professional as the 'quietest lad' they had ever had in the team.[32] Arthur Sellers scored the bulk of his career first-class runs during the summer of 1893, becoming 'one of the best amateur batsmen north of the Trent'.[33] J.T.Brown also started the season as a novice, having missed out on opportunities the year before through ill-health, but in 1893 his batting 'clicked.'[34] In addition, even after 20 years in the side, George Ulyett's performances pleased the journalist 'Old Ebor', despite some committee members being keen to drop him.[35] Less positively, Lord Hawke's position was the subject of some discussion, and 'Old Ebor' wrote, 'It is no secret that next season Mr Jackson will, in all probability, be asked to accept the captaincy of the Yorkshire Eleven. Lord Hawke is scarcely good enough in form for the position with a team of such all round excellence as Yorkshire.'[36]

As a result, in Coldham's view, whilst in 1892 'Hawke's young lions had whimpered their last, in 1893 they learned to roar and English cricket trembled. The honour and glory that had bled from Yorkshire cricket in the late 1880s and early 1890s now came flooding back.'[37] Such success caused considerable joy in the county. In June, the victory over Middlesex at Lord's was met with 'remarkable enthusiasm in local cricketing circles.' [38] In early August, at a fireworks exhibition at the end of a Bank Holiday event at the Botanical Gardens in Sheffield, one display contained the words 'Cricket 1893, Well Done Yorkshire', which was met with cheers.[39] Then, after Yorkshire had beaten Middlesex at Bradford, the *Sheffield Daily Telegraph* reported that there was 'feverish interest' in the remaining county games.[40] Later in the summer, 'Old Ebor' enthused that he could not remember:

> any occasion in modern cricket history in Yorkshire in which there was such general eagerness shown to learn the results of two cricket games as was the case on Wednesday last.....When the result was known, and it was found that Lancashire had been beaten, and the race was really over, the satisfaction felt by the public – and you could hear it in trams, trains and everywhere – was unbounded.[41]

A turning point?

Of course those celebrating the success of 1893 could not have known whether it was to be just a one-off triumph, and would probably not have imagined that it was the start of a glorious period of sporting success. Writing in 1904, Holmes commented 'For the following ten seasons, starting with 1893, Yorkshire's supremacy was scarcely once in peril, new batsmen and bowlers of the first rank appearing from time to time during this eventful decade.'[42] Between 1893 and 1902, they won the county championship six times, and over the 43 seasons to the Second World War, 21 times and were runners-up on another seven occasions. They were only outside the top three positions seven times. Then, after a barren period in the 1950s, the club also won the county championship seven times between 1959 and 1968.[43]

Thus, 1893 saw the emergence of one of the great sporting organisations. Yet there was nothing inevitable about the way in which the game developed or grew in popularity in the Victorian era, and in fact cricket in Yorkshire was characterised by patchy development in different parts of the county, after a slow start compared with much of the south of England. There were also ups and downs in its popularity throughout the century, contingent on a range of social and economic factors, and it also had to contend with strong competition at various times from other sports such as rugby, football and tennis, and from activities such as the rifle volunteers.

The performances of the county side on the field were also subject to considerable fluctuation. In an article in early 1893, *The Cricket Field* considered in detail Yorkshire's very mixed history in the three decades after the county club's formation in 1863. It noted the problems of the initial period when 'York, Sheffield and Bradford were each clamouring for the supreme control of the county's affairs' and when the five professionals refused to play against Surrey (discussed in Chapter 10). George Freeman and Tom Emmett then emerged as match-winners, and, between 1867 and 1871, Yorkshire 'could point to the fine results of 22 wins against only six defeats.' The article then divided the period from 1872 to 1893 into three seven-year blocks. From 1872 to 1878, there were 28 defeats and 36 victories, the county struggling in particular against Nottinghamshire and Gloucestershire, but dominating games with Surrey and

Sussex. The next seven years – between 1879 and 1885 – were considered at that time perhaps 'the most brilliant part of Yorkshire's career, sensations cropping up in such profusion as to make any selection a difficult matter.' Results were mixed with Nottinghamshire and Lancashire, but they lost only three times against Middlesex and Surrey, defeated Gloucestershire and Kent twice as often as they were beaten, and won three times as many games against Sussex as they lost.

The final seven-year period to 1892 was not a happy one. The county lost on 12 occasions to Surrey, seven to Lancashire and six to Middlesex. Results were only better against Sussex, Derbyshire and Gloucestershire.[44] These years were characterised by failure, discord, ill-directed efforts to improve, and an inability or unwillingness to harness the talents of the entire county. In 1891, *Lillywhite*'s commented very generously that Yorkshire cricket was 'to say the least of it, an uncertain quantity' and argued that little could be said by an impartial chronicler in praise.[45] The side lost 11 out of 16 games in 1889 and 11 out of 17 games in 1891, whilst across the whole of 1891 and 1892 combined, they won just 11 out of 36 matches. Yorkshire cricket was in crisis.

In contrast, the years after 1893 saw a significant change in performance. Whereas between 1883 and 1892, Yorkshire played 193 games and won only 36%, in the following 10 seasons they played 306 matches and won well over half. Defeats fell from 33% to 15% over the same period.[46] The transition in Yorkshire cricket in the early 1890s can also be seen in terms of the make-up of the county side. Names that had characterised the team since the 1870s and 1880s disappeared (not necessarily happily), and in their place were those whose reputations would resonate through Yorkshire cricket history for the next decade and beyond. Bates (202 games), Peate (154) and Grimshaw (125) played for the last time in 1887, while Joe Hunter (143) and Tom Emmett (299) followed in 1888. The next year, Preston (79) made his last appearance, followed in 1890 by Lee (105). The careers of two of the most significant figures of the period – Ulyett (who made 355 appearances) and Hall (275) – ended slightly later, in 1893 and 1894 respectively, but both were clearly on their way out after heroic service.

In their place, almost an entire side of talented players made their first appearances between 1888 and 1891. The 1888 season saw David Hunter, Moorhouse, Smith and Wainwright take the field for the first time; between them they played for Yorkshire on 1,229 occasions. In 1889, J.T.Brown (of Driffield) was first tried (345 games) and in 1890, F.S.Jackson (207). Hirst and Tunnicliffe (717 and 472 games respectively) began their careers in 1891. Denton – who appeared 676 times – made his debut in 1894. Only a few players – Lord Hawke, Bobby Peel and Bobby Moorhouse – straddled the divide of 1893 to any great degree.[47] The make-up of the county eleven had been transformed in a short period.

Yet the improvements in performances on the field and the changes in the composition of the county XI were just the most visible signs of a transformation in cricket more generally in Yorkshire. The players who started to make their names did not appear from nowhere. They were nurtured in towns and villages throughout the county, and were only the best of the thousands who played the game in hundreds of clubs on weekday evenings and at weekends on grounds of varying quality, and for clubs which had developed through the efforts of an ever wider group of people. By 1893, a series of strands had fallen into place, which were the foundations for several decades of cricketing success. It is worth briefly considering some of these strands as they form the substance of this book.

Firstly, there was a new seriousness about the county club, with the changes to the organisation seen by many as a major contributory factor. In April 1893, 'Old Ebor' wrote in *Athletic News* that:

> The movement for reorganising the committee has had its influence in stimulating public interest, and I firmly believe that in the early time to come the management and organisation of the county's cricket will become as popular and generally interesting as is now the case with the Football Union.[48]

Lord Hawke's efforts to enforce greater discipline on and off the field also ensured that the game was taken more seriously. Coldham commented that 'In cutting out the dead wood and axing disruptive elements Hawke had cleared the way for a wealth of young talent to come into the county side.'[49] In addition, Yorkshire's interests came first and, although it led to some unhappiness elsewhere, when Jackson chose to play for Yorkshire rather than for England against Australia at Old Trafford in 1893, and the county refused to release Peel and Wainwright to the Test side, the moves were widely supported by Yorkshire cricket followers.[50]

The club also appeared to have better arrangements for identifying and developing new players. In 1893, 50 names were put forward to play in the Colts games, 'proof of the increased interest which is being taken in county cricket under the new scheme of management' according to the *Yorkshire Evening Post*.[51] So many applied that the format of the games was changed, with two teams of Colts playing each other at Dewsbury and Barnsley, and the pick of the players subsequently taking on Nottinghamshire Colts. Having a proactive approach was seen as increasingly necessary, not only to help identify new talent, but also to counter efforts being made by other counties such as Surrey to invite young Yorkshire players to trials. A drift of Yorkshire-qualified players to Lancashire also caused concern, and Tom Wardall taking up a professional position across the Pennines was seen as a risk, as it was considered he would be 'greedily taken up in Lancashire' if Yorkshire dropped him.[52] 'Old Ebor' reported approvingly that the first fruit of the new arrangements was the subsidising of the wages of four young players by the county committee – W.Ringrose, T.Foster, G.Mitchell and W.Fletcher. This retained them for the county if they were needed; otherwise the committee wanted them to play in the West Riding League.[53]

Despite this apparent progress, there was still disquiet. The *Leeds Mercury* noted that Sheffield had given way to reforms with good grace, but added that there had still been a lot of talk at Headingley during the Sussex game that control remained in 'old hands', and some new members were not impressed that committee meetings were still held in Sheffield during county games.[54] The summer also saw animosity over the state of the wickets, initially at Bramall Lane, and subsequently, at Headingley. What was dubbed as 'the battle of the pitches' – well-publicised complaints about the adequacy of the wickets – seemed to be a continuation of the inter-town differences that had stretched back decades.[55] Newspapers traded blows. In June 1893, at the height of the controversy over the Bramall Lane wicket, the *Hull Daily Mail* provocatively stated:

> Bramhall Lane [sic] is bad, whatever folk 'fra Sheffield' may say. Sheffield is surly and selfish in matters of cricket – somewhat of a boar with a sore head. She must have most of the matches and the pick of the important ones and yet her cricket ground is hardly good enough for golf. [56]

In August, 'Old Ebor' was accused of being unduly negative about the role of Sheffield, with the *Evening Telegraph* arguing that it was the town's efforts that had put Yorkshire 'top of the tree before some of the West Riding towns had begun to emerge from their native obscurity in cricket matters.'[57] Internal rivalry rumbled on, but other signs were good that the club was on the up, and from 1893, membership grew – 227 new members were elected in the first three months of 1894, 594 in 1895, 838 in 1896 and 976 in 1897.[58]

Secondly, the strong and competitive club cricket that had developed in the county acted as a fruitful training ground for potential players. In the 1880s, a number of cup competitions were initiated, with the Heavy Woollen Challenge 'that most exciting of all cricket contests', according to the *Leeds Mercury*.[59] In North Yorkshire and Durham, the Cleveland and Teesside Cricket Association was established in 1886 and organised a knock-out competition for the Cleveland Cup.[60] In January 1893, the draw for the York and District Challenge Cup competition was held, with 'no signs of interest falling off'[61], while Londesborough Park were proud holders of the Challenge Cup competed for by clubs in the North and East Ridings.[62]

Such contests generated excitement for a while, but inevitably teams were knocked out and returned to play routine games which attracted less interest. The response was the development of league cricket designed both to improve the standard of play as well as increase spectator interest. As one author has put it, 'if a more competitive type of cricket was played, necessary finance could be generated from a larger membership.'[63] Some clubs disliked the move, and were slower to participate, but even the traditionalist, R.S.Holmes, noted in his 1904 Yorkshire history that as league cricket 'is probably only second in importance and interest to county cricket, and as it is intimately connected with it (our young county cricketers come from the leagues), a brief space may appropriately be devoted to it in this work.'[64]

A third factor was the huge level of interest shown in the sport, and the desire of many to play and watch. Successive generations showed ever more interest, and enthusiasm built up, particularly from the 1860s onwards, so that there were numerous well-organised clubs with excellent facilities and long fixture lists. On 22 April 1893, for example, the *Leeds Mercury* listed 94 games in its area – presumably involving more than 2,000 players.[65] The following Monday, the paper was able to report that the weather had been perfect for the start of the season and included two columns of detailed match scores.[66] A couple of weeks later, the same paper listed 210 matches (presumably involving over 4,600 individuals).[67] The edition of 1 May reported the scores of matches in seven leagues.[68]

On 4 May, the *Hull Daily Mail* (serving an area with a smaller population) printed the teams for 44 matches to take place the following Saturday.[69] The same weekend, the *Huddersfield Chronicle* reported 22 matches in its area, mostly in the Huddersfield and District League and the Alliance.[70] There were substantial crowds for many such games and 'Old Ebor' noted that 'The West Yorkshire League games produced good gates and unlimited interest.'[71] Enthusiasm was also seen off the field of play as clubs held the annual general meetings, fund-raising events and concerts over the winter.[72]

A fourth factor which developed and sustained this enthusiasm, was the authoritative press which provided regular and extensive news of the doings of local clubs, as well as cricket more generally. Over the winter, the papers kept cricket visible by reporting on the progress of Lord Hawke's team in India and then speculated on the likely composition of the Australian touring party to England. As spring approached, they included news of prospects for the coming season. Long columns in the *Leeds Mercury*, for example, set out details of players moving between local sides and considered their prospects for the year ahead. The papers included columns of 'Cricket Notes', reporting on the doings of clubs and the county team, as well as printing national cricket stories.[73] The *Sheffield Daily Telegraph* had its 'Sporting Gossip' section with short news items, and 'Old Ebor' wrote his regular column on Yorkshire cricket in the *Yorkshire Evening Post*. His inside knowledge and understanding of the game showed in the insightful and gossipy columns which appeared each Monday.[74] The same paper included a series called 'Cricket Portraits' of local cricketers, accompanied by small sketches.[75] The press made cricketers heroes and increasingly reported in ways which brought them closer to the followers of the game.

Once the season was under way, the scores of matches appeared regularly, with papers giving detailed coverage on the performance of local clubs, and providing full reports of first-class cricket matches. The *Sheffield Daily Telegraph* and the *Leeds Mercury* often included six or seven columns of county and local scores and discussion, particularly on a Monday when the weekend's games were considered. The Saturday edition of the *Yorkshire Evening Post* included full scores of the day's games across several leagues, with a six o'clock updated edition containing details at close of play for many matches. Late editions of the *Hull Daily Mail* with cricket scores were available as far away as Driffield every evening. And in Middlesbrough, a cricket edition of the *North-Eastern Daily Gazette* was on sale at 8 pm.[76]

League cricket began to dominate press coverage of local cricket, and 'Old Ebor' warned that what he described as 'ordinary' cricket could only be dealt with briefly.[77] The updated tables of several competitions were included in many of the papers on a weekly basis.[78] A close relationship between league cricket and the press grew up, to the extent that in Huddersfield in 1891, representatives of the local papers were included on the sub-committee established to decide which clubs should form the new Huddersfield League.[79] Enthusiasm for the competitive league cricket helped sell papers, whilst the reporting of matches in the papers helped attract spectators. Papers and clubs thus had a mutual interest in ensuring coverage of their games.

The papers contained ever more material for the cricket follower. The *Yorkshire Evening Post* included the Yorkshire county averages throughout the season. The performances of star players were reported with enthusiasm – George Hirst's emergence, for example, featuring in the columns of the *Huddersfield Chronicle* – while the claims of local runmakers to a place in the Yorkshire XI were pressed with vigour. On a more sombre note, readers were also reminded of the problems that could befall some of the county stars of the past and present. In January 1893, it was reported that Irwin Grimshaw had been charged with drunkenness, assaulting a police officer and doing damage to a police uniform.[80] And Bobby Peel – whose greatest days and biggest problems were still ahead of him – was fined 10s and costs for using bad language in Morley at the end of March.[81]

A fifth factor was the development of a large number of high-quality grounds on which cricket at all levels could be played. Whereas in the late 1860s and 1870s, the county club had been handicapped by using small and poor quality grounds at Wakefield, Hunslet, Holbeck and Hull, by the early 1890s there were better facilities in a number of towns. Bramall Lane, Sheffield had been the leading venue since the 1850s and ongoing investment had made it a fine arena. Bradford established a new ground in 1881, Huddersfield's ground was 'in splendid condition' by the 1880s, and Dewsbury had made improvements around the same time. In 1887, Bingley Cricket Club acquired a new field, which was described as 'one of the most convenient and best appointed of any in the county'. Saltaire's ground was 'pleasantly situated' and Pudsey Britannia planted trees to give its home a 'quite a park-like appearance'.[82] In 1890, Headingley was opened and Leeds finally had facilities suitable for regular county cricket. All around the county, well-appointed cricket venues were a highly visible addition to local amenities.

This book focuses on the development of cricket in the county of Yorkshire from the 1820s to 1893. It is not a book about specific cricket matches; there are plenty of such books already available, and the scores of all the county's first-class cricket matches are available on-line (along with many lesser games) at www.cricketarchive.com. It is also not a history of Yorkshire County Cricket Club in the same vein as those written by the late Tony Woodhouse or by Derek Hodgson.[83] Rather, it is a study of the sporting, social, economic and cultural forces that nurtured and shaped cricket within Yorkshire, and made it great.

In taking this focus, I am guided by the frequently quoted words of C.L.R.James, who wrote 'What do they know of cricket who only cricket know?'[84] His insight seems particularly appropriate here because no consideration of the development of Yorkshire County Cricket Club in the period can look at the club in isolation. There are a number of reasons for this. For much of the period covered there was simply insufficient county cricket played for it to be seen as a world apart from the local game, and many of those who appeared for Yorkshire pieced together a living from games played at several levels, including club games and fixtures against touring sides alongside a small – albeit growing – number of county matches.

In addition, for the entire period under examination, the backdrop is intermittent arguing between representatives of cricket clubs in different parts of the county about who should have control over the game. The big divide was between Sheffield and the rest of Yorkshire, but at certain times, particular towns pushed their case to have a greater share of the top matches. Thus, the development of cricket in the county has to be seen in terms of internal pressures and interests, partly driven by local pride and a desire to see local players perform on the bigger stage, but also by financial necessity as clubs sought to host those first-class matches likely to generate a profit, rather than lead to a damaging loss.

I also believe that cricket cannot be examined without considering the broader social and economic developments in England in the 19th century. The game was shaped by forces of class, economic development and social inequality which determined who was able to find the time and resources to develop their game, who could afford to pay to watch cricket, who was able or unable to take the risk of playing the game professionally, and who was sufficiently wealthy to be able to play without payment. As Davies has argued, the rapid growth in cricket clubs in the second half of the 19th century was made possible by the rise of new social and economic forces. In particular, he has observed that the 'key resources of time, space, money and organisation only became available through continued economic growth and the development of new social ideas.'[85] In addition, fear of working-class unrest – particularly during the 1830s and 1840s – and concern amongst social reformers about the impact of industrialisation and how leisure time was used, meant that there were many who saw cricket as a healthy and morally uplifting activity, capable of reconciling the interests of different social classes.

Added to this, cricket was in competition with other leisure activities, and the game had to respond to the commercial forces which shaped the tastes of those who wanted to pay to watch others play. This was part of the emergence of a mass sports industry, which Huggins calls 'one of the economic success stories of late Victorian Britain.'[86] The excitement generated by rugby and football in the 1880s and 1890s, for example, encouraged those involved in cricket to introduce similar, more competitive forms of the game. Other activities such as the military volunteers from the 1860s, and tennis from the late 1870s, also had an impact by drawing some young men away from cricket. The York Cricket Club annual report for 1861, for example, lamented that the season had been very unfavourable and the volunteer movement had 'deprived the club of the services of some of the best and most valued cricketers.'[87] As a result, supporters of the game had to think how to respond in order to maintain and develop its appeal.

There are other reasons for this wide focus. The success that the Yorkshire County Cricket Club achieved in 1893 did not happen overnight. Rather it was the product of years of development of the game going right back to the 1820s, when cricket in Yorkshire first secured a national reputation and had facilities where it could host significant games. It was also not the result of the efforts of any one man, although W.H.Woolhouse, M.J.Ellison, J.B.Wostinholm and Lord Hawke to name but four were clearly crucially important in the history of Yorkshire county cricket. Others played their part. Lord Londesborough, for example, repeatedly appears in support of campaigns for what was considered a more representative club, and a number of lesser figures such as club officials like Charles Lonsdale of Bradford Cricket Club played small, but important, 'walk-on' roles at points in the story. The significance of a small number of individuals is not in doubt, but I would argue that ultimately the success of Yorkshire cricket was also the result of many people throughout the county who set up clubs, who travelled to play and watch games, and who nurtured young talent and brought them to the attention of the county authorities. It was also the result of those who raised money to keep cricket clubs alive, who tended the wickets and organised fund raising events.

To study these developments the book is divided into four parts. Chapters 2-5 consider the growth of a strong cricketing culture in Yorkshire. Chapter 2 examines the development of the love for the game and the passions and tensions it created. Chapter 3 highlights the spread of cricket in different parts of the county, whilst Chapter 4 looks at the different formats that developed. The next section – Clubs – looks at the ways in which the local game was organised (Chapter 5), and financed (Chapter 6), putting a spotlight on the bedrock of the game. The third part – People – focuses on different participants in the sporting arena – the players, particularly those who made it to the county side (Chapter 7), the crowds who came to watch (Chapter 8), and the press which reported on cricket (Chapter 9). The final part (Chapter 10) examines how a broadly-based county cricket club was established in the 19th century. Chapter 11 draws out some conclusions on how the game developed in Yorkshire.

CHAPTER TWO

THE PLACE OF CRICKET

Speaking at an annual dinner of Yorkshiremen resident in London in the early 1890s, the Marquis of Carmarthen commented that it was 'absolutely no exaggeration' to say that the county of Yorkshire 'excelled in comparison with every other county put together', whether it be in industry, scenery or sport. And he added, 'whatever sport they went in for they would find the best of it in Yorkshire.'[88] Ten years later, similar certainties were expressed by Lord Hawke when he stated that 'Yorkshire cricket is a thing of which not only every Yorkshireman but every Englishman must feel proud.'[89]

A Yorkshireman's identification with his own has a long history. In 1843, for example, a match took place in Upton, Essex between twenty-two Yorkshiremen – eleven living in the City of London and eleven in the West End – for the prize of a dinner. Afterwards they toasted 'Yorkshire friends.'[90] This regular, well-attended gathering was later transformed into the Yorkshire Amateur Cricket Club, which grew in size, and whose dinners were accompanied by fine wines.[91] In 1849, at the annual dinner of York Cricket Club, there was a strong sense of county feeling in the speeches, as well as some concern about Yorkshire's standing in the game. A speaker referred to 'the superiority of Yorkshire over other counties', but asked why they could not find eleven Yorkshiremen to play with eleven from the south, concluding that it was only a matter of time before 'Yorkshiremen would not be inferior to others in cricketing skill.'[92]

No doubt, to the neutral, such sentiments sound rather insular and arrogant, no more so than those of one Sheffield reporter in 1893 who suggested that:

> As is only natural, what we are most concerned about is the doings of our own county. We can look on the meetings of other shires with a certain amount of unconcern; but when Yorkshire are in it, then arises the anxiety.

Or another who, after giving extensive coverage to Yorkshire's early-season wins, continued by reluctantly stating 'Now just a reminder of what outsiders are doing.'[93] Such writers took it for granted that a love of cricket was widespread in the county. The *Sheffield Daily Telegraph* claimed in 1890 that there was 'scarcely a youth in Yorkshire or Nottinghamshire who is not tempted to exclaim, on seeing a tolerably level meadow, "What a jolly place to play cricket in".'[94] And Tom Emmett, one of the greatest Yorkshire cricketers of the 19th century, was asked in an interview in *The Cricket Field* when he had started to play. His response was as soon as he could walk, 'like all Yorkshire boys do'.[95]

Emergence of the game

The origins of cricket have been the subject of considerable debate.[96] Much of this has focused on the game as a popular recreation in rural communities in parts of southern England, as well as on aristocratic involvement and the way in which the game was the focus for betting. From this, it is clear that in its early days cricket was far from a nationwide sport. As Davies has written:

> the game remained constrained by the limitations of pre-modern society. The synthesis between popular interest, commercial investment and aristocratic involvement which pushed cricket forward during the period was only possible in London and the south-eastern counties of England where economic and demographic growth were heavily concentrated. These conditions were changed significantly by the increasing spread of capitalist industrial society during the first half of the nineteenth century and circumstances which could support the game's development in other parts of England being created.[97]

The great Yorkshire cricket historian, R.S.Holmes, suggests that the earliest reported reference to a cricket match in Yorkshire is from 1751, when the Duke of Cleveland's side played the Earl of Northumberland's Eleven at Stanwick, near Richmond, the Earl's seat.[98] In February 1757, in Sheffield, the Church Burgesses' accounts state that cricket players were paid on Shrove Tuesday to entertain the populace and prevent 'the infamous practice of throwing at Cocks.'[99] Three years later, an advert in the *Leeds Intelligencer* noted that 'The Gentlemen Cricket-Players' would be meeting in Chapel Town towards the end of May 1760, and invited all willing to become subscribers to attend.[100] Matches were played on Chapel Town Moor in the early 1760s, and at the start of the 1770s, Sheffield took on Nottingham on two occasions, although it would be another 30 years until they met again. In the late 1770s, the gentlemen's cricket club in Leeds was sufficiently well established to support a performance at the theatre in the town, and in 1780 a new dance was performed at the theatre entitled 'The Cricketers, or the Sports of Chapel-Town'.[101]

Elsewhere, Gentlemen of Beverley played those of Howden in 1778, and in 1784 a club was formed in York, whose highly prescriptive rules are preserved in Holmes's Yorkshire history.[102] Games involving men from Pontefract and Wakefield are recorded in 1784, Doncaster and York in 1786, and Benningbrough, Ouseburn and Shipton in 1788. In 1796, a large crowd watched the gentlemen of Doncaster take on the gentlemen of York for 100 guineas, and later that year Knavesmire, near York, was the scene for a contest between York and Wetherby. Teams of gentlemen from Knaresbrough and Burton Leonard competed in November 1796.[103] The summer of 1798 saw a match involving officers from the West York Militia against 10 men attached to regiments camped in the Holderness area. A full scoresheet of the game was published.[104] In 1800, Sheffield and Nottingham clashed again, with the latter side victorious on both occasions. Around the same time there is also some evidence that the game was played beyond the middle classes, with two factories in Sheffield contesting for 11 guineas in October 1802.[105]

The amount of cricket in Yorkshire newspapers appears to increase towards the end of the first decade of the century. Matches involving the Wetherby and Harewood clubs were prominent in the expanded coverage, and in 1809, the gentlemen of Wetherby took on the gentlemen of all Yorkshire at Knavesmire for 200 guineas. Two marquees were put up on the ground, and fine food and wine was provided.[106] The Wetherby Club challenged the Harewood Club in 1810, which was a source of controversy during the autumn. The same year, a Ripon Club started promisingly and was involved in a game in November, where some of its players refused to continue as a result of a disputed leg-before-wicket decision. Their opponents, Kirby-Fleetham and Scruton, subsequently took steps to recover the stakes.[107]

Around this time, clubs at York, Ripon, Harewood and Knaresbrough contested major matches, many at Knavesmire. In 1814, the Ripon club announced it was open to a challenge from any club in Yorkshire, and it was reported that they would play the Mary-le-bone Club in Nottingham.[108] In 1815, a much anticipated game between Ripon and Nottingham did not take place, supposedly due to the latter having 'evaded the match.'[109] Arrangements were made the following year for the game to be played, with Ripon paying 20 guineas towards Nottingham's expenses. The match was contested for 150 guineas a side over two days.[110] Other matches reported around this time involved Knaresborough, Bishop Monkton, Kirbymoorside, Leeds, Armley, Wetherby, Stainley, Boroughbridge and York.

It is hard to tell from the limited coverage in the Yorkshire press how widespread cricket was in the years around the time of the Napoleonic wars. There are indications from reports that did appear that some places had well-organised and well-connected clubs, often associated with local noblemen. The sums of money involved as stakes and bets, and the amount of effort made to travel some distance and play over more than one day, were also indications of the seriousness with which the game was taken. Certain contests – Gentlemen of Wetherby v Gentlemen of All Yorkshire in 1809, Ripon and Nottingham in 1816, or the 'grand rubber' between Harewood and Tadcaster in 1821, for example – attracted large and wealthy crowds.[111]

It was from the 1820s onwards, however, that cricket seems to have seeped into Yorkshire life, in leisure time and workplace conversations, in newspapers, in petty disputes (some of which ended in court), in the education system, where some children were taught the rudiments of the game, and on Sunday school outings. Many observers commented favourably on cricket's apparent widespread appeal, frequently referring to it as the 'manly' or 'national' game, and alluding to what some already argued was its long (albeit murky) history and traditions. It became increasingly visible and started to have an effect on the landscape as grassy areas were enclosed and turned over to sporting purposes, cricket pitches were marked out in fields, and roads and inns (such as the Cricket public house in Darnall, the Cricket Ball public house in Savile Street, Sheffield, the Cricketer's Arms in Eccleshill and the Cricket Ball Inn in Attercliffe road, Sheffield) were named after the game.

Throughout the 19th century, cricket was widely seen by contemporary observers as developing and spreading, at a time when many traditional sports and recreations – such as bloodsports like bull-baiting, and violent and destructive football matches – were discouraged or actively surpressed.[112] In August 1827, the *York Herald* reprinted an article which commented that cricket 'was never more in favour than now. Some very excellent matches, in all parts of England, have been played during July, and many others have been advertised for the month upon which we are entered.'[113] These included games at Darnall, where Sheffield had beaten Nottingham by 154 runs that year. In 1830, a reporter commented favourably on the excitement generated by another Sheffield v Nottingham fixture, a reminder he said 'of the great days of the game, when the announcement of a grand match rendered it impossible for any master to calculate upon proceeding with his ordinary work until it was finished.'[114]

Sheffield was also the source of comments four years later when, in advance of the Yorkshire v Norfolk match, the *Sheffield Independent* reflected that:

> The popularity which this game has obtained in almost every town in England is greater than that of any other sport. Should you be on a visit at a friend's, a question sure to be asked is 'Can you play at cricket?' If you say no, the wonder is, where have you lived; for the game of cricket (if you play well) introduces you to the highest society, and it is become the duty of all the great schools to engage a person competent to teach the game.[115]

Elsewhere in the county, the *Bradford Observer* enthused in 1841 that in the last few years the game had made 'astonishing progress in public favour. Where it was almost unknown, it has now a large and increasing body of admirers.'[116] Nearly two decades later, a speaker at the end of season dinner of York Cricket Club remarked that cricket 'has made rapid strides during the last few years, and there is hardly a town or village that does not boast of its cricket club.'[117] In 1861, the *Bradford Observer* again noted that cricket was growing in popularity in agricultural areas, and by the end of the decade, a commentator in the Leeds press considered that the country was 'almost insane on the subject of cricket.' The following year, it was suggested that the young men of Whitby had 'gone stark staring mad after cricket.'[118]

Others pointed to specific signs of development. In an article in 1865, one writer noted 'the overwhelming number of cricket clubs that have been established, and the still greater number of names that are enrolled in those clubs.' This was despite competition from the Volunteer movement 'that occupies all of the leisure of hundreds of patriotic and athletic young men.'[119] The *Yorkshire Post* measured the growth of the game in the 1880s in terms of the number of fixture cards it received from local clubs, enthusing that they showed that the sport had never been more popular. The writer remembered a time when the paper had received 50-60 cards a season, but in 1885 his office had had 220 in three weeks, many apparently elaborately produced. And he added, 'the various towns are fringed with cricket enclosures, where the click of leather upon willow may be heard any time of an evening.'[120]

The following year, the same paper considered that there:

> never was a time since England became a nation that cricket commanded so much attention as now. The tendency of the age is in favour of the game, and as long as it is not indulged in to undue excess it will ever have a beneficial influence on the character of our Yorkshire youths.[121]

Predictably, some observers feared that there was too much of it. In 1881, for example, the *Leeds Times* complained that the levelling work on Hunslet Moor would have been far more effective 'if the cricketers could have been induced to keep off it for a while'. Hundreds of men played each night, damaging the newly prepared ground.[122]

Notwithstanding some reservations, cricket entered the lives of people of all walks of life. Teams were established by men who worked in mills, dye works, manufacturers, tan houses and foundaries. Mechanics set them up, as did law clerks, butchers, printers, tailors and moulders. There were church teams and sides formed by temperance movement supporters, as well as cricket clubs based around public houses and debating societies, and representing schools. A team of barristers of the Northern Circuit was established and town police forces put out sides. In 1860, there were complaints that a piece of land at the Leeds Infirmary that should have been used for the welfare of patients was only available for medical students to play cricket on.[123] In 1862, a match was played in Sheffield between teams of unemployed file grinders, and another between the paupers of the Eccleshill Union and those at Hollow Meadows, which raised sufficient money to enable 1s 4d to be given to each player.[124]

Mechanics' Institutes established cricket clubs as a way of keeping in touch with members during the summer months when their classes and reading rooms were less attractive places than being outdoors. In its annual report in 1873, the Yorkshire Union of Mechanics' Institutes reported enthusiastically that cricket clubs connected with the institute had greatly increased in number.[125] Local Conservative and Liberal party associations took on each other, and in the 1880s, members of the Primrose League (organised to spread Conservative principles) played cricket at their events.[126] In 1885, the Doncaster Board of Guardians decided to obtain cricket equipment for the boys in the local workhouse to provide exercise.[127] To some, cricket appeared to be replacing more traditional sports. An article on the lives of colliers in the West Riding in the 1880s, for example, noted that they were 'cultivating a taste for cricket and football, and the ranks of the 'knur and spell'[128] players and the pigeon fanciers are dwindling.'[129]

Cricket was associated with all manner of events. In May 1835, thousands gathered in Wakefield during the hustings for the West Riding parliamentary election. Included among the banners on display was one showing two cricketers, one in blue, the other yellow, with the motto 'Fair Play' over their heads. Underneath the blue cricketer the banner stated 'Take care, my lord, or I shall bowl you out', a reference to the ongoing debate about cricket playing on a Sunday.[130] During Queen Victoria's coronation celebrations in 1838 and those for her Golden Jubilee in 1887, games of cricket were part of the festivities in many towns and villages.

In 1845, at the Temperance Association annual gathering for Sheffield and Rotherham at Roche Abbey, boys passed the time playing cricket in front of the speakers, and the following year, matches were enjoyed as part of the celebrations in Hemsworth on the passing of the Corn and other relief Bills.[131] In 1848, children played cricket among the 'dark and unhappy concourse of men' listening to the orators at a Chartist meeting in Bradford.[132] When James Hall, a Sheffield man who had killed his wife with a hatchet, was executed at Armley Jail, 'the only sounds that broke the stillness' were the voices of cricketers playing outside the prison walls.[133] And, when the Local Government Board investigated allegations of misconduct by the workhouse master at Holbeck, part of his case that he had not neglected the children was that they had been allowed to stay up in the summer until 8 o'clock in order to play cricket.[134]

The game was a feature of many public holidays and village 'feasts' and 'wakes', those traditional celebrations that had been an important break from routine for ordinary people for many years.[135] By the 19th century such events consisted of galas, day trips, eating and drinking, when the factories and shops were closed, and stalls and bazaars were set up along main roads and streets. In August 1850, for example, teams from various Barnsley cricket clubs contested for prizes of bats and balls, generating a lot of interest at the local feast. A popular feature of the Woodhouse wakes were 'rural sports, particularly cricketing'.[136] In Dudley Hill and Eccleshill, cricket was part of the holiday events in 1865, where 'Beef was roasted, tankards flowed with heady ale, and all the etceteras usual at country fairs were brought into full play to the especial delectation of the young.'[137]

In 1880, the *Leeds Times* commented on the refusal of people in Holbeck to be dictated to about when they should have their holidays, insisting on holding their feast in September, as they had always done. Although some went away on cheap trips, 'the bulk of the natives remained at home to feast their friends and to enjoy the cricket matches promoted by the Holbeck Club', the main interest being a game with Lascelles Hall. In the evening, there was a gala and dancing, and a display of fireworks.[138] Cricket was thus seen variously as a civilising influence on traditional events, an alternative to what some considered were new, debased entertainments, and as a way of livening up an old-fashioned feast.[139]

Even when people were not involved in playing or watching cricket, they could not avoid being increasingly aware that the game existed and took place near where they lived. Events of all kinds frequently ended up in cricket fields. W.H.Woolhouse used his Hyde Park cricket ground in Sheffield for a range of other money-making activities, opening it at Whitsuntide 1832, for example, for displays of horsemanship, rope-dancing and leaping, with a military band in attendance.[140] Coronation festivities in Leeds ended up in the new Victoria Cricket Ground on Woodhouse Moor in June 1838, where refreshments were provided and games were played.[141]

The Hull Town club revived what were described as 'Merry Old English Sports and Pastimes' in celebration of Queen Victoria's birthday in 1856, and spectators paid 6d to gain access to the Anlaby Road ground.[142] Grounds were lent out or rented for festivals, horticultural events and to the local volunteers for parading as, for example, in Beverley in 1860 when hundreds made their way to the cricket ground, dressed in holiday attire, to witness the review by the East Yorks Rifle Volunteers.[143] In May 1867, 4,000 marched to the cricket ground in Holmfirth for a meeting to discuss the proposed alteration to the timing of their feast, which as elsewhere had provoked opposition.[144] Around 10,000 people met in a cricket field in Harrogate for the North of England Bicycle Meet in 1885.[145] Thus, cricket fields became a gathering place and a focus for many communities.

The growing popularity of cricket inevitably meant some sought to make money by providing for the spread of the game. Increasingly, many of those playing wanted to have at least some appropriate equipment and suppliers emerged to meet the demand and offer increasingly sophisticated products. Shops of all kinds saw their chance to make money. In Doncaster, 'Joseph Clayton's Repository of Fashion' (which more normally sold cosmetics and cut hair) advertised bats and balls in 1829, as did the offices of the *Doncaster Chronicle* in 1839 and a bookshop in the town in the 1840s.[146] In 1835, Carrall's Bazaar in Queen Street, Hull advertised the 'very best' cricket bats at 5s each and cheaper ones at 1s 6d, with treble seamed balls at 3s 6d. Orders from out of town had to be post-paid and the amount enclosed. The following April, the same outlet announced the arrival of 300 of Clapshaw's very best bats.[147] Specialist suppliers such as John Hall in Bradford and William Duthoit in Leeds were established. In 1863, Hall was offering 'the largest and best-assorted Stock of Cricketing Materials in the North of England', and a full list of items was available, post-free, on application.[148] In Sheffield at the same time, Edwin Jackson's Cricketers' Depot, which had been going since 1830, claimed to sell equipment at 'the Lowest Remunerative Profit possible'. In 1873, on moving his warehouse to new premises, Duthoit boasted of 25 years' of service, and promised 'none but first-class London-made goods'. Hall's described itself as the 'oldest House in the trade in Yorkshire'.[149]

Other businesses saw a chance to make money. The owner of the Yarborough Arms public house in New Holland, for example, put a notice in the *Hull Packet* in 1835 to announce that he had attractive accommodation for playing cricket, and a Jeremiah Millwaters advertised that he was moving his hostelry to a better site in Leeds where he had, 'in addition to the cricket ground previously provided, laid down a very convenient bowling green, in close proximity to the hotel.'[150] The makers of Measam and Co.'s medicated cream advertised that it could relieve severe bruising in five minutes. This was useful, it suggested, for dealing with blows from a cricket ball.[151] In 1857, Pablo's Circus, Bradford advertised that there would be a 'Cricketers' Night', when three complete sets of bats, balls and stumps would be given away.[152] Notices for schools such as the Queen Elizabeth's Grammar School in Gainsborough and Park Hill School, near Wetherby, highlighted the quality of their cricket fields in order to attract fee-paying parents, and in advertising for a young teacher many years later, the Commercial College in York specified 'abstainer and cricketer preferred.'[153]

Cricket was sufficiently familiar to be used for other commercial purposes. In 1850, an advert for a tailors appeared in the *Sheffield Independent*, shamelessly exploiting the excitement around the recent Sheffield v Yorkshire game. Using numerous puns on contemporary players' names, it announced:

> nor can anyone wonder, since R. Levy and Sons commenced their unrivalled business in Yorkshire, that they have called out the most admirable skill and furnished the people with every elegancy in clothing, thus placing Yorkshire in a position superior to "All England".....B.Wake [a Yorkshire amateur] showed himself '*wide awake*' in the game, and fully proved that Yorkshire abilities were

> not to be '*shut up*' by a '*Box*' [the Sussex wicketkeeper]. But R. Levy and Sons are always wide a-*Wake* to the selection and production of the best articles which can give grace and elegance to the human figure; in this way they have a 'Waked' the inhabitants of Sheffield and its vicinity to their real interests, which are only secured when they fix their "Stumps" in 24, High Street, and utter their determination not to be "bowled out" until they are rigged out in the fashionable clothing prepared by R.Levy and Sons.[154]

Similarly, several decades later the game and its language clearly had meaning to sufficient people to make it suitable again as a marketing device, with a firm of Leeds clothiers employing a cricketing reference during Queen Victoria's jubilee when it spoke of 'VR 50 – not out.'[155]

From the late 1840s, an increasing number of games between touring teams such as the All-England Eleven and local sides were as much commercial opportunities for some as a sporting spectacle for many. As West put it, local businessmen:

> could look forward to the opportunity of making a welcome addition to their annual income – the printers, the dealers in cricketing goods, the suppliers of tents, marquees, and in some instances massive canvas screens erected around the perimeter of the playing area to prevent spectators from watching the match without paying for admission. Above all, there were the caterers, anticipating a temporary boom in the sale of food and drink, and it comes as no surprise to find that matches often took place in a field adjacent to an hotel.[156]

Cricket could thus provide a valuable boost to trade of all kinds.

As well as a commercial exploitation of the game, cricket also had a philanthropic side, and on many occasions money generated by teams was given to needy causes. A match between Halifax and Huddersfield in 1826, for example, raised £3 for the fund for the relief of the poor in the area.[157] In April 1854, at the time of the Crimean war, cricket was played on Woodhouse Moor in Leeds between teams of friends who met regularly at the Bee Hive, Woodhouse. Afterwards, a dinner was held, and a sum of 11s 6d subscribed by the cricketers present towards a fund for the wives and children of men sent to fight.[158]

In 1856, the *Leeds Times* reported that 'Cricketer benevolence is solicited on behalf of George Armitage, a very clever professional bowler, and a member of Dalton club, who it is feared will never leave his room again. A subscription list has been opened at a local pub and another list at the *Bell's Life* offices.[159] The Emsley Challenge Cup in Leeds also generated funds that were disbursed to deserving causes – in 1882 to the General Infirmary (£50), the Dispensary (£20), the Women and Children's Hospital (£10), the House of Recovery (£10), the Eye and Ear Infirmary (£10), Cookridge Hospital (£10), and Meanwood Convalescent Hospital (£10).[160] Cricket was also seen as a solution to other social problems. When 4,000 men in Bradford received outdoor relief during the economic downturn of 1879, the *Leeds Times* asked why, amongst other things, they could not be put to work in draining, levelling and re-laying the cricket ground in Peel Park or Horton Park.[161]

Regardless of the value and pleasure that the growth of the game provided, cricket could also create tensions. One concern was its impact on the local environment, and cases of alleged destruction of property were heard by magistrates on a regular basis. In 1844, complaints were made in the Rotherham court about damage to trees caused by boys playing cricket.[162] A case was brought under Sheffield bye-laws by a woman whose house adjoined a ground where a group of youths had formed the 'Peep o' Day' Boys Club. The boys were accused of banging on her door and annoying her (and on one occasion, firing a pistol), but said they were all clerks in offices and had set up the club for healthy exercise. They added that they paid £2 10s rent for the year, but the complainant had tried to extract more from them every time the ball went into her garden. They were fined 2s 6d and costs, although it was accepted that they had a right to play on the site.[163]

In 1851, the Huddersfield Cricket Club prosecuted a former employee who had made holes in the wall around the cricket ground so as to see through to watch.[164] The same year, five boys appeared in front of magistrates in Sheffield charged with damage of property caused by playing cricket in Holland Street. This had become a nuisance over a period of years, with windows allegedly broken 'almost daily'. An attempt by one resident to drive them away led to him being forced back into his house under a hail of stones. The five boys were fined 1s and costs, and the police were asked to be more vigilant to prevent such behaviour recurring.[165]

In July 1859, the Barnsley Board of Health discussed the state of the church field, 'which was becoming a great nuisance to the surrounding property. On Monday, there were no fewer than eleven sets of cricketers playing there.' Warning notices had been issued and measures were taken to stop the games and prevent 'obscene language' being written on the church gates.[166] Over 20 years later, three boys from Golcar were fined and ordered to pay compensation following an incident in which their cricket ball was taken by the complainant after it went into his garden. They then threw stones at his hencote and pulled up the boards, causing extensive damage.[167]

Complaints about vandalism by cricketers on Woodhouse Moor became almost a permanent feature of Leeds life. In 1882, for example, the turf was reported to be in a 'sad state' as a result of holes made by cricketers and pathways formed in every direction. Changes to arrangements on the moor were debated for several years.[168] Leeds County Court also heard a case of a farm steward who had claimed £9 as sick allowance for 18 weeks from his lodge of the Independent Order of Oddfellows. He occupied a field in Horsforth where a cricket club had taken to playing. After asking them to leave, he was shouted at, and so returned with a plough and horse with which to dig up the field. He was then attacked, the plough thrown aside and the horse let loose. The plaintiff broke his leg and could not work. The friendly society refused his claim, believing he had been drunk. However, the jury was sympathetic and he was awarded the whole amount, with costs.[169]

These were just a few of the many examples which reflected the stresses and strains of living and playing together in rapidly urbanising Yorkshire. A longer lasting dispute occurred in York. During July 1859, concerns were expressed about trespassing by youths and schools playing cricket and other games.[170] That summer, a case was considered by magistrates, who found against a group of cricketers who had refused to leave Walmgate Ward stray when asked to do so by the pasture-masters. Although witnesses claimed cricket had been played there for nearly 50 years, they were accused of damaging the grass in June and July when it was needed for grazing, and cricket was only allowed from August onwards. The men were fined 6d each and costs.[171] By September, all had paid up, and could play on application to the pasture masters.[172]

Cricket also caused annoyance for travellers, with players blocking roads, leaving debris behind which was a risk to traffic, and sometimes injuring passers-by. Steps were taken to control this activity. In the early part of the century, turnpike legislation outlawed football, cricket or other games by the roadside, but for some this was a natural place to play, and in Sheffield, at least, the police commissioners and their officers allowed cricket in the streets in the 1830s, even though pedestrians received knocks from the hard wooden balls.[173]

Elsewhere, the authorities were not so generous. In 1835, two young sweeps and another boy were brought before the court in York, charged with playing cricket in the New Market to the annoyance of residents. They were reprimanded by the Lord Mayor, who hoped that further offences could be prevented.[174] There were other incidents in York, where the public was reportedly constantly annoyed by cricket matches being played on the roads leading to the railway station, including one occasion which saw:

> a large group of boys busy at the game, and amongst them might be seen a proprietor of one of the cabs...... actually batting, and striking the ball in all directions, whilst the public were wending their way to meet the train then due.[175]

In Huddersfield in 1861, six boys were charged by county police with playing regularly on the highway to the annoyance and danger of passengers. Part of the danger was that they left 'wicket-stones' on the road which were a danger to traffic, and this finally prompted the police to intervene. Each boy was fined 1s and costs, a total of 8s each.[176] A few months later, another lad was fined 1s and expenses for obstructing the highway playing cricket, although the principal offence was reportedly insulting a policeman.[177] Occasionally, injuries did occur in the streets. In Manningham, a man was hit in the face while walking down a road where cricket was being played. He suffered such damage that he was unable to go to work. The court gave a verdict for £5 and costs, stating that the injury had arisen from 'careless play in an improper place.'[178]

For some people cricket was too visible for other reasons. In 1876, an argument ('an extraordinary tombstone dispute') broke out at Wadsley Bridge, near Sheffield, when the widow of Benjamin Keeton, a local cricketer, erected a tombstone to her husband's memory on which were carved a set of stumps about a foot high, with bat and ball below. The vicar and churchwardens objected, and ordered its removal. The paper debated the merits of the matter, arguing that if war and weapons could be represented on tombs, why was it sacrilege to mark the dead cricketer's grave? It asked 'Can it be that cricketing is viewed at Wadsley as a frivolous, idle amusement, which it is profanity to name, or represent, or think of within a consecrated enclosure?'[179] The following week, Mrs Keeton was given seven days to remove it or be prosecuted.[180] Subsequently, in an attempt to mediate, the Vicar of Wadsley asked if the images could be cut out so Mrs Keeton could keep them with her all the time, but she refused. Although it was then reported that the church authorities had backed down, the tombstone was later secretly knocked over. A local resident restored it at his own expense and eventually the matter was dropped.[181]

Cricket also turned up in unpleasant or tragic circumstances. Particularly shocking was the four-year-old boy who fell into a coke oven at Coal Ashton (close to Sheffield, just over the border in Derbyshire) and was seen in the flames, with his cricket bat on top of him.[182] Serious injuries were not uncommon when boys were messing around with a bat and ball, or in local matches as batsmen were hit, often on the temple, or fielders ran into each other, damaging ribs. There are occasional reports of deaths from injuries.[183] In 1882, for example, a Sheffield man died from the effects of being hit on the knee by a cricket ball when keeping wicket, and in 1883, a young man from Morley was hit behind the ear. He carried on but died later at home.[184] At the Yeadon Feast in August 1883, in front of a large crowd, a 29-year-old man called Albert Luty, who was a Saturday professional for Bowling Old Lane, was hit on his temple by Joe Preston, the county player, and died, despite treatment on the field. The streets of Yeadon were lined with mourners for his funeral.[185]

One match between Denby Dale and Clayton in 1865 saw three, less serious, injuries. Firstly, two batsmen collided so violently that one broke his arm and was taken to a doctor to have it set. Then, another batsman had his nose broken by the ball. Two other players were injured in the game, and, unsurprisingly, it was reported that 'it is proposed to lay the ground properly preparatory to the next season.'[186]

Other impromptu games ended in tragedy. One afternoon in September 1838, some youths were playing cricket near Sheffield when their ball disappeared down a disused coal-mine. One entered the shaft on a rope to look for it, followed by another. The second was pulled out alive and treated by a doctor, but the first boy was dead when he was returned to the surface.[187] In 1851, a twelve-month-old boy died from an injury sustained from a cricket ball. His sister had been asked to move away but had stood with the child behind the wickets where he was struck on the temple. The jury at the inquest returned a verdict of 'accidental death', but also censured the girl for not moving when asked.[188]

At times, cricket was linked to criminal behaviour. In 1826, a police constable from Huddersfield, who had been sent to arrest a man called Denton Marsden at the ground where the Manchester and Huddersfield clubs were playing, was assaulted by a mob and had stones thrown at him.[189] In 1830, a Mat Gunston, described as the 'notorious dwarf boy', who was apparently well known to those who attended cricket matches in Sheffield in the 1820s, was arrested by the police and charged with theft.[190] In 1835, a number of men pretended to be playing cricket in a road near Sheffield, using a stick for a bat and stones for balls, and then attacked a group of shoemakers as they passed by.[191] A case was heard the following year of two men charged with stealing a silver watch from a man playing cricket on Woodhouse Moor, who had employed one of them to take care of his clothes and watches.[192] A cricket bat was used in the assault during a late-night dispute between locals and a group of Irish labourers who had been employed to reap a field of corn near Thirsk in 1845, and in 1849 two men from Holmfirth got involved in a fight during a game of cricket, one hitting the other so hard on the head that initially he was not expected to live.[193]

There were also incidents in the second half of the century. In 1856, two men were charged with brutally assaulting a constable after returning from a cricket match in Kirkstall. When they reached Pudsey they were very noisy and, having been remonstrated with by the policeman, struck him with a cricket bat and kicked him on the ground. They were found guilty, ordered to pay a fine of £5 or go to the House of Correction for two months.[194] The following year, two men were charged in Wakefield with assaulting another policeman after he tried to remove a drunken man using vulgar language on a cricket field.[195]

A different form of crime was perpetrated in 1883, resulting in a Bradford man being sentenced to 15 months in prison. He had approached a Manningham manufacturer known for his interest in sport, saying he had been tasked with asking him to become a vice-president of a Manningham Victoria Cricket and Football Club. The manufacturer agreed and handed over a subscription for the club, which turned out not to exist.[196]

Cricket grounds could be the scene of crimes. Tents and sheds erected, often on a semi-permanent basis and in isolated places, were vulnerable to theft. In July 1838, not for the first time, the tent on the York ground was broken into, despite being protected with locks, and bottles of porter, ginger beer and gin were stolen.[197] The following year, a shed used by Bradford cricketers to store equipment on their field near Mannville was broken into, equipment (and gin again) was taken, and damage done.[198]

The booths at Sheffield were also broken into in 1868, although apparently the authorities were unsure whether anything had been stolen since they did not know how much alcohol had been stored there.[199] In 1879, a man was charged at the Hull Police Court with breaking into a booth at Hull Town Cricket Club pavilion and stealing bottles of wine, aprons and other items. Later the same year, a husband and wife were charged with stealing about 80 yards of canvas, two cricket bats and a pair of leg guards, the property of Barnsley Cricket Club. They then sold it all on, along with stolen goods from other properties.[200]

Clearly, some clubs were sufficiently prosperous to have things worth stealing, as it seems did individual players. Cricket matches, like many gatherings, attracted pickpockets, and in 1850, a man was charged and committed for trial for stealing silk handkerchiefs at a game at Hyde Park.[201] In the 1880s, the *Leeds Times* warned of 'the affable stranger who looks in upon the ground just as the match is beginning, and speedily ingratiates himself with members, who helps out, then leaves before the game ends having stolen watches, rings, cash and purses.' It added that 'robberies of this kind have been very numerous, and they still continue to increase.'[202]

What did the game offer?

Looking back over a period of almost two centuries, it is hard to explain exactly why so many people took to cricket so enthusiastically, but we can make some educated guesses as to what the game had to offer, both for those playing it, and also for those who gave it their support. Sandiford has commented that 'All classes of Victorians were encouraged to play cricket simply because it was seen by the social and cultural leaders of the day as the perfect recreative pursuit.'[203] This may have been true, but it is clear that thousands of people in Yorkshire did not play or watch the game – in many cases, for decades – simply because they were told to do so.

Instead, it was clear that cricket became an interest for many, and an obsession for some, for many reasons, providing pleasure and excitement. No-one, for example, made a Job Robinson, a tailor's foreman who had moved up to Leeds from London for work, take time off without asking permission to play cricket at Harewood and Woodhouse Moor in 1825, leaving other men idle. He was dismissed, the jury finding against him when he took his employer to court. They suggested he be awarded costs for the journey to Leeds, although this was literally laughed out of court according to reports.[204]

No-one forced an unemployed Sheffield man with seven children (whose journal of his search for work was published in the local paper) to divide his time between job-hunting and playing cricket with five or six other men, in order to distract themselves from 'the ever haunting images of bread and hungry mouths.'[205] No-one made a William Britain of the Ripon Gentlemen's Cricket Club set off one evening in September 1842 to get to Ripon for a game with Thirsk the following day, when he was set upon by three men and kicked insensible.[206] And no-one made a Joseph Dickenson from Bradford get up at four o'clock in the morning in August 1843 to rouse his friend to play cricket, only to come across what turned out to be burglary of pistols, which ended with the culprit being transported for 10 years.[207]

Some were very open about their passion for the game. In April 1874, a case was reported in the *Leeds Times* from Liverpool Assizes of an action brought by a woman to recover damages of £8,000 for breach of promise of marriage. The defendant was a Liverpool cotton broker who had called off the courtship because of 'her disregard for the game of cricket, of which he was passionately fond'.[208] The *Huddersfield Chronicle* wrote a detailed (and rather tongue-in-cheek) editorial on the case, commenting that 'The mind shrinks appalled at MARY'S condition, at a young lady not sufficiently alive to the glories of cricket. Well might poor Mr ECCLES break off the match...If MARY has possessed any fine feeling she would have spent her days in studying LILLYWHITE'S Guide, and have cheerfully attired herself in flannels with leg-guards and gloves on, whenever she expected the cricket-loving ECCLES.'[209]

Cricket clearly appealed in different ways to different people, offering physical, social, aesthetic and other pleasures, and being the basis for many friendships. A teenage Richard Daft, apprenticed to a draper in Driffield, years before he became one of the finest players in England, used to 'gather a few kindred spirits' together at six in the morning so they could practise in a small paddock on the Beverley Road.[210] Attempting to stir interest in the game in Hull in 1868, John Leak, the President of Hull Town Cricket Club, called on those who had played when young to 'call to mind the many happy hours they have enjoyed, the many life-long friendships they have formed, and the physical good they have obtained on the cricket field.'[211]

For others, the game provided excitement and pleasure, often of a rough-and-ready kind. The *Bradford Observer* noted in 1858 that any vacant land 'immediately becomes an extemporised cricket ground on summer evenings, for groups of boys from the overcrowded 'back slums' of an adjoining locality.' The author regretted that notices were going up prohibiting trespassing, although he had some sympathy with those disturbed by the noise.[212] In 1849, a Bradford clergyman commented that in his neighbourhood 'the boys and young men were anxious to spend their leisure in the recreation of cricket', making use of vacant building land.[213] As a youth, Luke Greenwood, one of the great Yorkshire players of the 1860s and 1870s, recalled that he had 'made cricket his constant recreation, playing on turnpike roads, with crewelled balls and such primitive bats as it was possible to improvise from hedgestakes and palings.'[214]

As well as playing anywhere and with anything, some showed their enthusiasm by enjoying the game whatever the time of year. Indeed, it is clear that cricket was not necessarily a summer game, particularly in the first half of the 19th-century. This was linked to the desire to use it as a focus for betting, but was also a consequence of more opportunities for leisure arising in rural areas once harvesting was completed. As a result, many matches were conducted in the autumn and into November and December.[215] In 1841, for example, games were still played into late November between two Wadsley teams, almost certainly for money.[216] A match was reported in December in Otley in 1843, and in Sheffield, single-wicket games continued into November of 1844.[217]

There were a number of matches in the North Riding over several winters in the 1840s[218], and at the end of November 1844, the *York Herald* published a notice stating that Thirsk Junior club was keen to play Sowerby Junior club any day in Christmas week.[219] In January 1843, a game between Nether and Over Stilton, and Kepwick and Cowesby was played for 11 sovereigns a side. Unsurprisingly, 'the wind was boisterous and very cold', but more surprising was that 'a great number of spectators assembled to witness a much talked about match'.[220] Elsewhere, in October 1851, a game between Sheffield and Rotherham was played in bright sunshine, although it was so cold that a large bonfire was built on the ground for spectators to gather around.[221]

During particularly bad winters, when rivers and lakes had frozen hard, games of cricket were played on the ice. Over the winter of 1837, this was sufficiently inspiring to lead one man to verse, published by the *Sheffield Independent*:

> With crowds (although the frost was keen)
> The banks were cover'd o'er,
> And all declared that ne'er had seen
> A treat like that before.
> Indeed, I heard Tom Marsden say,

> As umpire he did stand,
> He never saw much better play,
> Not even upon land.[222]

In 1838, a number of well-known York cricketers played near Lendal Ferry on the frozen River Ouse, and around the same time, a game was played on the Earl of Harewood's fishpond.[223] In 1841, Sheffield's 'winter cricketers' played a series of games on the ice at Little London Dam, with Harry Sampson making 162 in one game. Cricket on ice was sufficiently popular that Farnsworth has suggested that cricketers carrying skates in the depths of winter was a common sight in Sheffield.[224]

For the more capable or enthusiastic players, messing about with a bat and ball on whatever surface led on to participation in competitive games and offered an opportunity for ordinary people 'to acquire prestige and self-respect' and 'to perform publicly for the esteem of their peers.'[225] The pleasure of making a significant contribution on the cricket field appealed to many, as did the camaraderie and the thrill of victory or the run chase, and the emergence of regular fixtures between particular teams added to the significance of certain matches. As the *Yorkshire Post* put it:

> There is no more enthusiastic supporter of the game than the clubman – the player who submits without a murmur to many inconveniences in pursuit of his favourite sport. The pitch upon which he plays may not be as level as a billiard table; the width of the wickets or of the bat may not reach regulation size; but for all that, the enthusiasm he displays is great.[226]

Cricket also helped establish rituals amongst colleagues at a time when work was an increasingly structured influence on people's lives. Malcolmson has argued that popular recreations 'served to foster social cohesiveness and group unity. Competitive team sports, for instance, often reinforced the sense of solidarity of the communities from which the opposing players were drawn.'[227] Work teams were easy to arrange within warehouses, mills and offices. The Hull Railway Clerks' cricket club, for example, started in 1873 when a Mr Milsom posted notices in the various departments of the Hull Goods Station, and as time went on the club recruited from other parts of the railway in Hull as well as associated agencies.[228] Places of work offered ready-made groups of sufficient men, and matches could be organised easily during the working day with identifiable opposition from other workplaces. Such teams required no new formal structure in the shape of a cricket club, equipment could be kept at the place of employment, and games played on a willing employer's property.

In some cases, employers gave broader support to help a club's development. In September 1853:

> through the kindness of their employers who had given them the day, the clerks and warehousemen in the employment of Messrs Stansfeld Brown and Co, spent it at a game of cricket between the married and single...Afterwards they partook of the annual dinner provided by the employers, at the Stansfeld Arms.[229]

In 1856, Mr G.J.Crowther, a manufacturing chemist, gave his workmen a half-holiday on a Saturday to play cricket on Woodhouse Moor, after which they returned to the works, where 60 people sat down to a substantial dinner, provided for them by the owner.[230] In 1855, the Sheffield United Law Clerks' Cricket Club was established, with 50 clerks enrolling. They played on several mornings and evenings a week, as well as Saturday afternoons. It was also reported that their employers had arranged to close their offices at two o'clock on Saturdays, and some of the members were allowed to stop work at six o'clock every evening, having given up the hour allowed for tea.[231]

Cricket thus provided a chance for men to pit themselves in the sporting arena against others with whom they came into contact in the course of their working lives. A report of one match stated that the joiners and corn millers of Brighouse had been on friendly terms for some time, and in order 'to cement the friendship still stronger each party has formed a cricket club and on Saturday a match was played'.[232] Cricket was a way of socialising and competing with people in the same occupation – for example, teams of butchers, livery lace weavers and confectioners played colleagues in York in 1845.[233] The same year, employees of Messrs Kearsleys, coachbuilders, sought a game with men employed by any other coachbuilders in the city.[234] In 1855, the steel refiners of Messrs Thomas Turton and Sons works met with Messrs Naylor, Vickers and Co for a match. The report (perhaps oddly) suggested that the result in favour of the former might have been due to them having worked all night, whereas their opponents had been on holiday![235]

Many of the contests reported in the *Bradford Observer* in the 1850s appear to be workplace matches, and the *Sheffield Independent* in the 1840s and 1850s contains numerous reports of similar games. A couple of decades later, other teams representing the police in Bradford and Hull played each other, and it was noted that the Hull people received their Bradford colleagues in 'a sumptuous and bountiful manner.'[236]

Cricket also had a strongly social aspect. Many games ended with a supper for the teams, invariably described in the papers in glowing terms. When Dunnington played Escrick in 1834, the latter club made a considerable effort, meeting their opponents with a band as they approached their village. The match ended with supper in the pub, where the teams spent the evening singing and 'no one thought of separating till an early hour in the morning when, after playing for a short time, principally on two bugles, some very beautiful tunes, the Dunnington players took their leave of the Escrick ones.'[237] In a similar vein, after a match between two teams from William Tyzack and Sons in Sheffield made up of 11 filesmiths and a team of saw and scythe smiths, the players ended up in a local public house:

> where upwards of eighty of their workmen sat down to a good English dinner of roast beef and pudding...After dinner, the health of the partners of the firm was drunk, and was cordially responded to by the senior partner who addressed the workmen at some length, referring to the relations of masters and workmen.[238]

Clubs often held annual events, where the results of the past season were celebrated (or lamented) and the annual accounts considered. These usually took place in a school room, public house, or in a room described as the 'clubroom' if there was an enduring relationship with a pub landlord. They were frequently accompanied by singing, music or some other form of entertainment. Wider social activities developed around cricket clubs. In January 1870, for example, 500 people attended the annual tea party of the Marsden Mechanics' Institute Cricket Club, the entertainment consisting of readings and comic singing.[239] Such events often included patriotic speeches. When the Bradford King Cross club held its annual dinner in the Old King Cross Inn in 1857, the room was decked out with Union Jacks and cricket items were suspended from the ceiling and walls. The chairman gave toasts to the Queen, the Army and Navy.[240] More aristocratic clubs organised events with more glamour. In December 1845, the Castle Howard Cricket Club held its annual ball, attended by around 100 people. Supper was brought out at midnight and dancing went on until 5 o'clock the next morning.[241]

Cricket also became an accompaniment to many other social activities or work trips. In 1846, Messrs Shellcross, British plate manufacturers in Trinity Street in Sheffield, entertained its staff at the Bagshawe Arms in Hemsworth, and prior to the dinner the men played cricket, while the women 'amused themselves with other pleasant and agreeable sports.'[242] Ten years later, Messrs John Kenyon and Co gave 300 employees a day of entertainment at the Hyde Park cricket ground in Sheffield, with cricket, football, rifle shooting and jumping part of the amusements.[243] Two years later, 700 colliers and workmen from Wombwell Main Colliery, along with their families, made a trip to Thorne, taking bats, footballs and fishing rods. They went on the river, and then played cricket against the local team, when 'the muscle and skills of the colliers was more than a match for the natives.'[244] Cricket also was a part of an excursion for the Yorkshire Penny Savings Bank, Bradford Church Branch in 1869, as it was of the Bradford Festival Choral Society event in August of that year, and for the children of North Frodingham Congregational Sunday School on their trip to the seaside in August 1874.[245]

Many people's enthusiasm for the game was stirred by the chance to experience something unusual, and a cricket match could be a break from the constraints and routine of normal life. Triumphant teams returning home created a stir. In 1834, the York players arrived back from beating Thirsk to be:

> warmly greeted by some hundreds of persons who had assembled in St Helen's-square. Indeed, so great was the anxiety manifested, that a large number of people went as far as Clifton to meet the coach, and followed it with acclamations to the city.[246]

Victories were the cause for celebration. When Huddersfield Old Club beat Manchester New Club in August 1826, church bells saluted the Huddersfield players after the game. And when the Knaresborough team returned from beating Otley in August 1842, they were 'hailed by the excellent Brass Band of Music, and welcomed by a demonstration of public feeling.'[247] Four years later, when the Otley Junior side beat Leeds Wellington, the town resounded to the 'shouts of victory' when people heard the news.[248]

It is easy to underestimate the boredom of small town or village life in the 19th century, so that a significant cricket match with a local rival or touring team was a major event. In Hedon in 1857, for example, 'the peaceful and unexcitable inhabitants of "Sleepy Hollow" were startled by the distant sound of a horn... Dames and daughters, men and boys, all rushed out to see the prancing greys, and cheer the musical old general and his band of heroes.' This was a prelude to the arrival of two cricket teams from Hedon Wellington and Beverley and East Riding.[249] The excitement can also be sensed from a report on the Bradford v Knaresborough match in 1840 which explained that:

> at half-past seven in the morning the martial notes of the bugle gave notice of the arrival of the Knaresborough gents., who entered the town by way of High Street in an elegant coach-and-four, with postillion, the bugleman playing 'See the conquering hero comes.' On passing Church Bridge the musician struck up the merry tune of 'We won't go home till morning.'....On entering the room at the White Lion Inn, where the Bradford youths were assembled, they gave utterance to their feelings, and declared "they had come to take the laural and carry the bit of tin over Pool Bridge."

After a good-natured match, the players dined together until it was time for the Knaresborough men to leave, the bugleman playing 'O dear what can the matter be' as they departed.[250]

Particular games acquired importance and stimulated strong local feeling. Reflecting on one particular example, the *Leeds Times* commented that few who lived outside of Holbeck and Hunslet could conceive of 'the intense rivalries that exist between these two clubs in cricket.' As a result, 2,500 were on the ground for the match in 1881.[251] In 1842, when Dalton lost to Sheffield, it was reported that 'The issue of this game also brings another first-rate club into the field to contend for the 'championship' of Yorkshire; and most probably, next summer, the Sheffield, Dalton, Bradford and Harewood clubs will make attempts for a final settlement of the palm of victory.'[252]

A decade later, the match between Bedale and Stockton-upon-Tees was described as for the 'championship of the North'.[253] At a lower standard, in 1843 a match was played at Millhouses near Sheffield between Upper and Lower Heeley to decide which of the two villages 'should have the championship'[254], and a match between Newstead and Saltaire was described as 'for the honour of the championship of firms.'[255] In 1843, although the *Bradford Observer* refused to print a statement from the 'Strugglers Cricket Club' because it had arrived too late, it still noted that 'the 'Strugglers' are ready to play their rivals, the butchers, for 10s a man any day – barring no member of either club.'[256] It was even claimed that efforts were made to sabotage preparations for a big game, when the (untrue) story was put around in Bradford in 1842 that one of the best Rochdale players was dead, allegedly in an effort to 'throw a cooler upon the exertions of our townsmen.'[257]

The downside was that such competitive spirit could create bad feeling. The Bradford v Leeds match in 1841 was 'unexpectedly, and disagreeably terminated in a dispute' over an umpire's decision, which was the subject of adjudication by *Bell's Life* newspaper, a trusted role it played along with acting as stakeholder for prize fights and for bets in a number of sports.[258] The paper concluded that Bradford had won and the bets should be paid, so that the winning club refused to consider a further game until the payments were settled.[259]

A dispute in 1844 in a match between Bradford and Harewood over the timing of the close of play led to the two clubs not playing each other for three years, when the outstanding stakes were contested for a second time, along with fresh ones from a series of three matches.[260] When a much-fancied Bradford side lost by one run to Dalton in August 1846, the Dalton players left in an omnibus. They gave 'three tremendous cheers, and although hundreds of people surrounded their vehicle, not one solitary response issued from the crowd.' The local paper considered that those who played cricket 'might afford to be a little more magnanimous.'[261] A game between Holmfirth and Nether Thong for £5 10s came to an abrupt finish 'when a disputed ball gave rise to a spirited and general fight between the antagonistic sections.'[262] A few weeks later, another game involving Nether Thong could not be finished, this time against Honley, 'the Netherthongers, as usual, kicking up a 'fratch'!'[263]

The opportunity to bet was a crucial factor generating interest in cricket. Betting on fights, races and local events had long been popular and cricket had many attractions for those keen to wager. In considering Sheffield in the 1820s, Farnsworth notes that 'The players were chiefly interested in claiming the stake money; and if spectators delighted in seeing their own favourites triumph, for them the real attraction was the gambling available on the sidelines.'[264] In 1834, the MCC instructed that no bet was payable on any match unless it was played out or given up, due to the number of disputes generated, and betting at cricket was so commonplace that the *Bradford Observer* sounded surprised that the All-England v 18 of Yorkshire game in 1846 was 'purely out of good-will' with no money at stake.[265]

Every form of the game was the focus for betting, and newspapers commonly reported the odds on offer before and during the games. Huge sums were sometimes involved. In 1866, a single-wicket match was arranged at York between George Freeman and Henry Terry after 'lively badinage' between the two players during the game between Malton Amateurs and Hull Town. Freeman staked £50 and Terry £25, and such was the excitement in Hull and Beverley that as much as £1,000 was reportedly riding on the game.[266] There was, however, growing disapproval of betting and details became less visible in match reports in the 1860s. Some papers were keen for it to be ended altogether. The *Leeds Times*, for example, was unhappy at what it called 'the pests of the cricket field', following an incident at the Horsforth Athletic Sports where some men assaulted a policeman who tried to stop them betting. It called for all such activity to be banned from cricket and athletics events.[267]

On occasions, betting disputes ended up in the courts. In 1833, a number of Yorkshire papers reported the case of Hodson v Terrill in the Court of Exchequer in Warwick, brought for the recovery of a sum of £20, which had been deposited as the stakes for a game of cricket. It was argued that cricket was considered one of the games captured by a statute of Queen Anne to prevent excessive gambling, and that anyone who lost over £10 could recover it. The grounds for this action was that the game was illegal, although the Chief Justice declared it was not.[268]

Two years later, a case to recover a wager from a match at Tadcaster appeared in the Yorkshire County Court. The plaintiff was a butcher, and the defendant was described as a former butcher who was now 'addicted to cricket playing'. The case was due to be tried one day in August 1835. The courtroom was reportedly full of lawyers and cricketers, 'but the defendant would not play it out'. Instead, the case was removed to the Court of Common Pleas in London. There, the judges would not try it because it was too small a debt and it was returned in March 1836. The defendant did not attend but the jury found in favour of the plaintiff, awarding damages of £1 19s 11d.[269]

As well as active participants in the game, cricket attracted the attention of other people who considered it had many great strengths. Some simply had a love for the sport, but for others it had values well beyond those of a game, and they sought to use it for their own purposes, often making quite considerable claims, in particular, for its moral value. An article from the *Chambers' Journal*, reprinted in the *Leeds Times* in 1877, summarised what many thought, arguing that cricket 'is a pastime so extensively and deservedly popular as to rank among the foremost of English institutions. It is physically an excellent test of wind, strength and endurance, and is intellectually attractive from the opportunities it affords for the exercise of scientific skill.' The article went on to argue that cricket encouraged prudence, temperance and fortitude, stimulated a love of justice, and acted against the growth of arrogance and self-assumption.[270]

The merits of cricket as a counter to the perceived social problems of the 19th century such as alcohol or self-indulgence were also a widespread point of debate. During the election of 1835 in the North Riding, a candidate, Edward Cayley, spoke about the Sabbath Bill and admitted under pressure that he could see little harm in a few young men playing 'an innocent game at cricket' on a Sunday, rather than sitting in a public house.[271] A speaker at the York Cricket Club annual dinner in 1852 suggested that 'cricket was one of the most manly recreations in this country' which he considered was valuable since the age was 'somewhat prone to be luxurious and too effeminate.'[272]

For many, cricket was a healthy activity and a counter to the damaging effects of industrialisation in reducing physical activity. When two teams of tailors played in Bradford in 1847, the local paper mused that it would be good if other employers would support such games because it would strengthen the physical powers of those leading confined and sedentary lives, would make the public house less attractive, and would raise the 'moral condition' of the working man.[273]

Amongst evidence gathered on the moral and physical condition of working children in 1843, a 50-year-old cutler lamented that urbanisation was taking its toll on places for recreation in Sheffield. He observed that 30 years earlier there had been many places where youths and men could play cricket, quoits, football, and other sports. Hardly any remained and he argued that as a result there had been a great increase in crime in the town and neighbourhood.[274] In 1868, a speaker at a Marsden Mechanics' Institute gathering commented that local cricket clubs were 'shown to be greatly in favour of the manufacturer, who, being shut up in workshops all day, required out-door enjoyments in the evening, while the agriculturalist was in the open air all day.'[275] As well as the health benefits of playing cricket, watching the sport also had its advocates. As the *Leeds Times* put it, there are many worse ways to spend time than watching the game since not only did it provide 'healthy excitement' for spectators, but it also offered those living in a smoky town 'a taste of pure air.'[276]

To others, cricket had barely disguised political benefits in that it was seen to bring together different classes of people. Industrialisation and urbanisation in the 1840s created concern amongst the ruling classes at the prospect of social strife. To some, cricket was a way of overcoming some of the class conflict which they feared might result in revolution in England of the kind which had spread across Europe in 1848. Thus, the scene at the supper after a match between workmen of two firms at Hemsworth delighted one reporter, who wrote that it was wonderful to see:

> employers and employed interchanging kindly and respectful sentiments towards each other, and strengthening that bond of union which ought ever to exist between those whose mutual interests are inseparable.....The working classes, feeling that they were cared for and appreciated, would be much more easily governed through their affections than their fears.[277]

Cricket was also considered a counter to crime and disorder. In 1851, a magistrate addressing the jury at Lancaster assizes remarked that in the neighbouring county of Yorkshire, where cricket was popular, crime was very light, and he recommended the same 'manly and invigorating exercise' in their part of the country.[278] At a dinner in York in 1856, one speaker said cricket:

> tended to preserve the national character, and sustained England in the position it now held, for Greece and Rome had their manly and national sports, and when these vanished, those countries fell...In no country as in England could they see the aristocracy blending with the greater part of society as in this country, for in neither France, Germany, or Italy would they find noblemen mixing with them as the noble Chairman had done that evening.[279]

Thus a direct link was drawn between providing space for cricket and other sports, and combating political unrest. In 1840, during evidence gathering for a parliamentary investigation into the health of towns, one witness commented that there was strong feeling against enclosure of open ground in Bradford. The witness stated that there was just three acres for recreation for 120,000 people. Asked what games these people played, he stated that they played cricket and 'spell and nur', and 'they cannot play at those game in three acres.' And he added, although political unrest was dying away, 'if the lower orders have not places where they can engage in sports, it is the very thing to drive them to Chartism.'[280] In Leeds, at a public meeting of the Early Closing Movement in September 1853, during discussions about the need for recreation, one speaker quoted a candle manufacturer, who commented, 'I think the mixing of the boys and myself with the men in cricketing and gardening, has produced much good and kindly feeling among us all, and has made many work together in winter as friends, who felt like strangers before.'[281]

Some politicians saw the value of cricket. In April 1846, during a speech at the Birmingham Athenic Institute, Lord John Manners MP, later Chancellor of the Duchy of Lancaster and in the early 1840s a leading member of the 'Young England' political movement, spoke of the importance of recreation for peace in England. Commenting that many people were concerned that any change in society indicated a sign of revolution, he observed 'a cricket-match does not necessarily imply the bowling-down of the pillars of state'.[282] Two years earlier, Manners had taken the future Prime Minister, Benjamin Disraeli, to the cricket ground at Bingley and joined in the game himself.[283] Others were more cynical about the role assumed for cricket. John Arthur Roebuck, the independent-minded politician and one-time MP for Sheffield, attacked what he described as the fictitious means of satisfying the demands of working people, suggesting that the ruling classes would not offer them genuine power, but instead 'wash-houses and a game of cricket'.[284]

Yet if cricket provided fun for many, it is clear that others found its presence an annoyance, taking up too much time and space. In 1852, an article reporting an educational series of lectures, complained about the small attendance, bemoaning that 'Electioneering, racing, cricket etc seem to absorb more attention at the present time than anything else.'[285] Even those who claimed to like the game feared it was already corrupted. In 1858, for example, in a book entitled 'A Month in Yorkshire', one writer commented gloomily that one could hope to be as:

> merry at a funeral as at a game of cricket, improved into its present condition; when the ball is no longer bowled, but pelted....when gauntlets must be worn on the hands and greaves on the shins... That twenty-two men should ever consent to come together for such a mockery of pleasure, is to me a mystery......Read Miss Mitford's description of a cricket match on the village green; watch a schoolboys' game, consider the mirth and merriment that they get out of it, and sympathise with modern cricket if you can.[286]

Around the same time, prior to a game between Nottingham and All-England, a critic of the game ('a delirious fanatic' and an 'oily-tongued bigot', suspected the *Leeds Times*) put out a 'bilious-looking handbill, condemning such contests and all who attend them.' The paper responded with nine reasons to go to cricket matches, arguing that 'on moral and sanitary grounds' it deserved support.[287] Others wondered whether it had different and more material benefits, the *Leeds Times* musing in 1883 that parents who complained that schools wasted time on cricket might consider that the Australian players had received between £600 and £700 for a few months in England, so that their children might do worse than take up the game as an alternative to classics.[288]

A wider objection to cricket was to it being played on a Sunday. The evangelical movement in England grew from the 1730s onwards and by the start of Queen

Victoria's reign had a great influence in English society. Strict observance of the Sabbath was an essential element of the evangelical position and 'the main moving force behind the appreciating regard for a disciplined Sunday which became so deeply rooted in nineteenth-century society.'[289] Many Yorkshire papers included letters from those unhappy with the 'profanation of the Sabbath', as a correspondent put it in 1834, having seen young men playing cricket in York.[290] Eight years later, the *York Herald* reported that boys and man had taken to assembling on Bootham Stray, in the suburbs of the city, on a Sunday to gamble and play cricket, and as a result much damage had been done to the grounds and hedges.[291]

At times action was taken. In 1842, four Ripon boys appeared at the Court House charged with the offence by a constable. They were part of a group who had reportedly been caught playing the previous Sunday and, appearing before the Mayor, they were fined 4s 6d each. However, these boys had not been seen by the constable, and as there were no witnesses they were discharged with a reprimand. This left the constable to pay the costs of the summonses 'to his no small chagrin, and the delight of the lads and several old cricketers who had attended the court.'[292] In the 1850s, extra policemen were often deployed on Sundays in York to prevent young men from gambling and playing cricket. A speaker at the York Working Men's Sabbath Protection Society meeting in 1851 (albeit to a small audience) called for cricket, football and other games to be done away with, adding he did not object to a man and his wife taking a walk after church, but 'when they went into the fields, played at cricket, and engaged in other exercises, excitement was created; they then, in all probability, from becoming thirsty, went to the public-house and got drunk.'[293]

The Lord's Day Defence Association was established in 1856 in York and elsewhere in response to the formation of the National Sunday League, set up to promote the opening of the British Museum on the Sabbath. Members expressed concern that it would not stop there and that theatres, billiards rooms, new rooms and cricket grounds would soon have an equal claim to be open.[294] In 1869, a case appeared in front of the West Riding Police Court of boys playing unlawful games on a Sunday in front of a school. They refused to stop when asked by a police officer. Apparently, it was common for boys to play cricket on Sunday in front of the school premises, although no action had been taken until now. They were fined 1s and costs of 7s.[295]

The relationship between cricket and the sale of alcohol was also the cause of some anguished debate, but was not straightforward. In 1861, the landlord of the Shoulder of Mutton Inn was reported by the police for selling alcohol on the Lockwood cricket ground. The police advised this was illegal and wrote to the Board of the Inland Revenue. The Revenue said they did not want to interfere and the magistrates were asked if they were content for the matter to pass. The police were unhappy that this was allowed to happen despite the law, but the officer who reported the matter said he would leave it until he had consulted the Chief Constable. The magistrates said they could not act unless there was a charge, which there was not, and encouraged the policeman to act on his discretion.[296] Two years later, when the same landlord applied for permission to sell liquor on the Lockwood ground for the game with Morley, there was no objection from the police and the application was granted.[297]

To some, the benefits that could be derived from cricket – that it was a healthy activity that could discourage people from drinking – were undermined by the way in which alcohol was then made available at games. In 1887, at the Brewster Sessions in Huddersfield, the Chairman reflected that there had been an enormous number of applications for licenses, particularly for cricket matches, adding 'it used to be thought that cricket matches were advantageous in giving the people rational amusement, and took away the facilities to drink, of which many used to take too freely; but it appeared that the drinksellers were following the people to every cricket match, and he was not sure they were not defeating the very object some of the magistrates had in view in supporting cricket clubs.' The police apparently had no complaints as to how the licences had been used, but the Chairman felt that magistrates should not grant them so frequently.[298]

It seemed there were no simple answers to the tensions associated with changes in Victorian society. At the same time, it is also clear that cricket had secured a very significant place in the lives and emotions of many people in Yorkshire in the 19th century. The game meant different things to different people. For some, it was a traditional game, evoking a simpler past; for others it was a force for change and modernisation.

CHAPTER THREE

THE SPREAD OF THE GAME

The county of Yorkshire is a large and very varied part of England – one-sixth of its land mass. Some of it became highly industrialised in the course of the 19th century, while much remained rural. It has a long coastline, but a majority of the population lived miles from the sea. Many people were pressed into a relatively small part of the county, while large areas were uninhabited. The role of geography in the development of cricket has been examined elsewhere. Underdown's history of 18th century cricket emphasised the particular geographical and economic circumstances in which the game emerged in the south of England, whilst Hignell took a geographical perspective in order to explain how cricket developed in south Wales in the 19th century.[299]

We therefore turn to examine how cricket grew in different parts of Yorkshire. This is inevitably impressionistic, but it is fair to say that it grew fastest and most intensely for much of the century around Sheffield, and in towns such as Bradford, Leeds, Dewsbury and Huddersfield. Elsewhere, in the North and East Ridings, cricket was played with enthusiasm, for example around York, Scarborough and Hull, but the game took different paths, influenced by geography and the ways in which particular areas developed economically.

The Ridings of Yorkshire

The three Ridings of Yorkshire were very different in the 19th century. Kelly's Directory for 1881 described West Yorkshire as 'one of the greatest manufacturing districts in the world'. It noted that Sheffield was the centre of steel converting and refining, as well as home to the cutlery trade and the manufacture of machine tools, spades and shovels. The West Riding also had coal fields. In contrast, the East Riding – the smallest of the three – was an agricultural and fishing area. Potatoes, flax, cereal crops and peas, beans and turnips were common, along with horse breeding. Hull was the major manufacturing town of the Riding, involved in shipbuilding, seed crushing, oil refining and the manufacture of oil cakes, as well as paint and sail- making. The North Riding was very large – at 1.36 million acres only smaller in size than the West Riding and the counties of Lincolnshire, Norfolk and Devon. However, its only significant manufacturing industry was pig iron based around Middlesbrough. Wheat was grown in large quantities, along with oats and seeds around York and Ryedale. On the moors, sheep-rearing was common, and North Yorkshire was also well known for horse-breeding and its grouse moors.

The population was very unevenly spread. In the West Riding it grew considerably in the 19th century as people moved to meet the demands for labour for the developing industries. In 1801, Sheffield had 45,755 people, but by 1871, 239,947, an increase of more than five times. The population of Leeds in 1801 was 53,162, but 70 years later was 259,912, a similar increase. Bradford grew more than ten times from 13,264 in 1801 to 145,830 in 1871, with the period from 1841 to 1851 particularly dramatic – a more than 50% increase. In contrast, other places experienced little change in their population. Skipton remained at around 32,000 people between 1861 and 1871 and Wetherby actually reduced in size over this period.

In contrast to the West Riding, the East Riding had a population in 1871 of 209,505 and in 1891, just under 400,000, spread across an area of 750,000 acres, with around half living in Hull. With a population of 199,991 in 1891, Hull was 16 times the size of Beverley, the next largest town. Finally, the North Riding was very thinly populated in proportion to its area, with much of its hilly countryside and bleak moorland uninhabited. In 1861, its population was 245,154 and in 1891, 368,237. The principal towns were Middlesbrough at 76,000 in 1891, followed by Scarborough at 34,000, but with only Thornaby-on-Tees and Whitby also above 10,000.[300] In some places the population declined, with young men abandoning quiet villages for the opportunities of better paid work in Middlesbrough, but overall it remained an area 'pursuing a way of life whose rhythms were orchestrated by the passing seasons.'[301] Finally, the population of York grew throughout the century from around 20,000 in 1811 to 51,000 in 1891.

A third factor which affected how these people came together for both work and pleasure was the ease with which it was possible to travel around and between the different Ridings. The West Riding was 'well supplied' with railways, according to Kelly's Directory. The Great Northern, the North Western, the Midland, the Lancashire and Yorkshire, the Manchester, Sheffield and Lincolnshire and the North Eastern companies all had a significant presence in Yorkshire, and thus lines ran out from the principal towns, providing communications with all parts of the country. There was also an extensive canal network. In the East Riding, the railways were less extensive, although Hull was well connected to Leeds, Manchester, Liverpool and the West Riding, and to London and the south. Lines radiated out to Hornsea, to Withernsea and northwards to the North Riding. The North Eastern Railway company had its head office at York. Lines branched out to many of the main towns such as Thirsk and Northallerton on to Darlington, and to Malton, Thirsk and Boroughbridge. Yorkshire was thus highly varied in many ways, and any examination of the development of cricket there should be seen against the background of this rich and diverse picture. We start with the traditional West Riding, then move to the East Riding and end up in the North Riding.

Sheffield

In an article published in 1829, it was suggested that 'Cricket has been introduced into Yorkshire little more than half a century. The principal place in the West-Riding, where the game was first practised in imitation of Hampshire, Sussex, and other southern Counties, is the district denominated Hallamshire; known, however, only to strangers as the beautiful country which surrounds Sheffield.'[302] As mentioned earlier, Sheffield took on Nottingham in the 1770s, which were hard-fought games but not repeated until 1800.[303] Farnsworth points to Hallam being the oldest club in Sheffield, with records dating back to 1804 and evidence of matches in the 1810s.[304]

Also looking back to that time, a senior member of the Sheffield Wednesday club claimed every village around the town had a cricket club, and players from these clubs were selected to play teams from elsewhere. Defeat of the best players of Sheffield by Nottingham in 1801 was a major blow and apparently led to the game declining for some years, but the peace of 1815 (following the defeat of Napoleon), and the return from the army of a number of good cricketers, led to a revival. In 1816, Sheffield played an important game with Mansfield, but they struggled without a good ground or benefactors, and had to play on stubble fields after the corn was gone (hence the match was played in October). Nevertheless, it was noted:

> the Mansfield match gave renewed vigour to the game, but they had no cricket ground until 1820, when one was opened by George Steer. In 1822, Nottingham played 15 of Sheffield, and scored in one inning 122, while Sheffield scored only 121 in two innings. Sparks was then sent for from the south, and he first introduced here the new style of playing. In looking round subsequently for men to play in a match with the celebrated Nottingham players, they, by good chance, fell upon Tom Marsden, who then played with a club in a brickyard in the Brocco, and subsequently so distinguished himself that his fame became known far and wide.[305]

In Farnsworth's opinion, the 1820s saw a 'cricket boom' in Sheffield when handicap, sweepstake and challenge matches were popular.[306] In 1820, the Sheffield Wednesday club was formed[307] and the following year, the ground at Darnall ('Old Ground') – soon considered the best in England – was levelled and prepared, opening with the match at the end of August 1822. There was a 'peculiar interest' around the game between 15 of Sheffield and 11 of Nottingham, and it was suggested that 'never, perhaps on any occasion, was witnessed an assemblage at once so numerous and respectable. Sheffield seemed almost to pour out the principal part of its population, the roads being literally covered all the morning with crowds hasting to the scene of the expected enjoyment.'

Unfortunately, the game was marked by an accident when, at 4 o'clock, a large amount of seating collapsed, injuring many people. According to reports, the arrangements:

> for the accommodation of several thousands of spectators, having nine tiers of seats, and being nearly forty yards long, suddenly gave way, and precipitated its unfortunate tenants one over the other to the ground. Shrieks, screams and groans, rent the air on all sides; and the scene of confusion which ensued was indescribably affecting. Every hand was instantly engaged in extricating the sufferers; every possible accommodation offered; and every vehicle put in requisition to convey them away to their respective homes.[308]

Despite these unfortunate events, George Steer prepared a second playing area at Darnall ('New Ground'), which opened in August 1824, and games in Sheffield attracted five-figure crowds of paying spectators.[309] In 1825, the All-England XI played in front on an average of 10,000 people a day over five days against a 'Twenty-Two of the county of York, with Sparks (from London) on the side of the Yorkshire players.' The All-England side won by 28 runs and, reflecting on the result, a contemporary commentator stated, 'though we concede that much progress has been made by the players of the town....we doubt if any chance would exist in an even match, from which alone reputation could be gained.'[310] Nevertheless, the enthusiasm generated led to the establishment of many new clubs in the town. So great was the interest that in 1830 'nine double-wickets were pitched on the Hyde Park Ground, where upwards of two hundred players were at work at one time.'[311]

Farnsworth suggests two possible explanations for this cricket boom in Sheffield in the 1820s. The first was the absence of alternative attractions. He commented that for years 'Sheffield races had kept people away from cricket, but then, during a period of acute trade depression, many of racing's leading patrons were forced to withdraw their financial backing.' The race track lost its attraction and many of the punters turned to cricket. As a result, games like the All-England contest saw large amounts of betting. The second reason was the interest generated by the controversy over round-arm bowling, considered dangerous at the time. This came to Sheffield when an England XI against Sussex match was played in the town in 1827, creating much excitement as two of the leading protagonists – Lillywhite and Broadbridge – were in the Sussex team.[312]

Davies adds a third, broader economic factor which was that Sheffield (like another increasingly important cricket town – Nottingham) was based around industries in which independent trades and small-scale production continued well into the second half of the 19th century. As a result, 'a considerable proportion of the labour force was free to determine its own pattern of work and leisure and set time aside for watching and playing sport. Both consequently became important centres for producing professional players and also enjoyed a significant market for commercial cricket matches.'[313]

Darnall saw some great matches and was well regarded by visitors. A report of the match between All-England and 11 Men of Yorkshire, Leicestershire and Nottinghamshire in 1828[314] noted that the ground was very popular with spectators and players. 'Few bowling-greens in the county presented a finer surface. The new stand was graced by the presence of a number of ladies; and Lord Milton and his family, with many distinguished admirers of the game from London and Doncaster, were likewise present, who expressed their admiration of the beauty of the place and the excellence of the general arrangements.'[315] At Darnall 'old ground' a grandstand holding 2,000 people had been built, and on the 'new' ground, artificial terracing with seats for 8,000, with a large area of level ground and a pavilion. This appears to have housed a lot of material because when W.H.Woolhouse, its owner, was bankrupted in 1828, the effects sold included working tools, warehouse and shop fixtures, a large stock of bricks, live and dead stock, valuable household furniture, chandeliers, silver plate, books, china, glass, linen, brewing utensils and other items.[316] In 1831, the cricket stand was sold by auction. Made of 'the best materials and workmanship, and finished at a great expense' it had a Tuscan colanade and balcony, strong timbered roof, as well as fixtures, cooking apparatus and a pump. It was described as suitable for any person wanting to erect public rooms, or for families or innkeepers.[317]

In 1826, a new ground at Hyde Park was completed at a cost of £4,000, and subsequently became Sheffield's most popular venue as Darnall declined. It continued with this status for around 20 years, and not just for competitive cricket as Woolhouse opened it up for pigeon shooting (3,000 attended a competition in 1833) and fireworks displays, and advertised its availability for anyone wanting to play friendly games of cricket on certain nights of the week. There was also a wrestling contest in 1834, although cricketers were reassured than any games organised to take place that day could go ahead uninterrupted.[318] At the end of the 1833 season the *Sheffield Independent* noted the 'very excellent manner' in which Woolhouse ran the ground. However, he struggled to make it pay and the ground was put up for auction in 1836. The advert stated that it had a large and commodious stone gallery extending the whole length of the south side, which commanded a view of the ground. The five-acre site was surrounded by a tall stone wall and was on a 21-year lease from 1826 at a yearly rent of £16. A tavern was part of the sale.[319] In January 1839, however, part of the wall at the entrance of the ground was blown down, and such was the violence of the wind that the thick bar of wood which fastened the gates was snapped in two.[320]

Not everyone liked the Hyde Park ground. In 1833, in evidence to a parliamentary committee on amusement and recreation for the inhabitants of large towns, one submission on Sheffield complained that the town was in a hole surrounded by high hills, and on one hill was a cricket ground 'surrounded by high walls'. There, the existence of entrance fees excluded it 'as a miscellaneous walk, and makes it rather a theatre for seeing cricket and other games, than a place of general exercise itself.'[321] The ground deteriorated in the 1840s, and in 1847, after some players were injured, there were complaints that:

> the ground was not in such good condition as we could have wished to see it; and we trust that before another match of the like importance, the spirited proprietor, who is generally 'awake' as to anything which tends to promote the convenience of his patrons, will see that the ground be properly mown and rolled.[322]

These were not the first complaints. In June 1845, for example, when Bromhall played Milton 'the ground was by no means in first rate order, owing to the unusual length of the grass'.[323]

The problems with the Hyde Park ground were part of a decline in Sheffield cricket in the 1840s, and according to an 1844 article, the second part of the history of Darnall was characterised by 'decadence'. It conjectured that perhaps:

> the public got tired of a pastime too frequently repeated, and certainly many of the supporters of the game made it the vehicle and medium of certain speculations....Darnall cricket field is now sown with wheat – its handsome stand and viranda may be partly found amongst the stores of old dealers – its tavern doors are closed, and its license fallen from the sessions list.[324]

Further evidence of the low standing of Sheffield cricket in the 1840s can be seen in tributes made to M.J.Ellison in 1851. Looking back, one speaker commented that in 1841 or 1842 the Lead Works Cricket Club slowly declined. Subsequently, in 1843:

> some members who appeared to have been in a state of somnolency for two years, all at once rose again, and in the autumn of that year was laid the basis of the present Sheffield Cricket Club. Other clubs in the town had still continued to play, but....the game of cricket was then at a very low ebb – perhaps lower than it had been in this town for 25 or 30 years before.[325]

The mid-1840s appears to have been a nadir for Sheffield cricket and the organisation of a game between Twenty of Sheffield and the All-England Eleven in 1846 can be seen as an attempt to rectify the decline. One reporter wrote that

'The match has already caused considerable interest in the town, and it is hoped, may be the means of materially forwarding the exertions now making to restore the game to the degree of popularity it enjoyed in this town during the time that the celebrated Darnall ground was open.'[326] Efforts were also made elsewhere in the town. Around £1,000 was spent on developing the Barrack Tavern cricket ground and bowling green in 1848.[327] Work was carried out on the Hyde Park ground over the winter of 1847/48, with the low side raised and trees planted. In 1848, the Sheffield Cricket Club reported that as a result the ground 'will now be worthy of the town of Sheffield, and of the games of which it will be the arena.'[328]

Things were improving by the early 1850s. At the end of the 1851 season, the *Independent* was positive about developments in the town, commenting that 'every exertion was being made by the Sheffield club to render the Yorkshire side, on all occasions, as strong and efficient as possible, and many thanks are due to them for their liberal patronage of this manly and athletic exercise.'[329] The *Manchester Guardian* was also very complimentary about the prowess of Sheffield cricketers, commenting after they had beaten Manchester that they 'presented those features of cool determination and abstracted attention... which, if not resulting in certain success, are the best means to secure it: features, too, we venture to say more peculiarly characteristic of Sheffield players than of any other provincials'. As a result, 'Sheffield has lost none.....of its high credit in the noble game.'[330] Despite this, the growing population of the town as well as industrial and housing development put pressure on cricket grounds, including Hyde Park, and for a while the Sheffield club moved from ground to ground.[331] Elsewhere, in 1854, the annual meeting of the Sheffield Athenaeum heard that its cricket club had not been successful, in part because the ground at Royds Mill had become unsuitable due to its proximity to numerous large factories.[332]

The turning point was the establishment of a new ground at Bramall Lane after the Duke of Norfolk made land available. At a meeting on 30 January 1854 it was announced that the Duke would give a 99-year lease for land on which to build a pavilion. However:

> owing to the strict nature of the family settlement, he could not give a lease for that portion which would be required for the formation of the ground. The rent for this portion would be £5 an acre......It would be for the meeting to consider how the money which was necessary for the formation of the ground should be raised, and also to appoint a committee to receive applications for shares, and also to draw up a report as to the most desirable manner in which the ground should hereafter be managed. He had roughly estimated the cost of the undertaking at from £1700 to £2000, which included the erection of the pavilion, the fence walls, and the levelling of the ground.[333]

With all its widespread hills and dales, it was not easy to find a suitable ground in Sheffield, so the Bramall Lane site was very attractive, the same speaker observing that it was near the town without being close to any factories as at the old ground. The Duke of Norfolk's offer was thus seen as very reasonable and it was accepted unanimously at the meeting. A provisional committee was established of men representing a number of Sheffield clubs – Sheffield Cricket Club, Adelphi, Milton, Wednesday, Exchange, Broomhall and Athenaeum – to finalise the arrangements.[334]

By September 1854, around half of the field had been permanently laid down, and a contract entered into for £700 for booths and sheds for spectators at the lower end of the Ground.[335] The ground was eventually opened on 30 April 1855, having cost around £2,500. Of this, £1,715 had been subscribed and £1,426 actually paid.[336] It was opened with a game between the first eleven and twenty-two selected from the Sheffield, Wednesday, Broomhall, Milton, Caxton, and Shrewsbury clubs, and it was reported that the 8.5-acre ground was:

> in excellent condition, and when completed, will be inferior to few, if any in the kingdom. Already an ample platform has been erected for spectators on the exclusive side of the ground, and on the other side is a building, the four lower compartments of which are occupied by publicans, while the upper form a sort of covered gallery for the convenience of spectators.[337]

There was also a new 'telegraph' on the ground so that the crowd could follow the score.[338] Once opened, the ground was used by different clubs on each day, with general practice on a Saturday. Such was the amount of early usage that 1,600 square yards of turf had to be applied to repair the ground after only five months.[339]

Impressed by the new arrangements, the *Sheffield Independent* commented that 'the convenience afforded by this ground will give a new stimulus to the practise of this national sport' in the town. In fact, the game was already widespread and in May 1855 the proprietors of the booths invited clubs within 20 miles of Sheffield to compete in a sweepstake competition, each club to contribute £5 10s, with a £20 prize for the winner. Professionals were not allowed to participate and no player was permitted to play for more than one club.[340] This seemed a good way of generating interest in the new facilities, although not everyone was happy. The following year, there were complaints from the Shrewsbury club that the sweepstake matches had caused inconvenience by being played on the day it was due to practise.[341]

Other developments took place in Sheffield around the same time. At Easter 1854, the New Hall Cricket and Pleasure Grounds were opened as a 22-acre site with cricket ground, billiard rooms, balconies, refreshment rooms, aviaries, bowling green, maze, deer paddocks, fountains, terraces, a lake for boating and conservatories. The first cricket match played here was between the United Eleven of England and XV of Sheffield. The site cost around £10,000 to lay out, but 10,000 people visited when it opened, being charged 3d each, which gave some basis for hoping it might pay its way.[342] It was not, however, a great success, and although highly thought of, the distance from Sheffield and a lack of seats, except on paying a second fee, were seen as likely to discourage attendance.[343]

The quality of the players and the facilities available meant Sheffield was the leading centre for the game in the county. During the 1860s and 1870s, Sheffield was the driving force in the development of Yorkshire county cricket, and M.J.Ellison and J.B.Wostinholm 'effectively ran Yorkshire cricket from Bramall Lane', even though, as we shall see in the final chapter, this carried with it considerable risks and pressures.[344] To many, Sheffield was the natural centre of Yorkshire cricket and in 1868, *Sporting Life* commented that whatever the claims of other towns, Sheffield had precedence, and was almost as famous for its cricketers as its cutlery. In addition:

> The Bramall-lane Ground is removed a nice easy distance from the town, and away from the smoke – except when the wind is in one direction. It is kept in excellent order, there is a commodious pavilion, a range of permanent bars, with ample covered sitting accommodation overhead.[345]

The game continued to grow in popularity in Sheffield in the 1870s. In 1873, 'An Impartial Observer' wrote that on fine summer nights, cricket was played 'on every vacant space' and 'some very fair players are sometimes trained in these rough and ready schools'. And the same writer felt that a visit to Bramall Lane 'would convince any doubter of the great hold which cricket has upon the affection of Sheffielders.'[346] Some even felt that the enthusiasm was going too far and, in 1870, member clubs of the Sheffield Cricket Clubs Association complained to the Ground Committee at Bramall Lane that it was difficult for its members to practise on Saturdays as so many factory matches were taking place.[347] During the winter of 1874/75, work was undertaken on the ground and it was anticipated that visitors would be astonished at the great improvements made. In particular, during the winter:

> about two more acres have been enclosed with a substantial brick wall, and the old unsightly rubble wall next the running track removed. The old decayed wood paling in front of the Pavilion has also been replaced by a very plain but substantial iron palisading let into a solid stone foundation. The enclosure has not only been subdivided, one part being set aside for shareholders and the

other for the general public, but it has also been furnished with comfortable seats arranged terrace fashion, thus giving all good view.[348]

The only problem with Bramall Lane was the environment in which it was situated. Economic development in the town continued and in 1873, Yorkshire's game with Lancashire was affected by smoke from the town brought on by a northerly wind, which made the light very bad.[349] In 1878, the *Leeds Times* reported observations from an Australian visitor that:

> the wind sent the smoke from the factories right across the ground, and occasionally it was so dense that the more remote onlookers could scarcely be seen from the pavilion. The smut rested on our clothing, and our faces were almost black with it. We were very glad to get back to our hotel and indulge in the luxury of a bath....The buildings, streets and the inhabitants have a smoky and unclean appearance.[350]

During the early months of 1881, a new pavilion was built and locally was considered the most complete in the country, being 'a splendid structure – most substantially built – and is as convenient and well-appointed inside as it is handsome and imposing outside.' The building had spacious storage rooms and a kitchen, with a cooking range with capacity to cater for 400 people. On the ground floor were gentlemen's rooms and accommodation for players and ladies, as well as a committee room, a large bar, approachable from the first enclosure, and a smaller one for use of those in the minor enclosure. On the first floor there was a dining room for 150 people or more, a promenade for members, a club room, a reporters' room, etc., and, at the front, a verandah with seats. As a result, one commentator suggested it was clear 'the Yorkshire Executive intend to be abreast of the age.' [351]

Developments continued. In 1885, the *Yorkshire Post* observed that:

> The turf in the playing portions of the ground at Bramall Lane has been well looked after, and is likely to play as true as in years past. Everything, too, has been done to ensure the comfort of the large crowds expected to attend. The seating accommodation alone will provide for 2,000 people, while a new printing and scoring box has been brought into requisition.[352]

Sheffield led Yorkshire cricket for thirty years and, throughout the period covered by this book, was the single most significant location for the game in the county. Men from Sheffield ran Yorkshire cricket, and the town's clubs were strong and produced many fine players. Sheffield cricket was admired and respected, but many followers of the game were unhappy about its domination.

Huddersfield

In 1874, the Chairman of the Huddersfield Athletic Club called Huddersfield 'a cricket loving town', and 30 years later, Holmes considered that, with the possible exception of the Sheffield district, 'no other corner of the County has taken so prominent a place in the development of Yorkshire County cricket from 1833 to 1903.' Holmes referred to several matches in the area in 1826; one between Huddersfield and Dewsbury, and others involving clubs described as Huddersfield Old Club and Huddersfield New Club. [353] In 1839, a club called the Morning Star Cricket Company was established, which took a field near the Highfield chapel, and required its members to meet to practise four times a week, including three times in the morning, with non-attendance resulting in fines.[354] Several village clubs in the area had their origins around this time, with Dalton Cricket Club, founded in the winter of 1831, six years after the beginnings of cricket in Lascelles Hall.[355]

Cricket was hugely popular around Hudderfield in the 1840s. Dalton was a very prominent side, taking on Sheffield, York (winning by an innings in 1845), Knaresborough and Bradford (bowling them out for 47 and 19 in 1846) on a regular basis. In 1844, it took part in 'The Great Cricket Match, For the Championship of Yorkshire, and £100' against Sheffield at Hyde Park.[356] The Huddersfield club was also active, for example, defeating Leeds Clarence in 1849, and the game between Dalton and Huddersfield in 1850 led the *Huddersfield Chronicle* to comment that 'finer skill and steadier play has not been witnessed on the Huddersfield ground during the summer.'[357] In addition, there were many smaller clubs appealing to different groups in the area. In 1842, for example, Huddersfield Caledonian or Socialist Club played against Huddersfield Beehive or Teetotal Club.[358] Other clubs with names such as Huddersfield Hope, Huddersfield Buffaloes, Huddersfield Alert ('with a little more experience, it will be one of the first minor clubs in the neighbourhood.'), Huddersfield Nelson and Huddersfield Brilliant operated at various points in the decade.[359] Work matches were also common. In 1845, for example, the letter-press printers of the town challenged the bookbinders.[360]

In 1851, Dalton played Sheffield in Manchester. The *Huddersfield Chronicle* reported that the former club had repeatedly tried to arrange a game but had been turned down, until it had inserted a challenge in *Bell's Life* for a match for £100, which was accepted. The local paper noted that the *Manchester Guardian* had been very critical of matches for stakes. The *Chronicle* commented it would normally agree with these reservations, but felt there were special circumstances since the Dalton men:

> occupy a position in life which prevents them from making pecuniary sacrifices such as matches purely for honour.....therefore

> if they are to come into the field at all to contest the superiority of clubs so notorious, it can only be by the generous support of the gentry, or by matches under similar arrangements as the game under notice.[361]

The game grew in popularity in the area during the 1850s and the All-England Eleven played local sides in 1850, 1851 and 1865, and the United XI visited in 1864.[362] In the early 1860s, there were many signs of progress amongst local clubs, and improvements to grounds in the area. In 1860, it was reported that Holmfirth is 'deservedly celebrated for its cricket club', and the game was also played by 'many gentlemen in the villages, amongst whom some exciting and well-contested matches occasionally come off with varied success.'[363] A couple of years later, the same paper commented that cricket was 'much in vogue in Holmfirth amongst all ranks of people, and matches are almost a daily occurrence – some of them worthy of notice, and others not.'[364] In 1861, Lockwood Cricket Club enlarged its ground, as did Kirkburton.[365] Lockwood enjoyed an increase in members, and it was noted that the club's ground, 'picturesquely situated beneath the shadow of the Lockwood Viaduct, has been considerably improved since last season'.[366]

The same year, Holmfirth Victoria Cricket Club was sufficiently confident to take on Glossop, said to be 'the best club in Derbyshire', beating them on the opposition's ground, and generating what was reported to be a 'mania' for playing cricket amongst men of all ages in the area.[367] Important games were played between Lascelles Hall, Lockwood, Bradford and Stockton-on-Tees, as well as the 'Mancunian Wanderers' side, which included many leading amateur players from Lancashire. In 1864, 'Ned' Stephenson, the Yorkshire player, acting as umpire in a game between Holmfirth and Sheffield Shrewsbury, was impressed by the 'mettle' in the home players and offered to return to coach them.[368] Thongsbridge Cricket Club built a new 'spacious wooden shed' as its pavilion and held a match in 1865 to inaugurate it, whilst the following year, the Clayton club had its cricket field relaid, the expense being mainly defrayed by the sons of a wealthy local man.[369] The club opened a new ground with a game against Denby Dale in the summer of 1866, having adopted a new code of rules and brought in fresh players to play on a ground which was 'excellently laid out [and] one of the best in Yorkshire.' Over the winter of 1867, the Kirkburton club also relaid its ground 'to make it more available for playing than it has ever been.'[370]

Despite all this activity, there was some concern at the lack of a really top-class ground in the area. In November 1871, when the Dalton Cricket Club held its annual meeting, the Secretary stated although there were many clubs in the district, 'there was not a field among them that was fit for an all-England match.'[371] In the end, the solution was provided by the Fartown ground. The Huddersfield Cricket Club started out in the form of Hillhouse St John's Cricket Club in 1866, which moved to Fartown in 1868. Over the winter of 1867/68, the re-named St John's Cricket Club spent nearly £70 on improving its ground and the *Chronicle* stated that many 'eminent' players had enrolled.[372] The club developed its facilities, putting in between 500 and 600 seats in early 1870.[373] Three years later, Yorkshire played its first county match at Fartown against Nottinghamshire, followed by a match against the All-England XI in 1874.

In 1875, the cricket club merged with the local rugby club to form the Huddersfield Cricket, Athletic and Football Club, and further work was carried out on the ground throughout the decade. First-class matches between the North and South, the United North of England v United South of England, and the Gentlemen of the North v the Players of the North were held at Huddersfield, and Yorkshire began to make regular visits. In 1878, following a match at Huddersfield, an Australian observer described the town as 'a perfect hotbed of cricket, every man, woman and child being conversant with the game.'[374] The same year, the secretary of the Lockwood Cricket Club commented that he felt that the game was 'becoming more and more popular every day' in the area. Spurred on by this enthusiasm, in the late 1870s, Huddersfield was at the forefront of efforts to challenge the Sheffield monopoly on Yorkshire cricket (see Chapter 10).

Further improvements were made at the Fartown ground in the 1880s. Over the winter of 1883/84 considerable work was carried out and a pavilion costing over £1,000 was built.[375] As result, by the mid-1880s the ground was an impressive sight. The pavilion was described as 'one of the most convenient in the county'.[376] In 1886, a new stand was erected built of brick, with a terrace in front of it to hold 2,000-3,000 people. A 'repeat telegraph board' for recording the scores was put up at the lower end of the ground. The members' enclosure was enlarged and the whole work, including refreshment rooms and dining room, was expected to cost a further £1,000.[377] The following year, the club was considered to be in a 'flourishing' condition, with a strong membership and a fine quality field.[378] In 1889, the Huddersfield Cricket and Athletic Club had 1,025 members and its application to the Board of Trade to increase to 1,500 under the Articles of Association was granted.[379]

Although it was Fartown that hosted the first-class games in the area, it was Lascelles Hall Cricket Club which overshadowed everything else achieved in the area, and played a hugely important role in the development of Yorkshire cricket more generally. Holmes described it as 'one of the most, if not the actually the most, remarkable cricket nursery in the whole country.'[380] Despite its small size, the village provided 21 county players between 1861 and 1890.[381] According to interviews with two important figures, Walter Haigh and John Jessop, the club began in 1825 when boys played on land near the village hall without permission. The trespassers were allowed to continue to play with the consent of the owner of the land and his wife until 1846, when the caretaker of the village hall would not permit the game to be played any longer. The privilege was restored in 1849, and the game went on there until a new ground was opened in 1866.[382]

The club punched well above its weight for many years. In 1867, Twenty-two of Lascelles Hall played the All-England Eleven, and in 1873 took on Yorkshire on level terms, winning by 146 runs. In 1874, the club beat H.Jupp's Eleven (virtually a Surrey side) and the following year played a North of England side.[383] The village was famous for the number of professional cricketers that it produced. In 1864, for example, the side to play in the Honley Feast match against Lockwood included Luke Greenwood (professional at East Lancashire), Job Greenwood (Dudley), John Thewlis (Great Harwood), David Pollard (York), John Ambler (Glasgow), Joe Thewlis jnr (Blackburn), William Shotton (Cheetham Hill), Ben Thewlis (Peterborough), Joe Brook (Earlsheaton), Henry Mallinson (Dewsbury) and W.Redfearn (Lascelles Hall).[384] According to 'Old Ebor', the 'zenith' of the club was around 1882, and the decline came as the traditional hand-loom weaving, which allowed the weaver to have much control over his time, was replaced by power looms situated in factories.[385] Nevertheless, Huddersfield played a major role in the development of Yorkshire cricket through the strength of its professionals throughout the 19th century.

Leeds

Holmes described Leeds as one of the first Yorkshire towns to play cricket. As was mentioned earlier, 'gentlemen cricket-players' were meeting at least as early as 1760 on Chapel Town Moor and the *Leeds Intelligencer* reported games in the 1790s in Leeds, Harewood and Wetherby. Nevertheless, it seems it was some 30 years later that the game became widespread. More than other towns, Leeds suffered from poor-quality facilities, and this may explain the view that the game was apparently less successful here than elsewhere for much of the 19th century.[386]

Cricket was commonly played on the moors in the Leeds area and efforts were made to develop a good ground on Woodhouse Moor, although this was not without its difficulties. In 1833, the *Leeds Times* noted that, although subscribers of the Leeds Cricket Club had gone to considerable expense to level part of the Moor for cricket, they were 'not a little astonished' to see the cavalry exercising on this land.[387] Such behaviour continued and there was further criticism of the cavalry in 1839 for destroying the turf and preventing cricket being played.[388] By 1838, the Victoria cricket field on the western side of Woodhouse Moor was enclosed by entrepreneur Robert Cadman, the local paper considering it was a 'beautiful ground, which has been formed at great expense.'[389] At the end of the 1830s, there were a number of clubs in Leeds including Leeds Oak, Leeds Brunswick and Leeds Cobourg, while again a sign of the Leeds Cricket Club's stability and prestige – as it had been in the previous century – was that a performance at the Theatre, Leeds, of 'Rob Roy' and 'Monsieur Tonson' was produced under its patronage.[390] In 1847, the Leeds Cricket Club was reorganised by W.Beckett Denison and held its first game in the new form on the Victoria Ground.[391] Cricket also took place on the Moor in the Holbeck area in the early

1840s. Holbeck had a strong side and an enclosed ground in the Beeston Hill area. The All-England Eleven played against a Leeds and District Twenty-Two in 1858, in a fixture hosted by the Holbeck club.[392]

In the 1850s, however, there were clear signs that Leeds was not at the forefront of cricket in the county. One commentator noted in 1853 that efforts were being made to raise money from wealthy townsmen, in order to try to:

> rescue Leeds from the insignificant position it has heretofore held in Yorkshire, in cricketing circles.....Whilst this dissentious spirit continues, and whilst raw "Greenhorns," who have scarcely learnt the right or wrong side of a bat are allowed to disgrace and lose our matches, we have little or no hope for cricket in Leeds.[393]

The *Leeds Times* was not impressed either by the standards displayed by those playing for the prestigious Leeds Clarence club, suggesting they were easily distracted during games. Sarcastically, it commented that it might be useful in future for players to remember that when playing in a tight game 'neither a horse floundering in a ditch, nor long-eared biped on a bank, should be allowed to distract their attention and induce them to "cut off" from the field....stick to the game, gentlemen, stick to the game.'[394]

Later in the decade, the Clarence club was without a ground and advertised for a new one 'at a convenient distance from Leeds (not to exceed a mile and a half from Briggate)'. Its facilities were taken over by the Leeds Royal Gardens, although it was still open for cricket matches and other entertainment.[395] The main team in the town was clearly seen as inferior to Bradford, and when they played each other in 1861, the local paper assumed 'Leeds stood very little chance of contesting successfully with the famous, well practised, and particularly powerful team of the neighbouring town.'[396]

On the other hand, although Leeds struggled for a premier team, informal games of cricket were clearly played widely in the town. Indeed, by the early 1860s, some considered cricket was almost too popular in some places. Following an incident in which a man was hit in the face by a ball, an editorial appeared in the *Leeds Mercury* about the dangers on Woodhouse Moor, observing that he would not have expected when out walking 'to find the path flanked on each side with formidable batteries of cricket and knor and spell, each pouring forth its deadly missiles in such profusion that it is almost a miracle of good luck if he gets through without being "killed or wounded." ' The paper called cricket a 'great nuisance', adding that whilst it did not wish to restrain the 'healthful and manly games of the Leeds youth', nevertheless they would not be worse off playing on a part of the Moor 'less dangerous to the skulls and limbs' of other people.[397]

In October 1861, the Council considered issuing regulations about playing cricket and other sports on the Moor[398], but the following May, there was opposition when they were brought in, with players telling the police to summons them if they wanted to prevent them exercising what they considered were their common rights.[399] Bye-laws were introduced in 1863 which banned knurr and spell, 'or any other game considered dangerous or likely to damage the surface of the moor except cricket', but cricket was only allowed in specific areas (marked with stones bearing the words 'cricket boundary'), and just one area when the volunteers were parading.

However, in the summer these rules were again flouted by six men who refused requests from the police to stop playing. They were charged with infringing the regulations and appeared at the Town Hall, represented by a barrister, who accused the Council of only pursuing the men because they were poor, whereas the wealthy were allowed to ride their horses where they wanted. Two of the men were fined 1s each and costs, with the case against the others dismissed.[400] The matter was not settled there. In August 1863, 11 more men appeared in court for playing cricket, having clearly tried to challenge the regulations. They were fined 5s each plus costs. Shortly after, a public meeting was held to discuss the matter, and their convictions were later quashed on the grounds that the magistrates had no jurisdiction in the case. The defendents presented three witnesses who claimed variously to have played without interruption on the moor from 1793 to 1823, from 1800 to 1843 and for the last 25 to 30 years. The Council Repairs Committee refused to leave it there and considered taking it to a superior court.[401]

Despite the enthusiasm for cricket demonstrated during this controversy, there was continuing evidence that the game was not in a good state in Leeds. At the meeting in November 1863 to set up the alternative, York-based Yorkshire County Cricket Club (see Chapter 10), the Chairman stated that it would be desirable to have gentlemen from the town on the committee, but feared that the 'spirit of cricket was very low in Leeds, there was no club in existence, and no ground to play upon.'[402] The following year, a correspondent to the *Leeds Intelligencer* asked:

> how it that Leeds, which once boasted of one of the best cricket clubs in Yorkshire ("the Clarence") never treats us to a game worth seeing? Where is the club which stands in the place of the defunct Clarence, and where are its matches played? Surely our young men have not lost all taste for this glorious sport. Have they no regard for their physical development ?[403]

A number of responses to this letter appeared. One argued that it was not surprising that cricket struggled in Leeds since, with the exception of the Grammar School and the Royal Park Gardens, there was no ground within walking distance of the town. He added that the Leeds Clarence club had now been revived and had a good fixture list, but was also struggling for lack of a decent ground.[404] Improvements began to take place in the town around this time. In 1864, the Leeds Football and Cricket Club had 500 members playing football and 65 cricketers, and in October it considered the offer of use of the Royal Park and adjoining field, but concluded they were too expensive. Nevertheless, it was 'subsequently agreed that a cricket club worthy of the town should be established', to be called the Leeds Borough Club.[405]

There were also developments in Holbeck and Hunslet. In 1864, with the old Victoria ground in decline, the Holbeck club obtained and developed a larger site on Holbeck Moor. The following season, the United England Eleven played XX of Leeds and District on the ground and, in 1868, Yorkshire took on Lancashire there in a match in which the visitors scored only 30 and 34, losing by an innings and 186 runs. In 1862, the Hunslet Cricket Club was reformed and in the late 1860s held matches against the Australian Aborigines and the United All England Eleven. In 1869, it too hosted a Yorkshire county game (its only one), this time against Cambridgeshire, when Yorkshire won by an innings and 266 runs.[406]

By the 1870s and the early 1880s, the game in the area around Leeds appeared more prosperous. In 1874, the *Leeds Times*, reviewing the state of Pudsey – mid-way between Leeds and Bradford – commented that 'the physical development of the inhabitants has not been lost sight of, for the noble English game of cricket has been largely fostered amongst us'. Foremost was the St Lawrence Club, which had 200 members and over the years had 'moulded and fashioned and grown in public estimation, and the present day finds it stronger than at any former period of its history.'[407] The Leeds Clarence club also looked in a good state in 1882, when it had 41 matches arranged, a new professional was available on the Kirkstall ground for practice, and a prospering lawn-tennis section was in place. The *Yorkshire Post* commented that it was about 30 years since it was considered 'almost a necessity' for every young gentleman living in Leeds and surrounding area to get himself proposed as a member of the Leeds Clarence Cricket Club, and 'many would like to see that old feeling revived.'[408]

Despite these improvements, tensions continued about the use of the moors for sport. In 1878, there were complaints that the surface of some of Hunslet Moor had been badly trampled by people playing cricket and knurr and spell over a long period of time. The matter was considered in court, where a 70-year-old man claimed he had used the moor for cricket in his youth and remembered his father saying he had done the same.[409] The old issue of the safety of those walking on Woodhouse Moor was then revived in April 1880 when a woman – holding a baby – was knocked off her feet by a cricket ball.[410] Steps were taken to provide particular spaces for sport. In November 1882, the *Leeds Times*, while approving of this arrangement, was anxious that the cricketers should not 'be 'crib'd and confin'd' by these changes, arguing that 'Cricket is too popular amongst us to be carelessly tossed aside.'[411] An area for cricket was eventually created, although the following year the paper complained about cricketers swearing within earshot of those walking past on the Moor.[412]

The problem of the lack of a decent ground in Leeds remained. The Australians visited Hunslet in 1878 and 1880, but the facilities were not popular, being small and deemed to be on the 'wrong' side of Hunslet to attract people from Leeds.[413] Efforts were made to improve Holbeck Recreation Ground over the winter of 1877 but these facilities also did not impress some visitors. The correspondent of *The Australiasian,* reporting on the visit of the Australians in 1882, commented that the ground is 'one of the smallest we have played on, and it is situated in a very uninviting neighbourhood. Noisesome smells, dingy tumbledown-looking brick houses, and unclean streets abound.' He was pleased to get back to the centre of Leeds.[414]

In the 1880s, the town's limited contribution to the county game was also an ongoing cause of concern to cricketers in Leeds. Members of local clubs got together in late 1882 to decide how they would select a representative to sit on the Yorkshire County Cricket Club committee ('the Sheffield committee' as the *Leeds Times* put it), and discuss whether the towns should have control over the finances of the Yorkshire club.[415] In February 1883, the same issues were covered at a meeting of the Yorkshire Wanderers Football Club and the Leeds Clarence Cricket Club, with the aim of forming a central and representative cricket, football and athletic club for Leeds.[416] The *Yorkshire Post* lamented the lack of progress in April 1884, agreeing with criticism made of Holbeck's facilities when it had hosted the Surrey game the previous year, and complaining that, although meetings had been held to discuss establishing a town club and purchasing Cardigan Fields, nothing had yet been done. Gloomily, it noted that local clubs 'will not sink their individuality and thus it is that Leeds falls gradually lower and lower in the athletic scale.'[417] Leeds then had no county game that summer, and the Holbeck committee received no response from the Yorkshire authorities to a letter asking what improvements it needed to make to secure one in future.[418]

At the start of 1885, the Leeds Corporate Property Committee inspected Woodhouse Moor with a view to selecting a piece of ground for cricketers where they would not be a danger to passers-by. The Council agreed to spend £400 on a selected spot despite objections about the burden on ratepayers.[419] Rumours began to circulate in spring of 1886 that a town club was being formed, and that a site was to be purchased for a ground suitable for county purposes. [420] Then, finally in 1888, land forming part of Cardigan Fields was bought at a cost of £25,000 by a group of businessmen who formed the Leeds Cricket, Football and Athletic Company Limited. During 1889, around £30,000 was spent on the site, which included a new pavilion and double-fronted grandstand.[421] It was considered 'admirably adapted for the purposes required', being a few minutes from Headingley Railway station and local tramway, and within easy walking distance of much of the borough.[422]

In May 1890, the Headingley ground opened with a match between the Leeds and Scarborough cricket clubs, and was hailed, with appropriate modesty, as 'one of the finest enclosures in Yorkshire, if not the world.' The first game of importance was played in September 1890 between the North and the Australians, a fixture notable for the reappearance of Edmund Peate, who was the groundsman. Yorkshire played a first-class match there for the first time in August 1891 against Kent, following a non-first-class fixture against Derbyshire earlier in the year.[423] The wicket was initially difficult, but in 1893 R.S.Holmes wrote that he liked the Leeds ground, particularly the row of evergreens and flowering shrubs in front of the pavilion seats, the club-room in the pavilion and a wide awning overhead to protect from the sun. He added that there needed to be better service at the refreshment bars, the pavilion could be better positioned and the wickets were not perfect, 'but only blind prejudice would dream of classing them with those provided at the old enclosure.'[424]

Others were less impressed. In 1893, 'Old Ebor' expressed concern at the size of the field, writing that the ground was too big for heavy scoring and for seeing the game properly, so that there were complaints at every match.[425] Despite these problems, the Headingley ground was the solution to the challenges that Leeds cricketers had faced for decades. Ten years later, the county club moved its offices to Leeds, symbolically bringing to an end the domination of Yorkshire cricket by Sheffield.[426]

Bradford

Cricket was popular in Bradford in the 1830s, and the 'Old' Bradford club was established in July 1836 at the White Lion Inn, playing its first game on 1 August.[427] Early matches were against Fairweather Green and Apperley Bridge, Horsforth and Guiseley, and in the following season, Fairweather Green, Keighley and Wakefield.[428] Forty years later, one observer recalled a match against Wakefield, when the Bradford side travelled in a coach and four decorated horses, driven by the landlord of the Hope and Anchor Inn. He was dressed in 'light buff kerseymere trousers', a large waistcoat to below the hips, a coat with numerous pockets, a wide semi-clergyman's hat and a white silk spotted tie. A new ground on Great Horton Lane was established in 1839, 'a little above Mannville', and a crowd of between 2,000 and 4,000 attended at different times during a game with Halifax.[429] The facilities were better than before, although the pavilion was still described as 'a ricketty old cow-shed, which did duty as dressing-room, warehouse, smoke divan, parlour and kitchen.'[430]

In the 1840s, cricket remained very popular amongst young men in the area, and in 1844, the *Bradford Observer* reported glowingly on the progress of the town's main club, noting that its members had stuck to their original objectives. These were:

> amusement to all classes...the creation of a spirit of emulation in other clubs, by selecting the best men in the neighbourhood to practise with and take part in matches; and lastly, the encouragement to young men generally to engage in the exhilarating exercise of cricket, in preference to a lax method of otherwise spending their leisure hours.

The Bradford cricket club was considered by some as 'second to none in Yorkshire.' It had played 44 games— 28 of which it had won, and 13 lost. The club had about 150 subscribers, including 'the *elite* of our gentry.'[431]

Over the winter of 1842/43, the main ground in Bradford was the subject of extensive improvements, including new sheds, railings and a 'greatly-improved play-ground.' It was noted that 'more members have been enrolled than at the end of any previous season. This is a good omen; and it is expected, that ere long, at least 120 genuine subscribers will be secured.'[432] As a result, the senior club developed throughout the decade, taking on sides such as Rochdale, Leeds, Dalton and Harewood, and competing (in a combined Bradford/Dalton side) with a powerful Sheffield team in 1847, after which Bradford players were reportedly held in high esteem. At times they were so strong they struggled to find opponents; in 1847, for example, no games had been played by the end of June as various clubs declined to compete.[433] Another positive sign was the success of matches against the All-England Eleven in the late 1840s and early 1850s.[434]

However, the 50% increase in the population of Bradford during the 1840s, noted earlier, started to have a negative effect on cricket. In 1851, the Bradford club lost its ground, which was sold for building purposes.[435] For a while the club faced dissolution, but a new venue was then secured in Great Horton Lane, adjoining a toll-bar, about 100 yards from the old field. It was owned by F. S. Powell Esq and taken on a 10-year lease. It was levelled, drained, walled and newly laid out and, by May 1852, much of the funding to cover the expenditure on the new ground had been subscribed.[436]

Despite the difficulties, enthusiasm for the game in the town continued into the 1850s and many clubs developed over the decade. The Bradford Moor club, for example, played at a good standard, attracting over 2,500 spectators on occasions. The *Bradford Observer* commented in 1856 that the Bradford club had never been stronger and noted the regular friendly games between the Saturday half-holiday clubs and warehousemen. Gradually clubs were established of the best players in each neighbourhood, and over a period of years they became increasingly successful and gained an air of permanence. Teams like Bradford Albion and Manningham built up reputations, while the Old Club was so strong that there was considerable disquiet among members in 1862 and 1863 when again they could find few opponents.[437]

The 1860s were a particularly good time for cricket in the town. The *Bradford Observer* noted that the expansion of the half-day holiday system had led to an increase in clubs. Initially, they were associated with particular firms, but later players were drafted into clubs that grew up in different parts of the borough and so became much stronger than those based around single mills or warehouses.[438] Attendances at the matches with travelling elevens also held up, the *Observer* reporting in 1861 that the All-England Eleven game showed 'that the game of cricket is not losing its interest in our neighbourhood.'[439] Added to this, Yorkshire county matches were held on the Great Horton Road ground, including against Nottinghamshire, which were highly successful, and added to the club's confidence. For a while Bradford was at the forefront of the challenge to Sheffield's dominance of Yorkshire cricket.

The late 1860s, however, saw something of a decline. In May 1867, there were complaints that the town Corporation was preventing cricket being played in the area marked out in Peel Park for the game because of safety concerns. The *Leeds Times* argued that 'the public ought to take the matter up and agitate for such a reform as will in future prevent clubs from having to trudge as far as Quarry Gap and other places, as the compositors of this town had to do last Saturday.'[440] Similar complaints were heard in 1869, when 'working men complained bitterly because they had been deprived of the cricket ground in Peel Park, which had, in a measure, been handed over to the local Volunteers.'[441] The *Leeds Times* kept up a campaign to allow cricketers to play in the Park, urging the Council Park Committee to consider the matter fully.[442]

There were other threats to the game. In 1874, two important clubs - Bradford Moor United and Manningham Amateurs - lost their grounds and ceased to exist as a result of building work.[443] Subsequently, the main ground was also disposed of for construction work. Efforts had been made to obtain a lease on the ground and then purchase it, but they were rejected by Mr Powell. A lot of money had been spent on bringing the ground into its 'present excellent condition' and it was suggested that it would be very hard to find 'so fine and level a field within so easy distance from the town, and every way so admirably fitted for the invigorating work of cricket.'[444] In August of the same year, Bradford Albion ceased playing at Horton Green as its ground was needed for the construction of the Bradford and Thornton Railway.[445]

Despite this the Bradford Club had a very strong fixture list for 1874 and looked forward to its 'best ever' season. Over the following winter it issued an appeal for funds to help it prepare a new ground, which was likely to cost £2,000. The

Leeds Times reported:

> The sum is large, and the members being young, and consequently, impecunious, the committee cannot carry out the serious responsibility they have undertaken without the earnest support of the public. But if the people will consider the claims which the club has upon them the amount required will soon be forthcoming.

Looking elsewhere in the town, it added that, because of building development, the Albion Cricket Club now played on 'a mere garden plot', whilst Manningham had only a yearly tenure, which was not likely to last much longer. Consequently, if Bradford had to abandon its plans, 'cricketers will be driven so far out of the town that practising will be out of the question and good play will become unknown.'[446]

By September 1875, the Bradford club had failed to put the new piece of land in order because of the cost. The money could have been raised but the lease was only for 10 years, and members decided it was not worth investing for so short a time. The club committee then negotiated for a piece of land at Longroyd, but was asked for £150 a year, which it also thought was too much, even though £400 was promised towards the cost of laying out the ground. As a result, the committee became very discouraged and determined that the club be wound up.[447] It was 'effectively defunct' by the late 1870s and many members drifted off to play for other clubs.[448] In April 1879, the gloom remained. One report observed that there had been no All-England or county matches, but instead:

> a multitude of minor affairs, promoted by clubs good enough in themselves but not equal to the cricket club that this town could once boast of possessing. Nowhere is the noble game more ardently pursued than in this town, and it certainly was a strange thing that first-class cricket here should have so long been under a cloud.

Eventually, however, things looked up thanks again to Mr F.S.Powell of Horton Old Hall, and a new field was found at Horton Green, well away from the smoke of the town.[449] A tender was accepted by the trustees in August 1879 for £2,400 for levelling, drainage and fencing of the new cricket and football field.[450] Considerable work was then undertaken over the winter of 1880 with a running track placed around the boundary, and provision made for tennis, archery and quoits.[451] The quality of the playing surface was given particular attention and the new ground was prepared with a slight slope to allow water to run off, while still appearing level.[452]

The new ground had an upper- and lower-level pavilion with spacious dining-hall and kitchen, besides a house for the groundsman. Another grand stand was promised on the lower portion of the ground with a double frontage, one side facing the cricket ground, with the other fronting the space for football. The field was enclosed with substantial boundary walls and there were three entrances, the entire works forecast to cost around £4,000. At the start of March 1880, subscriptions totalled £1,500 and much of the plan was dependent on raising more money.[453] The pavilion was built in a modified Italian style of architecture with overhanging eves, and the ground was formally opened in July 1880.[454]

The development work was a huge commitment for the Bradford club for whom outlay on the grounds and pavilions had been over £5,500.[455] Nevertheless, it soon attracted admirers. The club received a request from the secretary of the Melbourne Cricket Club in Australia for a sketch plan of the pavilion as it was designing a new one of its own.[456] The initial first-class game between the Players and the Australians was held in September 1880. The following year, Yorkshire played at Bradford against Kent and Derbyshire, but unfortunately the weather affected the latter match and the wicket was described as a 'morass'.[457] Nevertheless, the efforts paid off and in 1882 the Australian visitors described the new ground as 'the best designed place of the kind they have seen.'[458] Two years later, the club reduced the slight bank in front of the enclosure and added around 25 yards of perfectly level land to the playing field at the pavilion end. 5,000 seats were put in on three sides of the ground, and all were finished and painted before the county match in June against yet another Australian touring side.[459]

Despite problems with water, the Park Avenue ground became a regular venue for Yorkshire matches and the aspirations of the town were achieved to have a decent ground not threatened by building work. In 1883, the *Leeds Times* commented that the Bradford Cricket Club 'stands head and shoulders above all other clubs in this part of the county', although noting that there had been disquiet amongst some members at what was seen as the extravagance of the appointment of a paid secretary.[460] The number of club members rose from 520 to 790 in 1883, probably helped by reducing the subscription from 21s to 10s 6d.[461] After years of effort, Bradford was confirmed again as one of the most important cricketing towns in Yorkshire.

Other towns in the West Riding

Elsewhere in the West Riding there was also considerable interest in the game. Wakefield saw cricket in the 18th century and several teams played under the town's name – including Wakefield New Club in 1826 – before a stable club was established in 1847. In 1857, the town secured a new, enclosed ground and hosted a game with the All-England Eleven, which returned to play in 1864. The Wakefield Cricket Club leased a ground at College Grove in 1873, and that year W.G.Grace and the United South of England side visited, enjoying the facilities of a newly built, red brick pavilion. Yorkshire played there in 1878, but the ground was generally considered too small for first-class cricket.[462]

The game was also recorded in Halifax in the 1820s and several clubs played for short periods in the town, often on Skircoat Moor.[463] Halifax Clarence Cricket Club was sufficiently well organised that at the start of the 1837 season it held a ball attended by 50 members. The club stated that it was open to play any neighbouring town's club in friendly home and away fixtures.[464] A couple of years later, the club opened a new ground in Hopwood Lane, and was well supported by a range of influential honorary members, including a Member of Parliament.[465] Halifax Cricket Club hosted the All-England Eleven in 1863, and in 1876 moved to its Hanson Lane ground. It shared this with Halifax Rugby Club, with whom it amalgamated in 1878 to form Halifax Cricket, Football and Athletic Club. A short lease meant it was impossible to develop the ground, and a new site was obtained in 1885, opening with a game between Yorkshire and Eighteen of Halifax in 1886. A small number of first-class matches were played there between 1888 and 1897.[466]

Cricket was recorded on Dewsbury Moor in 1819, and there was a club in the town in the 1830s.[467] The beginnings of Dewsbury Cricket Club were in 1862, and in 1865 it moved to Savile Town. The Savile Town club developed as a force in the mid-1860s and organised a series of important games. Its new ground hosted the All-England Eleven in 1865 and in July 1867, Yorkshire played Cambridgeshire in a match organised by the Dewsbury, rather than Yorkshire county, committee. First-class matches between the All-England Eleven and United England Eleven for the Cricketers' Fund benefit were held in 1868 and 1869, and the North v South game was hosted in 1870.[468] The arrangements were much praised and the ground was described as a 'large, commodious, and well-laid out piece of land', with a wicket 'as level and as smooth shaven as a bowling-green'.[469]

The committee showed its confidence in the 1880s by pushing for county fixtures, although it continued to be dissatisfied with what it was offered. It invested further in its ground in 1886, building new terraces to accommodate 1,200 spectators at a cost of £400.[470] The Dewsbury & Savile club was particularly strong in the 1880s and featured prominently in the early years of the Heavy Woollen District Cricket Challenge Cup. It lost the first final to Heckmondwike and the second to Ossett. In 1885, it scored 448 against Mirfield St John's, who scored 15 in return, but again lost in the final, this time to Birstall. The following year, the result between the same teams was repeated, but finally in 1887, Dewsbury was victorious, leading to great celebrations as the cup was paraded between the town's public houses. In each of the next three years – 1888 to 1890 – Dewsbury won the competition to underline its position as one of the strongest club sides in Yorkshire.[471]

The game was recorded in Doncaster as early as 1786 when Eleven Gentlemen of

Doncaster took on Eleven Gentlemen of York for 100 guineas, and the fixture was repeated on a number of occasions, along with a game with Sheffield in 1801. A club was probably founded around 1814, playing on the race course, where use was made of the grandstand. By 1823, the club had nearly 100 members and matches attracted significant attendances. Other clubs were established in the 1820s and 1830s, probably for only short periods of time, providing a good example of the constant forming and reforming of clubs that was a feature of early cricket. In the 1840s, a Doncaster 'Gentlemen' team, supported by the gentry of the area, and Doncaster Town (later Amateurs) existed side by side. A new Doncaster Town club appeared in 1848, and four years later a union of the clubs was considered desirable, although subsequently there were still different sides competing for prominence in the town.

The season of 1856 saw the establishment of a South Yorks club, which leased land and built a brick pavilion. It was supported by local gentry and Members of Parliament and employed a professional. Further changes took place in the early 1860s, and in 1865 a new Doncaster club appears to have been formed and became well established. It tailored its subscriptions to different groups; tradesmen paid 10s 6d, artisans and mechanics 5s. Doncaster also saw a wide range of other smaller clubs based around the railway works after it was established in 1853, as well as different commercial groups such as butchers and fishmongers from the 1870s. A YMCA side had over 50 members in 1878, and churches also put out teams. In the 1880s and 1890s, the Doncaster Town club flourished, with membership of around 200 at times.[472]

Cricket was recorded in Knaresborough in the 1790s.[473] Some time later, Knaresborough Cricket Club played a number of games in 1814, including against Otley, Hovingham, and a combined Whixley, Hammerton, Ouseburn and Nun Monkton side. Two years later, the *York Herald* described the Knaresborough team as 'the first cricket players in the county'.[474] There appears to have been something of a decline, with clubs being sustained for only short periods, and Greaves notes that in 1839 players in Knaresborough were reportedly 'bestirring themselves to regain their lost fame as Cricket Players', with games played among local tradespeople and between married and single gentlemen. In the early 1840s, Knaresborough played Leeds Victoria and Otley, beating the latter by three runs over two days. Cricket in the town grew in strength and in 1845 the club had the best of a game against Sheffield.[475]

Efforts were made from around this time to develop a club in Harrogate, and a match was played against Knaresborough in June 1846. The first Harrogate club did not last long and a new one was established in 1852. It went into decline and another was playing in 1862, the year the game was given a push when the All-England Eleven made the first of six visits, playing on three different grounds between then and 1867. The current club was established in 1877 with a home at St George's Road, and by the end of the season it had a total of 140 members.

The United South of England Eleven visited in 1879 and matches between an England XI and the Australians took place in Harrogate in 1882 and 1888. Shaw's Australian Eleven also played an England XI there in 1885.[476]

There was significant interest in the game in Ripon – then in the West Riding, now in North Yorkshire – where it built up a considerable reputation in the early decades of the 19th century.[477] A game was played in October 1810 between the Ripon club and players from Kirkby Fleetham and Scruton in the North Riding following a challenge. This contest ended in a number of Ripon players refusing to continue over a disputed umpiring decision – three of the umpires considering the batsman was out ! – leading to their opponents taking measures to recover the match stakes.[478] The Ripon club – described as 'recently instituted' in that year – played matches with Kirkby Malzeard in 1811, Harewood in 1812, with York and, on three occasions, Harewood in 1813, and with Nottingham in 1816.[479] In 1814, the Ripon club offered to take on any other side in Yorkshire, and Holmes described it as 'almost the strongest club in Yorkshire' around this time.[480]

In 1829, a match between Ripon Friendly Cricket Club and Sheffield Wednesday provided a stern test, and before the game it was noted that 'the Ripon men looked with much reverence at their more southern antagonists, and the Sheffield side had almost the ill manners to openly express their contempt for them in return'. Despite this, Ripon won, albeit helped by driving rain during the final stages which slowed the ball on the grass and reduced Sheffield's scoring.[481] The same year, a match between Ripon and Knaresborough ended in acrimony, with a player hurling his bat down and leaving the field, which brought the game to an end and led to demands that Knaresborough should forfeit the stakes for refusing to continue.[482] In 1833, the Ripon feast saw a high-quality game for 50 sovereigns between an eleven of Nottingham and twenty players from the clubs of Ripon, York, Wetherby, Bedale, Thirsk and other clubs within 30 miles of Ripon. This was Ripon's first contest against Nottingham since 1816.[483] Three years later, as a sign of its significance, the club issued a book with the scores of all its games from 1813 to 1836.[484]

The game in Ripon then appeared to go into something of a decline. In 1841, a match between Ripon and Bishop Monkton and Skelton was considered to have 'excited considerable attention among the lovers of this manly sport, which being a novelty in Ripon brought back to the mind those bygone days when it was carried out to a considerable extent.'[485] Later that summer, further efforts were clearly being made by cricketers in Ripon to regroup. A meeting was held in the town, when 'several of the bowlers and batters of former celebrity attended with other younger aspirants to future fame to form a society, with proper officers of management, to engage suitable grounds, and other arrangements for the establishment of a first-rate cricket club.'[486] The following season, it was noted that the club:

> which has been in *statu quo* for the last six years, is again about to be revived with renewed energy....The first practice took place on Friday last, and drew together a respectable assemblage, among whom we noticed many individuals, who in by-gone days were wont to take such a lively interest in the prosperity of the club.[487]

In 1847, it was again noted that the club was being restored, with 'a respectable party of young men' forming a club and beginning to practise. As a result, it was hoped that the Ripon club, which had in the past been 'noted for its excellence in the game', would 'produce many aspirants to fame.'[488] The All-England Eleven appeared in Ripon in September 1848, winning by 36 runs, but the glorious days of the early part of the century were not regained.[489]

East Riding of Yorkshire

As highlighted earlier, the East Riding of Yorkshire was predominantly a rural area, populated by small villages and towns. The pace of life was slower than in the West Riding, and old traditions continued. Holmes suggests that stool-ball – a possible precursor to cricket – was still played in the East Riding after the middle of the 19th century, an apparent sign of its backwardness.[490] The earliest reference to the game in the East Riding comes in 1778, with a match between Beverley and Howden[491], but in Howarth's view little cricket was played in East Yorkshire even in the 1830s, and the game 'only regained popularity and achieved a secure footing' after 1841. From that date there are signs of progress and, referring to cricket in the Bridlington area, he suggests that the crucial period was the 1840s, 'when there is a definite sense of a revived interest in the game.'[492]

Cricket developed around Beverley at the start of the 19th century, and the Beverley and East Riding Club was a force in the 1820s and 1830s, playing influential sides, including as far away as Lincolnshire.[493] In 1852, the game was so popular that Beverley players pitched their wickets at 4am in April in order to practise, and showed 'a spirit of enthusiasm never before witnessed in this town.' This appears to be linked to the forthcoming game with All-England.[494] However, in 1856, the local paper commented that it was 'rather a disgrace (considering the natural advantages for this game possessed by the town of Beverley) that we should be without, at least, *one* cricket club.'[495] In 1862 Beverley Town Cricket Club was formed, bringing together men from a number of smaller sides in order to end the arguing between local players.[496]

Cricket was also played by boys at several schools, including at Pocklington Grammar School, which may have resulted in boarders spreading the game when they returned home to their villages around the East Riding.[497] It was played by different clubs in Driffield in the 1850s[498], and took hold along the east coast of Yorkshire at different times. In Bridlington, an apparently well-connected but short-lived cricket club was in existence in 1820, although it was not until the 1850s that the game appears to have become properly established in the town.[499] There was no recorded cricket in Hornsea until 1859, and no formal club until 1865, shortly after the railway had linked the town more effectively to Hull. Subsequently, it became strong there in the 1870s, drawing in players from Hull and around the Holderness area.[500] Further down the coast at Withernsea a club was formed in the 1860s.

There was more of a history in the Hull area, where the population was much larger. There is evidence of cricket around Hull just before the start of the 19th century, with reference made to 'the cricket-ground' in the town in 1798, but it was not until the 1820s that the game became well established.[501] In 1828, the *Hull Packet* expressed great pleasure in seeing a revivial of cricket in the area, contrasting it with 'the folly of certain modern inventions entitled *gymnastics*, lately imported into this country from the continent, and which can only be viewed with contempt by those who properly appreciate the merits of the noble and truly British sports, cricket and archery.'[502]

The Hull Union Cricket Club was revived in 1832, and was described as 'a most excellent cricket club', with around 40 members. Its ground on Spring Bank was 'rolled and kept in order for the purpose.'[503] The club had access to marquees for spectators and, in 1833, several new players joined and the ground was improved. A game against the Officers of the Garrison in August was well attended by 'genteel company, as well as a large concourse of the population.'[504] In 1835, there was a game between Sheffield Wednesday and the Hull Club at Hyde Park, the visitors 'being strangers to us' as the *Sheffield Independent* put it, suggesting this was the first such contest. A match also took place in September between Hull Tyro Club and the Sheffield Junior Club.[505] Two years later, however, one reporter lamented that cricket 'has been on the wane here of late years.'[506]

In the 1840s, the Hull Cricket Club, Hull Kingston club, and the St George's club were all strong sides, and the creation of a cricket club was one of the first actions when the Hull Athenaeum was established in 1848.[507] The club had 70 members the following year.[508] Matches were played by Hull sides across the River Humber against Grimsby, Barton, Caistor and Gainsborough, steamers taking the players over to Lincolnshire.[509] In 1847, the Hull Cricket Club was considered to have as strong a fixture list as in any previous season and was described as 'flourishing.'[510]

Despite this, cricket in Hull struggled at times. In 1848, Hull Cricket Club, which in the previous November had been described as in a 'prosperous condition', was suspended and its accounts wound up. Members were encouraged to join the Athenaeum club and negotiations then took place to lend the stock of the club to others.[511] The following year, the *Hull Packet* argued during the visit of the All-England Eleven that, although cricket had always been a favourite amusement of young people, it was not carried out into later life or 'made a matter of science and skill as in numerous, other towns.' Hull had had some clubs but had never succeeded in consistently turning out players like Nottingham and Sheffield, or even Leeds and York.[512]

Despite this, the Hull Town Cricket Club was formed in 1853, playing on Anlaby Road on what was known as Brown-Cow Field, and in an early game, a Hull player scored a century, described as unprecedented in Hull cricket.[513] The All-England Eleven visited this ground three times between 1855 and 1858, but the club gave it up for building purposes in 1859, moving further out to land adjoining the Borough Lunatic Asylum, owned by the North Eastern Railway Company.[514] In 1863, the *Hull News* bemoaned the 'lax condition into which cricketing matters have been allowed to fall of late in Hull' and suggested that the public of Hull were 'very cool' in supporting the game.[515] The *Hull Packet* also commented that with the decline of the Hull Town Club 'the game degenerated amongst us, and for the last few years we have only had small clubs in the town of indifferent fame.' Nevertheless, Kingston Cricket Club's efforts to bring the All-England Eleven to Hull in 1863 were seen as a sign of the 'old spirit for cricket' being revived, and in 1868, the President of Hull Town argued that it was no longer the case that sports had been 'habitually neglected in Hull, to the detriment of the rising generation'.[516]

The ground in Argyle Street gave cricket in Hull a new impetus, being within easy reach of many parts of the town. In 1874, a substantial pavilion was opened, and the *Hull Packet* again suggested that year that cricket had never been in such a prosperous condition as it was now, seemingly enjoying the support of many employers.[517] Things appeared to be looking up. In 1875, the first team scored a massive 375 against Scarborough and, in 1878, the club hosted the visiting Australian side on equal terms, albeit bolstered by outside professionals. Howarth presents other evidence to support the view that the game was on the up, with the Hull Town side playing games with places like Durham, Otley, Sheffield Pitsmoor, Hunslet and Retford, and clearly, as the leading side in the East Riding, capable of attracting 2,000 people to some games. There was also a wide base of smaller clubs, linked to churches and workplaces, which drew in many men to the game.[518] The Arygle Street ground was the venue for North v South matches in 1875 and 1877, United North v United South in 1876, and Yorkshire played Surrey there in 1879. However, as with a number of other grounds tried at this time, the playing surface proved too small and Yorkshire did not return except for matches with second-class counties.[519]

Despite this, there were still complaints of a lack of interest in the game, the *Hull Packet* commenting in 1878 that Hull people showed little interest in many matches which did not include the 'cracks' of the country.[520] The game subsequently prospered in the 1880s, including a Grand Cricket Week in 1884 and, unusually for the East Riding, around this time Hull players B.C.Bolton and H.W.Hart got opportunities to play for the county, albeit generally against lesser opposition.[521] In the late 1890s, however, the Argyle Street ground was taken over for railway development, and cricket moved a short distance to The Circle, where Yorkshire began to play matches more regularly.[522]

North Riding of Yorkshire and York

If cricket in the West Riding was heavily shaped by urbanisation, and the East Riding game generally remained a less well-developed rural activity played in numerous small towns and villages, cricket in the North Riding also had its own distinctive characteristics. As we saw earlier, the game was first recorded in the area at Stanwick near Richmond, at the seat of the Earl of Northumberland in 1751.[523] The village of Scruton, near Northallerton, was also an early centre. A great match was played in 1797 between Wetherby, under the patronage of the Hon. George Monson, and Scruton, supported by a Mr Millbank, for 100 guineas a side. The contest was apparently 'severe', ending in favour of Wetherby.[524] In 1829, Scruton was described as one of the oldest 'crack' clubs in the North Riding, whilst at the end of the 1830s, Yarm and Hovingham were regarded by some as the two best clubs in the area.[525]

Elsewhere, Easingwold (founded in 1829) and Bedale (founded in 1828) had early clubs, and the Thirsk club was established in the late 1820s, being referred to in 1834 as 'far-famed'[526]. In 1831, the *York Herald* stated that the Bedale Club are 'acknowledged to be expert players and we are informed, that in all their engagements, they have never once been beaten.'[527] They took on Sheffield Wednesday, paying their opponents £35 towards their expenses, and playing for 20 sovereigns a side, as well as erecting a grand stand for the occasion.[528] In 1832, the victory of a team of Twenty-Two Gentlemen of the North of Yorkshire over eleven of Sheffield was ascribed to 'the superior bowling' and 'excellent batting' of the Thirsk and Bedale men.[529] The following year, Sheffield played at Bedale. The local side's 'jerking' style of bowling was criticised by the *Sheffield Independent*, which noted that W.H.Woolhouse had to leave the wicket after being hit twice in the first innings, and Marsden lost his wicket in the second innings from one of the 'most rank jerks ever witnessed.' One of the causes for Sheffield's defeat was also reportedly that Woolhouse was given out in the second innings 'for telling the umpire where the ball hit him' (which presumably was interpreted as dissent).[530] Like a number of other sides, they went through a period of decline, but in 1858 the *Leeds Times* suggested that Bedale was 'the first club in Yorkshire beyond doubt, if not the first in the north of England.'[531]

Scarborough saw cricket in the 1820s, but Scarborough Cricket Club - originally known as the Queen's Club - dated from 1849, with the first recorded match taking place against Filey. Other opponents in the early days included Settrington,

Castle Howard, Wykeham, Sherburn, Pickering and Hutton Buscel.[532] In 1863, the club was reformed and played on an unsatisfactory ground, grazed by pigs and cows, with the teams changing in the Queen's Hotel. According to Hall, by the 1860s the finances of the club were very dependent on matches involving visitors to the town, 'who recognised certain social advantages of being involved at Scarborough.'[533]

The All-England Eleven played in the town in 1862, and Castle Hill was later used for matches with the Australian Aborigines and the United South of England Eleven.[534] The arrangements at Scarborough were, however, far from satisfactory prior to the 1870s. The Castle Hill ground was used by the Army for rifle practice, while the North Marine Road site was rough and at this time was 'no more than a small meadow with a roped-off square in the middle. A stone wall separated the field from North Marine Road and the other bounds were made untidy by a straggling hedge. Unauthorised entry was far too easy for the taking of gate-money to be attempted.'[535] The field was so small that one player of the time recollected that the long-stop used to stand in the ditch.[536]

The early 1870s saw the beginnings of the involvement in Scarborough cricket of Lord Londesborough, who arranged a game between his side and a Scarborough Visitors XI in 1871. It generated considerable interest and following this, given the limitations of Castle Hill, which was owned by the War Office, Londesborough encouraged improvements to the Queen's Ground. It was enlarged and levelled over the winter of 1871/72, and a perimeter fence and pavilion built prior to the 1874 season. In 1877, the club raised £7,000 to purchase the ground and further significant alterations were undertaken.[537]

Yorkshire played its first county game at North Marine Road, against Middlesex in 1874, and, following a visit by the MCC in 1875, the Scarborough Festival was held the following year, becoming a major fixture in the cricket calendar, with its first-class games marking the end of the season for many people.[538] The festival was key to the prosperity of cricket in the town; in 1879, for example, the favourable financial situation of the club was considered to be due to the 'unabated interest taken in his lordship's matches.'[539] In 1886, Scarborough Cricket Club had a net balance in its favour of £192 after paying expenses, including £100 interest on the mortgage. It was therefore in a position to pay off debts due to its bankers of £191. The net proceeds of the festival that year were nearly £400.[540] The ground continued to develop, with a new pavilion built in 1896.

Along the coast, the cricket club at Whitby was sufficiently well regarded in 1838 to be included in the procession for the Queen's coronation celebrations in the town (albeit behind the quoit club), when it was reported that the 'unique appearance of the Ancient Foresters and of the Members of the Cricket Club excited much attention.'[541] Later, in the 1860s, cricketers in the town looked jealously on developments in Scarborough, which had held All-England games. A report on the annual meeting of the Streonshalh Cricket Club in 1863 discussed the importance of making changes to put Whitby on a level with other coastal resorts. That year, four clubs in the town held their field days on Good Friday.[542]

In Malton, a club was formed in May 1833 and by the following July had between 60 and 70 members. The Kirkbymoorside club challenged them and they accepted 'notwithstanding the disadvantage under which the Malton club labours, from the want of practice.'[543] The game was played for 50 sovereigns. In 1839, however, Malton Cricket Club was described as 'recently established', and a club (possibly a further new one) was formed in 1842, consisting of residents from the town and Norton.[544]

As in the East Riding, parts of the North Riding appear to have seen a revival in cricket in the 1840s after a period of decline, with a number of sides returning to their former glories. The game was reportedly on the rise in Helmsley and Norton in the 1840s.[545] In January 1848, the latter club was presented with a portrait of 'renowned Lillywhite' and a blue silk flag by a number of local ladies. The justification given was 'the gratification which the subscribers had experienced, by the revival in the village of the manly pastime of cricket, and a desire to see it carried to the highest possible perfection.'[546]

Elsewhere, in 1852, a report on a game between two juvenile teams – from Leyburn and Middleham – commented that the young Leyburn team 'will gain the renown which that place, a few years ago, possessed in the game of cricket.'[547] In 1862, Thirsk Cricket Club, which in the 1850s had been one of the best in Yorkshire, but which subsequently declined 'either from indifference, or the pressure of other and more important matters', was reinvigorated, and benefited from an active and efficient committee, and had a good amount of cash in hand.[548]

The York area had a vibrant cricket scene, with many of the villages outside the town supporting a team during the 1830s and 1840s. A game in 1833 was played involving representatives of clubs from Linton, Alne, Aldwark and Whixley.[549] Cricket was played at Sheriff Hutton and Green Hammerton in the 1820s, and Escrick, Fulford, Poppleton, Nun Appleton, Haxby and Skelton in the 1830s. In one game between the latter two sides, the stakes had to be withdrawn because the scorers could not agree on the details.[550] A club at Selby played against York in 1834 and there were two in Stamford Bridge in 1845.[551] Clubs also existed in 1835 at Askam Bryan and Tockwith.[552]

In the city of York itself, the players were apparently 'assiduous in their practice' after a fixture with Harewood was announced in May 1833, and the ground at Knavesmire was in 'excellent condition'. At that game, it was noted that amongst the crowd were several men who had played for the old York club which 30 years earlier had contended with some of the best clubs in the kingdom.[553] A new club was formed in the city in the winter of 1833, involving 'a considerable number of respectable persons', and it established a new ground at North Street Bar Walls, playing an opening game in April 1834.[554] The following year a York Tradesmen's Cricket Club was in existence.[555]

Many observers considered the York ground particularly attractive, one enthusing that 'Nature and art have combined to add an interest to the scene.' Despite the views, the club was beaten by Ripon in 1834, which was considered superior in every department. York players had apparently taken to bowling in a style they had seen used at Yarm, although not yet being proficient in it, it did them little good.[556] In 1836, the *Yorkshire Gazette* congratulated fellow citizens for the revival of cricket in York, hoping that before long, the York club 'may acquire deserved celebrity.'[557] The club attracted both new men and past players as members in 1836 and 1837. This gave it the confidence to challenge any club in Yorkshire (inevitably, with the exception of Sheffield), and to announce it was organising a sweepstake competition (see Chapter 4).[558] By the end of the season, the York Cricket Club, 'having proved themselves the masters of the principal clubs in Yorkshire, excepting Sheffield', organised a match with the crisply named 'Twenty-Two players from clubs of Tadcaster and Boston and within four miles round including Wetherby.'[559]

Cricket continued to develop in York in the 1840s. Further efforts were made to involve a wider group of supporters, and the club appears to have been on a sounder footing. In 1847, it was reported that 'a very spirited committee' had been appointed and several influential gentlemen of the county had agreed to be patrons. A large building was erected on the cricket field and 'every arrangement has been made to promote the comfort of the players and their friends.'[560] When the York Cricket Club met in 1849, Hon. B.R.Lawley, president of the club, noted that it was only recently that they had secured a 'respectable local habitation and a name among the cricket clubs of the North of England.' In addition, Richard Letby, a celebrated player of the period and longstanding official, observed at the Club annual dinner in 1849 that without the assistance of the 'higher classes of society', cricket would never flourish. In 1841, the club had had 17 members and the figure was now around 160. This growth 'was mainly attributable to the patronage and support they had received from the gentlemen present.'[561]

During the 1850s the standard of the game continued to improve in the town and in 1861, a new York Cricket Club was established, which by the end of the season had 386 members.[562] Two years later, it was in a very satisfactory financial state, as well as providing facilities not only for members but also for students of St John's and St Peter's Colleges.[563] In 1863, York became the centre for efforts to organise an alternative county cricket club to the one established in Sheffield and, although this pressure came to nothing, the Yorkshire Gentlemen club was established there, with strong aristocratic backing. The Wigginton Road ground was laid out for the club in 1864 at a cost of around £700. Twenty-six years later, Yorkshire County Cricket Club played its only first-class fixture there, against Kent, but poor weather and a weak visiting side meant the game was over in two days and not a great success.[564]

There was a strong element of aristocratic support for the game in the North Riding. The Hovingham club played in front of the mansion of Sir William Worsley, where the United England Eleven appeared in 1853 and the All-England Eleven in 1858. Games at Castle Howard were played in front of the castle and attracted wealthy supporters.[565] The club was established in 1843 under the patronage of Lord Morpeth and made up of young men from his estate. One report enthused that:

> Too much praise cannot be given to the noble spirit, of wishing to afford pleasure and amusement to the more humble individuals around him, which prompted his Lordship to provide a cricket ground in the beautiful park at Castle Howard and for having, by his personal attendance at their meetings, and his constant anxiety for the promotion of the game, given that encouragement which must eventually produce such players as will prove formidable competitors against their neighbouring clubs.[566]

Food and drink were often provided from the Castle, laid out on long tables. When Castle Howard challenged the Langton Wold club in 1845 it was made by Lord Morpeth in person, and it was reported that a newly laid-out ground in the park at Castle Howard was 'now approaching a perfect state of completion.' In addition, a banner of orange and blue silk, on which were emblazoned Morpeth's coronet and motto in gold letters, had been presented to the club by a number of ladies from the neighbourhood.[567]

Elsewhere, the Earl of Mulgrave was a big supporter of cricket in Lythe, near Whitby.[568] The 1840s also saw the establishment and development of the Langton Wold club. The *York Herald* commented in 1845 that it had been going for two years, made up of young gentry and clergymen from the neighbourhood 'who, if we may judge from the expense that must have been incurred in laying down the splendid ground on which they play, and the extensive and permanent accommodation recently erected, are determined to establish such a club as will become . . . an honour to the county.'[569]

Further north in Middlesbrough, organised cricket was seen in the 1830s, although an early club in the town was set up by the Mechanics' Institute in 1847. Two sides were playing in the 1850s and amalgamated to form Middlesbrough Cricket Club in 1855. A new ground was levelled and opened in 1857, and the following year, Jonathan Joy (the well-known north-eastern player who appeared for Yorkshire until 1867) was engaged as professional, a post he held for nearly a decade. In 1861, the visit of the All-England Eleven boosted the game in the town, and in 1863 a combined Middlesbrough and Stockton XI took on a Yorkshire side and, later, the United England Eleven. Because of where Middlesbrough was located, the club often looked outside of Yorkshire for its games – to Darlington, Stockton, Bishop Auckland, Northumberland, and even into the south of Scotland.

The club was sufficiently well organised to host and fund – through Thomas Vaughan, the owner of local ironworks – the county match between Yorkshire and Kent in 1864 and between Yorkshire and Lancashire in 1867, two of the games initiated by clubs other than Sheffield in the period. The latter match proved a financial disaster and forced the club to consolidate for a while. With the improvement in the local economy in the 1870s, it became more ambitious, employed Tom Emmett as professional between 1870 and 1874, and was one of the most successful teams in the north of England. As with many clubs in towns experiencing economic development, Middlesbrough lost its ground to building work in 1874 but found a better one and built a new pavilion. The club experienced some internal turmoil during the 1870s, and was heavily in debt as a result of its relocation and redevelopment. In 1880, however, the Australian touring side played in the town and a second powerful club – Ironopolis Cricket Club – was formed.[570]

Factors shaping developments.

Overall, there is no doubt that cricket grew enormously in Yorkshire in the 19th century. Many more games were played at the end of the century than at the beginning, and the standard of play was considerably improved. More people participated and enjoyed facilities of a higher standard. However, this brief examination of the game in different parts of Yorkshire has underlined that its history in the 19th century was never a story of consistent progress in any one place, and developments across the county were far from uniform.

We have seen that Sheffield, Huddersfield, Bradford, and Leeds were strongholds in the West Riding, and places like York, Bedale, Thirsk, Ripon and Middlesbrough were strong further north. Only Hull was even close to being an equivalent force in the East Riding. Yet even the strongest clubs experienced fluctuations over time; indeed, the game ebbed and flowed in different places. Sheffield experienced a boom in the 1820s, and was seen as the strongest cricket area in Yorkshire into the 1830s, but experienced a decline in the following decade, before re-emerging again in the 1850s to dominate Yorkshire cricket for several decades. Bradford cricket was strong in the 1830s and 1840s, but experienced a decline in the 1860s, from which it did not recover until it had developed a new ground in the early 1880s. Leeds was generally weaker than the other major towns of the West Riding for much of the period, lacking a single, high-quality ground or club, but the establishment of Headingley at the start of the 1890s gave it the impetus which enabled it to come to greater prominence in the early 20th century. In the North Riding, the 1840s saw the revival of a number of clubs which had been successful in the 1820s but had subsequently lost momentum. The East Riding also appears to have experienced something of a cricket revival around the same time, with clubs being put on a more stable footing.

It is hard to explain precisely why there should be such fluctuations in the early decades of the 19th century. There is perhaps some evidence that initially in the 1820s and 1830s the game failed to embed itself deeply enough in many local communities to withstand the loss of even a small number of enthusiastic players who had been the mainstays of early clubs. In some places, while people played cricket as children, participation did not continue into adulthood, perhaps as work and family responsibilities ate into their time, or because the game was not seen as an appropriate activity for adults, especially in areas with more conservative traditions.

Where the game was revived in the 1840s, there is some evidence that, as well as a new generation of participants, those who had played earlier were involved again, perhaps only as supporters of the new clubs, but possibly as senior players too, spurred on by happy memories of the game. A new wave of players, inspired by stories of past glories, and increasingly aware of cricket through the press and the reports of the doings of the touring sides, may have found it easier to attract the numbers needed to maintain a presence for cricket in a town or village, even if specific clubs collapsed and were replaced. The 1860s saw the creation of far more stable clubs, many of which continue today, with constitutions and committees, more robust structures, and facilities which were not so dependent on individual contributions, and thus less vulnerable to decline. They became seen as an important community resource and secured wider financial support which made them more robust. Many clubs still disappeared and were replaced or amalgamated with others, but the existence of the game in a particular location was no longer in jeopardy to the same extent.

This chapter concludes by considering what wider factors shaped the changes that took place. Three are highlighted here – the influence of geography, changes in working patterns, and wider modernisation in society – before Chapter 4 considers the flexibility of the game.

Geography

The chapter started with a description of the industries, population and transport network within each Riding. Clearly, the growth of cricket was not solely determined by such factors, but indirectly it seems likely that the number of people brought together in concentrated areas, and the ease with which they could travel to meet and play each other, helped to shape how the game developed in different places and at what pace. The pattern of population change in Yorkshire seems likely to have been an important element in the development of cricket during the 19th century, affecting the speed at which it grew in different parts of the county, as well as the standards reached. There were simply far more men in the West Riding available to play the game. They lived closer together and worked in larger numbers in close proximity.

There were also many more organisations – schools, churches, factories, workshops, offices, etc. – that brought them together, and could potentially be the basis for a team. The distance between significant towns and villages was considerably smaller in the West Riding, for example, than the East Riding, making it feasible to travel by foot to play, rather than require any form of transport. Thus, in highly urbanised areas it was simply easier to arrange cricket matches. In turn, the scale on which the game was played helped to raise the standards and made it possible for improvements in approach or style to be seen and shared. And it was easier for good players to be spotted and recruited to higher-quality teams and, ultimately, the county side when it was formed.

In contrast, a smaller population acted as a constraint on the game. Howarth provides a possible explanation for the lack of development of organised cricket on the Wolds, for example, despite their similarities with the Downs in southern England. Although cricket was played as a popular children's game throughout the 18th century, he conjectured that the sparse population and the long working hours of farm workers were not conducive to organised team games. He argued that only when the demand for corn rose in the early part of the 19th century, and landed families grew wealthy on the profits and so built their homes on the Wolds, did things change. Sons of many of these landed gentry attended public schools and universities, where they gained a taste for the game.[571]

However, the size of the population was not always essential for a strong cricketing culture. As we have seen, the Lascelles Hall club – based in what was described as 'a little village, made up of a country gentleman's hall and a few hand-loom weavers' cottages' – had very specific reasons for being remarkably strong at cricket and for producing many Yorkshire players in the 19th century.[572] On the other hand, Hull, had a large population but generated few significant cricketers. It was physically out on a limb, although, because it was well connected by rail, its major club did play against towns in the West Riding. Geography thus appears to have presented an obstacle to the game developing in Hull. In 1849, one commentator, writing at the time of the visit by the All-England Eleven, argued that the town's inferiority at cricket:

> may be found in the difficulty in obtaining, at anything like a moderate rate, and within easy distance of the town, a suitable ground for the exercise of the game....[In addition] it would really

> appear as if cricket did not flourish in maritime and commercial districts, but is indigenous to the agricultural. The best players in 'All England' have for the most part had their training in rural districts, and the exceptions to the rest are all in favour of inland domestic manufacturing towns.[573]

The long distance from the north of the county to Sheffield, and later to Leeds and Bradford, was also an issue, and a number of potential county players were considered not to have had opportunities because they lived well away from the heart of Yorkshire cricket. The position of Sheffield, situated in the far south of the county, was itself a cause of some dissatisfaction for many of those who campaigned for a more broadly based county club from the 1860s onwards. Many complained that it was costly and time consuming to get to for many followers of cricket.

Working patterns

Another crucial factor that helped in the development of cricket was changes in working patterns and working hours. The modern working week was not established until after the 1850s and previously work was dictated by the agricultural and religious calendar. As a result, regular time for playing was restricted by local variations and seasonal demands. Spontaneous, rather than planned, holidays were therefore common.[574] Some historians have also emphasised that the pre-industrial economy was very poor at providing full employment and that there was uncertainty over available work, with intense periods of hard graft – for example, during the harvest – and long periods of under-employment with accompanying concerns about having sufficient to live on. For many, this is likely to have worked against thinking beyond immediate needs to sporting pleasures.[575] The traditional agricultural existence thus provided irregular opportunities for organised sport. In the East Riding again, Howarth considers that the slow progress in the development of cricket was related not only to the limited population, but also the working hours. Referring to the early 19th century, he suggests 'Knock-about games on a Sunday evening on the wold would be all the time that was available. It seems clear from other evidence that inter-village matches became common only at a later date.'[576]

Hours of work for the growing number of workers in factories, workshops or in outwork trades in the early 19th century were also long, and leisure time largely restricted to Sundays, when much time was taken up with recovery, giving limited time for pleasure. The impact of industrialisation can be seen in different ways. On the one hand, it led to a more organised regime and reduced the amount of free time enjoyed by many in pre-industrial times. On the other hand, it has been argued that pre-industrial leisure was often 'not the kind of free time that anybody wants. Unasked-for leisure was unpaid. It left families without adequate food, lodging or fuel.' Industrialisation thus provided an expanded amount of work to be done in a more structured manner, although it also subjected many to an economic climate prone to boom and bust.[577]

Despite industrialisation, however, some workers resisted regimentation by taking short days, or by continuing to follow traditional, informal customs such as 'Saint Monday', when workers would not turn up at the start of the week, and would leave work for fairs, local sporting events and for hangings and elections. In August 1879, this was clearly still happening. When the sun finally came out that summer, 10,000 attended the Monday of a Yorkshire match, and it was noted, 'In Sheffield Saint Monday is ordinarily a loose day, but when there is bright fine weather and a good cricket match on many observe the custom rigidly, and enjoy it.'[578] Over the century, however, such behaviour declined. Ad hoc and informal time off work was not satisfactory from the point of view of the factory owner or other employer, and it was combated where possible. At the same time, it was also not suitable for the development of organised sport.[579]

Working conditions also varied between towns. In Sheffield in the 1820s, many working men were employed for piece rates in small workshops or as outworkers. In his excellent study of the development of cricket in the West Riding, Light argues that a large proportion of the Sheffield workforce was not subject to the long regular hours which were being introduced by the capitalist system, and so 'could enjoy time away from work to spend on leisure activities such as watching or playing cricket. Indeed, the Cutlers of Sheffield developed a reputation for their 'sprees' at the Darnal matches.'

In contrast, changes in processes in the textile industry elsewhere such as in Leeds saw the introduction of mechanisation and large-scale production within a growing number of large new mills. Consequently, many people were subject to heavily regulated working hours and poor working conditions. By the 1840s the development of textile mills in Leeds had begun to place severe restrictions on a significant proportion of the Leeds workforce and, as a result, there were smaller crowds at commercial cricket matches and fewer teams active.[580]

Only those who were outside the regimented timekeeping expected of the factory system had greater control over their time. Thus, an explanation for the excellence of the cricketers of Lascelles Hall, near Huddersfield, has been that they continued to work in a pre-industrial manner, using hand-looms at home, where they could decide their own working hours. As Holmes put it, 'the weavers being masters of their time, could practise to their heart's content at their favourite game.'[581] And in his piece based on interviews with Walter Haigh and John Jessop, long-time President and Secretary of the club, 'Old Ebor' reported Haigh's recollection that:

> the men were so keen on practising that they would commence at dinner time intending to have just half an hour, but would end in playing right on till dark. Then they would go back to their looms, and by the light of a farthing dip, which shed its lava of grease in thick lumps down the loom side, would make up at night the time they had lost at cricket during the day.

In addition, the demands of the work were considered a benefit; hand-loom weavers were repeatedly training their hands and eyes, and their feet were in constant motion. As a result, 'Between shuttle and pick and treadle a weaver had his power of sight, smartness, and endurance very considerably sharpened.' This led to the 'remarkable quick timing of the ball and general activity in the field' for which Lascelles Hall cricketers were noted. Subsequently, Jessop commented that technical change removed the conditions that had led to success, arguing that it was the 'fast looms that have destroyed our fast bowling.'[582]

More widely, however, changes (and reductions) in working hours were important in providing more people with the opportunity to spend their time in organised leisure, and were seen by some contemporaries as likely to lead to improvements in cricket. In 1848, the report of the directors of the Sheffield Athenaeum, delivered at its first annual meeting, noted that they had established a cricket club on the ground belonging to the gentlemen of Royd's Mills Club. They were convinced that 'if the young men engaged in offices or counting houses, were allowed to leave business, merely one day per week, not later than five o'clock in the afternoon, the cricket club would be greatly reinforced in numbers.'[583]

Many in Bradford saw reductions in their working hours after the 1840s, ranging from just an hour for boilermakers to 16.5 hours for plumbers, glaziers and gas-fitters.[584] More generally, Thompson suggests that 'most working people enjoyed more free time from the 1870s onwards, although the increases were unevenly spread and for some were slender'.[585] Just as important as the number of hours was that leisure time was centred on particular parts of the week. Half-day working on Saturday was established by law in 1850 in the textile industries, where factories had to close by 2 pm, although this was largely consolidating existing practice from the 1840s.[586] Some other industries copied the approach, although not required to do so by law, and by the end of the 1850s it was firmly established in many places. As a result, Saturday afternoon and evening became the high spots of a worker's week, 'the time for exercise and sport, for spending and bargain-hunting, for drinking, fighting, and loving, for sociability and enjoyment.'[587]

These changes gave more opportunities to play cricket. In 1852, for example, under the heading 'Weekly half-holiday', the *Bradford Observer* reported games played on Saturday afternoons by employees of local businesses, noting a match between the young men from the two largest foreign shipping houses in the town had generated great interest. Saturday afternoon was generally a holiday in stuff warehouses and so lots of people were present.[588] In 1858, in advertising the annual excursion of the Saturday Half-day Closing Association to Temple Newsam to celebrate the weekly holiday, opportunity was offered to play cricket and other rural sports in the park.[589]

Traditional holidays also provided the chance to play the game. In 1862, the *Leeds Mercury* reported that at Whitsuntide in the town, 'The mills were suspended, most of the shops were closed, heavily-laden excursion trains ran to almost every neck and corner of the land which afforded any temptation to pleasure-seekers, galas and fetes were announced, cricket and other games were played, and indeed, there was an ample provision for every variety of taste.'[590]

Similarly, at the end of August that year, Barnsley celebrated the annual feast. All the mills and manufacturers were closed on the Monday and Tuesday, and a large number of the inhabitants went on rail excursions. To celebrate the feast, the All-England Eleven played XIV of Yorkshire and drew a large crowd.[591] Other developments presented opportunities. Early closing on a Wednesday was beneficial for some. In 1871, drapers and grocers in Holmfirth began to close at 1 o'clock on a Wednesday, and to celebrate the early-closing movement a friendly game of cricket was played between teams representing the two groups.[592] Bank holidays were established in 1871 for bank clerks and spread to other groups of workers.

In Bradford between 1871 and 1873, during a period of economic prosperity, a number of local employers – anxious about the possibility of shorter-hours protests that were affecting other places – granted Saturday half days without labour-force pressure. Later in the decade, the local norm was a 55 to 60-hour week with a free Saturday for skilled and semi-skilled workers.[593] In August 1879, mill owners, ironfounderers and other employers decided simultaneously to close their works on Saturday until the following Wednesday, and most clubs in the district arranged to play day matches with the best clubs on their fixture lists.[594] Conditions were thus increasingly favourable for ordinary people spending time playing cricket in a more organised manner. Referring specifically to Bradford, Russell concludes that a 'new overall pattern had been created. Working hours had been reduced and new focal points for recreation had emerged. After 1850, and even more so after 1875, the conditions were established which facilitated the paid expansion of leisure activity.'[595]

Modernisation in society

Wider developments in society also helped the growth of cricket. An article in the *Leeds Times* in 1867 highlighted the quality of the grounds, where 'a good wicket is now as true as a billiard table, and is all against the bowler and in favour of the bat.' In addition, grounds did not wear out due to lack of preparation as they used to do.[596] Expectations around the standards of the playing surface grew as technical improvements were made and popularised. In May 1876, the *Morning Post* commented that 'Men refuse to play cricket now except on wickets levelled by repeated applications of heavy rollers and made as absolutely true as turf can be.'[597] Such conditions meant a dramatic shift from bowler to batsman, and contemporaries marvelled at the ever-increasing scores made, which helped to make the game a more attractive spectacle.

In his study of the touring elevens, West also considered other factors were essential to the way the game spread in the 1840s. He wrote of the importance of the contribution of *Bell's Life in London*, the leading sporting newspaper of the day, which was helped by the introduction of the penny postage in 1840, creating a cheap and quick way of getting match reports to the press and making it easier for clubs to arrange fixtures. In addition, the military decree in 1841 that all barracks should be provided with a cricket ground led to a significant increase in the number of venues.[598]

The development of easier transport was also crucial. It allowed for a wider fixture list, which helped increase the calibre of opponents that could be reached. An article in 1876 written by Pycroft, looking back on 50 years of cricket, argued that the expansion of the railway system had been essential. Previously, the cost and time involved in travelling 30 or 40 miles had been a major barrier to games, mostly played by 'juveniles and drawing on the long-suffering father's purse.'[599] Better transport allowed the higher-quality players to travel to representative games. Holmes noted that prior to 1850 only two Yorkshiremen – Marsden and Sampson – had appeared in the Gentlemen v Players series, but 'as time wore on and locomotion became more easy, and matches more numerous, Yorkshire cricketers had no reason for complaint.'[600] As we will see in Chapter 8, better transport also allowed some people to travel some distance to watch. In contrast, parts of the county with limited rail travel suffered. At the North and East Ridings County Cricket Club AGM in 1893 complaints continued that 'the present difficulties of travelling from place to place at reasonable hours was very detrimental to cricket.'[601]

However, economic and social changes could also bring a variety of problems. On the one hand, in Bradford and other towns, the game was constantly threatened by the demands for land as the economy boomed. On the other hand, economic decline could also take its toll, affecting the ability of people to play and watch, and at times ensuring they had far more important concerns. In 1862, for example, the Sheffield Wednesday club experienced problems due to the depression in trade, which had a 'pernicious effect' on local cricket clubs.[602] In the late 1870s, many clubs appeared to have trouble getting members to pay their subscriptions, which was put down to current economic conditions.

In addition, other activities could impinge on cricket. In 1869, areas set aside for cricket in Bradford were apparently 'monopolised by the volunteers', the movement which became popular in the 1860s.[603] In the 1880s, lawn tennis grew considerably. The *Yorkshire Post* commented it was 'fast becoming a national institution', with interest on a par with football and cricket.[604] Some saw it as a threat, but the *Yorkshire Post* dismissed this, stating 'it answers a requirement, and is in many ways a fine form of exercise – especially for ladies.'[605] Many cricket clubs thought it wise to embrace the game and establish a tennis section, and in 1886 the *Yorkshire Post* suggested many cricketers and footballers had taken to the game.[606] Cricket could not be insulated from change.

CHAPTER FOUR

DIFFERENT FORMATS

As well as changing social and economic conditions, a further and more direct factor in the growth of cricket was its flexibility. Put simply, cricket could be played in different ways, for different lengths of time and with varying numbers of people. It was normally played on grass, but could – and, at times, was – adapted for less permanent surfaces such as ice-covered rivers or ponds. It did not always need to be played to a conclusion for those involved to derive pleasure, and it could be stopped and restarted, sometimes even the following weekend. Thus, it could be tailored to the prevailing circumstances. It also meant that over time it could be adapted if aspects of the game – for example, the pace of scoring - became unsatisfactory for those playing and watching.

Sandiford has highlighted how the Victorians developed the game of cricket – in terms of the grounds, styles of play and the equipment used – but they also innovated in the formats of the game.[607] The 19th century saw several variations, some of which found favour over the long term, and others which flourished briefly and then faded. The conduct of each format was, however, influenced by a number of common factors – the rules which were used and whether players adhered to them; the time available for play; the make-up of the teams, including whether there was the need for some form of weighting to equalise the sides; the terms for the contest, such as whether it was for one innings or two; and the balance between the effectiveness of the bat and ball.

The team format

By far the most common form of cricket in Victorian Yorkshire was a simple contest between two teams generally played with eleven men on each side. For most people, this was cricket. Typically, a game would consist of one or two innings a side (and occasionally, three[608]), which could be fitted in during a day, an afternoon, or after work, before it got dark in an evening. Matches could be adapted considerably in terms of time, sometimes starting as early as 9am to allow for a long day's play, or at other times – where the players were sufficiently independent or wealthy, or prepared to lose wages - last two or three days to provide sufficient space for two innings each.

There were a number of basic requirements for all games. At least two hours were normally needed to allow both sides the opportunity to bat once. Certain basic rhythms also needed to be respected such as teams taking it in turns to bat unless one was a long way behind on first innings. Essential aspects of competition also had to be observed – batsmen tried to score runs or protect their stumps (unless they were deliberately trying to get out in the absence of being able to declare the innings closed, which was not permitted until the law change in 1889), bowlers tried to take wickets or limit scoring, and both teams sought to score more runs than the other.

Before the start, competing teams agreed the terms on which they would play. Reports of early games often stated, for example, that 'the first innings were to decide it, provided there was not time for either parties to take their two innings in one day.'[609] Thus, even if there was not time for both sides to have two innings, games could be considered won or lost, rather than drawn, which was important when money was at stake. A second innings was common, either agreed in advance, or as a natural consequence of both teams being bowled out quickly before the time for close of play. In theory, two- or three-day games made it easier to fit in four innings, but even this did not guarantee a result as games were often not run to a tight timetable, and late starts, long lunches and other delays and timewasting consumed the time available.

For shorter games, there were practical timing issues. Referring to the East Riding, Howarth suggested that the length of the game was a problem in the 1860s when 50 or 60 runs a side was a normal total and so a single-innings match could be over quickly. However, a two innings game:

> was not often completed before stumps were drawn, a time that was often dictated by the local railway timetable and the need of the visiting side to catch their train home. The practice in unfinished games was not to call them a draw, but to judge them on the basis of the 1st innings. This could produce some strange anomalies to modern eyes.[610]

As batsmen became more proficient and harder to dismiss, the time available in an afternoon fixture became insufficient, and there were complaints that games could not be completed. On occasions, teams batted throughout the available time, leaving little opportunity for the opposition to respond. In Todmorden, for example, there were 22 matches between 1865 and 1887 where one side either did not bat at all, or spent most of the match in the field.[611] In May 1888, Bradford Cricket Club batted all afternoon against Brighouse and scored 490-9 wickets, which included 73 boundaries, making the reporter wonder whether this was the biggest score ever in a Saturday afternoon match. The same day, Castleford batted all afternoon for 392-9.[612] There was no mention of how the fielding sides felt.

On other occasions, pragmatic arrangements were made to allow for satisfactory conclusions. In 1841, when Bradford and Bradford Moor could not finish their game because it was too dark, they agreed to resume the following Saturday as the players could not stay overnight to conclude the contest the next day.[613] The main problem with such flexibility occurred when players did not stick to an agreed timetable. For example, when Stockton played Lascelles Hall in 1863, there were complaints that Stockton asked for stumps to be drawn at 2.45pm in order to catch a train 'to great dissatisfaction of all in the field.' The *Leeds Mercury* wrote that the Stockton players had 'hardly returned the courtesy shown by those of Lascelles last year, in arriving in Stockton the day before the match and staying till it was finished.'[614]

Games were generally played roughly in accordance with the laws of cricket, as outlined by the Marylebone Cricket Club, which Sandiford suggests, 'naturally superseded older, oral, and therefore less articulate, traditions'.[615] How closely they were adhered to, however, was dependent on the players and umpires being aware of the laws, and the umpires being prepared to enforce them, even when this meant they were unpopular or would disadvantage their own side. As is clear in looking at the causes of disputes in matches, it could not be assumed that even professional or experienced players knew all the laws or necessarily wanted to abide by them. In 1840, for example, matches between the Otley and Dacre Banks team and their opponents from Boston and Tadcaster were dogged by the bowlers of the latter side deliberately throwing as the game slipped away from them. *Bell's Life* commented that the Boston and Tadcaster club was alone in the area for not displaying 'the gentlemanly demeanour and love of fair play.'[616]

Some laws were easier than others to interpret, with the definition of leg before wicket unsurprisingly being problematic, and the rules around throwing being controversial for many in the 1840s. In 1845, Law 10 was revised to emphasise that the ball must be bowled, not thrown or jerked, and the hand must not be above shoulder in delivery.[617] Some players clearly pushed the boundaries of what was acceptable; in 1858, for example, Lascelles Hall players bowled overhand contrary to the amended Law 10.[618] At times, though, it was questionable how widely the laws were understood by spectators. Although allowed under the laws, Hallam were hooted and hissed by the Bramall Lane crowd of 6,000 when William Slinn changed ends to bowl in a match in September 1856.[619]

Disputes over points of law arising from matches were sometimes referred to the newspaper, *Bell's Life in London and Sporting Chronicle*, as an independent and respected source. In 1841, when Bradford played Leeds Victoria, the game ended in a dispute when the former side claimed victory as no new batsman appeared at the fall of a wicket. The *Leeds Mercury* noted that a decisive answer would appear in *Bell's Life*.[620] Shortly afterwards, that paper determined that Bradford had won and the bets were to go with the stakes.[621] Subsequently, the *Bradford Observer* gleefully included an article about the decision, adding that the outcome did not reflect well on 'some of our Leeds friends, who loudly boasted of being "deeply read and far learnt in the law" - of cricketing.'[622] The matter did not rest there, and in November, the same paper reported that there had been long delays in handing over the stakes.[623]

On the field, how well the game was conducted was down to the ability of the players. In many local matches skills would be quite rudimentary, and players lacked practice or teams included men just to make up the numbers. In many cases, playing conditions were not conducive to skilful play. Nevertheless, as we saw in Chapter 2, there is evidence of many men and boys playing and practising enthusiastically to refine their skills.

Bowling was transformed over the 70-year period under examination. At the start, under-arm bowling was common, often quite fast. Round-arm bowling was increasingly used in the 1820s and became legal in 1835, as long as the hand was not above the shoulder. Some players employed both styles; Tom Marsden for example was a 'fast under-arm bowler' who also did round-arm medium pace. Bowlers were praised for particularly accurate bowling – using the 'insinuator' (Sampson), bowling an 'irrestible' (Wake)[624], throwing up a 'teezer'[625]', or bowling close and well on the wicket'[626] Looking back at the time of the 1887 Golden Jubilee, the *Yorkshire Post* commented that, during Victoria's reign, bowling had improved and had 'far more 'work' in it, more spin, more dodginess and difficulty than in the days of our forefathers.' As a result, 'So straight is the simplest bowling, and so good the wicket-keeping, that long-stop's occupation is well nigh gone.'[627]

Sandiford highlights the importance of the legalisation of over-arm bowling in 1864, arguing that, by allowing it, the MCC 'compelled batsmen to develop superior forms of defence.' Such bowling on uneven surfaces was sufficiently dangerous that improvements were made to the preparation of pitches and technology transformed the science of groundskeeping.[628] At county level, standards were raised in the 1860s and 1870s, as new, more effective, styles developed. Tom Emmett employed the whole width of the bowling crease or bowled from behind it to vary the length of the ball, whilst George Freeman made it come back with a whip of the wrist.[629] George Atkinson and Luke Greenwood were straight and accurate, while Thomas Armitage bowled high lobs which could, at times, break dangerously.[630] Ike Hodgson developed a highly effective slow, left-arm spin style which enabled him to take hundreds of wickets in games for district sides against the All-England and other touring elevens.

Batting too became more sophisticated. Different styles were employed by certain teams. In 1833, the *Leeds Times* contrasted two Leeds sides, noting that the junior club 'build on their hard hitting system of batting – the Leeds on science.'[631] Reports were full of praise for batsmen for their 'usual graceful and masterly character' or 'usual effective manner', 'first rate forward play', and 'steadiness, science and good hitting'.[632] Sampson's 'insinuators' were countered by batsmen getting both legs in front of the wicket.[633] In the same reflections from 1887, the *Yorkshire Post* considered that batting had improved immeasurably, with larger scores as a result, and it feared 'batsmen have apparently so developed the science of defence as to obtain at times a permanent advantage over the bowlers.'[634]

Clearly developments with both bat and ball did not occur in isolation, and the period saw a constant shift between the two elements of the game. For perhaps the first 60 years of the 19th century, at least, the ball was overwhelmingly on top, and newspaper reports often simply described a procession of dismissals. Holmes commented that, in the 1820s, 'owing largely to the rough wickets, heavy scores were almost unknown.' Before 1826, only one innings of 200 had ever been scored, and no centuries were recorded between 1829 and 1833. In the latter season, Holmes also claims Marsden's 53 against Norfolk was the second-highest score achieved that summer.[635] In the East Riding during the period from 1850 to 1869, Howarth suggests that at every level of cricket there are only 29 scores of fifty or more recorded. Two of the 29 batsmen went on to make centuries.[636]

An analysis of the reported scores of two July weekend's worth of games in Leeds in the fourth summer of each decade from the 1840s to the 1890s (1843, 1853 etc) also gives some impression of the changes that occurred over time in terms of run-making.[637] Accepting that not all games played would have been recorded in the press, and that this is only a small (albeit random) sample of matches, nevertheless we see a steady increase in the amount of cricket reported. Whereas in 1863, around 15 matches were mentioned, in 1883, both weekends saw around 80 matches listed. By July 1893, cricket in Leeds had been subsumed within leagues and fewer matches were reported, but the game was now fully formalised and structured.

In general, team totals were under 100 for much of the period, with many a lot less, and it was only in the 1880s that was there a significant increase in the number of larger team scores. In the 31 games reported in July 1863 there were only nine team totals above 100, in 1873, five in 26 matches reported, but in July 1883, 32 in 70 games. In July 1893, 28 reported matches saw 38 team scores of over 100 including three over 200, and the second weekend saw 29 scores over 100 in 26 matches, with four over 200. There was a similar improvement in individual scores. Although one match in July 1863 did see a century, it was something of an aberration and, even in 1873, individual scores over 40 were rare. In 1883, however, more batsmen were reaching this mark, and both weekends reviewed saw centuries and other scores above 70. In July 1893, four centuries were recorded in one weekend's fixtures, and two in one match on the subsequent weekend.

Improvements in the quality of the wickets at some clubs, associated with the employment of professionals to look after them, led other clubs to copy their approaches and take their facilities more seriously. As a result, after 1870 there was a marked increase in team and individual scores. Writing about East Yorkshire cricket, Howarth suggested that over-arm bowling may have been easier to score from because it opened up both sides of the wicket. This, better coaching and more care with the wicket may explain why, at all levels, 'the balance tilted in favour of the batsmen in the 1880s.'[638]

The *Yorkshire Post* also put heavy scoring down to lack of practice on the part of amateur bowlers. It argued that such players are 'too much given over to the delusion that while no preparation for the wicket can be too assiduous and severe, bowling is a kind of gift of the gods.' It advocated a half-hour practice on a well-prepared wicket, without which professionals would always be on top.[639] Not everyone saw the dominance of the bat as a good thing. Heavier scoring led to more draws, and in the mid-1880s there was concern at the excellence of cricket grounds and the 'now universal practice of allowing so many runs for boundary hits.' As a result, bowlers were 'heavily handicapped by the smoothness and hard surface of the wicket and the batsmen are relieved from much of the fatigue of running, and escape the danger of being run out.'[640]

Sweepstake matches

Although some clubs played one another in 'rubbers' or the best of three matches in the 1820s, most cricket matches in the early decades of the century were one-off and ad hoc events. 'Sweepstake' games, however, were mini-competitions in which a small number of teams played in what were effectively semi-finals and then a final of the two winners. They were designed to stimulate local interest in cricket and, of course, provide the opportunity for betting.

It is unclear where the idea originated from but an early example came in 1837 when the York Cricket Club announced a 'Grand Sweepstakes'. An advert stated that 'The Members of the York Cricket Club, wishing to promote the noble game of Cricket, have agreed to invite any Five other Clubs (except Sheffield) in Yorkshire who may be desirous of entering into the following proposal.' The idea was for the clubs to contribute 11 sovereigns each, with a further 34 sovereigns being added by members and friends of York Cricket Club. The ultimate victor would receive £50, the second £30 and the third £20. Umpires would be provided by each club, but to avoid delays, a referee would be appointed at the start of each match and his decision would be final. Each game would start at 9am to ensure it was completed in the day. Money had to be deposited in advance along with a list of names of competing players.[641]

In 1844, a 'great sweepstake' contest took place in York, generating considerable betting.[642] York, Leeds, Malton and Knaresborough were involved and contributed £80, the home club putting in £50. Thereafter, York beat Knaresborough, who left with £5, and Leeds beat Malton, who got the same. The final was played for £70, which was won by Leeds, who received £50 and York £20.[643] In June 1845, another sweepstake competition was announced with Dalton, Yarm, York and Hovingham taking part, to be followed by 'a conquering game', with the side winning two out of three being entitled to £50. The contest was spread over several weeks and attracted large crowds.[644]

The opening of the Bramall Lane ground in Sheffield in 1855 was also the justification for a sweepstake contest organised by the proprietors of its refreshment booths. They advertised for any clubs within 20 miles of Sheffield to enter, for a prize of £50. This was designed to draw in the (hopefully thirsty) crowds and two-day matches were held during June.[645] Broomhall and Milton played in a deciding match, when 'great excitement prevailed among the partisans of the respective clubs.'[646]

A similar competition was set up the following season by the same organisers for clubs within 24 miles of Sheffield. The successful club would receive £20 and half the entrance money, and again professionals were not allowed to play.[647] In 1857, one sweepstake match was affected by disputes. Milton objected to several of Wednesday's best players appearing, including William Prest, on the basis that 'gentlemen players were not to take part in the sweepstakes matches. '[648] Such games did not necessarily attract large crowds but the template had been set for competitive cricket amongst a selection of teams which would take off in the 1880s.

Single-wicket cricket

Alongside team cricket, another very popular form of the game until the 1870s was single-wicket cricket. It could take a variety of forms and involved different numbers of players. The format involved pitting generally high-quality cricketers against each other in a challenge match, usually associated with betting on the outcome. It was essentially a gladiatorial contest, with elements of a boxing bout or duel as much as cricket. The description of the Grange-Sadler match in 1857 at Leeds, for example, noted that 'the competitors' arrived with their friends, and commented that the match had originated 'in some 'chaff' during which one of the players boasted of his prowess.[649]

Games were organised through challenges. In August 1828, for example, 'friends of a Mr Pinckney' of the Ripon and Boroughbridge clubs made a challenge to play any member of the York club. This was taken up by a Mr Collier, and the match took place watched by many friends of both players, with much money changing hands.[650] Richard Letby of York was a noted single-wicket player, and in 1833 he offered to take on any man within 50 miles of York,[651] while more than a decade later, in August 1845, he played two men from the Castle Howard club for £10 a side. Letby had not been beaten before at single-wicket and reportedly 'played in a manner which had never been excelled on the York ground'. He was defeated, however, in the view of his friends, because of the slippery state of the ground which meant he could not bowl 'overhand' and had to resort to the old style with which his opponents were very familiar.[652] Single-wicket cricket was not confined to two players. In September 1864, for example, two matches were reported in the *Leeds Times*, one involving three against three at Harrogate over two days.[653]

Single-wicket cricket could be very demanding for players, with results often being determined by luck or the lack of it. Fuller Pilch batted for nearly five hours against Tom Marsden in the single-wicket game at Hyde Park in 1833, facing 198 balls in his first innings and 202 balls in the second. There were no fielders on either side.[654] In another single-wicket game in Leeds in 1864, it was reported that Smith bowled 208 balls before he took a wicket, and with each player doing his own fielding, 'some idea may be formed of the heavy work he had to perform.'[655] In addition, some considered there were particular approaches to being successful and not all players were suited to the format. In 1843, when Hunt played Chatterton for £50, the *Sheffield Independent* commented that the result would teach the latter 'that, though a man be a first rate player in an eleven, he may cut but a sorry figure in a single match.'[656]

The format could also result in very defensive cricket or one-sided contests. In a game in 1848 on Woodhouse Moor, one player, Simpson, batted for two and a half hours for 7 runs.[657] In 1841, Sampson batted for 293 balls, making 207 hits, while his opponent, Tom Marsden faced only 82 balls over two innings. On the second day, Sampson batted from 11.30 until 5pm.[658] The same year, Hall of Bradford played against Dewhurst and Dalby of Bradford Moor in what was described as 'the much-talked of' match, but Hall was out first ball.[659] When George Atkinson played John Grange in November 1857 for £29 a side, the match was concluded in just over an hour, and in October 1861, a game took place between Swain and eleven of the Burley club, which the former won by bowling out his opponents for no runs and a single wide.[660] In 1873, a game at the New Wortley ground between Farrands, the Holbeck professional, and J.Blackburn of the home club lasted just half an hour, with the former player receiving only three balls.[661]

Despite this, there is no doubt that for a while, single-wicket games were popular, both as contests and as the opportunity for extensive betting. Marsden's matches with Fuller Pilch were the cause of great excitement in 1833. He was involved in constant practice in the run-up to the game at Hyde Park, and had a bowler travel over from Nottingham to help him prepare.[662] In 1857, the *Leeds Intelligencer* commented that the single-wicket match between John Grange and J.H.Sadler for £50 a side (mentioned above) created 'an unusual amount of interest, partly from the fact that a single-wicket match for so large a sum is quite a novelty in this district.' [663] In 1861, a single-wicket match was played for £400 between

Hayward and Carpenter against Robinson, Darnton and Hornby. Apparently, the 'match attracted an unusual number of professional cricketers and sporting gentlemen as spectators, and the betting was very heavy.' So pleased was the crowd with the batting of Hayward that there was a collection for him on the spot.[664]

In late September 1862, another 'Great Single-Wicket Match' was played (reportedly for either £200 or £400 depending on reports), at Stockton involving three of the All-England Eleven – Carpenter, Hayward and Tarrant, against five of Stockton – Robinson, Darnton, Hornby, Atkinson and Halton. The *Leeds Mercury* described it as the greatest single-wicket match ever played in the north, noting that the Stockton players had practised for some time and approving of the appointment of John Lillywhite as umpire because it is 'a guarantee that the game will be played strictly in accordance with the laws of cricket.'[665] George Atkinson (mistakenly recalling the game as being in 1861) told 'Old Ebor' that the match 'caused a lot of excitement and betting. Mr Jackson, the backer of the Cambridge Three, made some extraordinary bets, and won a lot of money. One of the bets was £1,000 to £1 that neither of the Five got 100 runs.' He also remembered that the crowds made so much noise when he ran out Carpenter that a pair of horses attached to an omnibus bolted, scattering the crowd. Halton and Frederick Lillywhite climbed on the roof of the vehicle and managed to stop the horses.[666]

Despite the enthusiasm shown for single-wicket cricket, not everyone was keen about this form of the game. In 1861, the *Sheffield Independent* observed that it was 'decidedly tame in comparison with matches between "teams" of the usual number.'[667] Two years later, the *Bradford Observer* also commented that it was 'to say the least of it, not cricket, and playing for money is now generally repudiated by respectable cricketers.' Because of the money involved the paper suggested that too often such games ended in arguments.[668]

One such incident ended up in court in 1866 in Huddersfield as a dispute between two players and the stakeholder, who had been trusted with the money. Articles were drawn up and signed, and £10 was placed in the hands of the third party. The match could not take place on the agreed date and was only partially played out later. When they could not finish it the players asked the stakeholder to return half of the wager, which he refused to do. The defendant's representive stated that the agreement had not been stamped and the Court held that as the agreement had been signed by all parties it could not be admitted without being stamped. Apparently, 'after a long argument between the parties the plaintiffs were non-suited.'[669] Such disputes were common. Despite gaining a reputation through this type of cricket, George Atkinson commented that 'There is no doubt these money matches did harm to the game in that they created a lot of heavy gambling and unhealthy excitement.'[670]

One of the most infamous games was that played in Leeds in October 1857 between James Sadler of Leeds and John Grange of Dacre Banks for £100. Hundreds watched four hours' play on the first day, with Grange batting for two and a half of them. On the second morning, the umpires stopped the contest because of heavy rain. The players had lunch with Grange well on top, but it was decided they would not start again unless the weather improved. As this did not happen, the players agreed not to continue, but this decision was not communicated to some of Grange's supporters in the field. According to the *Leeds Times* there were disreputable scenes:

> Numbers of forgemen crowded into the room where the umpires were sitting, in company with Sadler and his friends. A breach of the peace immediately threatened, the forgemen being furiously excited, and the umpires refusing to withdraw from the decision they had come to. Hard words were used, the umpires were accused of collusion with Sadler, and that individual himself was obliged to bolt through the window in order to save himself from worse usage.

Things deteriorated and Sadler had to hide in the kitchen before escaping in a cab. The police were called and peace was established, although Atkinson, Sadler's fielder, had disappeared. The *Leeds Times* was appalled, commenting that 'we may say we shall not care if we never witness another single-wicket match – more particularly when such riotous and disgraceful conduct takes place as that above referred to.' Grange won when the game resumed, to the 'unbounded and boisterous joy' of his supporters. Despite the unhappy scenes, the paper commented that it could not remember a single-wicket match that had excited such interest and estimated that not less than £1,000 had been staked on it.[671]

Single-wicket matches were still being played in the 1870s but the great days seemed to be over. In September 1873, there was excitement at the result of the game between John Hicks of York and Alfred Brown of Malton for £100 a side, with a great deal of money changing hands in bets.[672] Apparently there was 'an immense number of spectators not only from the district, but also from York, the West Riding, and the north of England.'[673]

Matches were also played in the Huddersfield area the same year, still attracting positive comments from the local paper. One involved two locally known gentlemen – one a noted Liberal, the other a Conservative.[674] Another at Kirkburton in 1876 involved players aged 58, 66 and 70 in front of several hundred people, and much amusement was caused 'by the manner in which the old folks handled the implements of the game.'[675] Writing about the East Riding, Howarth suggests that single-wicket cricket remained popular and a game was often improvised when a normal match ended promptly. He suggested that the last single-wicket match to be recorded in the area was in 1899.[676] This format had, however, lost the appeal that had made it popular for several decades in the mid-Victorian period. Tarnished by links with betting, and with a reputation for creating 'ill-will', it became increasingly overshadowed by the team game as standards rose.

Games with touring elevens

The itinerant elevens of England played a hugely important role in generating interest in cricket across the country, not least in Yorkshire. Games between the touring elevens – the All-England Eleven, the United All England Eleven, the United South of England Eleven, the United North of England Eleven and other less significant sides – and local teams of between 14 and 22 players were played from 1846 (the first such game was played between the All-England Eleven and 20 of Sheffield in late August/early September) and continued on a regular basis until the middle of the 1870s, and occasionally, thereafter. The games were commercial enterprises, initially on the part of William Clarke, who saw that money could be made by taking the best players around the country. To start with, Clarke took the initiative to organise matches, but as they became an established feature of the game and more club sides wanted to test themselves in this way, so it was local clubs which approached the touring sides over the winter to find a place in their itineraries.[677]

This was exhibition cricket, the chance to sell the game as a spectacle. The games themselves were of varying quality, dependent on the balance between the visitors and the local team. This was determined by whether a correct assessment had been made of how many were needed to oppose the touring side and by the ability, in particular, of the professional assistance engaged for the occasion. The role of 'given men' – professional bowlers such as William Slinn, Isaac Hodgson and Luke Greenwood, who would often bowl throughout the visitors' innings – was crucial to balancing the teams.

On the other hand, the organisers needed to avoid over-stocking the local side. Having up to 22 fielders often made it hard for even the finest batsman to make a big score, even if the fielders did get in each other's way, as frequently happened. The *Sheffield Independent* reported in 1858 that the All-England batsmen struggled to score against Hallam and Staveley, noting that 'the provincials were so thick on the ground and fielded so ably, that the chances of scoring, except by an occasional drive right over the field, were indeed small.'[678] The tourists were not slow to complain if the local side looked too strong. On arriving at Leeds in September 1848, the All-England Eleven objected to playing 20 men, with Clarke stating that he had not been aware when arranging the match that the Clarence club intended to enlist help from other towns. He also stated that the games lost their interest if many of the same players opposed the tourists on a regular basis. After considerable argument, it was agreed that all 20 could bat, but only 18 field.[679]

In order to be a match for the professionals, some local sides stretched the boundary of their district to include good players from elsewhere. In 1853, the Twenty-Two of York and District included men from Bradford, Dalton, Bedale, Redcar and Harewood.[680] The *Leeds Times* commented disapprovingly a few years later that it was not aware that places such as North Shields, Bedale, or Stockton were in the districts of Bradford and Leeds.[681] The physical state of members of the touring side could also be a factor. As West notes, although efforts were made to arrange games carefully to keep distances down, professional players often needed to travel overnight to fulfil the next engagement the following day. Consequently, they were known to fall asleep on the field or in their changing tent, and bad weather 'was secretly welcomed, provided their wages were guaranteed, for the jaded professional could then enjoy a day of unexpected rest and relaxation.'[682]

Nevertheless, there is no doubt that many of these games created excitement locally and were eagerly anticipated events. Richard Daft commented that 'one never sees such holiday-making and high jinks as we used to in the old All-England days, especially at those matches played in small country towns.' Games were talked about for months, entertainment was organised for the evenings and on the day 'the excitement was often intense.'[683] Interest was encouraged by the language in the adverts for the games such as in the *York Herald* in August 1847, where the match committee assured spectators that 'there will be a display of Talent never equalled in the Annals of Cricketing.' In recognition of the anticipated interest, the directors of the York and North Midlands railway announced cheap tickets on trains from Newcastle, Hull, Leeds, Bradford, Scarborough, Whitby and all intermediate stations.[684]

Local communities made considerable efforts when touring elevens visited. In 1858, the All-England Eleven match at Hovingham was combined with the annual village feast, with the game played in front of Sir William Worsley's mansion. A number of bazaars, stalls, shooting galleries and other marquees lined the street, the inns were full during the evenings, although 'all passed off peaceably.'[685] When the All-England Eleven played against Rotherham in 1854:

> Galleries had been erected at each end of the ground for the accommodation of the visitors; and also, in addition to two marquees for the players, a marquee had been provided for exclusive accommodation of the ladies. Near to the refreshment booth...was stationed a brass band, which played at intervals. The church bells were set in motion.[686]

The following year, the bells of the parish church also rang at intervals at the start of the game with the United England Eleven, and a drum and fife band was in attendance.[687] When the same side played Otley in 1863 there was a gala at the close of play which went on until dusk, with dancing and amusements 'kept up with great spirit.'[688]

The arrangements had to be well organised or else they could lead to significant losses. The Rotherham Howard club suffered financially in 1855 when it played the United England Eleven, although this did not deter it planning a match the following year.[689] After rain reduced the gate receipts for the August 1862 match between XXII of Doncaster and District and the All-England Eleven, which consequently failed to match the £100 guarantee put up by supporters, the local Council agreed to vote five guineas towards expenses.[690] In contrast, the financial side of the Sheffield Shrewsbury match with All-England in 1862 was a great success and apparently did not involve 'any loss upon those gentlemen who so kindly allow their name to be placed on the list of guarantors'. One report suggested that only one previous match between a local club and the All-England Eleven in Sheffield had paid its own way.[691]

Arranging such games was a test for many of the host clubs or especially established district committees, and success was often dependent on subscribers and supporters making considerable efforts to sell tickets in advance. At the same time, it was also a recognition of a coming of age for a club. When Batley hosted the All-England in 1862 it had only been properly organised for about two seasons.[692] Hornsea Cricket Club was just six years old when it organised a match with the United South of England Eleven in 1871. The club's annual autumn sports were cancelled to allow the members to concentrate on their big day. In August, tenders were invited for provision of the refreshments and a contract entered into for the marquees. Special trains were organised from Hull, and the ground near the seafront was carefully prepared by Andrew Crossland.[693]

As with single-wicket games, despite the excitement generated, aspects of this form of cricket were unpopular. Some complained that matches did not start on time because the travelling team arrived late.[694] In 1854, the All-England Eleven took on a side of Yorkshire Gentlemen and Noblemen at York. It was announced that the wickets would be pitched at 10.30 each day but there were so many 'preliminaries' to be sorted out that they did not begin play until between 12 and 1 o'clock.[695] The following year, the United All-England Eleven missed its train and the game at Langton Wold could not start until 3.30pm on the first afternoon, while in 1856, the match between the same side and Twenty of Bradford was marred by time-wasting, with players repeatedly visiting the refreshment tents towards the end.[696]

Similarly, there was unhappiness at the game between All-England and Hull and District in 1858. The *Leeds Times* reported that 'A good deal of dissatisfaction was occasioned by the conduct of the All-England umpire in drawing the stumps, in spite of the protest of the other umpire, a minute or two before the appointed time (seven o'clock), and thus preventing the twenty-two from converting their virtual victory into a nominal one also.' This may have been as a result of disquiet on the part of the travelling XI at the very wide range of players included in the home team as it was reported it was 'the merest farce to call it Hull and District – the England had little chance.' The Hull side had not even confined themselves to Yorkshire, including Sherman, an England player, in the team, who then took ten wickets.[697]

Gradually this form of cricket began to be contrasted unfavourably with the team game, particularly as standards and competitiveness of cricket grew in the 1860s. As early as 1858, the *Leeds Times* commented that 'there can be no first class play with 22 men in the field. The best two batters of yesterday – Diver and Clarke – could scarcely get a drive away, and all their score was got by sheer push and perserverence.'[698] In August 1863, the same paper quoted a London journal which described the touring elevens as 'trading companies' which 'may be lucrative to the managers, but they are not cricket. They are trading speculations, and very little more.' [699] Even those who acknowledged the value that had been derived from the touring sides in spreading a taste for the game, became concerned when further sides were established. The *Leeds Times* reprinted an article from *The Field* which commented that 'the players are beginning to look upon the game merely as a medium for making money...and.... care less for their county or their club than for their little Cricket Companies (Limited).'[700]

Standards also appeared to be slipping. In 1868, although the All-England game at Holbeck attracted a good crowd, the *Leeds Times* feared that 'the twenty-twos are weaker now-a-days than formerly, particularly in the batting element'.[701] Games could also be boring, Howarth suggesting that by the 1870s a sign of the growing maturity of the cricket scene in Hull was that the annual visits of the All-England Eleven were 'beginning to pall.' Matches often produced very dull cricket, and the reporter of the *Hull Advertiser* was not impressed by the long lunch hour or the quality of the visiting team, which contained too many colts. Local cricket followers wanted something more interesting to watch and this led to the Hull club committee negotiating with Joe Rowbotham, the Yorkshire captain, and James Lillywhite to stage a North v South match in 1875.[702] A few years later, commenting on a game between Yorkshire and Twenty-Two of Ripon and District, the *Yorkshire Post* added that 'The present generation requires something more exciting – something that will task the energies of our best players against celebrities of equal strength.' [703] The touring elevens had played a crucial role in increasing interest in cricket in Yorkshire, but the standards of the players and matches, and how they compared with the growing number of county games, meant that the novelty had worn off by the 1870s. Their time had passed.

Clown cricket

A shorter-lived, but nevertheless fleetingly popular, feature of Yorkshire cricket in the early 1870s was the 'clown cricket' phenomenom. It is clear that cricket was hugely popular at this time in a variety of forms, and was taken seriously by players and spectators alike. Against this background, however, there appeared briefly to be some appetite for a comic version of the game. In May 1869, the *Leeds Times* observed that among the 'cricketing novelties' of the new season would be a team of sixteen clowns appearing in their professional costume.[704]

Two years later, there was a clown cricket match at Huddersfield. The *Chronicle* reported that the public 'has no doubt been waiting with extreme impatience and anxiety for some days, nay weeks', and wondered why the town had not been visited before. It added that the clowns were driven around, preceded by a brass band, followed by a large number of boys 'who were delighted beyond measure with the extraordinary distortions of....some of the clowns'. Unfortunately, they were not particularly good cricketers and conceded 237 runs, before giving a performance of gymnastics, comic songs and dances at the close of play. Between 1,000 and 2,000 people attended in the afternoon.[705]

Similar events took place in Huddersfield in 1873, reportedly generating 'great excitement' and attracting an enthusiastic crowd. The Doncaster Town club sponsored three visits – in 1872, 1874 and 1875 – suggesting considerable local interest in both the games and the evenings of dancing and circus acts.[706] In 1876, 4,000 watched a game between Pudsey Britannia and Collegian Clown Cricketers.[707]

Inevitably, the manner in which the Clowns played cricket was not to everyone's taste and seems entirely contrary to the growing competitive spirit of other forms of the game. Holmes in *Cricket* wrote that it was the only cricket he could not respect, and Edmund Peate, who partly made a name for himself prior to becoming a county player by joining Treloar's Cricket Clowns, described it as 'booby cricket'.[708] The *Huddersfield Daily Examiner* reported strong criticisms in 1871, arguing that cricket had been seen as a manly activity, but it would be degraded to a 'mere burlesque' if there were many matches like that at the Savile Club, Dewsbury:

> On one side were thirteen clowns (motley their only wear) – good fellows no doubt in their way, capital hands at a sumersault, a comic turn with a song – but with the exception of four or five, certainly not cricketers – and on the other side an eleven described as the players of the Savile cricket club.

The author added that whilst it was no doubt very funny to see players fielding with an umbrella and large hat, such tricks became stale quickly, and were best kept to the circus. The writer concluded that there was 'much that was objectionable in a cricketing as well as a moral point of view' about the match, possibly including it seems the fact that one clown was dressed as a woman.[709]

Some years later, a correspondent to one East Yorkshire paper expressed his disgust at the second appearance of the clown cricketers in Driffield. He described their play as 'a senseless exhibition of folly' and added that 'I cannot see how any man, or body of men, could be parties in any manner to such a degredation of the grand old national game of cricket.' He hoped that it was the last time the town was 'disgraced by such a contemptible farce.' The correspondent was not alone in his unhappiness since according to reports only six clowns turned up, and local cricketers had to be recruited, whose play influenced the outcome of the match for which spectators had paid 6d. Few residents stayed to see their exhibition at the close of play.[710]

Other aspects of their behaviour did nothing to enhance their reputation. A report in the *Leeds Times* in November 1873 quoted a correspondent of 'a Manchester contemporary' newspaper who had travelled with a party of 'Clown cricketers'. Asked not to smoke in a train carriage they burnt – but did not smoke – tobacco, keeping the windows and ventilators shut. They made 'fearful and wonderful' noises with a banjo, and talked loudly about killing the reporter and throwing him from the train. When they got out at Bolton, the reporter complained to the station master, who simply took their names.[711] This form of the game died away, little lamented, although even in 1884 the Clarence Top-Hat Society and Clown Cricketers were still advertising for games in the *Yorkshire Post*.[712]

Cup cricket

In contrast to the fleeting interest in clown cricketers, the end of the 1870s saw the beginnings of knockout cup cricket which ultimately proved to be a lasting format. Although as we have seen 'sweepstake' contests had taken place in the 1840s, Holmes considers the earliest combination of clubs was the Emsley Challenge Cup, started in 1880 in Leeds.[713] In fact, in January 1880, Councillor Emsley, a supporter of local cricket in the town, had announced that he would present a silver challenge cup valued at 50 guineas, to be competed for by the cricket clubs of Leeds on similar terms to those which Sheffield cricketers already followed for the Wake Cup in that town.[714] At the start of March 1880, representatives of 26 teams met in Leeds and decided that the cup would be the permanent possession of the club that won it three times in succession and prizes would be given to the winning players. There was a discussion about when the games would be played since most clubs already had a full Saturday programme. Given the exceptional circumstances of the first year it was decided that the initial ties would be played in May, the second in June and the third in July, and that clubs could decide when was convenient to hold them. No professionals were to be used and no one could appear for any club unless he resided or was employed in the borough of Leeds, and played regularly for that club. The committee could decide on all questions, and the term 'professional' was defined as a man who received a weekly payment as wages from any particular club.[715]

The first final was played between Leamington and Armley, the former winning by 47 runs, in a game spread over a Saturday and Monday afternoon.[716] In 1882, Leamington won the competition for the third time in a row and thus kept the trophy. Shortly after, a Hunslet man (Alf Cooke of the Crown Point Printing Works) offered a cup to take its place from 1883. This was welcomed by the *Yorkshire Post*, which argued that the Emsley trophy had done a great deal to improve local cricket by encouraging healthy rivalry between clubs, helping to unearth hidden talent and raising the standing of some clubs as a result of unexpected wins. In addition, the paper enthused that the games had nothing of 'the gate money speculation' about them, with the profits instead going to medical institutions.[717] In 1883, 36 ties were played and the competition was won by the Leeds Constabulary. Gate money of £54 16s was raised, and after expenditure there was a balance in hand of £8 19s.[718]

The cup competition in the Sheffield area was the Wake Cup. According to its history[719], the idea came to members of the Sheffield Pitsmoor club committee during the 1879 season. The club's finances were in a bad state and committee members were looking for ways of increasing the game's appeal. One of them, W.R.Wake, was a keen football follower and had seen the excitement generated by the new English Challenge Cup. He had the idea of a similar knock-out competition for cricket in Sheffield and district. Wake and his brothers got the support of the Pitsmoor committee in July 1879 and W.R.Wake donated a silver trophy to the value of 50 guineas as the prize. To keep costs and travel time down, entry was initially limited to clubs located within a 10-mile radius (soon extended to 15 miles) of Sheffield Parish Church, and a total of 34 clubs entered in the first season – 1880. The competition was a great success – 3,000 attended the first final between Hallam and Pitsmoor United – and clubs reported record gates in many areas. At the banquet after the final, the first year of the competition was seen as 'adding strength to local cricket in Yorkshire.'[720]

Competitions were established elsewhere. In the summer of 1880 a silver cup was presented by Hunslet Cricket Club for the winners of a final between Hunslet and Pudsey St Lawrence, although it could not be finished due to the weather. Prizes were given to players from the previous matches.[721] In June 1882, the *Yorkshire Post* talked of the 'mania...for challenge cups' that had grown up in recent years.[722] That summer, the Heavy Woollen District Challenge Cup was established, initially for clubs within a six-mile radius of Batley Town Hall. This again excluded professionals and games were to be played on the first Saturday of each month unless teams already had fixtures.[723] Big crowds attended the final rounds, even though on a number of occasions in the early years the final was spread over more than one day. Some 5,000 saw the first final in 1883 between Heckmondwike and Dewsbury & Savile, when over £82 was taken on the gate.

The following year, between 4,000 and 5,000 attended Dewsbury & Savile against Ossett in the final, which spread over two Saturdays and a Wednesday because of rain. In 1885, 8,000 were present for Birstall against Dewsbury & Savile, and special trains ran to the ground.[724] The *Yorkshire Post* referred to this cup competition as the most successful in Yorkshire and again the claim was made that cup cricket had done a lot to bring some minor clubs to prominence and to unearth new talent.[725]

Other parts of the county took similar steps. At the end of 1883, David Bookless, a well-known north-east professional, offered a £50 challenge cup for clubs within a 50-mile radius of Middlesbrough.[726] In January 1885, a group of cricketers in the Kirkby Malzeard district decided to establish a cricket tournament 'for the benefit of county cricket', with prizes of not less than £15, the final to be played on the occasion of the local flower show in August.[727]

A few weeks later, the Hull and East Riding Cricket Challenge Cup was announced, organised by Hull Town Cricket Club, which reportedly excited great interest in the East Riding. Strict rules were introduced that no member who had not paid his previous year's club subscriptions or had not played in two bona-fide matches that year could appear.[728] A competition was also held around York,[729] and in the Huddersfield area after 1886, the Lumb Cup was the ambition of many clubs. Named after Edward Lumb, the Yorkshire amateur batsman who donated the cup, proceeds from the final were paid to the Huddersfield Infirmary.[730]

Cricket cup competitions continued the trend for more competitive forms of the game to find public and critical favour as long as they were suitably controlled and regulated. Some correspondents to the *Yorkshire Post* were even more ambitious, suggesting a challenge cup for the whole of Yorkshire, as in football, and urging that the County Committee support the idea in order to overcome what one writer saw as the overly localised nature of many club games, which reduced their interest.[731]

League cricket

If the 1880s saw the beginnings of cup cricket, the early 1890s saw the development of league cricket. It arose for a number of reasons. Creating a league structure provided regular fixtures and increased the certainty of a full season's cricket for clubs. It also reduced the endless, and at times fruitless, correspondence about fixtures for club secretaries by providing a framework within which officials could meet and arrange fixtures easily. And clubs realised that a more competitive type of cricket could generate much needed finance by increasing spectator interest, which tended to decline once cup matches were over and most teams were knocked out. League cricket also became to be seen as a way of imposing better discipline on the way cricket was played.

In the Huddersfield area, the Huddersfield and District Cricket Association was established in August 1886 as an administrative structure within which league cricket later operated. In 1891, the Huddersfield and District Cricket League was formed for the best clubs in the area (with the first games in 1892), and in 1893, the Alliance League and the Combination League were set up for local clubs of a lower standard. The organisers of the Huddersfield League took care to take advice from others and corresponded with the Football League, the Midland Counties League and the Hallamshire Cricket League. They also encouraged interest in the local press. From the outset, the objectives of the League were clearly stated as 'to promote the best interests of local cricket and club matches, consistent with loyal support to the Huddersfield and District Cricket Association and to County cricket.' It also sought 'the promotion of a greater interest in the game; the fostering and development of amateur talent; and the controlling of professionalism.'[732]

League cricket spread quickly. In April 1893, the *Leeds Mercury* commented that the most remarkable feature of the coming summer was the expansion of what it noted had been called the 'League disease.' The success of the Leeds and Huddersfield District Leagues had been imitated widely, including by the West Riding League, 'which promises to determine, on a definite basis....which is the champion Yorkshire club of the season.'[733] Similarly, the *Leeds Times* enthused that the establishment of leagues had given a wonderful stimulus to the game and could only get better now that teams had a year's experience. The West Riding League was considered second only in standard to the county game.[734] Lower leagues then developed. In Leeds, winners of the Leeds second-class cricket league were eligible for election to the Leeds League, and the side with the fewest points had to seek re-election along with others seeking to gain entry.[735] A Leeds Nonconformist Cricket League was created to 'deepen interest and create friendly rivalry between non-conformist clubs', and a £20 challenge shield was purchased.[736] A Yorkshire Postal and Telegraph Cricket League was established for postal workers.[737]

In April 1893, the Spen Valley Cricket League was formed and the Craven Cricket Union decided to form a league for 1894.[738] Around the same time, clubs in the Heavy Woollen District agreed to set up the West Riding Central League to start immediately, with earlier matches between the teams involved counting as league games.[739] In May, representatives of clubs in the Wakefield and District Cricket Union met and decided to establish a league with two divisions for clubs in the area, probably starting in 1894. Around 40 clubs were known to be interested.[740]

In North Yorkshire, spurred on by the creation of the Durham County League in 1891, the North Yorkshire Cricket League was set up the following year, involving Redcar, Middlesbrough, Constable Burton, Thirsk, Ironopolis and Northallerton.[741] In Sheffield, United played in the West Riding League but other sides competed in the Sheffield and District League, the Hallamshire League, the Barnsley and District League and the South Yorkshire Cricket League. There was also a Sheffield Millers' League.[742] As a result of all this activity, the *Leeds Mercury* commented in May 1893 that few clubs of note were not included in one of the major leagues, with some involved in two or three.[743]

The development of competitive cricket, with arguably more at stake, made resolving the issue of paid players more important. The Huddersfield League described the 'controlling of professionalism' as one of its objectives, and there was discussion about ensuring that no professional engaged with a club outside the league would be eligible to play for a club in the competition.[744] In April, the Sheffield Cricket Association also discussed the matter and resolved that a player 'would not lose his eligibility to play for the cup by occasionally receiving a reasonable amount to cover loss of a day's wages and expenses.'[745]

In contrast, the following month a meeting of members of the Hull Cricket League met to consider a charge brought by Hull Rovers against the Albert United club, which had played a professional in the game between the two sides. The case was considered proven and Albert United had two points docked.[746] The situation in another league was clarified in May 1893. According to the *Yorkshire Evening Post* 'The West Yorkshire League Committee have made important concessions to the clubs in membership allowing them to change either or both of the registered professionals in any match giving four days' notice, subject to the proviso that no player takes part in League matches with more than one club.'[747]

The establishment of league cricket was also linked to efforts to reduce biased umpiring and the resultant ill-feeling between clubs arising from disputes which had marked too many games for decades. This competitive form of cricket made neutral umpires more common, and some – such as the Leeds Cricket League – decided to adopt an examination for those wishing to officiate in league matches.[748] As a result, even those such as R.S.Holmes who had reservations about league cricket could see the benefits it brought. He wrote that competition had put new life into many clubs. The game was:

> played with a spirit which is delightful to watch, business-like methods are pursued, a game starts punctually and not an half an hour later than the advertised time, any time lost has to be made up, and, most important of all, neutral umpires are elected.'

As a result, he concluded that 'these modern competitions are responsible for a more rigid moral code, and for that they deserve our heartiest appreciation.'[749]

The team game prospered because it created a simple, competitive dynamic, and involved local clubs and players with whom people could identify. Gradually, the domination of ball over bat began to shift from the 1860s onwards, and was replaced by far higher scoring. Additional competition was added through the establishment of cup and then league competitions, designed to stimulate greater excitement and interest, and thus enhance takings at the gate. The lesson of developments throughout the century in Yorkshire was that serious cricket, played in a competitive manner, won over novelty cricket and gave people more of what they wanted to see.

CHAPTER FIVE

RUNNING THE CLUB

We now turn to look at how cricket clubs – the essential building blocks of the sport – developed in Yorkshire during the 19th century. Individual clubs arose from different sets of circumstances and, for just as many reasons, often faltered and disappeared. For all but the best organised, their existence, particularly in the early decades of the century, could be precarious. Many towns or villages were represented by many different teams or ad hoc groups of players before more formal clubs were established which kept proper records, and in the early years many matches were played by loose associations or groups of friends, rather than well-structured clubs. This helps explain why so many local histories note long gaps between games in particular locations, and cannot trace matches for some years. This chapter examines how clubs were established and run. The following chapter looks at how such clubs at all levels financed their activities.

Cricket clubs and their purpose

As we saw in Chapter 2, rough games of cricket could be played pretty much anywhere there was the space to swing a bat and chase a ball, be it in fields or open spaces, and streets in urban areas. This was how everyone started, in contests requiring little organisation, and for most this was as far as they got. For some, however, such fun led on to more serious forms of the game requiring greater organisation, and to the formation of clubs of like-minded individuals keen to play regularly. The 19th century saw what Sandiford has called 'The Great Cricket Explosion.' This involved what he described as 'an incredible upsurge of club cricket', which meant that, by 1900, 'virtually each town, village and hamlet boasted its local cricket heroes.'[750]

There is clear evidence to support the argument that in Yorkshire this growth occurred well before this, initially from the 1820s onwards, continuing to gather pace throughout the next three decades, and then particularly from the 1860s. Throughout the county, cricket was played in the name of villages and towns, places of employment or particular streets and areas in the larger towns, and a wealth of other organisations. In 1831, cricket clubs were so common in Sheffield so that when the *Sheffield Independent* observed that rifle societies existed in every locality in Switzerland, it drew the comparison with a cricket club being present in every English parish.[751]

Initially, clubs were established with little or no structure or organisation and it was only later they became more durable organisations. Howarth highlights quite how uncertain and informal things could be. In his words:

> like-minded individuals came together, hired a field, arranged fixtures almost casually and frequently played for more than one club in the same season. Usually they enjoyed a period of success before either waning enthusiasm, financial stress or the loss of the driving spirits, led them to wind up.

Thereafter, a new club might be formed which took on the old name and ground and was represented by many of the same players.[752] Davies, too, comments that initially, while the availability of more leisure time enabled more people to play in regular formal cricket matches, this did not necessarily lead to the formation of cricket clubs. In his view, this step required the involvement of outside agencies such as paternalistic local landowners, employers, religious groups, public houses, schools or social-reform groups. Each was able to offer some or all of the required assets: land to play on, financial support to buy equipment, and connections.[753]

Clubs could be got up and running quickly. Within a few weeks of being established in 1838, the Wharfedale Cricket Club consisted of around 30 members.[754] In October 1854, the Wakefield Manor Cricket Club met to celebrate its first year. Originally set up in April with around 10 members, it had between 50 and 60 by the end of the summer, apparently including 'very promising material.'[755] Armley District Cricket Club, organised in October 1856, had 120 members six months later.[756] In 1862, the *Yorkshire Gazette* called the speed at which the Malton Amateurs club grew 'almost unprecedented', noting that, 'Not above a month ago a cricket club was scarcely talked about, but at the meeting held on Wednesday night last it was found that 90 members had been enrolled, and that there was a prospect of many more.'[757]

Some showed early signs of being well organised and having standing through their clothing or off-field arrangements. In 1811, for example, the Ripon Club players were well turned for their games 'in their tall Dignity, White Waistcoats, with long Sleeves, Callico Pantaloons and Woollen Pumps bound with Morocco; accompanied by their Secretary, taking down the Particulars of the Game for Publication.'[758] In the 1840s, the Hull St George's Club also formalised its dress, playing in 'a cricket shirt, white flannel with red cross on left arm, white trousers and a hat bound in red.'[759] The Richmond Friendly Cricket Club met in January 1831 to audit the previous year's accounts, hardly the sign of impromptu arrangements.[760]

As a result, many followers of the game soon acquired expectations of what constituted a well-organised club, and expressed dissatisfaction when governance fell short. In 1863, for example, a supporter of the Hallam Cricket Club complained to the *Sheffield Independent* that it was two years since accounts had been issued, adding 'No club in the locality has been more liberally supported than the Hallam Club; and it is due to the subscribers and the public that a statement of its accounts should be annually submitted....It is the duty of the president and the officers to do this; and I can only say that I shall decline to contribute any further to its funds until this has been done.'[761]

Cricket clubs were formed for many reasons. For some, it was a way of formalising existing haphazard arrangements and bringing together like-minded individuals into some form of organisation which could be sustained. In 1856, it was reported that players in Armley 'intend infusing additional spirit into cricket in that village, and with that view we understand that a meeting will be held..... for the purpose of forthwith establishing a club of "the first order".'[762] Forming a club also provided a point of contact for potential opponents to allow them to arrange fixtures with confidence that someone would turn up. Other clubs were set up by collections of players tired of being beaten; in 1855, for example, a group of Sheffield printers organised the Caxton club and arranged practices after regular defeats.[763]

In other circumstances, there was a recognition that having several clubs in a small area was damaging the overall quality of local cricket and that a new one, consolidating the talent available, was needed. A letter to the *Leeds Times* in 1857 stated that between them Leeds clubs had never had such cricketing ability available:

> but the players are divided into so many clubs, and between one club and another so much jealousy exists, that it becomes almost an impossibility to play an eleven worthy of representing Leeds, and thus for seasons past matches have been lost.

The correspondent suggested several clubs should combine and a committee structure be set up to govern the game in the area.[764] In Beverley too, several clubs existed in the early 1860s, none of which could compete without assistance from others and it was feared that the game would decline unless a merger took place.[765]

In other cases, clubs were established to pursue a particular agenda by different groups which saw cricket as an opportunity to develop their interests. As Davies notes, 'many individuals and institutions established cricket clubs, observing that some benefited from the generosity of local figures, so that sometimes the paternalism of local landowners was crucial and key individuals saw support for their local community as a duty which came with their social status.'[766] Certain organisations saw a chance to influence young minds. Mechanics' Institutes, for example, saw the benefits of having a cricket club to attract young men to join their organisation, which might otherwise be off-putting given its strong educational and moral purpose. Cricket was also a way of retaining member interest over the summer, when men preferred to be outdoors, rather than in the reading room or class. Church clubs were also established to bind members to a religious denomination, as well as draw young men away from clubs linked to public houses.

Inevitably, there was a strong social aspect to the existence of cricket clubs. Matches were reasons to come together and have fun with friends and neighbours. Annual club dinners were often coupled with singing, dancing and recitals, while fund-raising events during the winter provided another reason for entertainment, perhaps in conjunction with more musical members of the club or a singing group from outside. In November 1851, for example, Lockwood Cricket Club organised a ball at the Shoulder of Mutton Inn – entrance 1s each – to celebrate the closure of the cricket season.[767] The Hunslet Woodhouse Hill club began benefit concerts in 1870 and attracted 'a large and fashionable audience'.[768] Larger clubs organised even more ambitious events. Bradford held a series of Grand Balls in the autumn and winter of 1844, with a lady and gentleman's joint ticket costing 10s 6d, and a single gentleman's ticket 8s 6d. The second ball, in February 1845, was even more expensive – 12s 6d and 10s 6d.[769]

Cricket clubs also arranged trips. In the summer of 1874, on the Longwood Feast Monday, the committees of the Longwood Mechanics' Institute and Cliffe End Cricket Club arranged a cheap excursion to Liverpool (3s 6d for adults), setting off at five in the morning.[770] In August 1877, the Dalton Cricket Club organised a visit to Scarborough and over 1,000 people went by train.[771]

Clubs celebrated individual success and joint achievement. Many awarded a wide range of prizes at the end of the season to celebrate the performances of individual batsmen, bowlers and fielders, or acknowledge sterling service by officials. In 1871, for example, the Great Horton club awarded bats with silver inscriptions to the main batsmen of the season, and a pair of boots and a belt to the best bowler.[772] The Hunslet Union club presented a 'splendid bat, with silver plate and suitable inscription' to its highest scorer, a cane-handled bat to the second highest, and a pair of leg-pads to another man for good attendance at matches and his all-round cricket.[773] In October 1883, the Hope Foundary club gave out £25-worth of prizes to the best batsmen and bowlers, and a marble timepiece to the maker of the highest score of the year. The same year, the Birstall Cricket and Football Club awarded a silver lever watch, a travelling bag and money to its prize winners.[774]

There was also a welfare element in the running of clubs, with many helping to raise funds for local causes. In 1849, a single-wicket match was played in Howden between two members of the Howdenshire cricket club for a certain amount of tea, the same quantity to be distributed among the poor widows of the town.[775] Other clubs raised money for their local hospital. In Leeds in the 1870s, a North v South of Leeds match took place annually in aid of the Leeds Infirmary. Players, scorers and umpires participated for nothing and in fact paid admission to the ground.[776] At other times, clubs responded to individual hardship. In 1887, Hull Town and Sheffield played a match for the widow and children of the late Len Jackson, who had been professional at Hull for 13 years and had also appeared for Derbyshire. The Hull club allowed use of the ground for free and paid all the printing expenses. The visiting team paid its own travel costs, and the family benefited from the tickets sold.[777]

A more surprising and wider welfare role arose in the terrible winter of 1879. During a period of economic downturn, when thousands in Leeds were receiving donated soup and other food, the *Leeds Times* reported that at Horsforth:

> the chief work of relieving the distress has hitherto fallen upon the two principal cricket clubs, which have already distributed to over 200 poor families a fair amount of provisions, comprising 250 loaves of bread, 2lb each, 280lb of bacon, 140lb of cheese, 150lb of sugar, 65lb of tea, 40 gallons of soup, and a small quantity of flour.[778]

Clubs became symbols of local pride, whose reputation and standing needed to be defended. In 1871, Lascelles Hall wrote to the St John's Club in Huddersfield to protest at the latter's claim to be the best club in the district, a label to which it considered it had more right. St John's claimed that it had meant with the exception of the Lascelles Hall club, although some present denied this caveat had been mentioned.[779] Some clubs took considerable offence at the suggestion that they had brought in outsiders to bolster their local resources. In 1870, for example, the Manningham Cricket Club annual meeting heard that it rigidly restricted itself to playing only the members of its teams, 'a rule which is not always adhered to by some clubs.'[780]

As we saw in Chapter 4, cup and league games added to the excitement between cricket clubs. During a game between Birstall and Batley in 1892, telegraphs and pigeons were sent to Birstall to relay details of the match. When it was known that their side was likely to win, residents put out flags and the Birstall Brass Band was sent out in a waggonette to meet the team in Dewsbury. The winning side was pelted with grass sods by opposing supporters on the way home, but celebrations reportedly continued for a week.[781] On occasions, the local transport arrangements were unable to cope. Despite the interest in the 1884 Heavy Woollen District final at Chickenley, the Great Northern Railway Company made no extra provision for the size of the crowd, and passengers were crammed

16 to a compartment. Once at their destination, frustrated spectators picked the ticket collector up and carried him from the gate, before throwing their tickets on the floor and walking to the ground. Here the number of money collectors in post was equally inadequate, leading to pushing and loud complaints.[782]

Efforts by clubs to play a role in the local community were praised, and many men associated with them made very grand claims for the importance of such organisations. In 1859, one observer stated great credit was due the committee of the York Club for the way in which it placed its ground at the disposal of those who wanted to play cricket. Several school and other matches had been played. He added that this 'not only encourages cricket, and advances its true interests, but tends to promote generous and friendly feeling amongst all who join in this popular amusement.'[783] Similarly, in 1877, Councillor Leak, the President of Hull Town Cricket Club, told the club dinner that it was the committee's duty and pleasure to support the game as best they could because such clubs were, he believed, 'absolutely essential to the well-being of a large community like the town of Hull.'[784]

Cricket clubs thus laid claim to possessing a significant place in the lives of their communities. Having an impressive ground with a pavilion and good accommodation for spectators added to the sense of standing, and were symbols of success and prestige. Conversely, not having a settled place to play created an air of uncertainty. St John's Golcar Cricket Club, for example, was established in 1871 but moved ground within a year, and again in 1874, before finding a more permanent home in 1877. It was only at this point that it could consider investing in its facilities and enlarging its ground.[785] In 1879, the President of the Huddersfield Cricket and Athletic Club reported that, although they could be proud of their ground, 'still they cannot be called complete without better pavilion accommodation; at present the committee do not feel justified in incurring a further large expenditure, but by and by hope something will be done in the matter.'[786]

Creating the rules

An early duty for any club was to agree a set of rules by which to run its affairs. Such arrangements had long been involved and prescriptive, as Holmes illustrated by quoting from the York club rules of 1784 which included, amongst other things, a fine of threepence on any member who was 'not within sight of the wickets each morning before the Minister strikes five o'clock.'[787] Clubs drew inspiration from different sources. In 1863, for example, Withernsea Cricket Club met to formalise the arrangements and took on the rules of the Roos Albion club, adding some new ones and modifying others to take account of its particular circumstances as a coastal resort. Special provision was added so visitors to the town could be admitted on payment of 2s6d.[788] Other clubs were influenced by the backgrounds of their founding members, and adopted rules from the schools and universities they had attended or read about. Reports in newspapers were also an influence, giving details of how others were organising themselves.

Rules were frequently very specific, regulating many aspects of club activity, and often incorporating a monetary penalty where broken. Detailed resolutions governing activities were established when Bradford Cricket Club was formed in 1836. Members were to meet on the playing field on the first Monday of each month between one and three o'clock. There was a penalty of 6d for failure to attend, with only absence from the town and illness regarded as adequate excuses. In 1839, the club passed Rules and Regulations which included that potential members could be voted on at any properly arranged meeting, but five black balls or a majority of those present at the meeting against would exclude the applicant. Two sets of players were not allowed to play on the field at the same time, and there was a fine of 1s if anyone used another member's private bat.[789] At Lascelles Hall in 1862, no-one was allowed to use any of the club traps to travel to a match without the consent of a majority of the committee of the club, and any member going in front of the Hall would be fined one shilling. A member chosen to play and then refusing would also be fined 6d.[790]

The behaviour of players was often carefully laid out. When the Mechanics' Institute in Middlesbrough set up a cricket club in 1847 it drew up a 'strict rule book', which forbid intoxicating drink, bad language and any form of gambling.[791] When Thornton Cricket Club was established in 1850, the *Bradford Observer* published a letter which enthused that 'one grand feature of the rules is no betting or playing for stakes is allowed; all bad language etc and public house meetings are disallowed.'[792]

This concern with respectability was important for many clubs. At the start of the 1846 season, the *York Herald* commented that: 'we are informed that great alterations have been made in the rules, which will have the effect of rendering the [York] club even more respectable than hitherto.'[793] Without such rules some feared clubs would fall short of such expectations for good governance. In 1857, a letter appeared in the *York Herald* about the Rosedale Cricket Club which the correspondent said was 'not well conducted' by a committee of only three, rather than seven, members, and was actually dominated by one person. In addition, it was desirable:

> that some statement should be made as to the outlay of the funds, and that when parties come from a distance to play a friendly game, they ought to be treated with some degree of courtesy, which was not the case with the Cropton club....With proper regulations, the club might be placed, as it once was, in a flourishing position.[794]

Others tried to protect themselves from actions and behaviour which could affect their interests or reputation. In 1840, the *Bradford Observer* reported that:

> the Bradford Club is determined to maintain the high character they have obtained by the same straightforward and honourable conduct which they have always acted upon, which is to meet their competitors with their own members, and with their own exclusively. They will not on any account hire superior players from any other club, and they would say to all competitors – do so likewise.[795]

Some even resorted to the law. In 1874, Lockwood Cricket Club decided to prosecute anyone who trespassed from the field they had hired. Many people left the cricket field via an adjoining one, and the owner said he would not let the club have its field any longer if the trespassing continued. The club decided to take action before it suffered damage to its reputation.[796]

Early grounds

Initially, the locations for many cricket matches were open land outside towns and villages, moors with unlimited access, such as Skircoat Moor near Halifax, Hunslet Moor near Leeds, or else racecourses such as at York and Doncaster.[797] In Beverley, the Westwood was used, as were the strays in York. Games might be played in fields with little or no preparation and, as a result, some were clearly unsuitable. Despite hosting a 'long talked of match' in 1829, Knaresborough's ground was dismissed as being 'as bad as could be found in the neighbourhood.'[798] In July 1834, York visited Yarm, whose ground was described as 'a ploughed field much more than a cricket-ground...intersected with ridges, in most places two and a half feet above the furrow.'[799]

Other venues were also unsuitable. In October 1843, when the West Riding played the North Riding in a highly publicised game, it was held on 'a large seed field', which was apparently not well adapted for cricket.[800] Eight years later, Sheffield Hallamshire played Swinton on the latter's ground, which was 'in a very rough state, and more than ankle deep in grass, which was very unfavourable to players accustomed to a ground like Hyde Park. In fact, the heads of the players were far more in danger than the wickets.'[801] When Leeds Clarence took on Hull in 1853, they also had problems scoring 'owing to the roughness of the ground and length of the grass.'[802] The weather could make things worse. When Leyburn played Fleetham in 1859, the ground, which was in any case poor, had been drenched by heavy rain and 'sadly damp'd the Leyburn players, whose stumps slipped down in rather novel style, as the majority of the players in the first innings were run out.'[803]

Dissatisfaction with the location, size or quality of some of the grounds used for games against the professional touring sides was common. In 1849, the All-England side was unimpressed by the conditions for their game with Hull, where the ground was deemed too small for such a match and the outfield, being ridged, was not an attractive prospect for a fielder.[804] The expectations of professional players clearly grew over time. Prior to their game against Pudsey in 1864, the All-England Eleven complained about the condition of the ground (described as 'disgraceful'). Although they went ahead with the contest, they were defeated so quickly that there was a financial loss for the organisers, and it was suggested they might have been better playing on a cart-road.[805] Even in the late 1870s, by which time many clubs were applying more scientific groundkeeping methods, particular venues hosting high-quality matches did not meet expectations. When the United North of England played Eighteen of Leeds and District at the Leeds Horticultural Gardens in 1878, the ground was so poor that the wicket was relocated to the older portion of the gardens, where significant matches had been played in the past.[806]

Although many early facilities fell short of acceptable standards, some were clearly much better and widely admired. In 1834, York Cricket Club opened its new ground at North-Street Bar Walls, which was considered excellent, the *Herald* commenting that despite a slight slope, 'no ground could well be more favourable for play; and for situation.'[807] The ground in the park of the Earl of Harewood was also far better than the norm when York played there in 1837. It was a wide open space of 12 acres which was mowed close and rolled smooth.[808] Achieving and maintaining such standards required costly efforts. Some wealthier clubs employed a groundsman who could manage all aspects of the ground. Andrew Crossland, the Yorkshire bowler, took on the role of proprietor of the ground at Hull in 1853, levelling out the ridge and furrow of the outfield and placing boundary flags to try to keep spectators back, although they had no significance since all hits had to be run out, including into the crowd.[809]

Elsewhere, club members toiled to produce a suitable playing surface, and by the 1870s standards of many club grounds were impressive. According to recollections, the Lascelles Hall members drew lots as to who would work on their new ground in the 1860s, and paid 3s 6d a day or worked themselves in laying a field which many years later was still being praised.[810] In Bradford too, an observer in 1877 noted how 'More care is bestowed upon the wickets, more attention is given to the comfort of the players and visitors. The well-fenced enclosures and commodious pavilions of a score or more clubs in this locality attest to their popularity and stability.'[811]

Organisation

The initial organisation of many clubs was rudimentary or non-existent. This was not necessarily a problem. Clubs based around workplaces could keep their equipment in the factory or warehouse. Those associated with a public house could use it as a meeting place, storehouse, venue for celebration, and a changingroom. The lack of any permanent clubhouse in which to store equipment in the 1830s was overcome in Bradford by the club being allowed to leave equipment in a local tollbooth.[812]

Those looking to flourish, however, needed to develop in various ways. As one speaker put it when the York Cricket Club met for its annual dinner in 1853:

> the good footing which the club had obtained among the institutions of York [was due to] to the patience bestowed upon it by the committee, to the peculiar constitution of the club itself, and its ability to be matched not only with the eleven of All-England, but also to accommodate, if necessary, any eleven of a second-rate character, as cricketers.[813]

Five years later, the Chairman of the same club commented that 'the success of this club during the past year was owing to the skill of the players, to the good management of the officers, and to the good feeling which had prevailed among all parties concerned.'[814]

Most clubs relied from the start on those members who were prepared to act in various capacities such as Treasurer and Secretary. The success of the Langton Wold club, which by the 1850s had enjoyed several years of improvement, was put down to its energetic secretary, Mr Trueman, who had 'untiring zeal' and brought out the energy of the club.[815] The York Cricket Club was particularly grateful to Richard Letby, with one speaker at the annual dinner in December 1853 noting that his name was intimately connected to the game in the town and without his exertions over 20 years, 'the game must have flagged, and could not possibly have occupied the position it has held and does yet hold.'[816] Similarly, Scarborough Cricket Club was heavily indebted to Robert Baker, who was secretary for 26 years, as well as the local Town Clerk.[817]

As valuable as the contribution of individual officials were, clubs were also kept going by the day-to-day efforts of a wider group of members and supporters. Club membership numbers grew in the 1870s. In 1873, for example, Dalton Cricket Club's membership was 155, up 17 since 1871. By 1879, it was 195, before dropping back in the early 1880s and then rising again to 224 in 1884. In 1873, St John's Huddersfield had 209 members (it had been 43 in 1870), of whom 26 were life members.[818] At the end of the decade, the Huddersfield Cricket and Athletic Club saw its numbers rise from 553 members of all kinds in 1877 to 748 in 1878.[819] It then dropped back when subscriptions were increased. Thereafter, attracted no doubt by new facilities such as a gymnasium, numbers rose again and by the late 1880s the total was over 800, and topped 1,000 by

1889.[820] In 1874, the Lascelles Hall membership grew by 30 to 177 in the year.[821] Middlesbrough Cricket Club had 179 members in 1869, an increase of 26 on the previous year.[822] The Todmorden club also grew from 157 in 1863 to 284 in 1864, interest stimulated as we saw in Chapter 4 by the match with the United England XI, but then declined significantly in the second half of the 1870s, falling from 270 in 1875 to 126 in 1878.[823] Membership numbers elsewhere were also subject to considerable fluctuation. In 1874, for example, Dalton Cricket Club had 163 members, including 21 new members and 17 additional subscribers on the previous year, but had also struck off 30 existing members for various reasons.[824]

Some observers reflected on the social make-up of clubs. In 1849, for example, Hon B.R.Lawley, the president of the York Cricket Club, stated at the club's annual dinner that:

> the game of cricket did not thrive so well amongst the upper as amongst the lower classes; but the advantage of the game....[was] that without destroying the degrees of rank which at present exist, it so equalises men that persons of every rank and station might play together, provided they conducted themselves respectably.[825]

In 1850, a new cricket club was established in Hull called the Caledonian Cricket Club, 'especially for the working class.' In Bradford in 1874, the *Cricketers' Journal* reflected on the subject, arguing that 'we are sorry to notice that there has been too much done in the way of confining the members of any one club to a particular class of society, but we believe even this does not exist to so great a degree as formerly.'[826]

Some clubs made an attempt to accomodate different social classes. In April 1853, a meeting was held in Hull to organise a senior club with membership open to all classes. The resulting Hull Town Cricket Club was formed with the subscription for mechanics half that of other members, described as 'an excellent inducement for working men to participate in this noble game.'[827] In 1875, a positive view was offered by one writer, who reported on the basis of 20 years' involvement with the old Bradford club that, 'associations of the most friendly character were formed between manufacturers, merchants, tradesmen and working men, without a shade of disrespect or overbearing assumption.'[828] Others, such as the Dalton Cricket Club, were considered accomodating to all classes, although there is a strong hint that this meant that working men 'knew their place'. In 1878, for example, it was suggested that the club possessed 'the element of equality among its members in the best sense of the term - all are ready to do their part, and no one seems to think himself superior to the other, while each one seems desirous of paying proper deference to another where it is due.'[829]

The cost of membership usually determined who could afford to join. In

Doncaster, club subscriptions in 1862 were 'tradesmen' 10s 6d and 'artisans and mechanics' 5s 0d, but by 1864 they were down to 5s 0d for all playing members. In 1871, they rose again to help pay the increased rent on the Belle Vue ground, but in 1877 fell from 10s 6d to 7s 6d.[830] In Todmorden, the cost of membership dropped by 1850 to 5s, 40% of that in 1839, which reportedly made membership affordable for the 'ordinary wage earner.'[831] Beverley Town Cricket Club's membership was 5s in 1862, with honorary membership 10s.[832] Elsewhere, however, the subscription at Middlesbrough in the mid-1870s was one guinea, and Baker suggests that 'this would represent over a week's wage for a working man.' As a result, most of the names in the team lists were tradesmen or senior employees with one of the iron companies.[833]

Involvement with a cricket club could also be time-consuming, which again influenced who could get involved. In 1836, the Ripon Club arranged two general practice games each week, and the York Club met for practice three times a week the same year.[834] In 1863, the *York Herald* commented that 'every exertion is being made to keep [the Bedale] club together. Mornings and evenings are devoted to practice, and now every Saturday afternoon an extra practice takes place.[835] There were also many tasks to be performed or meetings to attend. When the Hull Railway Clerks Cricket Club started in the 1870s, grass-cutting and wicket-preparation was performed at 5 o'clock in the morning or at night in the moonlight.[836] In 1873, the committee of the St John's Huddersfield club met on 58 occasions, with an average attendance of 14 members.[837] Such efforts probably meant committee members felt they had grounds for exhorting others to greater efforts. In 1877, for example, the Lockwood committee urged every member to:

> exert himself on behalf of the club; to get clear of debt; to increase its power, that greater facilities may be given to those who love the health invigorating game; to improve the ground, add comfort to the visitors, and bring in new members.[838]

Failure to sustain such enthusiasm and efforts inevitably led to problems for cricket clubs. At the St John's Cricket Club AGM in 1874, officials complained of difficulties in getting umpires and scorers, so that they had no proper record of the game on many occasions, and the services of anyone who turned up were used. They had also found it very difficult to get players to appear in away matches and promised to end them if this problem continued. In addition, they suffered a loss of income from the lockers in the club tent, due to members not returning their keys at the end of one season to avoid having to pay the following year.[839] Three years later, the Treasurer of Batley Cricket Club complained bitterly at the lack of interest in the town despite the signs of local economic success. He also bemoaned the way in which collectors had to visit subscribers three or four times sometimes to get them to pay their dues. Holding out the prospect of bankruptcy in the near future, he called on members 'to greater exertions and greater support, and asked them to bear in mind that all men have certain obligations.'[840]

Disputes amongst members about how a club was run were not unusual. In December 1851, the York Cricket Club held its annual dinner, and shortly after a letter appeared in the *York Herald* stating that many members had not known about it and that the attendance included many non-cricketers. There were angry exchanges about the inefficient manner in which the club had been run. The letter went on to state that it had been three years since the committee had been elected, and to question whether accounts had been produced over that period. It asked why matches were arranged without members' approval and why some players were able to draw 5s a day from the club to play despite there being no rule allowing this. The correspondent suggested that poor on-field performances were down to the committee selecting from only a small proportion of the 200-strong membership.[841] The following week, members of the York committee responded anonymously in the press, but this only prompted one correspondent to name the members involved and challenge many of their statements. The committee had denied that 'any one individual assumes the dictatorship', but the correspondent named Richard Letby, the club secretary, as acting in that way. The author added it was improper that he ('who has usurped all the power') had a public house on the ground and had sought to press bats and balls on the club at the highest retail price, having bought them cheaply himself. He called for an immediate annual meeting, scrutiny of the accounts and election of officials.[842]

In January 1852 a meeting was held to discuss the matters and in March the club met again to receive the report of a special audit committee appointed to examine the accounts since 1846. Although some vouchers from the early years could not be found, it concluded that the accounts had been audited and were largely correct. After discussion, it turned out that the balance sheet had in fact not been audited, and some members requested the past accounts be examined. There was a debate as to why the vice-presidents, rather than the members, elected the committee, to which Letby responded that in the past, some members had not acted honourably when voting. A motion was passed for the committee to be elected by members in future. Asked why members were paid to play, Letby said it was impossible to do otherwise since some players could not devote their time to cricket without remuneration. They got 4s at home and 8s 6d, plus coach fare, away. In response, one member argued that it would be better if they engaged two good professionals, and noted that the total cost of playing Knaresborough had been £9 8s.[843]

Internal club disputes occurred elsewhere. Howarth records a 'prolonged period of internal bickering and mismanagement' at Beverley Cricket Club in the late 1850s and early 1860s, which resulted in no games being played in 1858, hostile feeling between Beverley and other clubs, and many experienced players staying away.[844] In 1876, there was a well-publicised and long-running dispute amongst members of the Middlesbrough Cricket Club, involving very open dissatisfaction with the management about the club's financial state.[845]

At times, disputes could result in legal action. In 1872, the secretary to the Cleckheaton cricket club was charged with having embezzled £2 19s 6d. The question then arose as to whether the club had the power to prosecute someone who was essentially a partner of a firm. Based on advice on partnership law it was decided not, and he was discharged but advised to give the money back as soon as possible.[846] In late 1874, Leeds County Court considered a case brought by the committee of Hunslet Cricket Club against the club's former secretary. He had received £17 with which to pay for fencing around the ground and £24 in subscriptions, all of which he had kept. The defendant argued he had personally incurred significant expenses and asked for an indemnity for these debts before handing back the money.[847]

Support from others

If most clubs survived on the efforts of members and officials, throughout the county many looked for essential additional support – financial or in kind – from people outside the clubs. Better established and more middle-class clubs sought out wealthy and influential patrons such as MPs, local gentry or other local notables.

In the 1850s, York Cricket Club benefited from a number of wealthy patrons – including Lord Wenlock, the Earl of Carlisle, Sir J.H.Lowther Bart, G.Hudson Esq MP, J.G.Smyth Esq MP and W.M.E.Milner Esq MP.[848] The club also had a very close relationship with the local council, and the Lord Mayor and Town Clerk were strong supporters.[849] In 1850, Richard Cobden, manufacturer, radical politician and MP for the West Riding, allowed his name to be used as a patron of the Wakefield Mechanics' Institute Cricket Club, having enjoyed cricket in his childhood. He wished the club 'dry Tuesdays and Saturdays.'[850] When Scarborough's Queen's Cricket Club was revived in 1858, Lord Londesborough, Sir J.V.B.Johnstone MP and 'several other influential' people were listed as patrons and subscribers.[851] Middlesbrough Cricket Club had the support of the Earl of Faversham in the 1860s, and in 1869 two Members of Parliament and an admiral, while another MP granted a lease on a ground in 1875.[852] During the 1860s and 1870s, the role of President of Driffield Cricket Club was variously held by a local landowner, local magistrate and commanding officer of the local Volunteers.[853]

One of the most significant supporters of local cricket in Yorkshire was Lord Londesborough (1834-1900). William Henry Forester Denison was educated at Harrow School and elected to Parliament as a Liberal MP at the age of 23. In 1860, he succeeded his father as Baron Londesborough, at which point he took his seat in the House of Lords. He was a patron of many sports and boasted that he was personally acquainted with every noted sportsman in England. He was very interested in horse-breeding and racing, carriage horses, yachting and rowing, hunting and theatre, but is perhaps best known for his role in establishing the

Scarborough cricket festival, which he attended even in his final year. He owned over 50,000 acres of land, mostly in the north of England, and spent a part of almost every year at his Scarborough home, Londesborough Lodge.[854] Here he provided a stimulus to the development of a unique aspect of Yorkshire cricket, and a match in 1871 is often referred to as being the true origin of the Festival.[855] On that occasion, Lord Londesborough's XI played a team led by C.I.Thornton, the Kent and Middlesex player and a visitor to the town. Unable to charge spectators for attending the land on Castle Hill owned by the War Office, Londesborough incurred all the expenses himself.[856]

Londesborough's desire to shape the development of cricket in the county can also be seen in his involvement in the efforts to challenge the dominance of Sheffield in Yorkshire county cricket that will be covered in detail in Chapter 10. He was involved in the establishment of the Yorkshire Gentlemen's Cricket Club in 1863, and the attempts to create an alternative to the county club formed in Sheffield that year. In the autumn of 1869, he was appointed President of the United North of England Eleven.[857] He was made President of the Yorkshire United Cricket Club, offering strong support to another initiative which reflected dissatisfaction with the perceived bias in the selection of the county side. In 1882, he gave very public backing to the efforts, led by Bradford men, to challenge 'the Sheffield monopoly' of Yorkshire cricket.[858] Following a poorly handled meeting with Yorkshire county officials in 1882, Londesborough advocated a better organised approach to bringing more local clubs together. He was later elected President of the North and East Ridings Cricket Club which, although claiming not to be anti-Sheffield, nevertheless reflected widespread concern that cricketers away from the West Riding were not taken sufficiently seriously.

Another aristocratic supporter of cricket in Yorkshire was Lord Morpeth (George William Frederick Howard, 7th Earl of Carlisle (1802-64)), who held ministerial posts under several prime ministers. According to a study of his life, in 1845 he established the Castle Howard Cricket Club where he acted as scorer, describing it as his hobby. The club was made up of tenants and servants and his biographer commented that:

> Morpeth identified strongly with the team, even recording their results in his diary. This enthusiasm reflected his wish to promote social cohesion. Cricket was thought by its adherents to ease tensions in society by reaching across the class divide. Morpeth liked it 'for the way it brings people and classes together.'[859]

Other cricket-club patrons were less wealthy and grand, but in their own way provided much-needed practical support. In February 1850, a meeting of cricketers, their supporters and promoters (including many merchants and tradesmen) was held in Leeds to 'extend a feeling favourable to cricket' in the town. A subscription fund was established and more than £40 raised.[860] In the 1850s, the Hallam club in Sheffield was indebted to its patrons, a Mr and Mrs Laycock, whose 'play-ground was always open to the club'.[861] In 1869, at Farsley United's annual meeting one of the speakers commented that 'most of the influential gentlemen in the village were either playing or honorary members of the club.'[862]

Another source of support for cricket clubs came from churches. Davies has observed that in the 19th century, 'it became common for religious bodies of most denominations to provide recreational opportunities for their congregations.' This was part of wider attempts to reform working-class habits, 'increasingly seen as incompatible with the values of modern society.'[863] In his study of one such club – Illingworth St Mary's Cricket Club – O'Keefe tracked its history from 1884, after a period of a few years in which cricket was played informally in the name of the church. He suggests that 'the clergy made a virtue out of necessity by promoting 'rational' cricket and placing the stamp of the church upon it.' It aimed to be socially inclusive: the annual 5/- subscription could be paid monthly or on the basis of 6d during, and 4d out of, season. As a result, the membership included a large number of working-class men and youths.[864]

Local publicans also played a significant – and obviously not disinterested – role in supporting cricket, and without public houses, many clubs would not have survived. The public house has been described as 'the central social institution of the adult male working class and occupied a pivotal position in the world of sport.' They were places where games were played and talked about, and where teams could change and meet.[865] As well as offering refreshment, many public houses offered a fuller service, providing a playing field, making equipment available, being a place where stakes could be lodged and being a source of sporting news and gossip. Supportive publicans helped to sustain many cricket clubs. Hull players in the 1840s and 1850s had much to thank Mr and Mrs Beecroft of the Brown Cow public house for. The Hull Kingston Club played on a field behind their public house, and Mrs Beecroft regularly entertained local players to a post-match meal. In 1850, she 'expressed her grateful thanks for the uniform kindness she had always experienced at their hands and the pleasures it afforded her at any time, by any means, to increase the happiness and promote the welfare of the club.'[866]

The Dudley Hill Cricket Club was similarly well supported by the landlady of the Engineer Inn, who used her own funds to donate prizes to the top batsmen of 1864 and 1865.[867] The Lockwood Cricket Club near Huddersfield had a strong connection with the Shoulder of Mutton Inn, and the landlord provided refreshments on the ground for the biggest matches. He even ended up in court as a result of his involvement with cricketers. In November 1866, the club held its annual supper in his public house, where a police officer witnessed drinking still going on at 1.30am. The landlord was fined 5s and had to pay expenses of 8s.[868]

A more famous public house in the history of Yorkshire cricket was the Adelphi Hotel in Arundel Street in Sheffield, run by Harry Sampson and a meeting place for local cricketers, where numerous club gatherings were held for 20 years, including the Public Match Fund Committee in 1861 and meetings of the Yorkshire county committee.[869] Other public houses had significance. Jim Darley was another landlord who gave great support and who made his home, the Green Dragon Inn, Fargate, Sheffield, a headquarters for Yorkshire cricketers.[870] The Tandem Inn was the 'unofficial headquarters' of the Lascelles Hall players, and Joe Rowbotham was the long-standing landlord of the New Inn, Eccleshall Road in Sheffield between 1868 and 1898.[871]

Some landlords provided other support. In 1848, Mr Broadbent, the proprietor of the Barrack Tavern ground in Sheffield, gave prizes to the newly-formed Victoria cricket club, £2 each for best bowler and batsman, £1 for best fielder, but also – intriguingly – £1 for the best essay on the influence of cricket on the working classes by a member of the club. Sadly, no record can be found of what it said.[872]

As well as financial support to pay off debts or allow for developments, many clubs were provided with equipment by their patrons. A well-wisher gave the St George's Cricket Club in Hull a catapult in 1850, 'which can be regulated so as to send the ball any pitch and speed.'[873] As we saw earlier, Lascelles Hall Cricket Club were indebted initially to Joseph Walker and particularly his wife, who first let them use some land near the village hall rent-free from 1825 to 1846, and later to John Haigh. Haigh's son, Walter, was subsequently a great patron of the club, as was John Jessop, secretary for 30 years, and together they built the club up to a great power in the county.[874] In 1852, Sir John Ramsden agreed to become Honorary President of the Huddersfield Cricket Club and provide a suitable cricket ground (although their occupancy could only last until the land was needed for the extension of the town), and a decade later, Meltham Cricket Club was given a new pavilion, the gift of Charles Brook of Meltham Hall.[875]

Creating a fixture list

The quality of a club's fixture list was a signal of its standing. Club members often started by playing matches amongst themselves, for example, pitting Marrieds against Singles, or holding field days where ad hoc matches could take place and players could practise. Thereafter, they would play locally, advertising their availability or making challenges to other clubs, often at short notice, with games held within a few days. For example, Husthwaite issued a detailed challenge to the Knaresborough club in 1828, setting out previous rejections of offers to play and requesting a new game, for which it sought a response or else it stated it would play Hovingham.[876] At a higher standard, the Sheffield and Nottingham clubs issued challenges, specifying the money involved, the venue, umpires and the terms for expenses. These details might require some negotiation and could lead to wrangling; in 1828, for example, Nottingham wanted an extra allowance for travelling to Sheffield.[877]

This approach could mean that at times few matches were fixed before the summer was well under way – as occurred in Sheffield in the late 1820s and early 1830s. In June 1830, the *Independent* commented with some relief that:

> Signs of the commencement of the usual cricketing season have at length appeared. On Thursday, the principal supporters of the game had a meeting, when the acceptance of the following challenges, sent from Nottingham at the close of last year, was determined on, and official notices sent off to the parties concerned.[878]

The following year, the main players of the Wednesday club were still playing themselves on alternate Wednesdays in June as 'No public matches have hitherto been positively announced', although a three-a-side game with Nottingham was expected. Full matches with Leicester, Nottingham and Manchester had been offered but no response had been received, and Tom Marsden was still awaiting an opponent at single-wicket.[879] In 1832, it was not until August that a significant match was played at Hyde Park.[880]

Not surprisingly, clubs sought games with others located within reasonable travelling distance. Particularly in the days before the rail network was widespread, travel was not always easy. Cricketers walked, sometimes considerable distances, to play games throughout this period, although transport such as a wagon might be borrowed if available.[881] On occasions, better-off clubs could use faster means of conveyance. The Doncaster Amateur side that played Pontefract in 1849 left the town 'in great style in a coach drawn by four handsome bays', travelling the 15 miles in an hour and twenty minutes.[882] Not everyone could afford such splendour and so had to take into account distance considerations when deciding who to play. The Stilton, Kepwick and Cowsby Union Cricket Club, for example, announced it was open to competing with any club within four miles of any of the villages from £5 to £20. This was easily walkable.[883]

Decisions might also be needed on the composition of the teams, both who was allowed to play and, sometimes, who was not. When Ripon and Nottingham played in 1816, those involved had to be 'resident players, or within 10 miles of each place' and not now or in the past 'members of the Marylebone club'.[884] In 1844, the match between Malton and Huttons Ambo was contested for 11 sovereigns a side, with the latter allowed to choose from any players within 15 miles.[885]

On some occasions, clubs were allowed to exclude certain players from the opposition club. Where the line was drawn could make a big difference to the strength of a side. When York replayed Dalton in September 1845, it was agreed that only the same players would appear on both sides as in the previous game, and anyone unable to play for any reason, could not substituted. York had one player missing and asked for a replacement, but the Dalton club told them they would need to pay two guineas for this, which they refused to do.[886] A similar situation had occurred in 1830, when Hovingham refused to allow any substitutions when a man from Thirsk became ill and was unable to attend the return game.[887] However, other arrangements were more generous and designed to even up the sides. When York played Sheffield in 1849 they were allowed to choose three players from any club in the county, ultimately selecting three from Dalton.[888] Some announcements suggested there was suspicion between certain clubs. In 1855, Wetherby had no objection to playing Knaresbrough for any of the sums they named, but only on condition that 'each party confine themselves to bona fide residents for the last three months in each town.'[889]

At times, challenges could be very specific; for example, Lofthouse Albion sought to play a village club within seven miles, which had not been established more than four years.[890] York Cricket Club accepted a challenge from Bedale on the condition that two Sheffield players were umpires.[891] And in 1859, the *Leeds Times* reported that Dudley Hill Cricket Club had offered 'to any three junior clubs in Yorkshire an invitation to play on their ground on Monday and Tuesday, Aug. 15th and 16th, for an outfit consisting of a ball, two bats, three pairs of gloves, two pairs of pads, a square to mark out the ground, a whitening-brush and a bowl, all new, and to be presented by the Dudley-hill Club.'[892] In contrast, some challenges could be couched in very broad terms. In 1830, eleven licensed victuallers of Sheffield challenged eleven innkeepers of any city, town or village in the kingdom to play for £50 or £100.[893]

Agreement might also need to be reached on other matters such as the officials or venue, sometimes the request being to meet on a ground where neither side has ever played before, or which was equidistant between their grounds. In 1849, when Scorton arranged to play Northallerton, it was agreed that the clubs would toss a coin for venue, the umpires must reside 10 miles from either place, and half of the forfeit money was to be lodged with the landlord at Langton.[894] In 1852, when Dalton left a challenge in *Bell's Life* to any club in England, amongst the conditions required by the latter was that the umpires and scorers be selected by the committee of the MCC.[895]

While such specifications might seem excessive, without clarity, games could descend into confusion or disagreement. In 1847, in the Ripon v Leyburn game the first innings ended at around five o'clock:

> when some difficulty arose as to continuing the game; the Leyburn gents, however, were bound to play until eight, and this agreement

> was enforced; the second innings, therefore, may almost be termed a match against old time, and, eventually, proved a glorious victory for the Ripon gents, with four minutes to spare.[896]

Sometimes challenges were not accepted. In 1834, York rejected Thirsk's offer on the grounds that they alleged that the latter permitted and practised unfair bowling. Eventually, the dispute was settled and they played in June.[897] The tables were turned when York's challenge to Leeds in 1845 was refused, although they accepted the following year.[898] In 1862, the Birkenshaw Britannia club stated in the press that it would not recognise any challenge from Yeadon United that was posted in the papers. Rather, any club that wanted to play them 'must address the secretary...and at the same time, send a list of the names of the proposed players.'[899]

Nor were challenges always fulfilled. In 1826, under a heading 'Cowardice', it was reported that the game between Barton and Swinton did not take place, after the latter team went to Barton but then reconsidered, 'being afraid to meet their opponents in the field.'[900] There was disappointment too in 1834 when a Dewsbury side advised its Hunslet opponents that the match could not be played as they had some players missing. Thinking it was a ruse, Hunslet still turned up at the appointed time but were told again the reason. They then refused an offer to play for their dinners and half a dozen bottles of wine, and, giving three cheers, returned home.[901]

Poor communication could be to blame for problems. In 1856, a team from Captain Waud's colliery at Manston accepted the challenge from the cricketers of Messrs. Charlesworth's colliery, Lofthouse. It was reported that 'the Manston men mustered in good time, but to their great disappointment the Lofthouse deepmen never made their appearance. This is strange conduct, but the Manston men are determined to give them another chance, and will play them for any amount, and no shuffling, or they will play any other colliery in Yorkshire.'[902] The club at Charlesworth's colliery wrote to the *Leeds Times* shortly after, surprised at the item in the paper, pointing out that they had never received a reply to their letter and had assumed the opposition had declined to play.[903]

The ad hoc and, at times, complex nature of these match arrangements, as well as the effort that went into securing fixtures could be time-consuming. In 1838, a single-wicket match between two York and Harewood players was proposed. A member of the York club went to Tadcaster to meet a deputy from the Harewood club to arrange terms, but they could not come to an agreement and returned home. Letters were then sent between the clubs but still could not resolve their differences, so it looked unlikely the game would take place. York then contacted Sheffield to organise a game with them instead, although shortly after Harewood officials wrote to the paper to say they would play after all.[904] In September

1840, *Bell's Life* noted that organising the Bradford v Knaresborough match had involved 'long correspondence', although arrangements did include appointing a referee from a third club as well as two umpires.[905]

Such experiences eventually encouraged teams to formalise their fixture lists to give themselves more certainty. Establishing agreed fixtures with trusted sides also meant that arrangements whereby teams lodged money with one another as a guarantee of attendance were no longer necessary. And experiencing pleasant afternoons with another team of a similar quality encouraged clubs to replicate and build on their fixture lists year on year. Increasingly, clubs also looked to get fixtures arranged over the winter so that they took full advantage of as many spring and summer Saturdays as possible, and avoided weekends with no games. As a result, more and more clubs had better organised and regular lists of fixtures. By the 1860s and early 1870s, these had grown considerably. In 1870, for example, Leeds Rising Sun Cricket Club played 29 games and Knostrop Hall Cricket Club, 32.[906] In 1873, the Leeds Rising Sun club played 52 matches, which it was claimed was the largest of any club in the district.[907] Todmorden Cricket Club's fixture list grew from 'a handful of games' in the 1850s, to 20 a year in the 1870s and 38 in 1890, with the club exploiting the rail links along the valleys into Lancashire as well as Yorkshire.[908] In 1877, *The Leeds Cricketers' Guide* contained details of nearly 1,200 engagements of the main clubs in the borough.[909]

The scale on which the game was increasingly played led to calls for better arrangements. In June 1885, the *Yorkshire Post* listed over 160 matches for one Saturday (20 June), and later commented approvingly on a suggestion from the honorary secretary of Keighley Cricket Club for a meeting of club secretaries for the purpose of organising club matches in a coordinated manner, as was the case with football. It said the proposal would save 'an infinite amount of trouble' and endless correspondence. A meeting – referred to as a 'cricket Parliament' - was held in Leeds in July 1885, which 50 men attended. They decided to meet again in mid-August to complete arrangements for next season, when 150 delegates from 100 clubs wore cards in their hat bands stating the name of their club. They agreed to meet annually. In 1887, 130 clubs of different rank met in August, but it was noted that not all fixtures were organised through this means; many of the leading clubs still turned up with their fixture lists nearly complete.[910]

Length of games

Cricket matches could last varying lengths of time, and the format used could be very flexible depending on the working hours and availability of participants. Clubs with wealthier members could contemplate weekday matches which sometimes took up two or three days, and those whose members included independent shopkeepers or the self-employed could also hold matches on weekdays. Some clubs also benefited from continuation of the tradition of 'St

Monday' (even at times continuing into Tuesday), but for other clubs, the growth of more rigid working hours meant all-day, in-week matches were unsuitable for many members. As a correspondent to the *York Herald* noted in 1846, 'It is rather unfair to suppose men engaged in husbandry or trade will or can devote three or four days in the week to cricket….yet this sacrifice is frequently demanded from them.'[911]

In urban areas, regulated working hours increasingly meant that games generally took place on Saturdays at specific times, or after work and at holidays. In 1880, all matches listed in the *Leeds Times* had 2.30pm starts, except a small number of all-day games which began at 'about 10.30am', mainly on Mondays and, particularly, on holidays. On Whit Monday 1880, for example, 13 matches were arranged for 10.30am starts.[912] Nevertheless, many of the more senior clubs in urban areas did fix all-day matches, sometimes starting at 12 o'clock or earlier, on a more routine basis. Some thought this a good sign. The short-lived *Bradford Cricketers' Journal* commented in 1874 on the 'growing tendency' to arrange all-day matches, which it felt augured well for the progress of cricket. Further evidence of this, the paper noted, was the willingness of some to play on working days, sacrificing up to a day's pay.[913] Others, such as officials at St John's Cricket Club, Huddersfield, felt there were also financial benefits to all-day games compared to half-day games, given the heavy cost for so little play.[914]

If organising all-day games was a sign of growing enthusiasm, it also had its downsides, and in the early 1870s, timekeeping by players became a contentious issue. In the Huddersfield area, for example, many games were delayed by players arriving late from work. In June 1875, the visiting side turned up at 4pm for the Heckmondwike and Chickenley Young England match.[915] The following August, it was nearly 3pm when the Lockwood side appeared at the St John's ground, and stumps were drawn at 6.15pm, so there was no chance of playing to a conclusion.[916] Such problems were also experienced in the first-class game, with the start of the Yorkshire v All-England match at Huddersfield in 1874 (which was supposed to begin at 11.30am) actually taking place an hour and 40 minutes late. Prior to lunch, only 50 minutes' play was seen by some 2,000 spectators, and the following day the start was 50 minutes delayed, by which time the crowd was very restless.[917] In Todmorden, late starts were apparently 'commonplace', often due to home players, rather than visitors, arriving late.[918]

Not surprisingly, such delays were unpopular. When most of the Holmfirth side failed to appear for the match with Dalton in 1871, several strangers were persuaded to take part, including a young lad apparently still covered in dirt from his mill work. The crowd, most of whom had paid for admission, expecting to see higher-quality players, expressed their disgust loudly at the poor replacements. The *Huddersfield Daily Examiner* added its voice, suggesting that attempts at 12 o'clock starts should be abandoned and play instead begin at one and continue without lunch.[919] Some clubs acted to limit the bad feeling by reducing their fixture lists and the number of all-day matches except perhaps on Whit Monday.

Ten years later, however, poor timekeeping remained an issue and the *Yorkshire Post* commented that something needed to be done about time-wasting which was leading to matches being drawn, adding:

> There is really no reason, except it be one of habit, why time should not be accurately observed in cricket as in all other sports. Whatever the hour named for commencing a game may be the out side should walk out of the pavilion as the clock strikes. Unless this is done we are afraid that 'draws' will be the rule and not the exception during the ensuing season.

Amongst its suggestions for speeding the game up was a five- rather than four-ball over, and for an end to 'the ridiculous fashion of men bowling trial balls when put on.'[920] In August 1886, a conference ('the Yorkshire Cricket Parliament') was held to discuss changes to the rules for cricket in Leeds and included consideration of earlier starts and later finishes so more games could reach a definite conclusion.[921] The problem continued elsewhere, and at Sheffield Wednesday Cricket Club's AGM in April 1890, the committee was instructed 'to prohibit players who were not present at the time for starting from taking any part in the game, and to take steps to come to some arrangement with the other clubs playing on the ground to assist in this direction.'[922]

Experiencing problems

It is impossible to know how many cricket clubs were established in the 19th century in Yorkshire, and of these, how many disappeared. However, it is safe to assume that many did whither or collapse for a variety of reasons. In May 1848, for example, the Hull Cricket Club was wound up after difficulties securing sufficient interest and all remaining members were recommended to join the Hull Athenaeum club. The club agreed terms with Athenaeum for the transfer of its stock.[923] Others suffered from competition. In 1860, the well-established Driffield Cricket Club was threatened by the growing popularity of the local Rifle Volunteers, which drew from a similar social group. There were many resignations from the cricket club as men found they could not do both activities.[924]

There could also be any number of difficulties with a club's ground. Having a poor or badly sited ground was a problem. In 1879, the Lockwood Mechanics' Institution Cricket Club was wound up due to its poor facilities, its field apparently being unfit for cricket and the committee uncertain about the continuation of its tenancy. The club tent was sold to another club and all debts paid off, before the remaining funds were divided amongst members and the institution.[925]

Threats to its existence could blight a club for many years. The programme and souvenir of the Grand Bazaar in aid of the Manningham Cricket Club in 1892 explained that the club had originally played in a field near a public house, but had moved in 1863 to be nearer the town. The following year, it had moved on because of building work, although the members were able to stay at their next field until 1871 and had then relocated to Heaton Road. The club had played here until 1877, when a portion of the field was bought by the trustees of St John's Wesleyan Church. The club moved to land in front of Manningham Lodge and was safe until 1890, when it transferred to a field leased from the Midland Railway Company.[926]

Arguments over land used for cricket could eventually lead to the courts. In 1862, a case was heard at Huddersfield County Court in which Sir John Ramsden, a significant local supporter of the game mentioned earlier, sued the Huddersfield club to recover £50 in respect of rent due to him for the occupation of a field adjoining Greenhead Park. In 1852, Sir John had allowed the club to use his land, and accepted the role of president. The club construed this as being rent-free, but Ramsden's agent said they would be expected to pay a yearly rent. The club disregarded this and sent a letter to Sir John seeking to appeal. Ramsden's agent did not pass this document on, and when they realised this some time later, the members asked for an interview, which was refused. Ramsden insisted on past rent, and when the club did not pay, it received notice to quit. In February 1860, the players left the ground and their tents, grass rollers, and other equipment were retained by the landowner. The matter was taken to the County Court where the jury returned a nominal verdict in favour of Ramsden, which he refused to accept.[927] A new trial was held but three years later, it appeared that the expenses incurred in the case had still not been paid.[928]

Alternatively, disaster could strike with little warning. When, in 1859, the Rotherham Howard club was wound up quickly, it was reported that the 'formerly prosperous cricket club' had come to 'a somewhat undignified end.' Mr Moorhouse, the landlord of the cricket field, had seized the bats, balls, clothing, tent, and other property of the club in lieu of arrears of rent of nearly £30, and sold them by public auction.[929] In 1863, Langton Wold Cricket Club was summarily ejected from its field when its ownership changed hands following the previous owner's death, although it eventually found a ground elsewhere, thanks to the 7th Earl of Carlisle, who let the players use Castle Howard Park. Consequently, the club changed its name to Derwent Dale.[930]

Some clubs suffered a more gradual tailing-off of interest. In 1862, Thirsk Cricket Club, which only a decade earlier had been one of the best in Yorkshire, went into decline. Apparently this stemmed 'either from indifference, or from pressure of other and more important matters [so that] many of the leading members withdrew their patronage from the club, which gradually dwindled down till at length it died of sheer inanition.'[931]

For other clubs, problems were of their own making, following mistaken – if well-meaning – attempts to develop. Prior to 1877, Ilkley had been a strong cricket club with a good roll of members, numerous subscribers, a fine ground and a fixture list including games with some of the best clubs around. Then the committee decided to move grounds and problems began. While the new field was more attractive, it was not very conveniently positioned. The number of spectators declined and members began to complain of the distance involved in getting to home games. Gate money fell and funds began to dry up, although the club was still committed to playing as far away as Scarborough and Malton. Money had to be spent on the wicket, which turned out to have poor soil, and then £140 went on a new pavilion. Quickly the club fell into debt, and in 1880 decided to move again to a more central location to try to re-establish itself in the public eye. Another £100 had to be spent on the ground, the bulk of which was subscribed by supporters.[932]

In order to gain greater stability and an increased membership, some clubs attempted to diversify and add facilities which would broaden their appeal. As early as 1844, Bradford Cricket Club added archery to its offer at the request of members[933], whilst bowling greens were established at Bramall Lane to generate revenue. When Armley Cricket Club was established in 1856, one of its main supporters, a Mr.W.H.Porritt, encouraged the club to have a musical band connected to the club and promised to provide a large room for holding concerts.[934] Hull Town also announced that men who did not want to play cricket on its Argyle Street ground could alternatively find brasses, quoits or other amusements there for them.[935]

More widely, from the late 1860s, a number of clubs organised athletic events which became regular features of the year and attracted large crowds. The *Leeds Times* commented that since cricket could only be played a few months a year, establishing an annual festival would help to show that however valuable cricket was, 'other exercises may be combined with it by the same persons, and at different seasons of the year.'[936] In 1872, the festival organised by Bradford Cricket Club attracted 'some of the most famous athletes in Yorkshire', and helped to raise the club's profile with a wider audience.[937] Members of Kirkburton Cricket Club also organised an athletic sports contest in 1873, gathering a large number of subscribers, and generating such excitement that it was decided to incorporate a brass band contest as well.[938] In the late 1880s, cricket clubs took to associating themselves with other emerging sports, Barnsley, for example, promoting a cycling tournament at its ground in 1888.[939]

Behaviour of members

As well as financial and practical difficulties, a further threat to the well-being of some clubs was the risk of losing their reputation for respectability. The fear was that bad publicity would put off other teams from playing against them, or that it would discourage patrons from being associated with a club at a time when it needed their money. Such problems were considered by some to be widespread, the *Leeds Times* reprinting an article from the *Saturday Review* in 1871 that suggested that in country matches, 'where an innings is hardly ever got through without some opportunity occurring for raising a quibble, plenty of players are found ready to take advantage of the chance.' Referring to the most common cause of disputes – lbw decisions – it reported that games 'are continually reduced to a farce by the futile efforts of the umpires to execute justice on this point; and we are bound to say that their task is often rendered additionally difficult by the reckless and excited appeals of the bowler.'[940]

All forms of cricket were subject at times to some unruly behaviour, and the game was characterised by disputes and prematurely concluded contests. West referred to the period from the 1840s to the 1860s as 'a quarrelsome, bad-tempered age for cricketers.'[941] In fact, such disputes went back further and continued throughout the century.

Umpires were a major cause of disputes as a result of perceived bias or disputed decisions. A game between York and the Knaresborough and Scriven clubs in 1827, for example, was marked by an argument over a decision which, reportedly, was 'contrary to the opinion of the opposite umpire and nearly every person on the ground.'[942] A match between Knaresborough and Otley in 1842 ended in a dispute over an official's decision and the *York Herald* published two reports to provide balance. The Otley correspondent wrote that the Knaresborough players' conduct towards their opponents:

> was indeed disgraceful and cannot be too much condemned. As soon as the game was broken up an attempt was made to tear the tent belonging to the Otley players in pieces, but after a severe struggle it was secured with the loss of the flag and pole. The stakes were afterwards demanded by main force accompanied by most awful language, and in a short time they were paid over to the Knaresborough players, but notwithstanding when the Otley men started for home they began pelting them with stones and pieces of wood, and several of the party were more or less injured.

Legal proceedings were started against those who had destroyed the flag and pole, and detained Otley players. The Knaresborough version was very different, but despite all this, the club advised the *Herald* they would be happy to play Otley again.[943]

The same year, an umpire was 'roughly used' when a game between Malton and Kirkbymoorside came to an abrupt end over a decision. The Kirkbymoorside umpire held the stakes, which he was forced to give up after some manhandling.[944]

In 1843, the game between Ripon and Hovingham was not finished owing to a dispute. It was reported that the Hovingham umpire, 'who was evidently a stranger to the game, and who had betted a considerable sum on the event, came in for the whole blame. We understand legal proceedings will be commenced forthwith to recover from him the stakes.'

There were many other occasions when things got out of hand. In 1856, the game between Haley Hill and the Black Dyke club was abandoned because reportedly the latter team 'misbehaved themselves' and threatened some of the Haley Hill men with being 'pauzed'. In addition, 'oaths and imprecations were frequent and shocking, which made their opponents regret having accepted the challenge they had received.'[945] Predictably, the following week an alternative explanation was provided in the local paper by a representative of the Black Dyke club. He denied any rudeness and put the dispute down to the decisions of the Haley Hill umpire, who they had requested be replaced. This being refused, they decided they could not play on.[946] A further letter from the Haley Hill secretary called his correspondent 'stupid', questioned whether he was even present at the match, and stated that the cause of the final rupture was something that he did not feel able to explain in print.

The same year, there was suggestions of violence at a game involving Heckmondwike and Brighouse, with 'Brighouse savages' used to 'bully and unnerve' their opponents.[947] In 1854, another dispute in a game between Thornhill and Wakefield occurred over an umpiring decision. Things deteriorated, and 'from among the Wakefield party a plate of victuals was thrown out of the window.'[948] The participation of senior professionals did not eliminate such problems. In 1866, in a match between Bradford and Lascelles Hall, Luke Greenwood disputed an umpire's decision, and when both officials stood by the decision the Lascelles Hall side left. The local paper included an item which commented it was amazing that eleven men, including five county players, should be so ignorant of the laws of the game.[949]

Disputes were prompted by a number of other causes. A common problem was teams or players arguing over the arrangements for the game or leaving the field prematurely, usually when they were about to lose. In 1875, when Thongsbridge played Farnley Tyas, the former side made 92 and had their opponents at 28-9 with eight minutes to go when the Farnley side 'marched out of the field, contending that the match could not be finished and was a draw.'[950] Poor timekeeping was also a source of disagreement. In 1858, the *Sheffield Independent* reported on a match where it was agreed that there would be a six o'clock finish unless the band came, in which case it would end earlier. Following a request from the Eclipse Club the wickets were pitched at 10 o'clock. However:

> it was twelve before the whole of them came, and a quarter-past before a ball was bowled. There was no refreshment hour allowed,

> and I think seven hours and a quarter in such a bleak place as the top of Norfolk Park ought to satisfy any reasonable man. The Eclipse Club had forfeited the ball by not taking the field at the time appointed; they have not yet paid for it.[951]

The composition of teams could also cause arguments. Late in the 1833 season there was considerable interest in a game between Malton and York. The eleven of Malton was to be selected from a list of 14 names, including Taylor and Gatenby. On arrival, York refused to let the latter play and Malton would not start until Whimp of Husthwaite was involved. In order not to disappoint the large crowd, York eventually agreed to him batting and fielding, but not bowling.[952] Similarly, when Lockwood and Lascelles Hall met in 1868 for the benefit of a local cricketer, Ben Rushworth, the match was abandoned before a ball was bowled. Lascelles Hall had nine of their professionals involved including John Thewlis, Lockwood, Hill and Job Greenwood. The Lockwood side also had their best players but there was a dispute over whether one should be treated as a 'given' man. The matter could not be resolved so the game could go ahead, and Rushworth received a very much reduced benefit from a rain-affected scratch match involving players on the ground.[953]

As a result of these kind of disputes, some clubs got a reputation for bad sportsmanship and argumentativeness. In 1860, there was ill-feeling between Kirkburton and Thurgoland. The former lost the first game badly and reportedly 'acted very shabbily', but a return game was organised at some expense by Kirkburton. A dinner was arranged, the grounds were put in good order and a 'great many neglected their business to give the Thurgoland people a fair chance of showing their much boasted skill.' However, on the day a Thurgoland player turned up to say they would not play and gave no explanation.[954]

Bad feeling risked some fixtures not taking place. For example, in 1862, it was reported that, as a result of past disputes in games between Glossop and Holmfirth, 'it was desirable they should play no more together'.[955] The *Huddersfield Chronicle* commented in 1867 that the Savile Town side from Dewsbury had a wide reputation but 'it will soon be anything but an enviable one' if they continued to play like they had against St John's Huddersfield. They delayed sending in players to bat in order to secure a draw an hour earlier than the time agreed to end. In the scoresheet, the final batsman was given as 'would not bat'. [956]

The St John's club caused considerable irritation in 1875 when members of the Dewsbury & Savile side were required to pay threepence each to gain entry to the ground which the home club refused to return. They were also prohibited from having a few minutes' practice on the square.[957] The St John's club responded to predictable complaints by saying that to avoid unseemly arguments about who was and was not a player, they had charged everyone, and had then reimbursed the visiting team and umpires. The Honorary Secretary reported that the Savile players had refused to pay, but at the end of the game quite a few had requested the return of gate money, despite not having handed it over in the first place. He added that having not played Savile for some years, St John's were very sorry to have reinstated the fixture.[958]

Reports of disputes in matches generally occur less often in the 1880s, although incidents could still happen. In June 1882, the game between Huddersfield and Low Moor was marred by a row over the toss for first innings involving E.T.Hirst, the Huddersfield captain, and the umpires, and the game was abandoned. Around the same time, Almondbury and Lockwood argued over the interpretation of the law on hitting the ball twice.[959] In July, a game involving Leeds Police ended after four balls when a catch was disputed and the police side drew the stumps.[960] Later that summer, the *Leeds Times* commented that 'Scenes at cricket matches are happily not numerous', but noted that at the Wakefield v Ossett match, decisions of the Ossett umpire caused annoyance and he was 'hooted and hustled off the ground.' But for the intervention of the Wakefield umpire, he would probably have 'suffered personal violence at the hands of spectators.'[961] And in 1887, a match between Yorkshire Gentlemen and Scarborough Cricket Club at York had to be abandoned after the home captain refused to allow the match to continue after a particular umpiring decision. This created so much controversy and such strong feeling that the *Yorkshire Post* advised that it would not publish correspondence 'containing much personal matter'.[962]

To try to counter the bias shown by some umpires, more effort was made to appoint neutral umpires, particularly for challenge cup games, and to try to get them to apply the laws on throwing.[963] Payments were also made; for example, the North Yorkshire Cricket League decided to give umpires 5s and provide third-class return rail fares in order to try and raise standards.[964] By the late 1880s, other efforts were being made to strengthen the administration of club cricket in particular areas. The Sheffield Cricket Association was formed to bring together many leading clubs in the area, to play a small number of Association matches, to regulate the game (including deciding issues of eligibility of players), and to offer a challenge cup for affiliated clubs.[965]

Around the same time, Huddersfield and District Cricket Association was formed, initially of 20 clubs. Its aims included to organise neutral umpires and counter the use of professionals in club matches. The idea of the Association was also to help reduce the amount of correspondence involved in organising fixtures, as club secretaries could meet occasionally to make arrangements. The formalisation of the running of the local game in Yorkshire in such ways was a direct response to the disorderly practices that were common throughout the century. Efforts were made to make the game more respectable, in part, as we will see in the next Chapter, to attract and maintain outside financial backing.[966]

CHAPTER SIX

PAYING THEIR WAY

Playing the kind of cricket enjoyed by thousands during the 19th century cost little, if anything. Only when the game became better organised did cricketers start to incur costs. As the game became more competitive, a growing number of clubs paid for professional assistance and invested heavily in better facilities. Such clubs then needed to find ways of raising more revenue. Some became particularly ambitious, but at times hit financial difficulties. As a result, in 1886, the *Athletic News* reported that Wakefield Cricket Club was nearly £200 in debt, but added that it would be difficult 'to point to a cricket club which did not get into debt. It is one of their brightest privileges.'[967] This chapter looks at how cricket in Yorkshire was financed in the 19th century.

Early days

In the early decades of the century, most Yorkshire clubs incurred little or no expenditure. Many club's grounds were fields belonging to landlords of public houses and friendly farmers, or else spare land near railway lines as the network expanded, so that rents were often low or non-existent. In some circumstances, clubs paid small fees for the right to walk across other land to reach the cricket field or to allow for the retrieval of the ball during play. Pitch markings were often rudimentary or non-existent. Changing facilities might be a tent, and few players had special cricket clothing. Clubs played matches locally, and players thought nothing of walking to games. Sometimes a wagon was borrowed if the match was a distance away or hired if necessary. Thus, playing cricket was generally a cheap activity which people could enjoy spontaneously.

There were exceptions and in the early decades of the 19th century some of the larger and better organised clubs had at least some assets. In 1832, it was reported that Hull 'boasts of a most excellent cricket club' and its Spring Bank ground was rolled and kept in good order, presumably at some cost.[968] In the 1840s, the Kingston club in Hull owned a 'spacious marquee'.[969] The extensive improvements on the Bradford ground in 1843, including erection of new sheds, railings and a much improved playing surface, all incurred 'heavy expenditure.' The Bradford club suffered a break-in, which led to the loss of joiners' tools and cricket equipment, showing that it possessed material worth stealing.[970] For the better established clubs such activity meant financial arrangements were more complex, sometimes leading to the preparation of formal accounts which were subject to audit. Some clubs also gathered significant sums in gate money, necessitating a treasurer to keep it safe and present accounts.

As we have seen, lucky clubs benefited from influential and wealthy supporters who provided them with assets or assisted with purchasing equipment. In 1846, Lord Morpeth presented the Castle Howard club with a 'handsome new marquee' for its subscribers.[971] The Langton Wold club was 'completely out of debt' by the time of its annual dinner in December 1856, thanks to outside assistance.[972] Some clubs also received money to help with the cost of specific games such as those against touring sides. In 1852, Lord Londesborough contributed to Beverley Cricket Club's expenses for the match with the All-England Eleven, as did the Earl of Carlisle and the Hon B.Lawley. No expense was spared in preparing for the match, but local inhabitants 'subscribed liberally, and in other ways aiding the local committee.'[973] Lord Wenlock gave five guineas (and was followed by others) towards the cost of the All-England game against York and District in 1860 in order that funds would still be available for the usual club games.[974]

An insight into the finances of one of the better organised cricket clubs in the 1840s is gained by looking at the work of the special audit committee established by York Cricket Club to investigate its accounts going back to 1846. This resulted from the arguments highlighted in Chapter 4 about the running of the club. At a meeting in March 1852, the committee stated that, having gone carefully through the receipts and expenditure, they had established that the accounts had been regularly audited and were considered to be correct. As a result, it:

> has given your committee great satisfaction and pleasure to find that an actual profit of £96 3s 10d has accrued to the club during the last five years, in which amount is included £41 11s 5d., the balance in favour of the All-England match; thus showing that for the year's necessary expenditure for the game of cricket only, the revenue hitherto has been ample....During the five years the committee of management have expended the sum of £221 14s 6d in making improvements for the well-being of the club, and general comfort of its members.[975]

The York cricket club was still in an acceptable state a few years later. In November 1858, the Chairman commented at the annual dinner that the club's debt, which had still been around £100, had been reduced to £24, and he hoped subscriptions would remove it altogether. He believed that the membership and income were on the increase, and added that they had also benefited twice from a gift of five guineas from 'a perfect stranger' who just happened to love cricket.[976]

Further understanding of the finances of clubs can be gained from a summary of the affairs of Sheffield United for 1857. The *Independent* reported that:

> the expenses of the year had been – maintainence of the ground and material, £134; sundries, £21; printing and advertisements, £35; rent and taxes, £68; sweepstake matches, £59; shop matches, £4 5s; interest, £52. The receipts had been – match and gate money, £14 14s; rent of ground from various clubs, £130: rent of booths, £93; bowling green subscriptions. £17 10s; transfer fees, 15s; receipts from sweepstakes, £55; do. shop matches, £21. Total £339. The total expenditure, which is given above, was £376. The balance in hand, which at the commencement of the year was £112, was now reduced to £74. 18s.

The committee's report described a number of problems which had affected the club's financial position, in particular, diminished receipts from the sweepstake matches. There were also fewer shop matches than expected which generated revenue, and the committee encouraged subscribers to persuade their workmen of the great advantages of using the ground. The report said they wanted to provide better accommodation for members and their families, and had decided to propose a call of £1 in respect of each £5 subscription. The number of subscribers would be limited to 400 (they now had 329) and if they had sufficient support they would raise £755. After payment of all liabilities this would leave £359 to provide improved accommodation. In the course of the discussion, it was stated that no expenditure would be incurred on the new pavilion unless the whole amount was paid up, or until the subscribers had been consulted.[977] They agreed to go ahead, but in 1858, owing to the state of the local economy over the previous 12 months, the committee still had not called up the additional £1 per share, and were clear they did not want to go further into debt.[978]

If the cost of developing its ground was a common expense, there were two other important areas of expenditure that were incurred by some clubs – hiring professional assistance, and hosting the visit of one of the touring elevens. Engaging a professional was a significant investment decision. In 1848, for example, the Sheffield Cricket Club explained its rationale for employing assistance to pursue its objective of improving the quality of its cricket. Although it had added to the club's expenses, the committee felt it was justified 'to shew to the members and the town at large that those objects were not lost sight of.'[979] A full-time professional was beyond most clubs, but even small ones paid for occasional assistance.[980] Some also sought to protect themselves financially by establishing a separate fund into which subscribers could pay specifically to help engage a bowler. In Beverley in the 1850s, a Bowlers' Fund was established for the public to pay into which allowed a professional to be employed by the club in the town.[981]

Some clubs also took on considerable financial risks when pitching themselves against the touring sides in the late 1840s and 1850s, and again, often established specific funds with a district-wide subscription list to defray the expenses.

Significant investment was needed if a game was to be a success, and clubs were drawn into considerations of safety and order, and thus who should pay the associated costs. In 1850, a meeting of the Huddersfield Watch Committee discussed whether police officers should be deployed at the match between the All-England Eleven and Eighteen of Huddersfield and Dalton. They argued over whether men should be taken from the night force and thus have to do extra duty for which the managers of the cricket ground would have to pay. The alternative was to take men off day duty during fair time, which alarmed some.[982]

A spending spree

By the end of the 1860s, many of the clubs formed in the 1840s and 1850s had achieved some kind of stability. Many had settled grounds, strong fixture lists organised increasingly before the start of the season rather than on an ad hoc basis during it, and had gained a fair complement of players. The increased interest in cricket generated by the shift in the balance of the game in the favour of batsmen after the 1860s, and the celebrity that was accorded to W.G.Grace (and to a lesser extent, his brothers), meant that more people were interested in the game. As legislation on working hours was extended, more men had time for organised leisure, and club membership figures increased, bringing with it more revenue and confidence. To Davies, by the 1860s, 'many of the components which were to characterise leisure in modern society had begun to take shape.'[983]

Many clubs appeared to be in a good financial state by this point, with a small balance in hand at the end of the season. Reports of end-of-year meetings of various clubs in Leeds, for example, invariably indicated they were in a 'strong financial position' or were 'flourishing'.[984] Clubs around Huddersfield at the end of the 1860s similarly reported balances in hand. The result of all this was the confidence to embark on an unprecedented spending spree by cricket club committees all over Yorkshire, which resulted in more permanent sporting facilities in hundreds of towns and villages, and which, in turn, gave cricket clubs an even more established place in the lives of their communities. By the early 1870s, there were certain assumptions about what was needed to run a successful cricket club which could not be ignored. All involved spending money; as one official noted at the annual supper of the Spring Gardens United Cricket Club in 1874, the club 'have now a good tent and ground, and all requisites for keeping the same in good order, and their future opponents may rely upon having a good wicket to play upon next season.'[985]

Bolstered by some financial stability, many clubs aspired to greater things, and looked to be the best in their area. The Meltham Mechanics' Institute Cricket Club exuded ambition in January 1870 when it reported that, while it had a modest balance in hand of £4 after spending £16 on a tent, it nevertheless deplored the lack of better facilities. An official argued that if determined efforts were made 'there is no doubt but the committee will be well supported by the gentlemen of the town and the inhabitants generally...and the next report we hope will state that larger premises have been obtained, or that sufficient funds have been procured to erect new premises.'[986] Also in 1870, Dudley Hill Cricket Club announced that laying out the ground had cost it £80, 'but it was every way worthy of the expenditure.'[987]

Elsewhere that year the *Leeds Times* commented, 'Cricket seems to have received a fresh impetus. The Wakefield club has obtained a new ground and expended on it £200, collected for the purpose. The services of two groundsmen have been engaged and a number of important matches arranged.'[988] The annual report of the Yorkshire Union of Mechanics' Institutes stated that 'cricket clubs in connection with the institutes have greatly increased'[989], and at the end of the 1873 season, the Leeds Albion club reported that it was in a flourishing condition and 'after spending a considerable amount in fencing the ground a good sum would be available for further improvements next season.'[990] Holbeck Cricket Club had a particularly successful year in 1875. There was a 50% increase in gate receipts and a 40% increase in members on the previous season. As a result, the club was full of confidence about its future.[991]

Other activities suggested that cricket clubs were increasingly energetic organisations. In 1872, the committee of the Holbeck club was described as very enterprising for organising a match and grand gala for its annual benefit.[992] The following year, the Holbeck Recreation Cricket Ground was reopened and the local paper stated that the managers 'intend to introduce several new features during the ensuing season, which they hope will be the means of bringing a good accession of subscribing members.'[993] Around this time, various clubs in the Leeds area reported being in a flourishing condition, and were able to hand out substantial prizes to the top scorers and to long-serving members.[994] A gymnasium was opened in 1875 (run by a former army sergeant-major) for the use of Huddersfield Athletic and St John's Cricket Club members, with over 400 people eligible to use the facilities.[995] Elsewhere, there was even a hint of frivolity in some developments; in 1873, for example, Dewsbury Savile spent £250 on ornamental railings for its ground, the cost to be defrayed by subscribers.[996]

For many clubs increased expenditure followed on from the acquisition of more permanent accommodation, which provided greater security. In 1868, for example, Hull Town was assured the tenancy of its Argyle Street ground by the local railway authorities, and the committee set about adding to the amenities, culminating in 1874 with a new pavilion.[997] The St John's club in Huddersfield also sought reassurance before committing to more spending. At its AGM in 1871, it was suggested that they 'ought to take into consideration the propriety of securing from Sir John Ramsden, a lease of their ground, so that they might venture upon increased expenditure in order to make it second to none in Yorkshire.'[998]

Obtaining permanent facilities helped to strengthen a club's identity by allowing it to become more closely associated with a particular place over a period of time. It also provided somewhere regular to practise, gave an impression of solidity which encouraged investment from outside, and, in general, allowed committees to plan for the future. Without this, many clubs and their supporters were unsurprisingly unwilling to commit funds. In 1875, when Bradford was searching for a new ground, negotiations with one gentleman collapsed when he suggested only a 10-year tenancy. Few were prepared to put money in for so short a period.[999] Lack of clarity about the terms of the lease on the Savile ground was also discussed in detail at the 1877 AGM because of the effect it was seen to be having on the willingness of potential subscribers to get involved.[1000]

An insight into the financial balancing acts of two senior clubs of this time can be seen in the accounts of St John's Huddersfield for 1874 and Batley in 1880. Amongst the receipts of the former were donations for the use of the field (£26 9s), gate money, including from the All-England match (£332 9s), and subscriptions (£122 5s), making a total of £518 11s. Expenditure included the ground fund £79, printing, advertising, etc. £41, horse, ground and roller £26, horse upkeep £5 10s, joiners' and painters' work £32 9s, rent of field £22, bats, balls and pads, etc. £24 9s, ground and expenses of All-England match £187 2s 8d, professional pay £48, and other professional assistance £8 5s. This left a balance in hand of £26 18s and there was rent to come in for grazing and some outstanding subscriptions and money owed. However, there was also a half-year's rent to pay of £30, and the club owed £67 on the Extension Fund account and £78 on the Tent account. Overall, therefore they owed £139, compared to £236 the previous year. After the statement was read, there was a discussion about the desirability of subscriptions being large enough to meet ordinary expenses, as well as the viability of all-day matches, which reportedly cost six times as much away as playing at home. The club had also used five professionals for day matches, and although some of the money owed by the club had been borrowed on the security of the tent, they were paying 5% interest on much of it. [1001] There was a lot to think about.

Further insight into the financial demands on an ambitious club can be gained from the case of Batley Cricket Club, whose new ground was opened in June 1880. Development costs included £54 for cutting and laying sods, £28 for carting away the old sods, £50 for a new refreshment tent, £20 for seeds and hand tillage, a further £20 for clearing and preparing the field, £10 for fencing, £7 to children for gathering 160 loads of stone, and £53 for workmen and horses to move soil for levelling. At one time, the club had 15 horses and 38 men working on the field, conveying 800 loads of sods from an adjoining field and moving 2,000 loads of soil to help level the ground. To complete the work, they spent a further £50 laying down water and gas pipes, purchasing a new mower, and putting up a store for implements and cricket equipment. For the future, the club anticipated spending £300 on a pavilion and £60 on a circular cinder path, as well as £300 on a bowling green, croquet or lawn tennis lawn and swings for the children.[1002] Running a cricket club was now a demanding business.

Cricket club expenditure was not restricted to the ground and many clubs spent money in making other improvements to what they could offer their members. Fixture lists were extended in length, as well as in terms of the distances involved. Second or third elevens were created, and travelling to matches by foot might be replaced by use of the growing rail network, with the cost often deferred by the club. The employment of professionals also became even more common, with *Athletic News* noting in 1881, 'that almost every club of any pretensions whatever retains a professional.' For some, the alternative of not spending was considered potentially disastrous for a club. When the United Press Cricket Club in Huddersfield attempted to save money by not retaining a professional in 1874, the local paper wrote that it was very unwise to do without, as it would inevitably affect their status and results.[1003]

Clubs were also driven to incur expenditure by the feeling that what they were doing was for the good of the community, and thus financial concerns were of lesser significance. In 1878, the Hull Town President disputed with the local Watch Committee over who should pay for the services of six policemen who had attended the Hull Town match with the Australians. The Watch Committee had agreed that no men should be sent unless they were paid for, but they had still been present. It was then reported that the Australians had been asked to pay £2 18s towards the costs of the police and they had complained that in no other town had this happened. A number of unsympathetic councillors argued that the police had quite enough to do without supervising cricket matches, but the President confidently responded his club had a right to police assistance. However, attempts to get agreement to repay the Australians were defeated.[1004]

At times, it appeared, therefore, that during this period some clubs acted first and thought later about how to pay for their improvements. Many had only small balances in their favour, which could not really justify a large increase in expenditure. In December 1870, for example, the Dewsbury Savile committee reported a poorer financial situation than in previous years due to a large loss on the annual feast game, a decline in receipts from Saturday matches and generally poor support within the town. Despite this, one senior official made it clear that 'it was not, however the fault of the committee', and argued that if they had the support in the neighbourhood which they deserved, they would not have been out of pocket. The club proposed to invest in its ground, as well as appoint a paid secretary. Referring to the proposed new fencing, the Treasurer commented that the club committee had to decide how the cost was to be defrayed.[1005]

Similarly, Hull Town thought of acting first and finding ways of affording later when in 1874 it erected its new pavilion. Building work commenced in February, but in March it was announced that it will 'cost considerably more than was expected at first, additions and improvements on the original plans having been suggested and found desirable.' At the club dinner in November 1874, an official stated that 'he should be glad indeed to be a party to any measures that could be suggested whereby the debt might be paid off.'[1006]

Such an approach did not suit everyone, however, and many officials urged their clubs to pay their way to survive. In January 1872, Lockwood members were warned about indebtedness. One official commented that they had spent too much 'in attempting to keep up what they called the prestige of the club.....but he thought the real prestige was being out of debt and keeping its head above water.' Part of the problem was that they had been dependent on good players to allow them to take on strong opponents. When they could not play, the club had to find others, and 'the consequence was that if they gave a man ten shillings to play it became known to others and they soon had two or three down upon them for the same amount.'[1007]

Running a cricket club had become an expensive business, and some officials were concerned at the implications of getting into financial trouble, especially where, for example, a club had got into the habit of paying men to play or covering the cost of their railway fares. Many assumed that members would feel honour bound to pay their share of liabilities in the case of a club collapsing, although a county court case in 1884, involving Leeds Clarence Cricket Club, established that this was not the case, and that in the eye of the law, ordinary members ran no risk whatever. Despite this, the *Yorkshire Post* suggested they were morally responsible.[1008]

Income

As we have seen, cricket clubs raised their funds in a number of ways – subscriptions from members, gate money and assistance from a wider group of supporters and patrons. Some also gained some further income if they allowed others to use their ground or let it out for grazing animals. Acquiring members was an important aspect of running the club and raising revenue. Howarth refers to an 1820 document entitled 'Bridlington Cricket Club Accounts and Rules'. This stated that subscriptions were 10s 6d and in addition, 'members shall be answerable for the expenses incurred in equal proportions and shall pay such subscriptions and at such time as the President shall find necessary.' This made the club very exclusive, but also provided clarity about how it would be resourced.[1009] When Beverley Cricket Club was established in 1862, members paid 5s annually in advance, with honorary members, 10s.[1010] Driffield Cricket Club's subscription was one guinea, although this was reduced in 1877 to 10s when the club ran into financial difficulties and needed to attract new members.[1011]

In addition, clubs encouraged subscriptions from a wider range of people, who were supporters but not necessarily playing members. Beverley Cricket Club was given financial support by subscribers who paid into club funds. At the first AGM in 1863, for example, receipts were made up primarily of subscriptions from friends and admirers of the game (£12 2s 6d out of £20 12s 6d).[1012] In 1857, the Sheffield Wednesday club benefited from around 20 subscribers offering to double their contributions so that the club could pay the expenses incurred by players travelling to away matches.[1013] The same gesture was made at the annual meeting of the Batley Cricket Club in November 1874.[1014]

At times, gate money was a major source of income. Members of the Dewsbury Savile club were told that gate money had risen annually from £22 in 1874 to £106 in 1877, as a result of the efforts that had been made 'by increasing the attraction, by making people know if they came they would see something which would interest them.' In 1874, the St John's club in Huddersfield received 64% of its income from match takings, while Batley in 1875 obtained just £28 from subscriptions, the vast majority of funds being gate money, including £123 out of £263 from the match with the United South of England Eleven.

Inevitably such funds were subject to fluctuation and uncertainty.[1015] For those clubs which hosted and benefited financially from games with touring sides, the visits of the Australians in 1878 and 1880, for example, were a major boost to their finances, but these were not annual events, and in 1879, several club committees in Yorkshire regretted that their income that summer was nothing like the previous one. Nevertheless, the aim was to make such events more frequent. For the largest town clubs in the county, the ambition of hosting a regular fixture with one of the stronger counties such as Nottinghamshire or Gloucestershire fuelled the ongoing argument with the Sheffield-based Yorkshire County Cricket Club, which insisted that the major county games (and the highest earners) be played at Bramall Lane.

For smaller clubs, not able to justify charging 6d or even 3d, gate money was far less important. For Holmfirth Temperance Recreation Ground Cricket Club, for example, gate money was under 10% of its income in 1873.[1016] Not being dependent on people watching was important. The weather could have a significant impact on takings at the gate when matches were abandoned or curtailed, an experience, for example, for Huddersfield St John's in the 1871 season.[1017] George Anderson suffered from the effects of the weather when a benefit was organised for him in 1869 at Dewsbury. The previous year, a similar match had been played for Carpenter and Hayward, raising over £400. In 1869, however, takings were £69 and £60 on the first two days, and nothing on the third, all because of rain.[1018]

Since all income could be vulnerable to factors outside a club's control through poor weather or economic depression, there was considerable benefit in having different sources of income. The income of the Holmfirth club, for example, was divided 40% from subscriptions, 9% from rents, 22% from the athletics festival, 13% from teas, concerts and a ball, 3% from letting the field, and just 9% from takings at the gate.[1019] Thus clubs needed to find ways of spreading the financial risks associated with an increasingly sophisticated game.

Experiencing problems

Unsurprisingly, the spending spree which characterised many clubs caught up with some, and in the 1870s and 1880s many experienced financial problems. In truth, for most clubs there had never been much money left over at the end of each season. Thus, there was little margin for error, and raising additional money through a collection on the spot was a regular occurrence at club annual meetings. Clubs could get into debt as a result of rash decisions or choices. Bridlington Cricket Club found itself in trouble in the late 1860s after engaging professional assistance (costing £18 16s in 1867), meeting the travelling expenses of players and funding non-club members to play. The club folded in 1869. A new club was formed the following year, but soon got into financial difficulties and was in a bad way by 1874.[1020] The Yorkshire Gentlemen club also suffered financially in 1867 because of 'too many expensive matches having been played from, and at home – no less than thirty – and also from the absence of many gentlemen who had previously promised to take part in these matches.' The committee decided to play as many games at home as possible in order to reduce costs.[1021]

Some clubs were hit by unforeseen events. In 1874, Lascelles Hall went significantly into debt as a result of the need to repair its buildings following heavy winds the previous November. The club decided to move the buildings to the better protected side of the ground, which, along with other ground improvements, cost £250 and led to a deficit of £99 for the year. Poor weather over Whitsuntide, when they normally made a lot of money, added to the club's difficulties.[1022] In 1886, when Wakefield Cricket Club was £197 in debt, an appeal was made to clear it. The rent for the ground, which had been £50 per annum for twelve years, was reduced to £25, but the favourable balance for the year was just 1s 6d.[1023] Beverley Cricket Club got into trouble when it moved to its new Recreation Ground in 1884. By 1891, the club's history notes, the rent was raised to £66 15s 0d, which when added to rates and taxes became a real problem. It was only kept solvent 'through the generosity of a number of wealthy patrons'.[1024]

Other clubs suffered problems for different reasons. Some did not receive the backing anticipated. In 1873, for example, Dalton was in a poor financial position, mainly due to the professional fund not having the support promised. There was a general balance of around £2 in hand but £30 of subscriptions were owed.[1025] Wider economic problems inevitably took their toll. Looking back in 1877, the secretary of the Lockwood Cricket Club reflected that for some time 'the club was in a precarious and almost insolvent state, arising from a variety of causes, the principal of which was the inattention of both committee and members to the general interests of the club, and the consequent want of support from the public.'[1026] In November 1879, the financial secretary of Holbeck Cricket Club read out a report at the annual dinner stating there had been a 'considerable falling off in receipts of the year, no doubt largely caused by the severe depression in trade.'[1027]

Once in debt, clubs had two choices – to cut costs or to seek new means of providing for themselves. Some took the first option, for example, deciding not to re-engage its professional or scaling back its programme of fixtures. In 1878, the Hull Criterion club decided because of its debts 'that it would be prudent to rather restrict the number of matches played', although it still maintained a fair number of fixtures.[1028] Others decided to restrict the distance travelled to away games, and in 1885, the annual report of the Bradford Cricket and Athletic Club noted that it had organised only one all-day match, 'owing to the difficulty of raising a representative team on other than Saturdays.'[1029]

More clubs took the alternative, however, and sought new ways of raising funds. A number of methods were tried. Many clubs asked for additional donations at their annual meetings. St John's Huddersfield, for example, announced a debt of £24 in October 1870 and managed to collect £17 8s on the spot and the rest outside the meeting, so that it started the new season with a small balance in its favour.[1030] Others actively tried to increase the number of club members by advertising or soliciting for subscriptions on the assumption that new people could be drawn in. At Lockwood Cricket Club, the Secretary saw the increasing popularity of cricket in the late 1870s as a great opportunity and called on members;

> to bring in new subscribers, work as if success depended on you individually. Many improvements are required on the ground which cannot be done without money. Therefore put your shoulder to the wheel.[1031]

Still more took the decision to increase club membership fees, considering that a loss of members would be more than offset by the additional revenue from those remaining. Huddersfield Cricket and Athletic Club is a case in point. Although making a profit of £214 19s 10d in 1878 the committee reported that this was mainly owing to the success of the athletics festival and the Australian match, and it was well known that the ordinary subscription of 10s 6d was insufficient to make the club self-supporting. The committee told the membership that they would like to see the ordinary income meet ordinary expenditure, and therefore wanted to ask as many members as possible to double their subscription and become honorary members at £1 1s.[1032] After trying persuasion, the club let things continue for another year, but in November 1880 a special general meeting was hastily called as soon as it was known that annual income had fallen £250 below annual expenditure. Losses on county games, substantial alterations and enlargements on the ground which would cost £1,400, and loan interest, had all added to the problems. Given the benefits that members derived from the amalgamated club, an immediate doubling of the price of ordinary membership was proposed and passed by a small majority. A subsequent meeting confirmed the decision, although dissenting voices criticised club extravagance.[1033] In early 1881, members were asked to return their cards if they did not wish to rejoin at the new price. Out of nearly 800, 184 did this, but, as predicted, income from subscriptions increased, and for the first time for years, ordinary income covered ordinary expenditure, even though membership dropped to just over 600.[1034]

However, membership subscriptions could be an insecure source of income, particularly during economically difficult times. Many members were not necessarily in a position to pay more than a basic fee. As one member of the Batley club put it at the November 1873 AGM, many of the players 'were only working men, who were willing to give their time as well as they could, but were not able to do much towards expenses.'[1035] Downturns in the local economy inevitably made matters worse. Many clubs in the Huddersfield area suffered unusually large arrears of subscriptions as a direct consequence of the depression in the local economy in the late 1870s and early 1880s. Many men in a variety of industries were on short time in the factories, and tradesmen in the area suffered a knock-on effect in reduced sales. With less money to spare, men cut back on luxuries such as cricket club membership and club finances suffered.

In 1876, Lockwood had outstanding subscriptions of £21, a significant amount when considering that the club had a surplus of only £15 17s for the year without this income.[1036] The following year, arrears of subscriptions were £30 9s or 13% at the year end, while Lascelles Hall reported being £40 in arrears of contributions. There were 173 members at Dalton in 1880, but 24 had been struck off for non-payment.[1037] In 1883, Cliffe End Cricket Club, Longwood reported a favourable balance on the year of £33 in club funds, a position considered 'a satisfactory state of affairs, considering the slackness of trade and unfortunate strike in the district passed through some few months ago'.[1038] Membership numbers elsewhere were subject to considerable churn. In 1885, for example, Huddersfield Cricket and Athletic Club elected 153 new members, but 77 were struck off for various reasons.[1039]

There were other important ways of raising club funds. In 1882, Manningham Cricket Club issued 20 £10 shares in order to try and liquidate its debt which had reached £227.[1040] Alternatively, clubs simply borrowed from senior members, as Dalton did in the late 1870s. In 1876 it was reported that £79 had been secured from members and a loan of £40 had been given 'by a gentleman who generally stands foremost in anything for the good of the club, both of which have been borrowed to pay for the new tent and the seating of the field.'[1041] In 1877, Dewsbury Savile benefited from 20 members who had promised 10 guineas each towards the cost of a new tent.[1042]

A more common way of raising funds, however, was by organising entertainments such as benefit concerts, galas, choir recitals, conjurers, musicians, 'glees' and theatrical performances. Such events became increasingly popular from the 1870s as teams looked for additional finance and membership, and tried to tap into income sources from people who did not necessarily attend cricket matches. They also acted as a helpful way of keeping in touch with members over the winter.

In some cases, these events were simply routine fundraisers for the benefit of the club, but in others they were particular responses to financial difficulties. In the summer of 1867, for example, the Rastrick United Cricket Club organised a 'grand entertainment' on its ground and attracted over 2,500 people. A cricket match was held, but there were many other activities, including foot races, throwing the cricket ball and climbing the pole. A brass band played and there was dancing into the evening.[1043] Lockwood Cricket Club organised a successful concert in 1871 to defray the costs of expenses incurred in building a new wooden clubhouse. Between 300 to 400 people attended despite bad weather.[1044] In February 1884, Otley Cricket Club held a Bazaar and Fancy Fair 'to provide extra accommodation for visitors to the Otley cricket field, and to improve the finances of the club.'[1045] Two years later, Pudsey Britannia Cricket Club held a 'Persian Bazaar' for three days with the aim of raising money to defray the cost of relaying their ground. Yeadon Cricket Club also held a three-day fair that month, which was opened by Hon. M.B.Hawke, with the aim of providing funds for the new pavilion.[1046]

Some clubs looked to novelties on the field, as well as off it, to generate funds. After the disastrous relocation mentioned in the previous chapter, Ilkley Cricket Club teamed up with the town's Prize Brass Band, which agreed to play at the ground in return for the receipts of one game. Unfortunately, there was limited interest and the club's debts remained. In the end it was only when it introduced the novelty of an Annual Trademen's match in old fashioned clothing that the club was able to revive interest in its activities, and a sum of money was subsequently handed over to the club.[1047]

There was, however, a limit to how much could be generated in these ways and ultimately committees were looking for rather more stable ways of providing for themselves. The answer for many clubs was to attract more honorary members. This meant involving outsiders in the club who, although not necessarily taking an active part would subscribe a fee, which gave membership priviliges and a place of standing on the social side of the club. Increasingly cricketers turned to local businessmen, councillors and others, who were often prepared to support clubs out of feelings of civic pride or sympathy for the cause of healthy recreation. Some were very responsive to the request to be involved. In November 1872, a local businessman told the Birstall Victoria club that, as an honorary member, it was a pleasure to be present for, 'although not a cricketer, the game received his sympathy, and in fact more general sympathy than any other English game.' The club chairman noted that they had a long list of honorary subscribers 'who were always ready with their purse, and the committee therefore wished to give them the prominence they deserved.'[1048] At the Batley Cricket Club AGM in 1873, the club President commented that 'the club was much indebted to honorary members and subscribers, for it was from them that funds principally came.' He was very glad they had such a body of gentlemen who took an interest in the club; he wished they had more of them. It was a pleasure to him when he went up on Saturday afternoons to see them in the field.'[1049]

Involving local dignatories gave cricket clubs a greater status and visibility in the community, but of necessity it meant they needed to maintain an increasingly respectable image. Victorian society was noted for seeking to surpress what was considered disorderly behaviour associated with traditional fairs or the maltreatment of animals, and there was a similar desire to purge cricket of the kind of behaviour we saw in the previous chapter.[1050] In keeping with this, committemen of many clubs, in particular the more middle-class ones, repeatedly urged their members to give a good impression on the field, and appropriate behaviour and responsibility became vital requirements to retain patronage. A committee member at the annual dinner of the Hull Town Cricket Club, for example, said he 'hoped the club would receive the generous support of the honorary members who might desire to see it carried on with the same respectability as it had been hitherto.'[1051] In 1874, the President of the St John's club in Huddersfield commented that the public now looked on the club as 'something' and they must not disappoint them. It was therefore necessary to begin play on time and go on to the announced finishing time because when people had paid their admission money they expected to get something for it. In his view, too many clubs ignored this.[1052]

In 1877, a speaker at the Birstall Victoria Cricket Club dinner, urged cricketers to control their tempers when they were provoked by critical spectators. This and other petty jealousies needed to be avoided because it not 'only made them look childish, but prevented them getting on and making progress.'[1053] Behaviour was also of concern at the Dewsbury Savile club some years later. Triumph in the Heavy Woollen District Cricket Challenge Cup by 281 runs led to the cup being taken on a tour of public houses by a noisy crowd. The *Dewsbury Reporter* commented that 'it does not reflect the best credit on the Savile club that its members should be the cause of anything like what went on on Monday', and Sam Shaw, the winning captain commented later that, if they had encouraged drinking through their behaviour, he and the rest of the team would be sorry they had ever won the cup.[1054] Cricket's financial realities increasingly dictated how the game was played and presented to its growing audience. The game and its clubs needed support of all kinds, and in order to secure that they needed to ensure a certain amount of respectability.

CHAPTER SEVEN

MAKING THE GRADE

Most men who played cricket in Yorkshire during the 19th century did so for fun, pleasure and exercise. They appeared, often for many years, for their local team, fitting in games outside work hours and on holidays. For just a small number, however, cricket provided employment and, for an even smaller number, the opportunity to appear in the growing number of first-class county matches. A total of 209 men appeared for Yorkshire County Cricket Club between 1863 and 1893 – but fewer than one-third did so on more than 10 occasions.[1055] Of these, the vast majority were professionals. For most, it was the pinnacle of their sporting career, and one involving considerable struggle. In just 11 cases, excellence at county level led to international cricket. This chapter examines how players made the grade, looking firstly at the professionals and then examining how the small number of amateurs fitted into the picture.

The club professional

Sissons notes that there were limited opportunities in the early 1840s for a player to earn a living from cricket, with the best looking to secure positions at Lord's or The Oval, work for a wealthy patron, or be a practice bowler at a university or public school. Apart from these openings, a small number of local clubs employed bowlers.[1056] Most of these posts were outside Yorkshire, although he suggests that between 1846 and 1854 there was a rapid growth in the number of professionals in the county; some 27 out of 110 professionals listed as engaged or available in England were in Yorkshire in *Frederick Lillywhite's Guide* for 1854.[1057] August 1846 saw the first-ever match by the All-England Eleven, played at Hyde Park, Sheffield, and their regular appearances around Yorkshire (and later those of other touring sides) did much to stimulate interest in the game. Achieving high standards required instruction and practice, and professional players with skills and experience were increasingly in demand as clubs sought to develop. Employment opportunities thus grew considerably during the second half of the century.

The cricket professional's role varied. He could be engaged to strengthen the team, to help coach members of the club and, in many cases, to tend to the ground. He might need to have multiple talents. In 1882, for example, Sunderland Cricket Club advertised in the *Yorkshire Post*, looking for an additional professional, preferably a left-arm bowler, who was able to keep wicket occasionally and

☛ 172

From a Photo by E. Hawkins & Co., Brighton. London Stereoscopic Co. (Photomezzotype).

WAINWRIGHT. TUNNICLIFFE. TURNER *(Scorer)*. HUNTER. MOORHOUSE.
ULYETT. F. S. JACKSON. LORD HAWKE. A. SELLERS. PEEL.
BROWN. E. SMITH. HIRST.

YORKSHIRE, 1893.

The Yorkshire side that headed the County Championship in 1893. (Mick Pope)

Left: Lord Hawke, who led the side from 1883 to 1910, and had a huge on- and off-field influence. Right: George Hirst, who came to the fore during the 1893 season. (Famous Cricketers and Cricket Grounds)

For most people playing cricket progressed little beyond a game with friends. (Roger Mann)

Cricket on Beverley Westwood at the end of the 1860s.
(East Riding Archives and Local Studies)

A match in progress at the Yeadon Feast in 1892. (Leodis: photographic archive of Leeds)

Adelphi hotel, Sheffield, a home for Yorkshire cricket and cricketers. (Mick Pope)

Darnall 'New' Ground in Sheffield. (Mick Pope)

Bramall Lane in Sheffield, which staged its first game in 1855. (Mick Pope)

The Savile Town ground in Dewsbury was used for Yorkshire county matches from 1867 onwards. (Mick Pope)

Bradford Park Avenue, opened in 1880. (Mick Pope)

Headingley, Leeds, opened in 1890 and first used by Yorkshire the following year. (Mick Pope)

The United North of England XI visit Easingwold in July 1870 (Roger Mann)

Scarborough in 1878 before its development.
Iddison sixth from left, Atkinson in front with ball. (Roger Mann)

The 22 of Hallam and Staveley that took on the AEE in 1858, fielding so well that their opponents struggled to score. (Sheffield Galleries and Museums Trust)

The All-England Eleven, pictured in 1863, which did much to popularise the game in Yorkshire. (Roger Mann)

United Eleven of All England - created in 1852 as a rival of the All-England Eleven (Mick Pope)

Lord Londesborough, who backed several initiatives to broaden the base of Yorkshire county cricket and established the Scarborough Festival. (Roger Mann)

Lord Morpeth, who held senior posts under three prime ministers and was an enthusiastic patron of cricket at Castle Howard in North Yorkshire. (Reproduced by kind permission of the Howard family)

Harry Sampson was one of the great Yorkshire players of the 1840s and 1850s, and then land-lord of the Adelphi Hotel, where the county club held its first committee meeting. (Mick Pope)

Tom Marsden was Yorkshire's earliest cricketing hero and this cup was presented to him in 1831 in recognition of his achievements. (Sheffield Galleries and Museums Trust)

Yorkshire star of the 1850s and 1860s, George Anderson was at the heart of the dispute between the five professionals and the county committee. (Mick Pope)

George Freeman was a highly respected bowler in the 1860s and 1870s. (Mick Pope)

One of the many Yorkshire players from Lascelles Hall, Ephraim Lockwood was one of the county's best batsmen of the 1870s. (Mick Pope)

Tom Emmett played nearly 300 matches for the county over a 22 year period, and was a firm favourite with Yorkshire crowds. (Mick Pope)

One of Yorkshire's greatest wicketkeepers, George Pinder played 125 times for the county. (Mick Pope)

A mainstay of the Yorkshire side from 1873 to 1894, Louis Hall was renowned for his solid defence. (Famous Cricketers and Cricket Grounds)

A hero to cricket followers in Hull for his fielding alone, Charlie Ullathorne made a living as a professional on the edges of the county side but ended his life in poverty. (Mick Pope)

George Ulyett's 20 year career with Yorkshire was rewarded with a benefit which raised £1000 in 1887. (Mick Pope)

Spectators at a match at Hovingham Hall in the 1850s (By kind permission of Sir William Worsley)

Spectators at the Yeadon feast match 1892 (Leodis: photographic archive of Leeds)

Spectators at Headingley in the late 1890s (Mick Pope)

Admission token for Darnall cricket ground in Sheffield. (Sheffield Galleries and Museums Trust)

A handbill for the match at Darnall between Sheffield and Leicester in 1824 (Sheffield Archives)

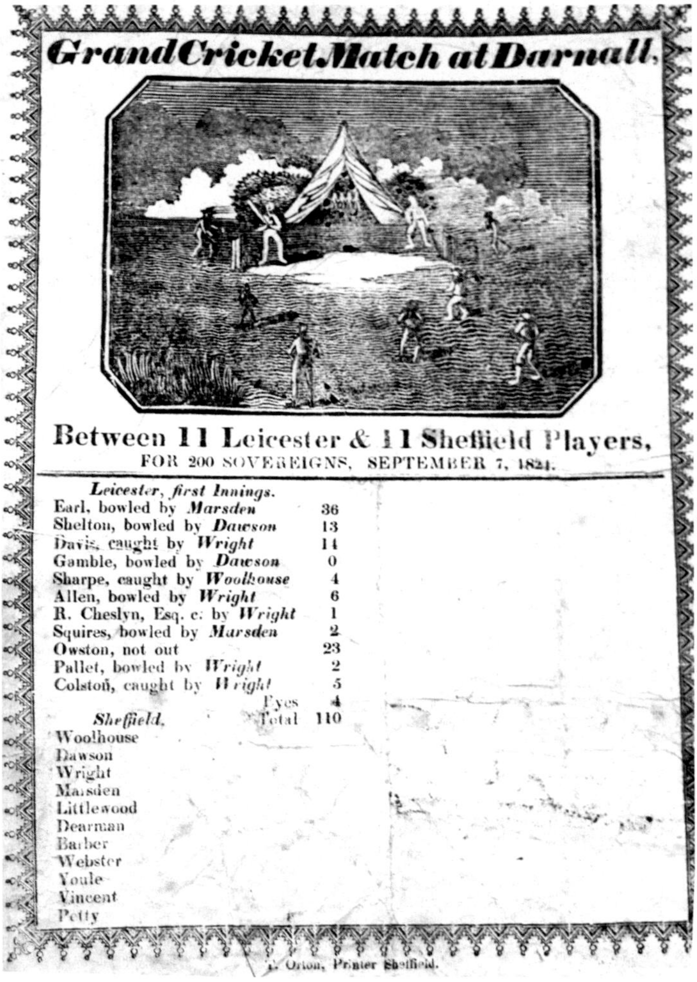

Grand Cricket Match at Darnall,

Between 11 Leicester & 11 Sheffield Players,

FOR 200 SOVEREIGNS, SEPTEMBER 7, 1824.

Leicester, first Innings.

Earl, bowled by *Marsden*	36
Shelton, bowled by *Dawson*	13
Davis, caught by *Wright*	14
Gamble, bowled by *Dawson*	0
Sharpe, caught by *Woolhouse*	4
Allen, bowled by *Wright*	6
R. Cheslyn, Esq. c. by *Wright*	1
Squires, bowled by *Marsden*	2
Owston, not out	23
Pallet, bowled by *Wright*	2
Colston, caught by *Wright*	5
Byes	4
Total	110

Sheffield.

Woolhouse
Dawson
Wright
Marsden
Littlewood
Dearman
Barber
Webster
Youle
Vincent
Petty

Orton, Printer Sheffield.

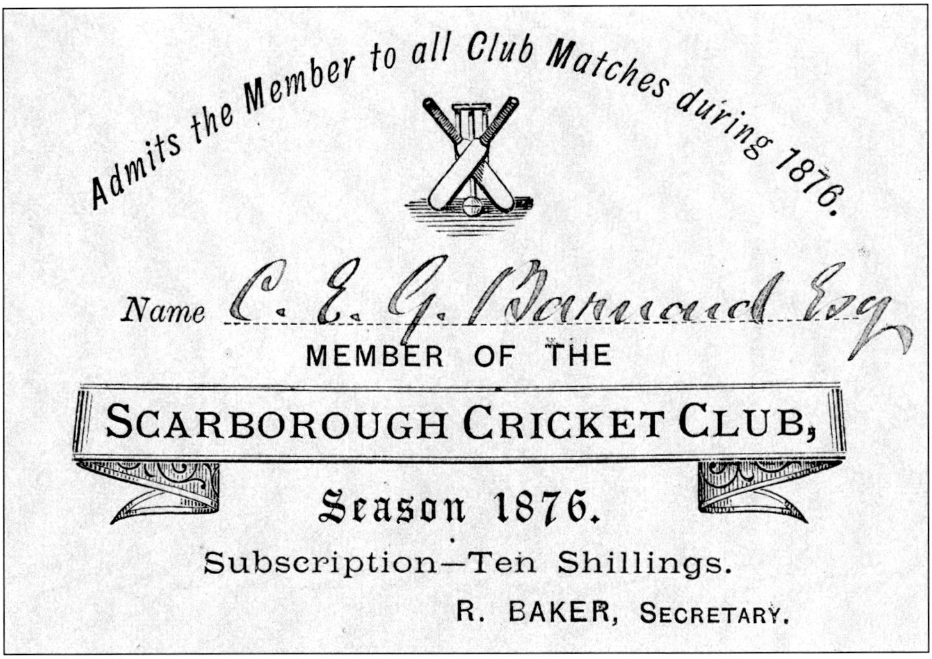

Admits the Member to all Club Matches during 1876.

Name C. E. G. Barnard Esq

MEMBER OF THE

SCARBOROUGH CRICKET CLUB,

Season 1876.

Subscription—Ten Shillings.

R. BAKER, SECRETARY.

Membership card for Scarborough Cricket Club 1876, which would have allowed admittance to the first Festival games (By kind permission of Hull History Centre)

CRICKET.—YORKSHIRE v. SURREY.

PLAYED AT THE BRAMALL LANE GROUND,

On MONDAY, TUESDAY, and WEDNESDAY, JULY 27th, 28th, and 29th, 1863

SURREY.	First Innings.		Second Innings.	
MORTLOCK	b Slinn,	21	c Thewlis, b Slinn	8
HUMPHREY	c John Berry, b Iddison	31	run out	29
H. H. STEPHENSON	b Slinn	15	b Slinn	12
CAFFYN	c Iddison, b Hodgson	43	c Brownhill, b Berry	30
GRIFFITH	c Iddison, b Hodgson	7	b Hodgson	2
JUPP	c Stephenson, b Slinn	17	not out	33
CÆSAR	b Idison	4	run out	11
LOCKYER	not out	30	b Hodgson	4
SEWELL	b J. Berry,	2	c Iddison, b Hodgson	1
GUNN	b Hodgson	11	c Berry, b Iddison	9
POOLEY	b Iddison	16	b Slinn	0
	w. ; b. ; l.b.1 ; n.b. ;	4	w. 1 ; b.2 ; l.b 2 n.b.	5
Umpire—T. SEWELL, SENR.	TOTAL	201	TOTAL	144

YORKSHIRE.	First Innings.		Second Innings.	
JNO. THEWLIS	c Mortlock, b Griffith.	17	b Griffith	0
T. BROWNHILL	b Griffith	1	not out	1
J. ROWBOTHAM	b Caffyn, c Lockyer	12	c Stephenson, b Caffyn	65
E. STEPHENSON	c Stephenson, b Caffyn	17	c Jupp, b Caffyn	3
B. W. WAUD, ESQ	c Griffith, b Mortlock	33	b Caffyn	0
G. ANDERSON	b Sewell	1	not out	26
R. IDDISON	b Sewell	51	c Caesar, b Stephenson	53
E. DAWSON	b Lockyer	20	c Caffyn, b Stephenson	12
JNO. BERRY	not out	8	c Stephenson, b Caffyn	4
I. HODGSON	run out, b Mortlock	2	not out	0
W. SLINN	b Mortlock	0	not out	0
	w. ; b 4 ; l.b. 5 ; n.b. 1;	10	w. ; b 3 ; l b.7 ; n.b. ;	10
Umpire—W. CUTTLE.	TOTAL	172	TOTAL	174

Printed on the Ground by T. S. ALGAR, of 23, Church Street, Sheffield.

Scorecard for Yorkshire v Surrey 1863 (Roger Mann)

Left:
A W Pullin (Old Ebor), whose journalism did much to popularise Yorkshire cricket (Mick Pope)

Bottom Left:
J B Wostinholm, who was Yorkshire CCC Secretary 1864-1902 (Famous Cricketers and Cricket Grounds)

Bottom Right:
M J Ellison, who was Yorkshire CCC President 1864-1897 and Treasurer 1863-1893 (Mick Pope)

The 1875 county side, featuring some of the greats of the early years of Yorkshire CCC. (Mick Pope)

The county side in 1884, a disappointing season despite the batting of Louis Hall. (Mick Pope)

The side of 1887 as the problems confronting the club were starting to come to a head. (Mick Pope)

The Ridings of Yorkshire

also assist the groundsman.[1058] Smaller clubs contracted professionals for specific games in order to beat their rivals. Others, frightened by the financial commitment of a full contract, employed a player by the week or for a fixed purpose.

Terms and conditions varied. The Beverley club employed a professional, W.Hind, for ten weeks in 1863, but then added an extra six weeks once reassured about his merits.[1059] The Yorkshire captain, Ephraim Lockwood, told *The Cricket Field* that he had started as a 'Saturday man', a player who was not engaged full time as a professional, but undertook to appear for a club on a Saturday over the season. He did this from 1867, after a short childhood in which he started work early, winding bobbins and then hand-loom weaving.[1060] For a select few – most notably William Slinn and Isaac Hodgson – there was the opportunity to act as a 'given man' for the district teams which took on the great touring sides to help ensure that games lasted the distance. Both frequently bowled all day against high-quality batting.[1061] Finally, some players were contracted to work for specific individuals. Luke Greenwood, who played for Yorkshire between 1861 and 1874, began his career as a bowler appointed by the Duke of Sutherland and later Lord Lichfield, while Albert Champion, who appeared on a few occasions for both Yorkshire and Lancashire, was described as a 'private and practice bowler' for a gentleman in Richmond for many years.[1062]

Many professionals were contracted for a whole season, usually 20 weeks from May to September, often from Monday morning to Saturday evening. During that time, the player was available to bowl at club members in practice sessions. In 1863, it was noted at the Beverley club's first AGM that it would again solicit financial support so as to engage 'an accomplished player as instructor', and thus bring out the 'cricketing capabilities of the members.'[1063] The professional was usually a capable addition to the club first XI, and so paid to help provide regular victories, but he was also regarded as a 'magnet' to help attract new members to the club. In the late 1860s, for example, Tom Emmett's presence at Keighley as professional was widely advertised in the area, and the Honorary Secretary emphasised that if anyone came to the ground any day of the week he would be ready and willing to bowl for them 'without any emolument other than that he receives from the Keighley club.'[1064]

The decision to engage a professional was not taken lightly by many clubs, concerned about their finances. In 1864, Lockwood Cricket Club's annual meeting decided to engage a professional player for the ensuing season 'after considerable conversation on the subject', and a subscription was set up to defray the expenses which raised 16 guineas in the room.[1065] In October 1876, the committee of the Holmfirth Temperance Cricket Club considered the matter, putting off the decision as to whether they had sufficient funds to engage a professional for the next season, but agreeing there was no doubt it was needed 'especially if the club is to maintain its standing amongst the clubs of the neighbourhood with whom it competes.'[1066]

Uncertainty often characterised the relationship between the professional and his employer. Injury or accident could lead to the contract coming to an end. Sam Berry, a Dalton professional, injured his arm in 1873 and could not bowl. As a result, despite his excellent past service, he was not reappointed as professional, the club's committee hoping 'the new one would do equally good service.'[1067] Contracts were also terminated where conduct was not considered satisfactory. After the 1877 season, Hornsea Cricket Club did not renew the engagement of John Briggs, later one of the greatest English bowlers of the 19th century, clearly dissatisfied with his efforts. The local paper noted that 'the committee intend to engage an older professional next year, as Briggs has been by no means as attentive as he should have been.' In fairness to Briggs, at the time his contract ended he was not yet 15.[1068]

There were pros and cons to the role of professional. While not well paid, there was the possibility of a benefit at the end of the engagement; for example, in 1867 the Bridlington professional, J.W.Sagar, received 30s in gate money and subscriptions from his benefit match, the equivalent of about two weeks' wages for an agricultural labourer.[1069] Wakefield offered 30s for a groundsman who was a good bowler for the 1883 season,[1070] and Sunderland Cricket Club offered £2 10s a week and a benefit for 1886.[1071] For some, opportunities to play cricket were a welcome contrast to a more routine working life. George Atkinson – who appeared for Yorkshire between 1861 and 1870 – said he had hated his work as an apprentice glassblower and had been very happy to run off to play the game.[1072] Many professionals were also treated with considerable respect by their employers. At the annual meeting of the St John's Huddersfield club in September 1869, for example, Joe Berry was thanked for his excellent work in preparing the ground. He was then re-engaged for the following season given that a 'great improvement would have been noticed in several of the players since Berry had been with club.' [1073] In 1873, he was described at the club annual meeting as 'their respected and courteous friend' and 'an excellent tutor'.[1074] The Meltham Mechanics' Institute Cricket Club also thanked its professional, W.Berry, for 'his readiness to impart information, and for the talent he had displayed in general as a professional.'[1075]

On the other hand, a professional had to be compliant, and it is clear that the attributes expected of a paid cricketer were those that emphasised his status as a servant. In 1882, the *Sheffield Independent* stated that Ephraim Lockwood's success 'never made him proud or presumptuous. He was ever the same simple, quiet-spoken, unassuming person – respectable in his appearance, respectable in his tongue.'[1076] And Louis Hall was praised for being popular just as much for 'his abstemiousness and unassuming manners as by the excellence of his play.'[1077] Even where professionals were held in high esteem there were limits as to how well they were treated. In 1878, for example, Tom Emmett was appointed Yorkshire captain, but, according to the county club minutes, only 'in the absence of a Gentleman', and it was further recorded that his complimentary tickets admitted him to the ground and enclosure, but not to the proprietor's enclosure.[1078]

Once in the public eye, a professional could also expect to be talked about, as much as to. In 1848, a rather pompous letter in the *Sheffield Independent* commenting on George Chatterton, one of the greatest of early Yorkshire wicketkeepers, praised his play but added:

> I was, however, not pleased to see him occasionally raise his head and hands with a sort of "Well, I never," "Did you ever," movement. Signs of astonishment are not tokens of perfection in cricket playing. Chatterton is so good a player at all points, and so remarkably efficient at the back of the stumps, that for the honour of the town and for the sake of his own reputation, I wish he would carefully guard against all unnecessary gesticulation.[1079]

Professionals could also become the centre of disputes between clubs. In September 1876, an article was published in the *Leeds Times,* following comments in the *Yorkshire Post* that Tom Emmett had been left out of the Yorkshire side against the MCC at Scarborough after not turning up for a game organised by Lord Londesborough. It said such treatment is 'but a poor return for the gallant manner in which the fame of Yorkshire cricket has been upheld throughout a long and arduous season and a poor encouragement to the rising talent of the county.' Lord Londesborough responded, saying that he had engaged Emmett but had received a letter the night before saying he would not be appearing. As president of MCC he said he felt the need to show displeasure and therefore did not engage him for Scarborough. The *Yorkshire Post* responded by stating that, in its view, the match was only of secondary importance and the punishment was excessive. This exchange provoked further comment. A representative of Keighley Cricket Club wrote that he had engaged Emmett in November 1875 to play against the United South of England Eleven in the match which clashed, and commented, 'I have always found him honourable, upright and truthful, and have not the slightest reason to doubt the statement he made over two months ago respecting his leave of absence from our match.'[1080]

Another player-club dispute occurred in November 1877, when Luke Greenwood brought an action in the Wakefield County Court against the honorary secretary of the Wakefield Cricket Club to recover £1 13s less 13s paid into court. Greenwood was the club's professional for 20 weeks at £3 a week, and it was agreed he could go away when the club did not need him so that he might play elsewhere. Having travelled to Huddersfield, Mirfield, Dewsbury and a number of other places he now claimed the above sum for fares and refreshment. The solicitor for the plaintiff was unable to prove that the secretary was liable.[1081]

As well as having to accept that many followers of cricket considered being paid to play was undermining the spirit of the game, there were other, more practical downsides to being a professional. A club's financial situation might threaten a professional's employment, some clubs considering under pressure that paid support was a luxury they could no longer afford, or breaking off contract discussions when their financial position was known, or while negotiations over a new ground took place. The professional was also dependent on a satisfactory reference for other clubs to take him on, which in itself was based on good behaviour – 'his obliging manner', as many newspapers put it - and a suitably energetic performance on the field and in the nets. In addition, despite all his contributions, the professional was not really a full part of the club. He might not be able to win the club's prizes as he was a paid employee. In 1878, the highly respected Hull Town professional, Len Jackson, was the best performer in each of the categories for which prizes were given – bowling, batting, total runs and greatest number of catches – but was not allowed to win any of them because he was the club professional.[1082] Other clubs were very explicit about what was on offer or not; the Savile club in Dewsbury, for example, advertised for a professional for 1883, but stated clearly: 'No benefit match allowed.'[1083]

As his employer, the club could also say whether he could appear elsewhere and take on other obligations during the summer. County or other representative appearances were at the employing club's discretion. When Richard Daft wanted to take his team to the United States and Canada towards the end of August 1879, the Yorkshire committee, unhappy at the prospect of several players going abroad with county matches still to play, eventually agreed on condition that Lord Londesborough gave his consent they could be absent from the Scarborough festival.[1084] The consequences of certain contractual relationships clearly rankled. George Atkinson was employed at Middlesbrough for many years, and lamented later, 'I wish I had never known [this] engagement. I wish I had never seen Middlesbrough. I should have been a different man, and much better off than I am now if I had not.'[1085]

If this paints a bleak picture it is clear that for some – the more skilled and ambitious – there were wider possibilities and greater levels of security than might have been obtained in other employment. Some could command two or more contracts, fitting in a coaching engagement for several weeks in April at a public school or college, and then returning for the rest of the season to their Yorkshire club side. In 1861, for example, William Slinn started the summer engaged at Christ Church College, Oxford, played as a 'given man' against the All-England Eleven, and made his Yorkshire debut.[1086] Others – like William Swain – had no problems moving from club to club, taking up 20 engagements in his career, including in Manchester, Halifax, Aldershot, Westminster School and also in Oxford.[1087] There were also many professionals, some at the edges of the county game, for whom cricket provided good, steady employment. A number stayed with the same club for many years and gained a degree of respect. James

Stubbings, who played for Derbyshire between 1880 and 1893, was engaged by Huddersfield Cricket Club for 27 years, later being made a life member of the club, whilst David Pollard was long-time professional at the Yorkshire Gentlemen Cricket Club.[1088] For others, unusual opportunites arose. In 1877, for example, George Ulyett was offered the chance of an appointment as a professional in India, although in the end he turned it down.[1089]

Other professionals stood out as particularly influential amongst their peers. Roger Iddison was one such player, who was trusted by Lord Londesborough to organise his sides.[1090] And, just occasionally, there were other hints that some players could use their celebrity to influence the conditions under which they played. A reporter at the United North v United South game at Huddersfield in 1876 feared that his complaints about poor timekeeping amongst the players might fall on deaf ears, observing that if he complained to the committee, 'they say these men will only come on their own terms, we are obliged to give them *carte blanche*, they won't stand talking to or remonstrance, and we are glad to get them on any terms.'[1091]

Additional games for other clubs and for districts against touring sides could all be opportunities for the better players, who could put together a complicated diary of engagements. Many clubs were dependent on professionals to put up any kind of performance against such teams and, importantly from the financial point of view, make sure the game lasted. For these men, juggling different roles could help to provide a reasonable living, and a willingness to travel ensured a full portfolio of appearances. In fact, some professionals had to refuse fixtures which clashed or required unreasonable travel. One who was in great demand was Tom Emmett. In September 1869, a misunderstanding meant that both Holbeck and Stockton thought he was in their side when he turned up for the game. As a result, considerable time was wasted before the game could take place and Stockton recruited another professional on the ground so that the game could go ahead.[1092]

Although many clubs employed one or two professionals, the situation at Lascelles Hall, where numerous professionals were members, was more complex. At times, more than 20 of the club's players were fulfilling professional engagements in different parts of the country.[1093] In November 1874, at the annual meeting, their activities were celebrated and a statement read out. This detailed what they had achieved in different parts of the world, including Andrew Greenwood's visit to Australia, the performances of Lockwood and Hill in the Gentlemen and Players matches, and Lockwood's record of scoring more runs in first-class matches than anyone except Grace and Jupp.[1094] Lascelles Hall was unusual, however, in the standing of those employed to play cricket, and except in particular circumstances, the professional's role was as precarious as that of the majority of working men in Victorian England.

Being noticed

There were a number of routes to being noticed by the county club. Some players were just lucky. A.W.Pullin's book *Talks with Old Yorkshire Cricketers* records how Ephraim Lockwood gained his first selection for the Yorkshire side in 1868. John Thewlis, his uncle, was playing in a match in London, with the Surrey v Yorkshire game to follow at The Oval shortly after. Ashley Walker was unable to fulfil the engagement and the county needed another player. Thewlis duly nominated Lockwood and, with further endorsement from Tom Emmett, he was called for. Opening on his debut with Thewlis, the two put on 176, after which Lockwood played for the county until his retirement in 1884.[1095] Other interviews with old Yorkshire players also bring home the element of chance associated with being spotted. George Pinder only took up wicket-keeping because the usual keeper at his club was missing. He did so well that he retained the role and was noticed after playing in some matches against the All-England Eleven. He became a regular in Parr's team and it was from there that he was taken on by Yorkshire.[1096]

Other players were spotted playing in the touring games. According to West, without the All-England Eleven many promising players such as the young George Anderson 'would have languished in the obscurity of districts remote from London.'[1097] Anderson was a solicitor's scribe in Bedale, where he played for the club in the late 1840s. According to the *Sheffield Daily Telegraph*, William Clarke was engaged to coach local players and, impressed with Anderson, he pushed him forward to play against the All-England Eleven. In 1850, he was noticed playing for Twenty-Two of Scotland, and was recommended to M.J.Ellison, appearing for Fourteen of Yorkshire against All-England. He subsequently turned out for the All-England Eleven for over 20 years.[1098]

Increasingly, players appeared first in fixtures where they could be tested amongst their contemporaries, such as Colts games. Matches between the County XI and a Colts side began in 1872, or were played between two teams of Colts such as in 1878 and 1893. After 1876, a Colts game was played against a Nottinghamshire side, and in 1877, those appearing were paid 21s for the two days and provided with a third-class return train fare.[1099] That winter, Yorkshire County Cricket Club advertised the game with Notinghamshire Colts, stating that 'Cricket Clubs desirous of recommending Colts...are requested to forward particulars of Name, Residence, Age, and special efficiency, before January 31st, to Mr.J.B.Wostinholm'.[1100] The games were taken very seriously and it was reported that spectators 'come from all parts of the county to rejoice with their favourites when they do well and sympathise with them in their misfortunes.'[1101]

Unsurprisingly, there were far too many names submitted for all to be included in the sides; in 1877, for example, there were 64 applications. As a result, many hopefuls fell at this stage. Of the 24 Colts who played in the match organised between teams led by Pinder and Lockwood at Bramall Lane in May 1877, for example, only 10 appeared for the county in a first-class match.[1102] Yorkshire also played matches against local teams, providing further opportunities to appear in a representative side. Success in such trials was not a guarantee of county selection, however, and there were accusations that certain players were discarded despite some success, because they were considered not quite right. In 1887, for example, T.C. Shepherd was seen by some to be in this category. Having been tried in several Colts games, he did not progress any further because, it was believed, the committee thought he was too short.[1103]

For all these efforts, in the mid-1880s the county side was visibly short of talent, and a renewed attempt was made in 1888 to discover new players. It was clear that the established ones were not enough, and following his accident in Australia, it seemed unlikely Billy Bates would ever play again. The Colts game was held in mid-May, providing Robert Moorhouse with an opportunity which led to a first-team place later in the season. Generally though it was not a success and the county committee issued circulars to a number of the leading clubs in Yorkshire to nominate their two best men under 24 to come to Bramall Lane to practise on a specially prepared wicket.[1104] There was an immediate response, and in mid-June the committee said that, while they were anxious to encourage young players, they would prefer that the sessions were well ordered and that only those invited came along as they simply could not cope otherwise.[1105] The following season – 1889 – the club tried another approach, and virtually the whole of May was devoted to Colts matches at six different venues. A full county side was put out and over 40 players were given a game. All the fixtures were affected by the weather, but several players including Luther Whitehead, David Hunter and J.T.Brown enhanced their reputations.[1106]

Lack of success on the field stimulated further consideration of the need for fresh blood. In a June 1891 interview, Lord Hawke discussed the idea of Yorkshire raising money to keep professionals by placing them at grounds where county matches were played.[1107] As we will see later, reform of the county committee was seen as part of the solution because it would help to increase the visibility of men from around the county. In 1893, the *York Herald* reported that J.B.Wostinholm had told members at Bradford that any club with a player who showed promise should be put forward to the committee as soon as possible and made available when called for. The committee was prepared to subsidise clubs where they could not afford to keep a player to ensure he did not go elsewhere. He also hoped the new Yorkshire League matches would help bring forward players.[1108] Two Colts games were held in April between teams led by George Ulyett and Louis Hall, and a selection of players turned out for Yorkshire Colts against Nottinghamshire at the start of May. Later in the summer, Yorkshire 2nd XI matches were played.[1109] A far more systematic process for identifying talent was falling into place.

The final step

For some players, being noticed by the county authorities was not the final hurdle. Instead, they still had to be released from their existing obligations, either with their club or another employer where they were not professionals. For some, progress into first-class cricket faltered here. The county committee came in for criticism for not playing certain players but, in January 1881, M.J.Ellison emphasised that there were 'private circumstances' sometimes which, unknown to the public, prevented the executive from securing the services of particular men.[1110] In 1882, for example, William Hampson did well in the game between Twenty-Two Colts and Yorkshire at Sheffield and was asked to play for the county, but apparently, his club, Middlesbrough, refused him leave. Other counties showed an interest in him, but his career was restricted to being a high-quality league professional.[1111]

Samuel Flaxington got slightly further. A schoolmaster from Otley, he was included in a Yorkshire XI against the Yorkshire Gentlemen in 1881, an indication that he was considered a strong candidate for a county place, and was duly engaged for four games as a batsman of great promise.[1112] He was then unable to play in the Yorkshire v Twenty-Two Colts match in May[1113], and was initially included in the team for the Kent game at Bradford, but had to drop out, unable to leave his teaching duties. No agreement could be reached with his employers.[1114] Circumstances improved slightly the following year, 1882, and he made four appearances for Yorkshire, but his county career went no further after that, and tragically he committed suicide in 1895.[1115]

Other players experienced difficulties getting released for county matches. Bobby Peel, who made his Yorkshire debut in 1882, was refused permission to play against Leicestershire in 1883 as he had club obligations. Harrison was also unavailable, and Hunter and Skilbeck injured, so the county struggled to put a side out. The *Sheffield Daily Telegraph* was unimpressed by those who declined, commenting that, 'I think that everything should give way when the county calls.'[1116] Thomas Walker from Leeds, a malster by profession, was asked to appear against Derbyshire in 1878, but had to refuse because he could not miss three days' work.[1117] Interestingly, when he did turn out for Yorkshire in 1879 he tried to play for a while as an amateur, but his later appearances were as a professional.[1118]

Possibly the most demanding of employers was Thomas Vaughan, the well-known ironmaster in Middlesbrough. According to Baker, Vaughan 'opened his mind and wallet to the idea of a cricket club, [taking] the line that if there was to be cricket then prepare the best ground and engage the finest professionals. The prospect of employment within the Iron Industry that usually accompanied such engagements was sufficient to bring many fine players to Middlesbrough.'

Between 1862 and 1869, he engaged George Atkinson privately for the club and clearly regarded the professional's loyalties as first and foremost to Middlesbrough.[1119] This led to controversy in 1863 when the player was selected for Yorkshire against Nottinghamshire at Trent Bridge. The *Bradford Observer* reported that, when the Yorkshire team came together, it was discovered that Atkinson was absent, 'though he was specifically engaged to play in both matches, and had repeatedly promised since the one at Bradford that he would be at Nottingham. On being telegraphed from the ground, his reply was simply: "Mr Vaughan can't spare me." ' The paper discussed this in detail, but considered that:

> We do not know we can question the right of the employer to keep the services of his bowler entirely to himself, but we think it should be the pleasure of any right-minded patron of cricket to place his professional at the disposal of the county whenever his services are required.[1120]

The paper warned that Atkinson would struggle to escape a 'storm of indignation' when he appeared again in the West Riding. Interestingly, his fellow professionals also took action and advised the committee at Sheffield that they did not want him to play with them in the game there against Surrey.[1121] Despite these examples, other clubs did not stand in the way of their professional getting an opportunity. When the Secretary of Nottinghamshire County Cricket Club wrote to the Bradford club in 1867 to ask permission to call up its professional John Oscroft, the Bradford committee considered they could not very well deny him the chance, even though it was likely to affect their prospects in a match with Kirkstall.[1122]

The county qualification

Another factor influencing whether an individual could make it to the Yorkshire side was the necessity of being born within the county boundary. Although this was breached on 19 occasions prior to 1893 – Lord Hawke being the most obvious example – it was not until 1991 that the county decided to abandon its policy of not employing an overseas player and other non-Yorkshire-born players.[1123] Having some form of restriction on who could, and could not, play for a team was nothing new when the county club started in 1863, as was demonstrated in Chapter 5. A key feature of the negotiations around matches in the first half of the century concerned who was qualified to play. Teams specified the distance from which they would allow their opponents to select players in order to ensure that they did not unfairly strengthen themselves. As a result, towns and villages were proud of their ability to put out teams based solely on their own resources, and complaints were often made when a side considered their opponents had breached the qualifying terms.

For many years, however, the county game was marked by considerable flexibility as to the county qualification. Roger Iddison, for example, played for both Yorkshire (1855-76) and Lancashire (1865-70), including in the same season of 1867.[1124] David Eastwood appeared for three counties – Yorkshire, Durham and Northumberland – in the summer of 1874.[1125] Intermittently, there were challenges to particular selections on the grounds of birthplace. In 1864, there was considerable discussion before the Yorkshire v Surrey game in Sheffield about the inclusion in the Yorkshire side of Tom Darnton, to whom the visitors objected on the grounds that he was a Durham-born man. They eventually gave way as Yorkshire did not have another player available.[1126] Henry Reynolds, who played for Nottinghamshire but had strong ties with Middlesbrough in the 1870s, was selected for Yorkshire against Middlesex in 1874, but the latter refused to let him play on the basis of his qualifications. Yorkshire retaliated by refusing to allow W.C.Wheeler, a former Surrey player, appear for Middlesex.[1127]

Frank Sugg was another player from outside the county boundary (he was born in Ilkeston in Derbyshire) who created controversy. His selection for Yorkshire in 1883 was widely debated when he failed to produce the kind of form in the county game that he had in West Riding club cricket. Sugg played in just eight matches for Yorkshire before joining Derbyshire in 1884 (although not before Yorkshire had large posters printed for a Colts' match with Sugg's name included, which then needed to be covered over), but then made his name with Lancashire between 1887 and 1899. (As an aside, in January 1884, an action was brought against Sugg - described as a clerk at Brocco Bank and member of the county eleven - for throwing cues in the billiard room of a café in Sheffield and, when asked to stop, for throwing pudding at a companion which damaged a billiard table. He was required to pay for the damage and costs.)[1128]

In the autumn of 1872, a meeting was held in London to discuss who was eligible to play county cricket, with Ellison and Atkin representing Yorkshire.[1129] In 1873, MCC and the county authorities agreed arrangements which determined a player's right to represent a specific county. A cricketer could only represent one county in a season and had to choose between his county of birth or his county of residence, where he had had to live for two years. Sissons commented that 'For the professionals these changes had far-reaching consequences. Their mobility of labour was immediately restricted and their earning potential limited. Further, the two-year residential qualification reduced the player's bargaining position.'[1130]

The limitations that adherence to the convention on home-grown players placed on Yorkshire cricket began to be discussed in the 1880s. In 1881, the *Bradford Observer* commented that it 'frequently keeps promising men in the background. Players who have resided for twenty years in one shire are unknown in another.'[1131] The *Yorkshire Post* also questioned the arrangements following poor Yorkshire performances in the 1882 season, and because the qualification could exclude amateur talent.[1132] Following further weak displays in the 1884 season, more agreed with these sentiments. The *Sheffield Independent* suggested that the county committee 'are fast coming to the conclusion that the birth qualification carried out *pur et simple*, without any reservation whatever, is a mistake'.[1133] Another observer called it 'an antiquated and almost incomprehensible piece of folly', although others pointed out that a similar approach was not doing Nottinghamshire any harm.[1134]

Despite this, the birth qualification was still enforced. In April 1887, a useful prospect, E.Southall, was mentioned by the *Yorkshire Post* as likely to appear in the Yorkshire Colts match. However, the player wrote to the paper later stating that although he had lived in Leeds since the age of four, he had been informed by J.B.Wostinholm that he was disqualified as he had not been born in Yorkshire.[1135] The *Post* later reflected that, while applying the birth rule strictly had kept some players out of the team, 'we do not think that the county has suffered thereby to any considerable extent.' The paper also criticised Lord Harris's recent suggestion that the residential qualification should be relaxed to 12 months, arguing that if this happened there would be no incentive to develop native talent. For this reason, it accepted Southall should not be allowed to play.[1136] On other occasions, however, the club could be flexible and the subject remained controversial at a time when the county side was struggling for new blood. In 1890, W.F.Whitwell played for Yorkshire under the residential qualification but many in the north-east had misgivings, with the Hon. Secretary of Durham County Cricket Club complaining that it appeared that Yorkshire would depart from the birth qualification at the first opportunity.[1137]

Nevertheless, the selection of Yorkshire-born players was a source of pride, and in August 1893, reflecting on the championship win, the *Yorkshire Evening Post* commented that the side were all Yorkshiremen, 'a fact which in these days of importation should not be overlooked and which should encourage the Yorkshire Committee to persevere in their policy of looking after native talent.'[1138] It would be another 100 years before the realities of the modern game led to a major change of heart.

Making it...and staying there

Having overcome all the obstacles and gained a first-team place, there were still problems and pitfalls for certain players. Some related to the immediate demands of the game itself such as finding and maintaining form at the highest level, but others came with the job such as the rigours of travelling the country, avoiding injury, the temptations of drinking and late nights, and the pressures of the new-found status and hero-worship. A graphic description of the problems for a professional came in an issue of *London Life* in 1863. Although not specifically about Yorkshire players, it nevertheless captures the challenges 19th-century cricketers faced, suggesting:

> A short life and merry one is all the professional can hope for, as regards his cricketing existence - younger and more brilliant men tread upon his heels. Popular applause is proverbially capricious, and the smoking, drinking and good living during the summer, contrasted with the greens and bacon – and not too much of the latter – all through the winter; all this is unfavourable to the preservation of a high cricketing condition.

Turning for evidence for these statements, the journal spoke to an unnamed professional's wife, who stated that if she could have her time again she would not have married a cricketer, despite what she described as the honour. But she could not live on honour, she insisted, and now her husband had finished playing, 'his past life makes him above bottling spirits and drawing beer. He has been used to living so well, being flattered and made much of; for a cricketer's life does always make a working man so lazy and so luxurious.'[1139]

As things became more organised at county level, the more successful players were engaged for longer periods of time. For some this meant the whole season, although this was only for the most reliable and effective. In April 1871, the county committee decided to engage Iddison, Rowbotham, Rawlinson, Pinder, Emmett, Freeman, Lockwood and A.Greenwood for every game, while Hill, Ullathorne, W.Smith, Clayton (as twelfth man) and Luke Greenwood (as umpire, a role he did not fulfil) were offered only the match at Lord's against the MCC on 22-23 May. The following month, Clayton and Smith were asked to play for all the remaining games.[1140] In 1878, the committee minutes noted that all engagements with professionals were to 'be made with the distinct understanding that should their services not be required in any or all of the Matches for which they are engaged they shall receive the Sum of Three Pounds per Match.'[1141]

In 1883, the chief members of the Yorkshire side were announced in March, but the performances of a number of players during that year did not impress the county committee.[1142] The following year only Ulyett, Bates, Peel, Hall and Harrison were engaged for the whole summer, while Lockwood, Peate and Hunter were given three-match trials. Emmett, now 42, was put on the reserve list and initially only offered the Colts game, which he turned down. He was then given three matches to prove himself, which he accepted. Subsequently, he bowled 'like a demon', taking six wickets in an innings against both Cambridge University and the Australians, and then eight for 32 against Sussex. To be able to play, Emmett had to get permission from the authorities at The Leys School in Cambridge, where he was engaged for a month, leading the *Yorkshire Post* to ask, 'Is this a just reward after the splendid services he has rendered in bye-gone days?'[1143]

Income and expenditure

Cricket professionals were not well paid and most had to put together their income from different sources. The nature of their working circumstances also meant that it was easy to eat into their earnings in getting to and from games. Sissons notes that for county cricketers £5 for a home game and £6 for an away match was well established as the rate for the job, and Yorkshire did not agree to the proposal that an extra £1 should be given where the match took place 100 miles or more away until 1898 (although an extra £1 was paid, for example, for the game at Clifton in 1877[1144]). For the best, more could be secured by being chosen to appear for the Players against the Gentlemen (£10) or in other representative matches.[1145] However, players paid all their own travel and lodging expenses – rail fares, bed and breakfast, tips, cab fares, evening meal, etc. – and George Anderson observed that after such expenses 'there was not much left to get fat on.'[1146] Atkinson made similar comments about the costs that were incurred, noting, 'I have reached home with only 7s or 8s in my pocket after paying hotel bills and railway fares.' He even recalled that on one occasion he and George Freeman had to borrow rail fares home from the station master at York.[1147]

At times, there was some negotiation involved in securing a fee. Tom Emmett asked for 7s 6d and rail fares to play for Todmorden v the All-England Eleven, but was refused as the match committee thought it was too much. He also asked for £5 to play for Yorkshire against Nottinghamshire in 1866 and was also refused on the grounds he was too inexperienced. Insistent that, given the cost of travel, he needed that sum, he got his way.[1148] In April 1862, Yorkshire negotiated terms with various players on a bilateral basis to play in four games that season. Some agreed to do so for £18, others to appear in two games for £9. George Anderson asked for £22 for the four matches, and the committee agreed.[1149] In May, the committee heard that the terms offered had all been accepted, except in three cases where players had asked for £5 per match, but it was thought 'probable that the Committee's terms would be finally agreed upon.'[1150]

A year later, the Yorkshire secretary was asked to write to George Atkinson to advise that all the players except Anderson had agreed to take on Surrey home and away for £9, and if 'he be disposed to play for that sum he might consider himself engaged for the two matches and if not he might have £5 for the one at The Oval'.[1151] Subsequently, as we have seen, he failed to appear to play at Bradford against Nottinghamshire. In mid-July, however, it seems that the county committee was prepared to include Atkinson as it was noted in the committee minutes that he had not replied to two letters inviting him to play against Surrey. Luke Greenwood was proposed as a replacement, but eventually Brownhill was included.[1152]

Players at all levels could obtain talent money for outstanding performances. Some got it on the spot. For example, Berry, the Batley professional, received

£1 talent money for his 55 against St John's in 1872 and £2 5s collected from spectators as he left the field.[1153] Several players scoring 50 or more in the game between the Sheffield Club and the Wednesday Club in August 1871 received 5s.[1154] Billy Bates received a sovereign for his century for Yorkshire against Nottinghamshire in June 1878, and 'double talent money' for his 118 against Lancashire in August 1879.[1155] Otherwise, prizes were awarded at the end-of-the-season dinners; in November 1882, the *Huddersfield Chronicle* listed the performances of the Dalton players who merited talent money for that year.[1156]

At county level, Edwin Stephenson appears to be the first recipient of a reward from the newly formed Yorkshire County Cricket Club when the committee gave him 20s for 'his splendid play' against Surrey in 1863 (he made 67 in the side's only innings).[1157] The following year, Luke Greenwood and Edwin Stephenson both received 20s for their performances against Cambridgeshire, and Tarrant and Pryor for the visitors received the same amount for their fifties against Yorkshire.[1158] In 1876, the county committee decided to give £1 to each Yorkshire player for their 'determined stand' against Nottinghamshire at Trent Bridge.[1159] In 1892, Yorkshire paid £1 for scoring 50, 30 shillings for a score of 75 and £2 for a century.[1160] Particularly impressive performances in games might also lead to prizes from supporters. Lockwood received a silver jug for being top scorer in the match against Surrey in 1869, the gift being given by 'an ardent admirer of cricket in Yorkshire'.[1161] In 1871, Rowbotham and Greenwood were awarded a silver cup each for their batting in the game with Surrey at The Oval, and Hill a similar prize for his bowling, awarded by a 'well-known and popular Yorkshire patron of cricket' who lived in London.[1162]

For the best players, the possibility of overseas tours from the 1860s onwards provided a chance for further income. George Anderson made £230 after paying expenses from the 1863/64 tour of Australia.[1163] In 1876, when Ulyett, Emmett, Greenwood and Hill went to Australia they received £200 each, a first-class passage, a share in the benefit matches and 25% of the net profits arising from the speculation.[1164] Each man who went on Shaw's Australian and American tour of 1881-82 received £200 for the trip (of which £100 was to be paid after the last match), with £20 spending money, as well as first-class passage paid out and home, and all hotel expenses covered.[1165] Again, however, it is not clear how much a player could, or more importantly, did save. Years later, Shaw recalled that the majority of players returned with practically nothing as a result of what he described as 'expensive habits.'[1166]

In any consideration of the financial position of professionals, it is also worth remembering that the vulnerability of cricketers to uncertain work conditions was hardly an exception amongst working people in Victorian England, many of whom had little or no protection from illness, poverty and disease. Here, an interesting comparison can be made between Charles Ullathorne, long-time Hull professional and occasional Yorkshire player, and his father Francis, a small businessman. Variously described as professional cricketer, clerk, draper, publican and brewer's representative, Ullathorne junior suffered the fate of many cricketers as he aged, and in 1882, some seven years after his final appearance for Yorkshire, a benefit was held for him after he was discovered in circumstances 'not of his making.' According to 'Old Ebor', in 1891 and 1892 Ullathorne fulfilled a professional engagement in Geneva, Switzerland, 'among the English colony', but on his return he dropped out of cricket, and for five years was engaged by the Sweetmeat Automatic Delivery Company. He then lost his job during hard economic times.[1167]

In 1899, Ullathorne used his interview with Pullin to mention that he had umpired in Lancashire League games, adding that he would be happy for this remark to be published 'as a hint to the Yorkshire authorities'. He emphasised that he could 'see and hear as well as ever I did in my life, and my nerves have not gone by any means. I did apply for a county umpire's post on my return from Switzerland. I was nominated but not appointed. Why, I don't know.'[1168] The previous summer, Ullathorne attended the funeral of George Ulyett (who credited the Hull man with naming him 'Happy Jack') and, when a Hull side played in Manchester, the team came across Ullathorne. Ominously, shortly afterwards another benefit was held for him, for which several players promised support.[1169] This did not have much effect, however, and six years later when he died, his wife was given £20 by the Yorkshire County Cricket Club committee, such was her financial position.[1170] Yet if Ullathome's life was one of ups and downs, so was that of his father. A dealer in fabrics, he was declared bankrupt, and spent time in a debtor's prison in London in the 1840s. In 1864, he was again adjudged bankrupt in a case described by the County Court Judge as one of the worst cases that had ever come before him. For both men, such was the reality of a society with little or no safety net.[1171]

Other players experienced difficult financial situations. In November 1867, William Slinn – described as a tobacconist and professional cricketer, and part of Yorkshire's first great bowling partnership with Ike Hodgson – was adjudged bankrupt the same week that Hodgson died. Slinn was still turning out as a 'given man' for local sides against the All-England Eleven and the United All-England Eleven, and was professional at Bolton Cricket Club, but also had business difficulties.[1172] Luke Greenwood of Kirkheaton, despite his status as a county player, was declared bankrupt in December 1869. Described as weaver and professional cricketer, his financial difficulties were principally caused by an action against him by someone alleging he had suffered a severe accident due to Greenwood. It was later discovered that the plaintiff had contributed to his own accident and, when ready for trial, abandoned the action on advice. The bill of costs had been incurred by the bankrupt, and no opposition being offered, the discharge was granted.[1173]

Some players ensured that they were not entirely dependent on their cricket income. As well as those like Joe Berry, the St John's Huddersfield professional in the 1870s, who was also landlord of the Thornhill Arms, others had sources of income inside or outside the game. Jonathon Joy was for many years a gamekeeper for Thomas Vaughan of Middlesbrough.[1174] Edmund Peate had a 'Cricket and General Athletic Sports Warehouse' in Leeds in the 1880s, and Ephraim Lockwood had a Cricket and Lawn Tennis Outfitters in Huddersfield. Tom Emmett advertised as a Cricket and Lawn Tennis Outfitter in Keighley[1175], while Joe Hunter offered both hotel accommodation and the 'best and cheapest cricket materials' in 1886.[1176]

Drinking and gambling

Cricket and alcohol have long been associated. As discussed in Chapter 5, many clubs were formed and met in public houses, used a field adjoining a pub, and often took whatever facilities were available to store their equipment or get changed in. Refreshment marquees were an essential facility for big games, generating much welcome revenue. For the county players, bars on grounds were an obvious attraction away from home, and improvements in catering facilities made them more appealing. In 1875, for example, the proprietors of the refreshment booths at Bramall Lane, Messrs Donoghue and Wilcox, regularly provided players and officials with a free post-match meal, 'in princely style', with champagne.[1177]

Those who disapproved of players drinking could be subject to scorn. In 1890, the *Sheffield Daily Telegraph* mocked the views of Alderman William Johnson Clegg who, when considering an application for the Bramall Lane booths, had commented that 'Cricketers who practise don't want a drink.' It added that it seemed unlikely that Clegg had ever played the game if he believed such 'a preposterous idea.' The paper argued that cricketers did want an occasional drink and would have one despite 'the fanatical enthusiasts who would ram their teetotal principles down everybody's throat and would treat every man who takes a glass of English ale as though he was a confirmed drunkard.'[1178] While many felt some alcohol was harmless enough and good for morale, others took a more puritanical view. Rev J.Pycroft commented on country players 'tempted to the night-houses of London', fearing that money was 'easily squandered, and a professional often comes headachy, and half sleepy from beer and tobacco-smoke, on the second day of the match.'[1179]

In the late 1870s, rumours began to grow that some of the Yorkshire county players were keen drinkers, and that this was affecting their performance. This was added to by suggestions that an enthusiasm for late-night card-playing after matches at Bramall Lane amongst several players meant 'they haven't turned up in very good order next morning. Perhaps Andrew [Greenwood] may have had a weakness in this direction, but if so, he wasn't the only sinner.'[1180] In 1880, when the Australians were entertained at Leeds Town Hall for a banquet, the Mayor asked the visitors how it was they were so successful, and whether it was related to their eating, drinking and sleeping habits.[1181] An editorial in the *Leeds Times* was impressed that, although they were not total abstainers, the Australians practise 'the golden rule of temperance' and were successful because they ate and drank in moderation.[1182] Not everyone was prepared to accept this, and in September 1882 a letter appeared in the *Yorkshire Post* stating that, having observed the Australians at Harrogate, there appeared to be not a single abstainer in the side. This provoked further correspondence asserting the importance of not drinking alcohol and playing cricket.[1183]

If the subject died away in the early 1880s, it resurfaced later in the decade when certain players were again suspected of enjoying themselves too much. As a result, action was taken. According to Thomas, Hawke gave professionals a certain amount of security and:

> he expected a sense of self discipline and self control in return. But many players were too much of the old hard drinking, hard living school, to change their ways. Hawke had no hesitation. They had to go, and once he made up his mind he carried out his duty with a singlemindness and determination that had never been seen in county cricket before.[1184]

Despite still having some years of cricket in him, Edmund Peate was described as the first of the 'victims' of Lord Hawke's clean-up campaign in 1887, although, according to the captain, dismissing him from the county side was one of his saddest tasks.[1185] The same year, Irwin Grimshaw played his last match, in 1889, Joseph Preston, and in 1890, Fred Lee and Saul Wade. In moving the adoption of the county club's report and statement of accounts in January 1890, M.J.Ellison, club chairman expressed his concerns that problems with the side were 'caused by those who called themselves supporters of cricket, who came to the ground and who could not see a professional cricketer without wanting to give him a glass of drink. They never thought that if they gave him a glass a thousand others would want to do the same.' And, in language which says a lot about the attitudes to players at the time, he added that 'the most serious thing they could do to a professional cricketer was to offer him a drink.' Equally censorious were the words of R.S.Holmes who argued that the players involved only had themselves to blame for the disappointment they proved to followers of county cricket.[1186]As a postscript to all this, in January 1893, Grimshaw appeared in front of magistrates in Bradford charged with being drunk and disorderly, assaulting a police officer and damaging his uniform. He was fined 12s 6d for being drunk and 10s for the assault.[1187]

Several players looked back on the accusations of excessive drinking with mixed views. George Anderson told 'Old Ebor', 'Most of our fellows were very steady. I only knew one who could get drunk and play the next day, but I won't mention his name. He could sleep it off, and come up smiling for his innings next morning....

You may take it that a man cannot indulge and play cricket. One glass of grog before bedtime was my usual allowance, and that was the habit of a good many of my comrades.'[1188] Luke Greenwood was less sure, telling 'Old Ebor', 'We are too often blamed, and rightly, for insobriety and improvidence', adding 'but neither charge can be brought against me.'[1189]

Travelling

When George Ulyett died in 1898, the magazine *Cricket: A weekly record of the game* estimated that he had covered 258,000 miles playing cricket, of which 157,000 had been during his five trips to Australia.[1190] Ike Hodgson also travelled long distances to piece together a living, crossing the country almost continuously from May to October in the late 1850s and 1860s. On average he travelled around 2,500 miles each summer and around 4,000 miles in 1863 – including five trips from Yorkshire to London - when he was much in demand. Tom Emmett was another who played cricket throughout the country, and made long and arduous overseas trips in 1876/77 (Australia and New Zealand), 1878/79 (Australia), 1879/80 (North America) and 1881/82 (North America, Australia, New Zealand).

The expansion of the rail network after the 1830s made travel more feasible and (slightly) more comfortable than it had been, but it was still a challenging experience to go far, particularly to remoter places. Tom Marsden's fame took him long distances to engagements. In July 1833, he left Sheffield on Friday 5th to go to London, where he played at Lord's on the following Monday and Tuesday, making the highest score of the match between Eleven Players and Sixteen Gentlemen. The following week, he appeared at Lord's again for a team of Left-Handed Hitters against the MCC (making the second-highest score of the match), then took on Fuller Pilch in Norwich on the 18th (losing badly) and in Sheffield on 5-7th August.[1191] Marsden's defeat in the single-wicket game in Norwich was put down to his being out of condition, having travelled the day before.[1192] Travel also brought risks, and Marsden suffered a 'severe accident' in 1836 when engaged to play for North of the Thames against South of the Thames at Leicester. The post chaise in which he was riding came into contact with a wagon driven by a boy who had lost control. The impact threw the driver and Marsden from the carriage, about six miles from Nottingham. He dislocated his wrist and had to be treated in the town. He was then unable to play in the Yorkshire v Norfolk match at the end of August.[1193]

Things got more demanding as the game took off and the rail network made longer distances more realistic. Players could often finish a game at 6.30pm in the south of England and be expected to play next morning at midday 200 or 300 miles away. Ike Hodgson's arrangements for 1866 demonstrate quite how much travel could be involved. On 7 May, he was engaged to play for Yorkshire at

Bradford. On the 10th he appeared in Glasgow, followed on the 14th by a game at Quarry Gap, Bradford. In June he was in Leeds, Bradford and Thorne over a ten-day period, followed by Seaforth four days later. July was the same, with games in Bradford, St Ives, Oldham, Dudley, Redcar, Lascelles Hall, Darlington and Keighley, while the first two weeks of August saw engagements in Nottingham, Kendal and Mansfield. He also turned down matches in Heckmondwike, Retford and Worksworth.[1194] Unsurprisingly, this itinerary took its toll and his health broke down in August of that year.

Both George Atkinson and George Anderson told 'Old Ebor' of the travelling they had experienced, and both thought the subsequent generation of players had, as Atkinson put it, a 'feather bed' time of it. He said he had travelled to as many as 38 matches in a year with the old elevens and the county side. Anderson added that cricketers who now travelled the country 'in saloons and express trains' had a much easier time than he had experienced. This had included trips from Dublin to London, London to Glasgow and Edinburgh, 'often in one night, to be ready for the next day's match.' He remembered getting lost in the dark in Lincolnshire, and also finishing in London on a Wednesday night and playing in Glasgow the next morning.[1195] In May 1861, Anderson travelled from Dublin to London overnight and appeared against Surrey at The Oval. He batted at number five within a few hours of arrival and top-scored in both innings, making 60 out of Yorkshire's 185 runs across the two innings.[1196]

The growing calendar got tougher for regulars in the county side. In 1882, the *Yorkshire Post* suggested that 'the convenience of the Yorkshire players is less considered in making the cricket arrangements for the following season than that of any other county.' The team played in Hove (14-16 August), then Cheltenham (17-18 August), followed by Sheffield (21-23 August) and then Gravesend (24-26 August).[1197] In 1887, the team finished playing Gloucestershire at Dewsbury at six in the evening on 27 July, and travelled overnight for a game with Hastings and District starting at 1 o'clock on the 28th. The journey was described as 'tedious, long and tiresome', and unsurprisingly the Yorkshire XI was in no fit state to field, conceding a score of 180 to a gentleman appropriately named Pigg.[1198]

Tom Marsden was not the only one who found that travel could be dangerous. Cricketers of all levels were just as vulnerable as anyone else to accidents when travelling. The wheels came off a coach taking a York Junior Club team back from a match at Selby in 1834. The players got themselves out with the only injury a slight sprain to one man.[1199] In 1858, Thomas Hunt, who appeared for Yorkshire between 1845 and 1851, was knocked down by a train and died as he walked along a railway line having played for Twenty-Two of Rochdale against the All-England Eleven.[1200] In 1868, following an appearance in a game for Somercotes against the All-England Eleven on the Derbyshire/Nottinghamshire border, Tom Emmett and Luke Greenwood were injured in an omnibus accident, along with a policeman and several other passengers. Greenwood was so badly hurt that it was initially reported that he was not expected to live, although thankfully later information stated this was exaggerated. The same article in the Sheffield press reported that, a short time after the accident, Tom Emmett was advised of the sudden death of one of his children.[1201]

Adulation

Some players became local celebrities as a result of their performances, and clubs and individuals found many ways of rewarding and celebrating them. In Sheffield in the 1820s, Tom Marsden was the 'idol' (sometimes referred to as 'glorious Tom'[1202]). In 1831, a silver cup was presented to Marsden at a dinner by cricket followers. The inscription stated that it was given in view 'of their estimation of his undeviating integrity in all public matches, his first-rate talent in every department of the game, of his unwearied diligence and undaunted resolution in the field, and as a trophy of the distinguished success which has attended his exertions in that noble and manly exercise.'[1203] Such was the esteem in which Marsden was held, that the *Sheffield Independent* found it very hard to believe rumours that he would abandon Sheffield for a match at Lord's which clashed with the game with Nottingham in 1831. The rumours actually proved to be well founded, although he was soon playing in Sheffield again.[1204] Marsden is also a good example of a player's celebrity living on. In 1854 – several years after his death – his friends and supporters organised a match to raise funds to build a monument 'for one of the finest cricketers of his or any other day.'[1205]

Another highly respected player was Richard Letby, described as 'one of the outstanding players from York' and, as we have seen, a well-known single-wicket cricketer. Born in 1809, he appeared for York Cricket Club from 1832, and was secretary for 35 years and treasurer for 25 years, frequently finding himself out of pocket through his responsibilities.[1206] In 1850, he was the subject of a full-length portrait, which was suspended in the ballroom of the Assembly Rooms at the Castle Howard Inn for the annual ball of the Castle Howard Cricket Club. A lithographic engraving of the picture was available to buy shortly afterwards.[1207] Nearly a decade later, Letby was again the subject of much adulation when a testimonial was presented to him supported by many local dignatories.[1208] More than £100 was raised, and the committee bought a number of items which were exhibited in a silversmith's shop in the city.[1209]

In the 1860s and 1870s, Charlie Ullathorne was the local hero in Hull, famed for his ability as a fielder, which alone secured him a place in the Yorkshire side. In 1878, after a critical piece about him had appeared in the press, a long response defending Ullathorne was published in the *Yorkshire Post*. The correspondent stated that, 'I think is my duty to say a few words in favour of our townsman, Ullathorne, who we are all proud of as a cricketer.'[1210] In Batley, a celebrity for many years was Louis Hall, who topped the Yorkshire averages in 1883, and was a leading professional in the country. That year hundreds waited for him to come home on the train after one end-of-season game, and the Temperance Brass Band greeted him with a rendition of 'See the Conquering Louis Comes.' When he arrived, a procession made its way to the Town Hall, where speeches were given. Modestly, Hall said if he had known this would happen he would have got out at an earlier station. Eventually the crowd went to his house, where he was forced to appear and wish everyone good-night.[1211]

Perhaps the biggest star of the period from the 1860s to the late 1880s was Tom Emmett. On his death in 1904 the *Leeds Mercury* stated that 'No member of the eleven was more popular with the crowd than the genial "Tom", who liked to "play to the gallery" occasionally.'[1212] Tom Emmett stories filled the papers for years after his retirement, and were endlessly repeated in serialisations from books and memoirs by Hawke, Grace and Daft, and interviews with 'Old Ebor', making him an early working-class sporting hero, whose image and character were magnified by the press. His idiosyncratic bowling style, his 'never say die' approach in a contest, and his famed rapport with the Yorkshire crowds all added to his popularity, and were in direct contrast to the widespread view that most professional cricketers were dour and conservative in their approach, made anxious by fear of failure.[1213]

Those like Emmett who reached the heights of international cricket were treated with even greater respect. On many occasions, Yorkshire's tourists were seen off from their home town, or met on their return from abroad. In September 1876, Emmett, Greenwood, Ulyett and Hill were among the 12 players who went to Australia on the tour which included the first-ever Test match. They were waved off from Huddersfield station by a crowd, before departing from Southampton to great applause.[1214] In 1879, a dinner was held for the Yorkshire members of Daft's American and Canadian team at the Paragon Hotel in Huddersfield. Many cricketers were present and Tom Emmett stated that, despite being on other tours, this was the first time he had enjoyed a public banquet.[1215] Bates and Lockwood returned from the same trip in November 1879, and were given an enthusiastic reception at the railway station in Huddersfield.[1216] Great international performances were also not forgotten. In July 1884, more than a year after his fine bowling for Bligh's side in Australia, where he had contributed a match-winning performance at Melbourne, an anonymous cricket follower sent Bates a solid silver tankard of considerable value.[1217]

Such interest was not without its downsides and players responded differently to the attention that came with the game. Bobby Peel clearly hated giving interviews and, having kept J.A.H.Catton of the *Athletic News* waiting, sent a representative to say he would not be coming to talk.[1218] In contrast, having experienced such adultation, some players felt its loss painful. After George Pinder ceased to play for Yorkshire, for example, he suffered the indignity of not being recognised at the pavilion at Bramall Lane, and reacted so forcefully that thereafter he was required to pay to watch the county following the incident.[1219]

Injury and ill-health

Injury was the great fear for the professional cricketer as it could mean the end to a regular income and, in the worst cases, the termination of his career. There were many dangers and players suffered all kinds of accidents on and off the field. In the early years of the period, most pitches were poor, particularly in local cricket, and there was no guarantee of a flat wicket and, even less likely, an even outfield. On-field collisions might also lead to injury. In June 1878, at the end of the Yorkshire-Nottinghamshire game at Sheffield, several players had a 'scrimmage' for the ball, during which George Pinder, the wicketkeeper, fell heavily and broke his collar-bone, missing two and a half month's cricket. At the July county committee meeting it was agreed that during his recovery he would be paid £2 a week as long as he was not engaged to umpire, for which he would get £3.[1220] Off the field, in 1867, Joseph Rowbotham cut a severe gash in his hand when attempting to slice a piece of bread, and was unable to play for some time, and in 1869, John Thewlis fractured one of his legs while at home.[1221] In early 1885, Allen Hill ran a rabbit bone into his thumb and suffered from blood poisoning. At one point, it was suggested that he could lose his right arm as the infection was so bad.[1222]

Injury brought Billy Bates's professional career to a sudden end. Although not particularly successful in the 1887 domestic season, he toured Australia over the winter. While practising, he was hit above the right eye by a ball played from the adjoining net by Billy Newham, the Sussex opener. Following stitches, it was immediately clear that he would not play again that winter and he was put on the return ship, arriving in England in March. Rumours spread that during the trip he had tried to kill himself. At home he was told neither to read nor write, and for some weeks he was only able to see 20 yards with his damaged eye. His problems were compounded by illness to his wife and son. During 1888, he struggled on, but when two members of the Yorkshire team visited him, they found him in a very feeble state, and eventually he lost the use of an eye. Luckily, while county cricket was impossible, he continued as a coach and a professional during the 1890s. However, his tragic story ended in 1900, when he caught a chill attending John Thewlis's funeral, and died a few days later.[1223]

The effects of playing the game often took a toll in old age. George Pinder's hands suffered a terrible battering during his many years as wicketkeeper. In 1898, 'Old Ebor' wrote that his finger joints are 'gnarled and distorted, and he can move some of them in a way which nature's anatomy never intended they should be used.'[1224] Charlie Ullathorne was another who told 'Old Ebor' of cricket injuries. He demonstrated how damaged his fingers were, and recalled a match in Wellingborough where he misjudged a catch and was hit on the knuckles. The team went on to Uppingham, where Roger Iddison insisted Ullathorne play or act as scorer, which would have meant he received £3 10s, instead of £6. So he played and as a result his fingers were permanently deformed.[1225]

Assisting each other

The increasingly competitive nature of professional cricket and the emphasis on personal performance within a team game generally seems to have worked against unionism amongst professional players. The Cricketers' Fund Friendly Society was established in 1857 to provide financial assistance to professionals who fell on hard times. It was not a great success, however, and in Sandiford's view English professionals were 'a proud group who traditionally frowned on the idea of establishing a players' union.'[1226] Despite this, there were many cases of players supporting each other on a more ad hoc basis. Specific assistance can be seen in 1865 in the way players clubbed together for particular causes, such as when Fourteen Gentlemen of the North played with the help of Grundy, Freeman, Wootton and Cuttell senior against the All-England Eleven at Hyde Park for the benefit of the five professionals who were in dispute at the time with the Yorkshire county club.[1227]

There was also considerable generosity amongst professionals when a player was injured or in trouble. Mindful that misfortune could all too easily befall any one of them, many put themselves out to assist others. The case of Isaac Hodgson illustrates how many were prepared to rally round a popular professional. In the mid-1850s, his health broke and he spent some time at Redcar recuperating, before returning for 10 more summers of seemingly endless cricket. His gruelling programme for 1866 was mentioned earlier, and under the strain, by August, his health had broken again. On the 18th, after a commitment in Shrewsbury, he went home, asking Tom Emmett to go to Tynemouth in his place for a match on the 20th. Over the winter, he was unable to take on any obligations for the 1867 season, and in the spring, news items began to appear in the press about his condition.[1228]

During the following months, the extent of public respect for Hodgson became obvious. The Bradford press suggested a benefit for him, and the idea was taken up across the town.[1229] In June, the Albion club played a game, which was attended by 1,400 people and generated £70. Dudley Hill Cricket Club raised money through another fixture, and the Bradford club hosted a match between 18 of the town and a Nottinghamshire XI, making £235. Members of the Manchester club sent £10. A subscription fund was set up, eventually eliciting £306 13s 6d, which, after expenses for the Nottinghamshire game, left Hodgson with £230. His contemporaries played their part. Hodgson's friend, Edgar Willsher, the Kent bowler, with whom he had stayed in Maidstone over the winter recuperating, sent £9 10s collected from fellow professionals in the south of England, saying that 'every cricketer in this list willingly subscribed his mite' for a much respected professional. A rough estimate of the sum raised was communicated to Hodgson just before his death and he was happy with the recommendations for how it should be used to provide for his wife.[1230]

Other players received ad hoc assistance. In 1864, Luke Greenwood fell ill when playing for Yorkshire against Surrey at The Oval and had to stay in London at his own expense. A match was organised and generated £18 for him.[1231] At the end of the 1882 season, a benefit was held for a former professional, Ted Hope, who had played for several Leeds clubs and had lost an eye in an accident. Around 2,000 people attended the match, in which several county players appeared, including Peate and Emmett.[1232] The Yorkshire county committee also made some discretionary payments, and showed concern for the wellbeing of players. In 1869, for example, £5 was awarded to Luke Greenwood.[1233]

Assistance could also extend to players' families. In June 1850, a presentation was made to the son of Tom Marsden (Marsden senior had died in 1843), to hand over 'the balance of certain subscriptions which were collected at the time of the celebrated cricketer's death, for the purpose of apprenticing the son to one of the staple trades of the town.' Young Marsden was presented with the silver cup, previously given to his father, and was promised that, should he find himself in difficulties, he could always turn to his father's friends for help.[1234] George Armitage, who played for Yorkshire in the early 1850s, died aged 32 after a lingering illness. During this period he was supported by friends, and over 200 cricketers and other people attended his funeral, many having come a considerable distance. His wife and child were left with very little, but a subscription was set up to help her open a shop.[1235]

After Thomas Hunt was killed walking back along the railway, considerable efforts were also made for his family by various clubs. Matches were held in York, where a committee was established to raise subscriptions.[1236] By the start of 1859, the huge sum of £890 had been raised, which was to be invested by trustees in the interests of the family.[1237] Included amongst those who contributed were officers and men of a regiment now stationed in India, as a sign of their gratitude for the many games they had played on the Manchester ground, which Hunt had managed when they were stationed in the city.[1238] In December 1866, Gotham Smith, a professional in Bradford, died, leaving his wife and family unprovided for. He was buried with his bat and a ball, and a fund was established to raise money for his family, organised by a Bradford club official. The local paper commented that it knew of 'no class of men more ready than cricketers to assist each other in seasons of adversity.'[1239]

Benefits for county players

It was not only injury and mishap that stimulated generosity, and more routinely benefits were arranged to recognise fine performances over time. These could be both one-off matches, or funds open for a longer period. An early subscription fund was established for Tom Marsden in the winter of 1836. Friends of Marsden (who had recently lost his wife) advertised in the *Sheffield Iris* that 'his committee' would wait at the Waterloo Tavern every day during the Christmas holidays 'to receive the amount of the Subscriptions already entered, and any other which the public think proper to forward for his benefit.'[1240]

Thirty years later, the All-England Eleven v United All-England Eleven game at Dewsbury was held for the benefit of George Anderson, but this proved to be a complete failure owing to the weather. There was only one day's play and the receipts at the gate were poor, resulting in a loss for the beneficiary. A private subscription was then set up on his behalf, and kept open until the end of the season.[1241] The following year, another benefit was held for Anderson in the form of a match between the North and South at Dewsbury. Again, however, it was not a great financial success, 'owing to the expense of securing the players.'[1242] As an aside, Anderson appears to have been a particularly unlucky player. In 1866, he returned home from a match in Kendal to discover he had been robbed of momentoes from his Australian tour.[1243]

Official county benefit matches started in 1870, awarded to the most successful players as recognition for services rendered over some years. Quite likely they were also regarded by the county committee as a useful way of encouraging players to stay loyal after the problems the county had experienced with professionals in the mid-1860s. George Anderson clearly believed his lack of a benefit from the county was 'on account of my declining to play against Surrey owing to the dispute about Willsher being no-balled. Several declined besides. I believe Roger Iddison did for one, and E.Stephenson, but they went back to the county, and each got a benefit.' However, he claimed he did not hold it against the club, and in 1895, the county club endorsed a match for Anderson between Yorkshire and Eighteen of North Yorkshire played at Bedale. He was 70 by then and, having ceased to work in a savings bank, was 'thrown on his own resources' so that friends decided to organise the game.[1244]

In 1869, both Stephenson and Iddison requested a benefit for the 1870 season. The committee decided that since the former had recently decided to retire, he should be supported first, and Iddison's request could not be considered unless Stephenson withdraw his request.[1245] Stephenson had his benefit in 1870 and Iddison two years later. In 1873, Joe Rowbotham was granted the match against Gloucestershire at Sheffield, in which the Graces appeared, and around 20,000 people attended over the three days.[1246] Requests for benefits were made some time in advance; John Thewlis made his in early 1873 for the 1875 season.

Others were turned down. In 1877, the county committee resolved that they 'cannot hold out any hope of a Benefit at Sheffield to Geo. Atkinson'.[1247] A year later, Tom Emmett (who had applied in 1876) had a successful benefit match against Gloucestershire. There was a large crowd on each of the three days and it was reported that he would receive £500 after expenses were paid.[1248] By May 1879, this sum had reached £616 and, added to the money he had made in touring Australia over the winter, he was considered to be in a 'very comfortable position.'[1249]

George Ulyett's benefit came in 1887, and at the time was by far the largest in Yorkshire's history. A benefit committee was set up in April and regular meetings held at the start of the season to make arrangements. In May, submission lists and books of one-shilling tickets were sent out, and those involved were urged not to take it for granted that Uyett would secure a 'monster benefit on account of his great popularity.' When it came, his match was also affected by the weather, but was nevertheless a considerable success. On the opening day, £347 was taken, on the second £226, but on the third, only £3 12s. In addition, over 340 donations of at least half a guinea were made and 700 one shilling tickets sold, and the subscription lists were left open until the last week of August. In May 1888, a cheque for £1,000 was presented to Ulyett during the game with the Australians.[1250]

Louis Hall was the beneficiary twice as a result of unfortunate circumstances. Originally, he was awarded the game with Surrey at Bramall Lane in 1889, a match almost guaranteed to attract a large crowd. However, he deferred his benefit in favour of the injured Billy Bates, and instead was given the corresponding fixture the following year. Unfortunately, there was little reward for his kindness. The whole of the first day was washed out, and play did not begin until 4.25pm on the second day, when there was a small crowd to witness the final hours. On the third day, just 1,500 attended, so that the money taken was just sufficient to cover costs. To add to this, the match finished early to allow Ulyett, Peel, Read, Lohmann, Wood and Shuter to travel to The Oval for the Gentlemen v Players match.[1251] Naturally disappointed, Hall asked the Bradford committee for the Middlesex game as a supplementary benefit, but the idea was rejected. Instead, he was offered free use of the ground for three days at some stage of the 1890 or 1891 seasons.[1252] Whatever value that would have been, he still approached the Yorkshire committee, which decided to give him another benefit in 1891. In the end he received £570, the fourth largest at that time.[1253]

Retirement

Most players slipped quietly out of the county scene, perhaps returning to years of club cricket, other employment and then retirement. For some this journey could take many years. After his county career came to an end rather abruptly in 1864, William Slinn's workload consisted of being a 'given man' against the touring sides for a while, engagements at public schools and universities (Oxford and then Cambridge), and professional posts at various north-west clubs – Bolton, Kendal and Burnley. As late as the 1881 census – by which time he was 54 – he was recorded as a 'professional cricketer' (whereas on previous occasions he had been described as a 'scissor grinder'). Some, such as Luke Greenwood, Louis Hall and G.P. 'Shoey' Harrison spent years as respected county umpires.[1254] Numerous players became landlords of public houses during their careers or took on that role on retirement. George Pinder took over the Nelson Inn on top of Sheffield Moor, later moving to the Lancers Hotel and another inn in Worksop in 1882.[1255] George Ulyett also took up a public house – the Vine Hotel – close to his birthplace.[1256]

For some though the story was one of poverty. Without doubt, the most famous story is that of John Thewlis, discovered by A.W.Pullin at the end of the 1890s. The journalist described the terrible circumstances in which he found him in Manchester and asked whether it was 'creditable to cricket at large, and to Yorkshire cricket in particular, that men, like John Thewlis...should be found so utterly neglected and forgotten?' Pullin wrote up Thewlis's story, causing such an outcry that the county club provided the former player with a pension.[1257] The attention given to his situation was sufficient to provoke old friends and admirers to come together and he was found a groundsman's job in 1898.

In the same series of interviews, Luke Greenwood's situation was highlighted, 'Old Ebor' noting he was 'ekeing out a precarious livelihood by laying cricket and tennis grounds, and is still more or less indebted to friends.' Offered a job with Ossett cricket club, he turned it down because he could not do the work alone and the sum involved was too small to allow him pay someone to help.[1258] Andrew Crossland was also largely forgotten by the time of his death. Described as one of the great early Yorkshire champions, he played for the county between 1844 and 1855, but Thomas notes that despite his successful career his death largely went unnoticed by any of the newspapers.[1259] Pope has chronicled the sad demise of many Yorkshire players of the 19th century, including several of those released by the club in the late 1880s and early 1890s and who died prematurely. In 1890, Joe Preston died aged only 26 after catching a cold. Irwin Grimshaw's death came in 'rather poor circumstances' in 1911, while Fred Lee passed away in 1896, aged 39, after a long illness.[1260]

Others had more productive retirements, although they were not without their stresses. Some took on coaching roles where their experience and skill was valued. Tom Emmett, for example, was a very popular coach at Rugby School until 1896 (when a change of headmaster seems to have led to him being let go in circumstances which clearly upset the player), although he later died after a period of ill-health.[1261] George Atkinson also coached at public schools – Marlborough and Rossall – where, like Emmett, he developed a number of boys who later appeared in first-class cricket.[1262] After county cricket, as well as umpiring, Louis Hall took up a post as a cricket coach at Uppingham School. He became a Liberal councillor in Batley, also taking over as Assistant Overseer of the Poor of the Borough. He was for many years a Methodist lay preacher, before dying in 1915.[1263]

Towards the end of the period under review, action was taken to try to address some of the problems which could adversely affect professionals. In his 'Introduction' to R.S.Holmes's history, Lord Hawke wrote at some length about the arrangements for the county's players, explaining – in language which we would now consider well-meaning but patronising – that his 'hobby in cricket has been the welfare of the County professionals.' He argued that insufficient attention had been paid to looking after them, and that the remuneration for professionals was 'even now none too good. He has to live well, for after a day's hard cricket he must have good food and good lodging. The wear and tear of the season, with its numerous journeys and the constant change, involve a strain of which the public have little conception.'[1264] According to Thomas, Hawke 'brought in revolutionary changes that made county cricket as we know it today.' Players had been paid talent money of £1 for a 50 or six wickets, but, appreciating that 20 on a bad wicket or three wickets on a good pitch were worth more than better performances on more helpful wickets, Hawke introduced merit marks. He kept a detailed record and distributed merit money at his annual gathering at Wighill Park. He also brought in winter pay.[1265] Thus, the county club took significant steps to look after those who had served it well.

Amateurs

Professional cricketers were the majority of those who turned out for Yorkshire in the 19th century, but the side also included a number of amateurs. The distinction between professionals and amateurs was the great fault line in English sport, going back in time to the 18th century when, as Sandiford put it, 'The amateur was the gentleman with the bat, and the professional was the labourer with the ball.'[1266]

Class distinctions and concern with social status were fundamental to the way in which Victorian cricket operated, shaping how it was played, who led the teams, the design and layout of county cricket grounds, and the way in which scores were reported. Middle- and upper-class views about how the game should be played, codes of conduct on the field, and changing social conditions which brought together 'the values of a striving, enterprising liberal elite with the refined and restrained world of upper-class good manners and style' all helped to strengthen and justify the role of the amateur in sport.[1267] Concern with maintaining status could be difficult and, as Sandiford has put it, snobbery led to 'shamateurism' in Victorian county cricket.[1268] Such hypocrisy did not go unnoticed in the Yorkshire press. In 1879, a long letter in the *Sheffield Independent* mocked the way in which 'gentlemen' players took payments well in excess of expenses, which the correspondent said was 'ridiculous'.[1269] Allowing such views to be voiced did not, however, prevent the same paper publishing first-class averages separately for professionals and amateurs.[1270]

A total of 62 amateurs appeared for Yorkshire in county games up to and including the 1893 season. Of these, 13 played in just one game and 35 in fewer than five. Together, they made a total of 1,228 appearances for Yorkshire, with Hawke, Jackson, Smith and Sellers between them accounting for 75%.[1271] Many played in the matches at the end of the season at Scarborough in Festival games organised by Lord Londesborough (H.E.Rhodes, for example, only played for Yorkshire in 10 Festival games between 1878 and 1883), and ten were born outside the county. Because most amateurs appeared infrequently for Yorkshire it was often argued by critics of the club that the committee was biased against them, and there was a significant body of opinion – regularly reflected, for example, in the columns of the *Yorkshire Post* – suggesting that the county needed to tap into the amateur talent of the county more.

There are grounds for thinking that the Yorkshire committee had a poor opinion of the ability of many amateur players of the time, and that these views were often justified. Many of those tried by Yorkshire were simply not up to county standard despite fine records in club cricket. Charles Landon, a great success with the Yorkshire Gentlemen and constantly pressed by those who wanted to see amateurs in the county side, made five ducks in the nine innings he played in first-class cricket. Frederick Andrews was invited to play for Yorkshire against the MCC and Middlesex during the 1870s, but declined because of his self-confessed poor-quality fielding.[1272] Despite strong recommendations from A.E.Stoddart, the Middlesex captain, George Thornton failed miserably on his Yorkshire debut in 1891, making a pair against Kent and taking no wickets.[1273] During the 1880s, even Hawke was the subject of criticism on a number of occasions, including when Yorkshire continued to pick him even after he had been dropped by Cambridge University.[1274]

Others were positive about the amateur talent that was available and there was much criticism of a lack of opportunity for such players amongst the complaints of the campaigners for the reform of Yorkshire cricket.[1275] In 1882, the *Yorkshire Post* bemoaned the feeble batting of the Yorkshire tail end, adding that it could not understand why the county 'should therefore persist as they have done in the past in almost entirely ignoring the claims of our best amateur bats'. It noted that several other county clubs found three or four gentlemen essential.[1276] A few weeks later, the same paper was scathing of the failure of the county committee to explain why Forbes and Leatham had not played against the Australians at Bradford, and was also critical of the selection of L.G.Hill, arguing that others such as E.T.Hirst and C.H.Marriott were entitled to be chosen first.[1277]

There were in fact obstacles to selecting amateurs. Firstly, many were born outside the county and so were not qualified to play. Clearly, this was waived on a number of occasions, most notably in the case of Lord Hawke (born in Lincolnshire), but the criticism expressed when 'outsiders' were played showed there was support for the convention. W.F.Forbes was widely admired in the 1870s and early 1880s, but was not from Yorkshire, while the fact that he had been born in Surrey was held against C.J.Gifkins when he was on the brink of county selection, even though he did appear twice in 1880 following success with Hull Town. Secondly, the demands of county cricket appeared increasingly incompatible with the lifestyles of many Yorkshire amateurs. With some exceptions they were not men of great private means, but many were businessmen or employees of Yorkshire firms.[1278] By the late 1870s, county cricket was establishing itself as a time-consuming occupation and few could afford to jeopardise a career for sport, particularly with no guarantee of a regular place and with only expenses reimbursed. In 1884, one young prospect, J.W.Hudson, wrote to the *Yorkshire Post* to comment on correspondence that had suggested other players should be tried. He said people overlooked the question of availability, adding that the public were unaware that he and others mentioned were not able to leave their professional duties to assist their county.[1279]

The county committee's concerns were also about reliability and flexibility. What this amounted to was expecting players to appear when needed, and with amateurs this was less easy than with professionals. In August 1881, J.H.Wood left early during the game at The Oval against Surrey and was absent when his turn came to bat. Yorkshire still won by nine wickets thanks to a second-innings 8-22 from Tom Emmett. Despite the victory, the *Sheffield Daily Telegraph* asked, 'Is there any encouragement to the Yorkshire Executive to play gentlemen in good matches? They have to be run after in the first instance, and when they are secured they are not to be depended on.'[1280]

The following year, the *Yorkshire Post* also noted that whilst there were a number of capable amateurs around, the committee 'after the many disappointments they have had on their not being able to play at the last moment, and consequent trouble etc., appear inclined to prefer relying on the professional class if they can secure adequate representatives.'[1281] Not dependent on cricket for a living, and so not having to be as 'obliging' as the professional, many amateurs did not fit the committee's idea of a compliant cricketer. Some were regarded as temperamental. Having hoped that they would be able to include Hawke and Lumb, the *Leeds Times* commented in 1884 'that all the committee could do was to offer them places in the county team whenever they feel disposed to play.'[1282] Lumb, an amateur who ran a worsted spinning business employing some 500 people, was quite open in 1883 in revealing that when first asked by Yorkshire to play he had said he would not do so, so strongly did he feel about the way amateurs were 'snubbed' in the county. Only when friends pressed him and correspondence on the subject appeared in the press, did he agree. Unfortunately, his county career was dogged by health problems and he died aged 37.[1283]

Another amateur, F.S.Jackson, caused quite a stir at the start of his Yorkshire career. After making his county debut in July 1890 aged 19, following a first year at Cambridge University, he was approached to play again. Initially, he advised Wostinholm that he had 'ricked' his back and so declined. Before this letter was communicated to the committee, Jackson wired Bramall Lane to say he could play. In the absence of Wostinholm, an emergency committee meeting was held at which it was decided to invite Jackson to play all the remaining games. For the match against Middlesex at Bradford in mid-August, Jackson replaced G.P.Harrison, who had recently been championed by Lord Hawke. It then emerged that Jackson only wanted to play up to and including the Surrey game, and end the season appearing for I Zingari. When he arrived at Bradford, Hawke was furious that his selection had been ignored, and resigned on the spot as captain, originally threatening not to play at all. He also objected strongly (and perhaps hypocritically in view of his own record in the 1880s) to amateurs playing only when they felt like it, and to Jackson not making Yorkshire his first choice. At a committee meeting on 19 August, Hawke withdrew his resignation once the misunderstanding was explained. It was then decided that since Jackson was already committed to I Zingari, he would not be selected by Yorkshire again until 1891. The matter was resolved.[1284]

Other amateurs dropped out at short notice and the *Yorkshire Post* commented on 'the many disappointments' Yorkshire had experienced with 'amateurs failing to keep their appointments at the last moment.'[1285] Robert Sidgwick, who appeared for Yorkshire nine times in 1882, was chosen against the Australians at Dewsbury and 'though on Thursday expected to play, did not put in an appearance', being replaced by C.W.Landon. He was clearly forgiven as he played in the game with the Australians at Middlesbrough, but his poor performances limited his appearances.[1286]

Eleven years later against Essex, there were more problems. Hawke was unable to lead the team, and Arthur Sellers was appointed in his place. Over the weekend preceding the Monday start, he too dropped out and it was arranged that F.S.Jackson should play in his place, although on the morning of the game he did not appear. (The shambles was added to by Mounsey and Waller fielding initially but with injured hands, and eventually being replaced by Wilson and Needham, although the latter was recorded as 'absent' in the Yorkshire first innings of 44).[1287] Such behaviour from professionals would not have been tolerated and when, for example, John Wilson failed to turn up for a game at Huddersfield in 1887, there was an inquiry, although it found that his absence had not been due to any fault of his own and he appeared later in the season.[1288]

Amateurs were also often unable to play at short notice. R.W.Frank from Scarborough, the long-time 2nd XI captain, objected strongly to committee attempts to make use of him at the last minute. This, and an injury picked up when facing Sammy Woods, help explain his limited first-class appearances.[1289]

Others felt the way the club organised itself worked against them. E.W.Hirst, an amateur from Huddersfield, who appeared for Yorkshire in 1881, questioned why the club could not follow the example of southern counties and arrange a series of away games in a two-week tour, adding that if this was done, 'I feel sure the committee would have the pick of the best amateur talent in the county, as many gentlemen would be only too glad to take their holiday in this way.'[1290] Only on odd occasions, such as when Henry Hill visited Sheffield in 1889 to watch a game with Surrey and found himself playing in place of an 'indisposed' Fred Lee, could amateurs respond at the last minute.[1291]

Finally, there were other, specific reasons why certain amateurs did not make it. Joe Frank was seen by many during the 1880s as suitable county material. He was arguably the best medium/fast-medium bowler of his day in local amateur cricket, but his career was dogged by controversy over his bowling action. In 1880, this issue blew into a storm when he appeared for Scarborough and District against the Australian tourists. During their second innings, Alec Bannerman objected to his style and suggested he threw the ball. Frank appeared for Yorkshire against I Zingari at Scarborough the following season and for the Gentlemen v Players at The Oval in 1883, but, in Thomas's words, 'It is almost certain that the doubt about his action meant the committee refrained from playing him in championship matches.'[1292] Thus, despite the ongoing critique of the dangers of professionalism threatening the spirit of the game, the influence of amateurs in Yorkshire cricket was quite limited. Few except Lord Hawke made an impact until the 1890s. Led by an amateur, an increasingly well-drilled county side made up mainly of professionals emerged in the last decade of the 19th century and came to dominate English cricket.

CHAPTER EIGHT

WATCHING THE GAME

The 19th century saw the emergence of mass spectator sport, a phenomenom which has continued to this day. According to Vamplew, 'Gate-money cricket had its origins back in the eighteenth century, but was further stimulated from the 1840s when the peripatetic professional teams took advantage of the railways to tour the country playing local sides, often giving them odds.' He argues that for two decades they dominated gate-money cricket until the paying public showed they preferred to watch more competitive cricket between teams with which they could identify.[1293] To Collins, until the 1870s commercial sport found it hard to develop a sustainable structure or national mass market. Thereafter, the rise in real wages for the British working class in the last third of the nineteenth century, along with urbanisation, helped create this mass market with 'the spending power to support regular, continuous sporting events throughout a season.'[1294] This chapter examines what attracted Yorkshire people – mostly, but not always, men – to attend cricket matches in the 19th century and what they found when they got there.

What attracted spectators to watch cricket

At this distance, it is hard to say exactly what encouraged people in Victorian Yorkshire to watch cricket, but it seems clear that there were a variety of reasons. It is fair to assume that, just as much as for those playing the game, cricket provided excitement and fun, and was the focus for socialising for many who watched. There was the anticipation of the big game, as well as the experience of the event. In the early days of Sheffield cricket, contests such as that between All-England and Twenty-Two of Yorkshire in May 1825 created a significant stir in the town, and at 'an early hour every path which led to Darnall was crowded, and the fields presented lines of active pedestrians. The anxiety to reach the ground of contention was singularly contrasted with the eager debates upon the various merits of the players, which caused many at intervals to pause upon the road.' Six thousand people had entered the ground by eleven o'clock and 'the influx of persons at the various entrances continued at a rate of more than fifty each minute.' Such was the interest that the *Sheffield Independent* complained that no-one had sent it any correspondence for publication, commenting, 'They must be all gone to the Cricket Match. Mr Steer must bear the blame of this.'[1295]

Twenty years later, the match between the West and North Ridings in 1843 at Thirsk generated huge interest (which turned out to be unjustified as most of the promised stars failed to appear). It was reported that, 'This is truly an event in cricketing affairs, and since we intimated a fortnight ago that arrangements for such a match were in progress, excited expectation has been on tiptoe; the gathering from all parts of the county will undoubtedly be immense.'[1296]

The excitement was added to where the local side defeated a local rival or supposedly superior opponent. In 1841, when their team beat Leeds, the joy of the inhabitants of Dalton was 'most excessive', and at the end of the game between Bradford and Dalton there was the 'most tremendous cheering, shaking of hands, waving of hats, and hearty welcomes greeted this triumph.' This was added to because of the 'unfair means' resorted to by some of the Dalton men.[1297] In 1855, towards the end of the United Eleven's game with 20 of Bradford and District (won by one wicket), 'the most intense excitement prevailed amongst the spectators during the last half-hour, as it was equally uncertain up to the last ball who would be victorious.'[1298] In 1870, the Sheffield and Lascelles Hall game for £100 aroused considerable attention. People in Huddersfield followed news of the game and:

> on Tuesday night a crowd of people assembled on the railway station platform, expecting that the match would be terminated and that the victors would be returning home by the late train. Some disappointment was experienced when it was reported that the contest would be renewed on Wednesday, but in the evening of that day a still larger crowd assembled at the station, and hearty cheers broke out from them as the cricketers stepped from the carriages.[1299]

As they grew in number and significance, county matches also generated a lot of excitement. When Yorkshire beat MCC by one wicket at Lord's in 1870 the victory was 'hailed with frantic delight by the Yorkshire element of the spectators.'[1300] In 1879, reporting on the win against Gloucestershire, the *Sheffield Independent* commented that the scene which followed:

> beggars description. The spectators gathered in a crowd round the pavilion, and cheered the Yorkshiremen to the echo, the names of Peate, Bates, Ulyett and Emmett being called out....It was nearly half an hour before the excitement calmed down. The ladies and gentlemen in the pavilion were in a state of wild enthusiasm, handkerchiefs were waved and hats thrown up on all sides, while the Yorkshiremen came in for the most generous personal congratulations.

The *Sheffield Daily Telegraph* added that 'there was a perfect babel of noises, hats, sticks and umbrellas going up in the air', and reported 'How the gallery yelled, how the pit roared, how the boxes gruffly shouted "Hip, hip, hurrah!" and how that wildly exciting display called a 'sensation' pervaded the private box of the ladies.'[1301]

A pre-requisite for many spectators was some element of tension created by the balance between the competing teams. Despite the availability of cheap excursions elsewhere, it was reported that at the match between the Gentlemen and the Players of Yorkshire at York in 1850 there was a respectable company present, 'amongst whom the celebrity of the competitors, and the equality of the sides, excited much interest.'[1302] In contrast, in 1851, when Yorkshire played Lancashire shortly after a game with Surrey, 'little interest was excited', especially on the first day, when hardly any spectators turned up. Efforts were made to balance up the sides, and four players were given to Lancashire.[1303] The absence of the five Yorkshire stars from the side in 1865 for the game with Surrey also meant the game apparently 'excited little or no interest.'[1304] When they were all present, however, the chance to see some well-known names and watch high-quality performances was an attraction which drew the crowds. When Grange and Sadler played their famous single-wicket match in October 1857 on Woodhouse Moor it was noted that 'a great number of workpeople were neglecting their work, and betting money which they could ill afford to lose.'[1305] In September 1860, the All-England against Twenty-Two of Leeds match saw a large crowd, 'attracted, no doubt, by the deserved reputation of the England Eleven, particularly George Anderson, now considered by many the first batsman in the world, and Hayward, who so astonished the Yankees in the Transatlantic matches.'[1306]

The arrival of the Australian team in 1878 created a lively atmosphere in Huddersfield. It was their first tour of England and at all the railway stations on the route into the town scores of people waited to catch a glimpse of the team as it passed. At the main station, the Secretary of the Huddersfield Cricket and Athletic Club, several JPs, club patrons and members, as well as numerous cricketers, waited on the platform. Around 300 were present in total, even though the Australians turned up over two hours late and many people went to the wrong platform. Once the train had arrived, the crowd quickly enveloped the carriages and watched with great interest as each cricketer walked through the crowd, to be greeted by 'that sort of lull which generally precedes a salvo of vocal artillery on great occasions.'[1307]

Novelty could add to the excitement but not necessarily guarantee a crowd, particularly as cricket developed and audiences appeared to become more demanding. Up to the early 1860s, matches between sides of men with one arm and one leg attracted large (if voyeuristic) crowds. According to reports, some 3,000 people turned up in Leeds for a game in 1863, when the 'running of most of the one-legs caused a great deal of amusement, some of them even throwing in their bats and turning a summersault to regain the crease.'[1308] When the Australian Aboriginal side played at Hunslet in 1868 there was also a 'pretty numerous gathering of spectators', although disappointment was expressed at the fielding, and the crowd appeared more satisfied with the demonstration of spear and boomerang-throwing at the conclusion of the game.[1309] On the other hand, the visit to Dewsbury of the same side did not attract much interest and the crowd was 'very meagre.'[1310] A similarly mixed response was seen in Middlesbrough.[1311]

For others, attending a game was just something to do, and the fact it involved cricketers was unimportant. For those who regarded themselves as fashionable, a match was an opportunity to see and be seen. In 1843, a match between teams from Leeds and Bradford involving officers of the 32nd Regiment drew hundreds of spectators, described as 'the wealthy, the beautiful, and the industrious – the day was specifically set apart as a day of pleasure.'[1312] Commenting on the Scarborough Festival 40 years later, the *Leeds Times* noted that some of those present saw 'cricket matches as legitimate occasions for small-talk and flirtation.'[1313] And as we saw earlier, the crowd that attended at Scarborough after Yorkshire had won the county title in 1893 apparently included many who were not regular followers of the game, but were there for the occasion and to be associated with something popular and successful.

Cricket matches were often an exciting opportunity for spectators to bet, which they did in huge numbers. In September 1855, when the All-England Eleven played Bradford and the game came to a tight finish, 'The spectators – many of whom had backed the Twenty at odds – now looked on with breathless anxiety.'[1314] As mentioned earlier, betting seems to have been the reason for cricket continuing throughout the autumn and into winter some years, especially in the 1840s. Even in 1860, one single-wicket game in Otley took place in early December and despite the very wet and unfavourable weather on both days attracted a great deal of interest in Leeds, Bradford, Otley, Guiseley and other places, largely for the betting.[1315] By the 1880s, it was becoming less visible at cricket matches and the *Yorkshire Post* reflected that 'the absence of betting is one of the most convincing proofs of the high and elevating tone of the game. At one time it was the custom to advertise the most important matches for so many guineas a side. At present we are free from the injurious associations of the betting man, and long may we remain so.'[1316]

Size of the crowds

Identifying the number of people who watched cricket in the 19th century is difficult, if not impossible, with any degree of accuracy. There is information in the press, although mainly for county games or the most important club matches, but it is hard to say how reliable much of it is. Journalists reporting the matches usually made estimates (which may or may not have been accurate) and almost all attendances quoted are in round thousands, suggesting their numbers involved a lot of guesswork. Where figures for the same match are given in two papers they sometimes differ. However, at the distance of over 100 years this data, and the more reliable official figures available towards the end of the century, are the best we have.

Most small club games throughout the period – for which data is generally not available – were probably no better attended than today. Club officials, friends and relatives, other players, interested spectators, passers-by and club patrons would attend games, but not many more. However, more important club matches were often well supported and attendances at many matches were large, particularly compared with today. They also measure up favourably with many county games of the time. Partly this was because the games were exciting spectacles which could generate much local feeling, but it also reflected the fact that many club sides included well-known professionals. Unable or unwilling to travel too far to watch the county side, the population of many towns had quality players who turned out regularly for their local clubs, and the cost of seeing them was either nothing or 1d or 3d, rather than 6d for the county match and the cost of a train fare.

A few examples give a sense of the numbers involved. In 1819, the *York Herald* reported that the game between Leeds and Boroughbridge on Harrogate Common was attended by nearly 3,000 people.[1317] Games between Knaresborough and Husthwaite in 1828 attracted 2,000 at Boroughbridge and 3,000 on Derring's plain near Helperby.[1318] The match between Leeds and Knaresborough in 1829 had an attendance 'more numerous....than we ever remember to have witnessed on any similar occasion', although reports suggested that some simply had too much time on their hands due to 'the difficulties of the times' and would have liked to have been elsewhere working.[1319] High-quality single-wicket games also proved highly attractive. In August 1833, when Tom Marsden and Fuller Pilch competed at Hyde Park, upwards of 12,000 paid to see two of the best players in England.[1320]

In the 1840s, matches in Bradford regularly attracted 2,000-4,000 people. In October 1840, 'Monday and Tuesday being what is termed Barkerend tide, the moor presented a most animated appearance', and two well-contested games were watched by 3,000-4,000 (although in comparison, 10,000-12,000 attended the Bradford Moor races later).[1321] The game between Malton and Kirkbymoorside in 1842 attracted around 1,000 spectators, paying 3d each, and when a single-wicket match was played the next summer in Ripon it was claimed that 'nearly the whole of the citizens [of the town] and several parties from a distance' were present.[1322] Big crowds viewed games in the Sheffield area. The Sheffield-Nottingham game in 1842 appealed to the largest crowd at Hyde Park for several years, helped by the day being 'beautifully fine and above all, *Saint*

Monday.'[1323]

Games continued to attract good crowds at all levels in the 1860s and 1870s, encouraged by the improvements in the club game and drawn by the many touring-team matches and growing county programme. The crowd might be even greater if a game was played at the time of a feast, or if it was a significant contest. For example, the 6d and 1s entrance fee did not put off 'a large circle of spectators' at the Rifle Parade ground in Huddersfield for Lascelles Hall against Stockton in July 1863. Even games played by smaller teams could draw in spectators. There was a 'very large' attendance of spectators at the game between Kirkstall Educational Society and Shipley in 1862[1324], and in August 1867, Brighouse Alexandra against Rastrick United was reportedly watched by a crowd of more than 2,000 paying spectators on a Monday.[1325] Between 4,000 and 5,000 watched the Holbeck and Hunslet match in 1879, a contest which was characterised by unrest in the crowd about certain umpiring decisions.[1326]

Cup matches attracted even more attention. In September 1882, between 8,000 and 10,000 people saw Saturday's play at the Emsley Challenge Cup Final at Holbeck, with many more returning on the Monday to see it finished after rain had caused a delay.[1327] Three years later, 8,000 attended the Heavy Woollen District Challenge Cup final at Dewsbury, some 3,000 more than the 1883 game.[1328] As a result, it seems reasonable to argue that a crowd of 1,000-2,000 was unremarkable in Yorkshire club cricket, and sides such as Lascelles Hall, St John's Huddersfield, Dewsbury, Bradford, Hull Town or the major Sheffield clubs could attract several times that number on occasions.

Games with touring sides – initially the professional XIs and then overseas visitors - were also big draws, as we saw earlier. Seeing the famous names and watching the local stars pitting their skills against them naturally aroused great interest. The All-England v 20 of Sheffield game in 1846 attracted around 5,000 on the first and third days and around 6,000 on the second.[1329] Some 2,000 gathered on one day at Boston Spa when the All-England Eleven played the local team in 1863, and at Holbeck in 1877, 6,000-8,000 packed the ground at the start of the game with the United South of England. In 1873, 14,000 paid for admission to the Twelve of All-England game with Twenty-Four of Yorkshire at Royal Park, Leeds, with 7,000 on one day.[1330]

On his own, W.G.Grace was a major attraction when he played in Yorkshire. In 1873, his first appearance in Bradford was the cause of the very large crowd at the United South of England Eleven v 18 of Bradford match.[1331] At Bramall Lane he was a huge draw the same year, and at lunch on one day 'an immense crowd' ran to the enclosure gate to get a closer view.[1332] Grace was also a big attraction in Huddersfield in July 1875 at the North v South game, despite the weather. The ground was full on the third day, with the top part lined with wagons covered with spectators. The fences at the bottom end were 'ridged with sightseers [and] the gallery of faces at the top part of the ground about fifty deep.' It proved to be a financial success, providing a large surplus with which to pay off the debt incurred in laying down the ground at a cost of £400 a few years before.[1333]

The Australians were an even bigger draw. When they played Eighteen of Bradford in 1880, at least 8,000 watched the second day's play, and similar crowds attended matches throughout their tours across Yorkshire.[1334] In 1882, despite the weather for the game at Bradford, the *Leeds Times* commented, 'Didn't the "tykes" muster in force!' A few weeks later, nearly 20,000 were present at Bramall Lane on the first day and 13,000 paid for admission on the second. Total gate money amounted to £930, of which half went to the Australian team.[1335] In May 1890, when Yorkshire played the Australians at Bramall Lane, 'so great was the crush in the enclosure that many persons were unable to find a seat.'[1336] More than 60,000 attended the Players of England v The Australians at Sheffield in 1884.[1337]

County cricket also gained in popularity from the 1860s onwards. In July 1881, there was a huge crowd at Sheffield for Yorkshire v Lancashire, when even the organisers 'were astonished to observe the immense stream of persons which poured through the turnstiles.' By mid-afternoon, the ground was full, 'with a complete square of people ten or twenty deep, and with every 'coign of vantage' more than fully occupied.'[1338] In 1887, the added attraction of it being local man George Ulyett's benefit match led to over 12,000 paying on the first day to see Yorkshire and Surrey at Sheffield, and 'attracted by the prospects of a good match and anxious to do the beneficiare a turn, an immense number of spectators had assembled long before the time fixed for a start'.[1339]

Composition of the crowd

No thorough analysis of the composition of the crowds which attended Yorkshire matches is possible, but some anecdotal evidence exists within newspaper reports of the county matches, particularly in the 1880s and 1890s as cricket coverage expanded. Some reporters liked to suggest that major games attracted a broad range of people. The *Sheffield Independent* commented that at the Marsden-Pilch game at Hyde Park in 1833 the crowd included 'every grade of society from the peasant to the lord, to witness a trial of skill between two such proficients.'[1340] In 1855, a reporter who attended the United England v 20 of Bradford and District game suggested that the crowd on the third day included both 'ladies and gentlemen of station, and a large influx of the working classes, from the town and district.'[1341]

Other references to the crowd were more specific. In 1848, when All-England played Sixteen of Sheffield at Hyde Park, 'many of the leading gentry, professional men, merchants and manufacturers honoured the proceedings with their presence.'[1342] In 1863, an advert in the *Leeds Times* for the All-England game against Twenty-Two of Yorkshire at Leeds Royal Park, under a heading 'Interesting to the working classes', stated that the All-England Eleven had agreed 'in order for the working classes to see them, they will play up to six o'clock on the Saturday evening.'[1343] Many years later, another writer commented that, a big match brought out many men who rarely attended other places of amusement:

> The grinder tears himself away from his wheel, the cutler's toil is suspended for a while, the forgeman and the miner leave their laborious occupations, and the manufacturer and the merchant throw in their lot with their poorer bretheren in their desire to do homage to the Genius of Cricket.[1344]

On days when play coincided with the half-holiday enjoyed by shop assistants, they came in after lunch, whilst towards the close of play, clerks were often noted hurrying in to catch the final overs.

The Sheffield press viewed spectators from out of town with some amusement. In July 1889, the *Daily Telegraph* reported that:

> Tuesday is generally the countryman's day. Bucolic looking farmers from the Doncaster and Worksop districts, looking as well fed and beefy as their choice cattle; pale-faced men from the mining districts, who have snatched a few hours from their gloomy working life to bask in the sunshine; and strong armed, ruddy-faced labourers fresh from the turnip fields, jostle each other in the race for a seat from which the match may be witnessed with the minimum of discomfort.

It also noted that excursionists from Rotherham, Mexborough, Worksop, Doncaster, Chesterfield and other places poured into Sheffield for the game.[1345] Four years later, the same paper described the holiday crowd in equally colourful terms, noting that 'grinders fresh from their unyielding horses.... cutlers with the stamp of the workshop writ large upon their dingy aprons and faces, swart forgemen from Attercliffe and Brightside, and cunning artificers in silver, crowd together with the marks of their calling fresh upon them.'[1346] For all this variety, however, the crowd was generally not a particularly lively spectacle. Dark clothing was almost universal, with only the military and some female spectators providing colour.

The vast majority of spectators were men, but women did go to cricket, making up a small but noticeable proportion of the crowd, albeit usually accompanied by fathers, husbands, brothers or friends. In July 1884, the reporter sent into the crowd for the Players of England against the Australian match at Sheffield, commented that 'many of the ladies seemed to be as familiar with the names of the performers, and to appreciate as keenly the leading features of the game, and generally to be as much interested as any of the gentlemen.' At the same match, the excitement led to one story of a lady receiving a message from her washerwoman to say that she could not come in as she was going to the cricket. On trying to find a replacement, the lady discovered that several others were 'going wi' t'mester to t'match.'[1347]

References to women almost always included mention of their appearance, journalists of the period frequently dwelling on the presence of 'the fair sex' in the crowd, as they put it. Occasionally, reporters noticed more than just colourful dresses. For example, the *Yorkshire Gazette* in 1834 regretted that there had been no accommodation for ladies in the new ground at York, although there were plenty of booths for gentlemen. It recommended that they erect a tent or stand for ladies in order to increase the number who watched the game.[1348] However, journalists often found it hard not to be patronising. In 1863, in a report on the Huddersfield v Holmfirth game, the reporter commented that 'Such was the interest taken by two or three beautiful young ladies, that they had books, in which they diligently noted down the progress of the game; their hopes, their fears no doubt, oscillating thermometer-like as their favourite swains excelled or otherwise in the game.'[1349]

At times, the make-up of the crowd appeared to worry seemingly easily alarmed journalists. At the same game against the Australians in 1884, one reporter commented that:

> the working class element was present in such force that the whole place was practically at their mercy - to go where they liked, to do as they pleased; but they really constituted themselves as the guardians of the peace, and quickly brought any offender to book who attempted to secure an advantage at the expense of his neighbours.[1350]

Another reporter was more concerned at the health of those he saw. In 1893, in an article entitled 'Stunted Weaklings at Bramall Lane', the *Manchester Guardian* feared:

> it would have been impossible to find in England such another crowd of stunted weaklings as that which we saw some time ago at Bramall Lane. Thousand after thousand of young fellows passed before us, not one of whom would have been accepted by a recruiting sergeant. When we see a crowd of Sheffield cutlers or Lancashire "hands" we are tempted to wish for the return of the "good old days" when Englishmen were compelled to practice martial exercises.[1351]

Getting to the game

Perhaps nothing illustrates the scale of change that took place during the reign of Queen Victoria than the revolution in transport. At the start of the period, stage coaches were still running; by the end, motor cars were just appearing. In between, we saw the rapid expansion of the rail network. Spectators got to cricket matches in different ways. When the All-England XI played in Sheffield in 1825, 'all routes to Darnall were thronged with pedestrians, horses, gigs and waterloos.'[1352] For the 1846 match between All-England Eleven and Twenty of Sheffield, 'vehicles of every description, and groups of pedestrians, thronged our streets early during the mornings of the three days, and hundreds availed themselves of the advantages of railway accommodation.'[1353] Using the roads was not always easy. In 1864, the *Sheffield Independent* welcomed the fact that spectators:

> will no longer have to wade ankle deep in mud to get to it [the ground]. The improvements in Bramall Lane will, it is expected, be completed in a short time, and the approach will be rendered easy and comfortable and *clean*, both for pedestrians, and the more fortunate people who go down to cricket grounds in carriages.[1354]

Transport companies responded to the increased demand for cricket. In 1846, the Sheffield and Manchester Railway Company put on cheap trips and thousands of people used them in early September to travel to and from Sheffield for the game at Hyde Park.[1355] In August 1864, trains were laid on when All-England played Harrogate, leaving Wellington Station, Leeds, at 10 am each morning. First-class travel to Starbeck was 3s 6d, covered carriages 1s 6d.[1356] On big occasions, excursion trains brought in thousands from many miles away. In 1869, for example, the crowd for the All-England Eleven v United All England Eleven game at Dewsbury (for George Anderson's benefit) included numerous spectators from Leeds, Bradford, Huddersfield, Wakefield and other West Riding towns, as well as from Lancashire.[1357] In 1875, a special train was laid on from Leeds to Hull for the North v South game, leaving at 7am and returning twelve hours later, for a fare of 2s 6d.[1358]

Linking up with the railway network became a concern for some clubs. In the early 1880s, when the Bradford Park Avenue venue was being developed, the ground committee sought a promise from the Great Northern Railway that they would place a station nearby, bringing it within five minutes of the centre of the town. The company opened a new station in late 1880, close to the ground so that visitors from Leeds could then ride directly to the cricket, although there were complaints that the journey between Leeds and Bradford was very slow after a game and involved inconvenient changes.[1359] In 1893, the availability of the rail system was still considered to have an influence on the game. Reporting on the North and East Ridings Cricket Club, the *Leeds Mercury* commented that

Middlesbrough and the towns in the North Riding are 'almost as inaccessible as in the old coaching days, and....no reliance whatever can be placed on the trains in this district arriving so that play can be begun at the advertised time.'[1360]

Once near the grounds the scene could be one of confusion for big games. When the North played the South at Huddersfield in 1875 the roads were packed with pedestrians, buses and waggonnettes as spectators struggled to get to the match to get a glimpse of W.G.Grace.[1361] In the 1890s, the streets around Bramall Lane were full some time before the start of play, often becoming unpleasantly congested. As a result, 'All along the main route, by means of Porter Street or the Moor, crowds filled the side-walks, all with a common goal, that of a seat inside the ground.'[1362]

Spectators then had to get through the gates, which might involve queuing. The basis for making a commercial success of organising cricket matches was the ability to enclose a ground to prevent people from watching without paying. Despite this, some still attempted to get in free. In October 1830, the owners of Hyde Park warned on their adverts for the Wednesday v County of York game that they would prosecute anyone found trespassing on the walls after damage had been done at an earlier game. Police constables were deployed to watch for people trying to sneak in. Similar warnings were made nearly ten years later.[1363] In 1848, a shoemaker was charged with doing 16s of damage to the new wall at the New Cricket Ground, where Dalton were playing Knaresborough. A large number of men had climbed over and damaged it. The shoemaker claimed that he had only gone to rescue a child in his protection who had been swept over by the pressure of the crowd. Perhaps unsurprisingly, the court did not believe him and he was fined 1s and 9s 6d costs.[1364]

For big games, tickets were available from a range of outlets such as shops (including tobaccanists and opticians), public houses, newspaper offices and hairdressers.[1365] However, even armed with a ticket, spectators had to wait, and manned entrances could become congested for big games. Occasionally, attempts were made to steal the takings. In 1853, an incident took place at the United England Eleven v Rotherham game, when:

> A party of suspicious-looking characters approached the entrance in a body, and, whilst Sergeant Timms was endeavouring to prevent any from passing in without paying, one of the men adroitly laid hold of the box in which the cash was deposited. Timms, who had from the first suspected some evil designs on their part, wisely kept an eye on the money, and, observing the movement, he seized hold of the box, whilst another policeman, who stood near, seconded his efforts; and thus the rogues escaped, but the cash was preserved.[1366]

Entry to the ground for Yorkshire matches became better organised in the 1870s as the crowds grew and the need to ensure entrance money was collected efficiently increased. In 1872, Bramall Lane installed a set of turnstiles, a relatively new invention, paid for by the county club, which meant that 'the old system of checking has been rendered useless.'[1367] During the decade, measures were also taken at Dewsbury to ensure that there was no unauthorised entrance to games, and turnstiles were used at Huddersfield in 1876, and at Holbeck for the Feast game with Lascelles Hall in 1878.[1368] In the early 1870s, it was impossible to charge admission money at the North Marine Road ground in Scarborough but after 1877 improvements were made and the field enclosed with a wall.[1369] The speed of arrangements for letting people in was not always considered adequate, and in June 1882 there were complaints at the Australian game at Sheffield. Around midday, people 'came into the ground in shoals' and the keepers of the turnstiles could not let them in fast enough. The queues increased for over an hour. Several hundred spectators then inspected the wicket before play started, only being dispersed by the sound of a gong.[1370]

Club members were often reminded in newspaper advertisements that they must have their subscription cards with them to gain admittance, probably because many forgot and added to the delays at the gates. Money and check takers were engaged to police the entrances, doing their best to keep certain people out. Men with dogs were barred from many grounds, and in 1863, one venue advertised very specifically that it would not allow in naval men – 'blue jackets' – presumably because they were considered to be trouble-causers.[1371] Occasionally, things got out of hand at the gates. In May 1845, a case was heard in Sheffield of a man refused entry at Hyde Park. He was charged with disorderly conduct after people complained about men assembling outside the ground and, on being refused entry, making use of 'very obscene language to one of the female servants'.[1372] Gate staff did receive some recognition for their efforts. As a show of gratitude for their work during the big Players of England v Australians game at Sheffield in 1884, money-takers were entertained to a substantial supper after the game, thanks to the Australian cricketers and their manager.[1373]

There is evidence that some spectators travelled significant distances to watch games. When Sheffield and Nottingham met in 1833 on the Hulme ground near Manchester, players from Liverpool, Sheffield, Leeds and other parts of Yorkshire witnessed three days' play.[1374] The town of Ripon was unusually 'thronged with visitors from different parts of the county' in August of the same year when Nottingham played the club for the first time for 17 years.[1375] In 1846, the crowd for the Leeds Wellington v Otley Juniors game included 'many visitors' from Leeds, Bradford, Harrogate, Knaresborough, Harewood and elsewhere [1376], and the same year, a 20-carriage excursion train travelled from York to Leeds, drawn by two engines, primarily to take spectators to the All-England game against 18 of Yorkshire.[1377] Some went even further afield. When Mynn and Dearman played at Town Malling in Kent in 1838 for £100, the crowd included supporters of the latter, who had travelled around 200 miles from Sheffield.[1378] And in 1851, when Yorkshire played Surrey at The Oval, the *Sheffield Independent* reported it recognised in the crowd 'a considerable number of Sheffield faces, many having availed themselves of the cheap trains to visit the Great Exhibition, in Hyde Park, and also, what was expected to be a grand exhibition of cricket.'[1379]

Paying to get inside the ground

Spectators had to pay to get into the more significant games. The amounts remained roughly the same for the entirety of the period under consideration, although the assumption was that spectators could pay more for greater exclusivity. To get into Darnall for a match such as All-England v XI of Yorkshire, Leicestershire and Nottinghamshire in 1828, for example, admittance was 6d, with admission to the tents 1s and the 'saloon' 2s 6d. Ladies introduced by a gentleman were 1s each.[1380] A few years later, W.H.Woolhouse tried a different approach, charging 6d for admittance to Hyde Park for a single-wicket game between J.Dearman and T.Heath, but 'Threepence of which to be had in Refreshments.'[1381] In 1830, the game between Wednesday and Eleven of the County of York was cheaper, admission being 3d to the ground and 6d to the Saloon.[1382] Lesser matches varied in price. The game between Holbeck and Calverley St Wilfred in 1868, for example, cost 1d, while Leeds Albion against Holbeck was 2d in 1872, with ladies free. Admission to Hyde Park for the sweepstake game in September 1862 was 3d.[1383] In contrast, the basic admission price to county games was 6d, with the enclosures 1s.

While there were many contemporary claims that cricket brought together all classes, in reality there were clear limits to this and Yorkshire cricket grounds, as much as anywhere in Victorian England, ensured that different social classes were kept apart, to a great extent separated by price. While they might watch the same game and urge on the same players, those able to afford to do so, could and did pay for a place in the enclosure or the pavilion, apart from the great mass of the crowd. When Tom Marsden played Jarvis in a single-wicket match in 1829, admittance was tradesmen 6d, working people 3d, and to the Saloon, 1s.[1384] For 6d, entrance was gained only to the ground, and access to the enclosures was an additional 6d, which for many was clearly prohibitive. As a result, many papers referred to the crowd in the enclosures as the 'upper ten', and it was here that the wealthier sections of local society sat. On occasions, exclusivity came at an even higher price. When the Australians came to Sheffield in 1884, the enclosure to the left of the pavilion was 2s, but was still overflowing, while to ensure 'the comfort and convenience of people in the central enclosure', a fee of 5s was charged for non-members.[1385]

For many, 6d was the limit they could or would afford. There was considerable surprise in Hull in 1849 when the entrance fee for the match with the All-England Eleven was set at 1s a day, especially when one of the professionals let it be known that the normal admission at their games was half that.[1386] In 1884, rumours spread in advance that the entrance fee for the Australians match was to be raised to 1s and there was much criticism in the press, one paper noting that 'a sixpence can be scraped together, but a shilling would have placed a sight of the match beyond the reach of the hundreds who were there.'[1387] In 1893, when the Australians appeared at Bramall Lane again, a reporter noted how reluctant many were to move at all once in their seat. They had paid their admission, 'the saving of which coins had, doubtless caused many cravings to an appetite mildly devoted to ale and tobacco, and they were determined to get their money's worth.'[1388]

Although the admission charge of 6d for important matches did not change during the 19th century, a sign that many were priced out of attending the game can be seen when the cost of admission was cut. When All-England played Leeds and District in September 1856, for example, the *Leeds Times* reported that 'to give the working-classes an opportunity of being present to-day, they will be admitted to the ground for threepence at two o'clock'.[1389] Similarly, at the ground in Kirkstall, Leeds, in September 1869, on the third afternoon of a game between Yorkshire and Eighteen of Leeds Clarence, the club committee cut the entrance fee and the gates at the lower part of the ground were 'eagerly besieged by the admirers of the noble game of cricket.'[1390]

A more generous arrangement was made when York and District played the All-England Eleven in 1860. The *York Herald* noted that to meet 'the means of all classes, the committee of the York club have reduced the charge of admission to the ground', encouraging many to attend who would have otherwise stayed away.[1391] However, the prohibitive cost for many of travelling to matches came up in 1882 when a correspondent to the *Yorkshire Post* recommended that rail companies should run cheap day excursions from Leeds and Bradford to allow those who could not afford the ordinary rail fares to get to Ephraim Lockwood's benefit match at Sheffield.[1392]

For their money, spectators got much the same as today – a simple seat and a view of the action. As the crowds increased, and the clubs and the game in general became better organised, facilities improved. The authorities at Sheffield showed some concern for spectator comfort, and in 1875 the enclosure was furnished with seats with backs. Since the cheaper seats – hard wooden forms with no backs – had only just been replaced, the local paper suggested 'we may now fairly say that Bramall-lane is the best arranged ground for spectators in the kingdom.'[1393]

Nevertheless, the distinction between the crowd and the field of play could be blurred. Without clearly defined boundaries, fielders retrieved the ball from amongst the spectators. Charlie Ullathorne recalled that at Bramall Lane in the 1870s he once 'ran after a ball which went into one of the booths....and in running in after it I jostled against a chap who was just drinking a glass of beer, and spilled the precious liquor over both of us. 'Where the deuce are you going to?' he growled. I picked up the ball, threw it in, and shouted to the man, 'Very sorry, old chap; will be round at lunch time and pay for another.'[1394]

Attending a match was generally a safe experience, although on occasions people did suffer injury. As mentioned earlier, the opening of the Darnall ground in 1822 saw a stand collapse and 50 people were injured. A similar occurrence took place at the match near Leeds between Sheffield and Twenty-Two of Yorkshire in August 1832, when a large stand holding 2,000-3,000 people came down with a tremendous crash. Many were badly bruised, and great alarm was caused, although the game went on.[1395] Ironically, a match in 1874 in aid of Huddersfield Infirmary between Lascelles Hall and Huddersfield and District saw two serious incidents where spectators were injured. Firstly, a boy from Huddersfield was struck on the side of the head when standing too close to the players as they practised, and had to be examined by a doctor. Then, a man [Mr Woodhead] was accidentally injured by a knife during the game when a ball was hit into the crowd. It was reported that 'from some unexplained cause Woodhead received a severe stab under the right arm above the elbow, and although only at first feeling stunned by the 'fielder' running against him, it was subsequently found that he had been stabbed.' He was taken to a doctor and not allowed to go home for the night.[1396] There were other dangers associated with cricket. In 1862, the *Sheffield Independent* warned that after lunch practices were times of 'considerable danger to the spectators, who press forward in close proximity to the batsmen.'[1397]

Seeing the cricket on big occasions could call for ingenuity. In May 1893, the Australians again attracted so many people to Sheffield that all seats were taken by the start and in the 1s enclosure people were standing 12 deep. As a result, early arrivals found that those coming later simply stood in front of them. Consequently:

> As those in the first seats rose to get a glimpse of the game, the people behind naturally complained that their view was shut off, and, rising in their turn, the growl of the blocked-out rose from tier to tier. Thus, for several hundred people the afternoon's enjoyment was unnecessarily marred, and not a few left the ground, including ladies who could not well stand on the seats, and were utterly unable to see through the opaque bodies of obstructives between them and the players. There was no such rudeness visible in any part the working men were massed, and it was surely the business of somebody to see that after people had paid their shillings and obtained their places sufficient attendants were provided to keep the course clear.[1398]

Despite this, more people came in the afternoon and spectators used anything to hand to watch the play. Some placed a ladder on the roof of a shed near the pavilion and the top of the building had a 'human fringe.' Others stood on ginger-beer boxes, wheelbarrows and piles of bricks, and unsuccessful attempts were made to construct precarious platforms. Competition for seats was intense. The *Sheffield Daily Telegraph* reported that once spectators sat down they would not move, even to share a drink. 'Armed with a daily newspaper which 'contrived a double debt to pay' – namely to hold beef sandwiches and to impart information concerning the game of cricket and the farce of politics – they were secure against temptation.'[1399]

The length of time over which a cricket match was played meant that for those who did not bring their own food, there was a need for refreshment facilities. Improvements to grounds during the period included the upgrading of these places and generally standards went up, although not always as quickly as some would have liked. During the 1860s, the authorities at Sheffield let out refreshment stalls or booths each season. In 1873, they made more lasting arrangements with Messrs. Harrop and Wilkinson to take over the catering.[1400] A wooden shed was erected near the score box for the crowd on that side of the ground, and a marquee was put up in the enclosure so that people did not have to cross the field.[1401] This was not sufficient, however, and lunch times at county games were still marked by an exodus of people from the ground, searching out places to buy food. Then, in 1876, the booths were extended and spectators were now able to obtain 'a very substantial feed at a nominal cost, at the north or booths' end of the ground.'[1402] The new arrangements were well received in July of that year[1403], but by the 1890s, as crowds increased, facilities were once again inadequate, and one writer noted that on many occasions the 'luncheon interval was more a purgatory than a meal-time, and lunch to most was a delusion and a snare.'[1404]

An observer was no more impressed by the facilities at Huddersfield in 1876. He commented that the refreshment tent was not inviting, and 'where numbers are so great, feeding is all hurry and confusion, and first come first served, comfort being out of the question. Scramble is a necessary condition of things at such times. I blame nobody, I only say it is not a pleasant thing to contemplate.'[1405] In the early 1880s, the refreshment department on the ground was still described as 'ludicrously inadequate'. On one occasion, sandwiches were soon sold out and 'at luncheon time there was not a morsel of anything to set before the hungry crowd. In the small and filthy shed which is dignified by the name of refreshment room, a roaring trade was, however, done in bottled beer.'[1406] Arrangements for refreshments at the new ground at Horton Park Avenue were also little better in 1880. One reporter complained at the lack of choice of drinks:

> Why any amount of beer, spirits etc; also non-intoxicants, such as horehound beer and ginger beer; but no signs of a cup of tea or

> coffee could I find. If the committee do not assume that all lovers of the game are beer and dram drinkers, why is not some provision made for those who abstain from such drinks?[1407]

In the crowd

Most reports of cricket matches do not mention the crowd, and it can be assumed that generally spectators behaved well and, as now, showed varying degrees of interest in the game, talked to those near them, and were usually entertained or not by developments on the field. Amongst Yorkshire county crowds, the atmosphere was mostly one of good humour, but also of patience. There was an eagerness to see good cricket and a willingness to endure play which fell short of this in order not to miss anything. In May 1890, the *Sheffield Daily Telegraph* noted:

> The love of a Tyke for a good horse and a close cricket match is proverbial. All sorts and conditions of men are in the habit of sitting through the longest county match. If a statue is ever erected to Patience the most fitting model would be a Yorkshireman sitting on a hard form watching Lewis [sic] Hall or Scotton compile a "century", the goal of every cricketer's ambitions.[1408]

When the rain ruined play in a game at Huddersfield in 1886, a sympathetic reporter spoke of the 'mournful patience of the more determined spectators, who sat stolid and immovable waiting for the break in the clouds which never came.' This was a sign that many had come a long way for the game. The occasional appearance of an Australian player looking up at the murky sky was, however, 'their only relief from the distant prospect of shining umbrellas and the patter of steady rain upon the empty seats.'[1409] At other times, spectators were keen to get a close look at the players. In 1875, for example, play against Gloucestershire at Bramall Lane was delayed after lunch on one day when many spectators followed the visiting team out to the wicket 'gazing their fill at them'. They had to be ushered off before cricket could resume.[1410]

Despite some reporters' fears, the crowds usually exercised considerable self-discipline and good humour. At the start of June 1862, when Yorkshire won a tight game with Kent, the visiting captain was subject to 'a good deal of good-humoured chaf' as a result of Rowbotham managing to get the ball through the tight field he had put in place. Some shouted that it would be advisable to station men on horseback at the four corners of the ground to assist in the chase, whilst others suggested bringing in a train to help or giving the captain powerful binoculars so he could trace the course of the ball.[1411]

The Yorkshire crowd was also considered to be very knowledgeable. The *Sheffield*

Daily Telegraph observed:

> they know cricket at Bramall Lane. Every point of the play – by bowler, batsman, or fielder – is keenly and critically noted. Though local patriotism is easily roused, good work, whether by home players or strangers, is promptly recognised......Anything loose or ill-judged is equally soon observed by "the pit", who have eyes for the play as sharp as the kestrel's for its prey.[1412]

In 1884, the *Sheffield Independent* spoke of a 'spirit of fairness' amongst the crowd and a 'willingness to give everyone the same advantage they enjoyed themselves.' When particular spectators prevented others seeing, 'they were immediately assailed with such a shower of dust that they were only too glad to beat a retreat amidst shouts of derisive laughter.'[1413] Crowds could be highly generous to visiting players, and it was remarked in 1874 that there was 'probably no town in England where the public are so impartial in their applause or better judges of cricket or football than Sheffield.'[1414] In August 1876, Richard Daft of Nottinghamshire batted well to win the match against Yorkshire, and his strokeplay was applauded 'with an impartiality which showed that the spectators who had come see the conclusion were true lovers of the game.'[1415] Two years later, an Australian observer reported that, in contrast to the Yorkshire players who had taken their defeat at Huddersfield badly, the crowd had warmed to the victors.[1416]

Yorkshire crowds could also be noisy and highly partisan at other times. During the same tour, the Australian observer commented that the Sheffield crowd was very one-sided in its applause and he had never seen 'a rougher-looking assemblage on any cricket ground, and the language used by some of them when our men planted a fourer was not exactly parliamentary.' They had nicknames for the team and he commented, 'I think the spectators at a cricket match in Australia would be considerably astonished if such names emanated from their midst as the Sheffielders showered upon us.'[1417] Banter amongst the home crowd and with any visiting supporters made for a good atmosphere. At the Nottinghamshire game at Bramall Lane in 1889, many visiting supporters were keen to make their presence known. Locals traded comments with them about the performances of their players, Sheffield men at times falling back on references to football victories over Nottingham clubs the previous winter.[1418]

Other things set the crowds off. Roars of laughter could be provoked by some 'wag' or vendor. Billy Whittam, the scorecard printer and seller, was a well-known sight and sound on Yorkshire grounds from the late 1850s, with his calls of 'Crickcards', 'order of goinin' and 'Nalysis of the bowling'.[1419] During the same Nottinghamshire match mentioned above, a reporter in the Sheffield crowd commented that 'The lives of the spectators in one portion of the ground were made almost intolerable by the antics of a would-be punster, who committed the most unprovoked barbarities with the surnames of the cricketers, such as 'Lee me aloan,' when asked questions, and 'Wade a bit,' when the inquiry was made by a companion as to whether he was about to depart.'[1420] The police also came in for regular, generally good-natured, baiting. In 1890, the Sheffield authorities arranged for officers to wear flat hats ('a plateau-like structure') to avoid obstructing the views of the spectators. All this did was to provoke laughter and led to calls for them to be taken off and passed round for inspection.[1421]

Drinking added to the good humour and loosened a few tongues. Luke Greenwood recalled the fun that weavers from his village had at the game. 'How those old weavers used to follow cricket!' he commented. 'There was a glee party among them who always came to the matches in Yorkshire. They would put up at the nearest 'pub' to the ground, and if we were batting and doing well the crowd always heard their music round the field. If things went wrong they kept quietly to the bar-parlour.'[1422] The bars on the county grounds did excellent business, and in 1890 during a dull stage of the Nottinghamshire match the 'visits to the refreshment tents were so persistent that......bets were freely made by some of the onlookers concerning the number of red noses in the crowd in a given area.'[1423] Occasionally, drinking got out of hand, and the police had to remove a drunk from the square in the middle of an over where he had collapsed with a friend who had gone out to rescue him. The two rolled around on the grass and were escorted off, provoking 'good-humoured badinage.'[1424]

Disrupting play

Despite the good nature of the crowd, there was the possibility of trouble and the police were present at larger games. In 1864, for example, Yorkshire County Cricket Club requested two detectives and four policemen to 'preserve order' at Bramall Lane for the game with Surrey. Similar arrangements were made for the following fixture with Cambridgeshire.[1425]At times, the good humour disappeared and there are many reports of disruptive and, at times, aggressive behaviour amongst the crowd throughout the century, particularly in the early decades.

Local games, fuelled by pride and betting, occasionally saw some trouble. In 1834, a match between Halifax and Huddersfield attracted a large crowd, 'the only drawback upon it being the highly reprehensible conduct of a drunken blackguard throwing a bottle into the midst of the crowd, which cut through a young man's hat and slightly injured him.'[1426] When Sheffield Wednesday played Chesterfield in 1837 at Hyde Park, an umpiring decision led to loud complaints from spectators who were in line with the stumps. Some came onto the field of play and expressed their views forcefully to the Chesterfield umpire. The ground was eventually cleared but by then the visiting team had left the ground. They were tracked down in Sheffield but refused to return to finish the game.[1427]

Spectators from Dalton seemed to acquire a bad reputation. In 1842, the *Bradford Observer* reported on the match with Sheffield, highlighting 'the stubborness and refractory disposition of the Dalton supporters' who, when their side was about to lose, 'closed in upon the players, threatening to do bodily harm to the Sheffielders.' The players did their best to keep back 'the uncouth assemblage.'[1428] The following year, a Bradford paper wrote:

> Monday and Tuesday last were stirring days at Huddersfield and Dalton; and the natives of those districts, being unaccustomed to such exhilerating scenes, displayed rather too much of those uncouth, domineering qualities, for which they are too truly celebrated. Oh, ye Daltonians, ye are expert, scientific, and praiseworthy admirers of the manly game of cricket, but ye "are a rough lot".[1429]

In 1843, a match between Idle and Junction Airedale cricket club ended with hundreds of people on the field, most of them from Idle, who, 'being mortified at the evident superiority of the Junctioners, treated them with great incivility and rudeness.'[1430] Protests could even occur on grounds such as York, which was assumed to be more genteel. In 1846, in a keenly anticipated game between York and Bradford, a run-out decision was given in the fielding team's favour because the batsman had not grounded his bat. The spectators thought otherwise, running on the ground and threatening 'extermination' to Mr Pearson [the umpire] with shillelahs, fists and "lots o' tongue".[1431] As was often the case, this was probably explained by the large bets placed on the game. Other decisions provoked the crowds. During the match at Woodhouse Moor in 1846 between an All-England Eleven and XVIII of Yorkshire, the objectivity of the umpires was called into question. When one umpire walked off having heard criticisms of his ability and honesty, his replacement – a Mr Girling from Manchester – was selected. However, he called 'no ball' and 'wide', 'till he was hallooed and scouted off the ground, which rendered matters unpleasant.' It was said he had bet against Yorkshire winning.[1432]

Yorkshire crowds were at their most restless on the occasions when play was restricted and spectators felt cheated of their entrance money. In 1861, a scene developed at Bramall Lane when spectators stopped Surrey and Yorkshire players bringing a close to play following a storm. Caffyn was reportedly brought back by some spectators, having already changed and left the ground after the captains agreed that there would be no more play. Angry at not getting value for their 3d admission and with money at stake, the crowd successfully had the match restarted, despite the wet state of the field.[1433]

In 1875, against Middlesex at Sheffield, the crowd got restless when there was no play for three hours, even though the weather had improved. The *Huddersfield Daily Examiner* remarked that 'As Sheffield 'fields' do not like to pay their money for nothing, many of the spectators gathered on the running course in front of the pavilion rails, and commenced to 'chaff' the players and to call upon them to resume.' When Buller, one of the Middlesex players, walked out onto the ground, he was 'hissed and hooted.' The paper had some sympathy with the crowd, commenting that teams of gentlemen were all very well, but 'there is one great drawback to such a team, and that is they will not come up to time.'[1434]

Eleven years later, it was decided to abandon play after a three-hour delay at the game with Kent at Bramall Lane. Spectators expressed their disatisfaction by crowding onto the wicket, pulling up the stumps and shouting at the players and officials, including Wostinholm, who was almost manhandled. Many beseiged the pavilion, banging on doors and windows, and eventually the authorities agreed to issue free passes for the next day after what was described as 'a violent demonstration of rowdyism.' 10,000 people turned up. [1435]

Other things sparked off groups of spectators, and at times, the Yorkshire crowd was noisy and irreverent. A crowd invasion took place in 1875 at Bramall Lane during the game against Nottinghamshire. Oscroft was given run out by the umpire when standing out of his crease. Both batsmen walked off and the crowd, highly excited, pressed onto the grass, surrounding the Yorkshiremen, who shortly left the field and were admitted one by one to the pavilion enclosure in order to prevent the crowd rushing in. The crowd tried to force the gate, but were resisted, and contented themselves with calling for the players to resume and abusing the Nottinghamshire team. There was a half-hour delay.[1436]

An interesting incident also took place at Bradford during the game with Kent in 1881, which was reported on by several papers. The *Leeds Times* observed that there had been a lot of talk on the ground about:

> the fact that the Kent professionals had their quarters in the lower pavilion, whilst their aristocratic comrades, as well as the Yorkshire team, were housed in the higher-class pavilion at the opposite end of the ground. It may be that the Kent professionals prefer such an arrangement, and, if so, there is nothing more to be said; but we must confess that the separation had a disagreeable appearance, and the sooner it is put an end to the better.[1437]

The facilities on Yorkshire grounds did little to restrain the crowd from getting on the field, intentionally or otherwise. In August 1832, the organisers of the match between Sheffield and Twenty-Two of Yorkshire at Kirkstall Bridge near Leeds warned in their advertisement that constables would attend to keep order. They also asked spectators to keep out of the space marked by the flags.[1438] At Bramall Lane in 1878, for the game with the Australians, it was noted that there were 'no chains or ropes to prevent encroachment on the turf', whilst the few policemen who were present 'were entirely ineffective in their efforts to keep the people back.'[1439] Subsequently, the county committee engaged numerous policemen for the big games in order to keep spectators off the field.

The best-known players were not immune from comments from the Yorkshire crowd. In 1874, spectators at Bramall Lane were riled by W.G.Grace sneering at Allen Hill's appeals and urging him to 'come on' when he was hit and disabled by the ball, sufficiently badly for him to miss the next game. Two years later, at Huddersfield for the United North of England v United South of England game, spectators mocked Grace's refusal to carry on fielding until the umpires had removed their white jackets, which they had not worn during the South's innings. He only agreed to resume play when the opposing captain, Lockwood, accepted that they should not be used.[1440]

Home crowds also did not distinguish between Yorkshire players and visitors in their criticism, and throughout the second-innings collapse to 40 all out against Nottinghamshire in 1884, a large group of spectators ridiculed their own side, 'laughing heartily at the utter breakdown of the Yorkshiremen.'[1441] In 1893, against Middlesex at Bradford, Lord Hawke made a mistake and watched the ball head towards the boundary. It did not get that far and he had to chase after it, with the crowd mocking his efforts.[1442] The same year, Hawke was also the subject of attention from the Sheffield crowd, which a writer in the *Sportsman* commented could speedily 'develop an unfriendly – I had almost said spiteful – tendency.' Unhappy with a decision made by Hawke, the crowd greeted his every action with ironical applause.[1443]

When the amateur G.A.B.Leatham took over from David Hunter behind the stumps in a match at Scarborough, the local crowd barracked him mercilessly until Tom Emmett went and remonstrated with them. He was believed to have told them 'Nah lad, Scarboro has allus had a reputation for being respectable. Don't loss your character.'[1444] Even Emmett himself was the subject of the crowd's attention. In 1893, *The Cricket Field* reported, 'The idol of the crowd, Emmett would, if necessary, talk to them as a father might talk to an erring child. On one occasion at Bramall Lane they ventured to express a difference with him as to a short run which he refused to make, and from the middle of the ground he addressed them, amid a dead silence, upon the virtue of letting him mind his own business. The crowd apologised, and the game went on. Such a circumstance could have happened nowhere but in Yorkshire, and probably nobody but Emmett would have dared rebuke a Yorkshire crowd.'[1445]

Dissatisfaction with the way certain players performed also created unrest. When the Gloucestershire batsman, Cranston, fielded for Yorkshire as a substitute at Sheffield in 1876, he was booed repeatedly when he made mistakes, even though the state of the field, rather than bad sportsmanship, was to blame. The paper called the behaviour of the crowd a 'dastardly exhibitions of spleen and malevolence.'[1446] Shortly afterwards, against Middlesex, George Pinder was jeered for batting carefully. The same paper reported with surprise 'that even some of the upper ten of the enclosure joined in the unseemly exhibition.'[1447]

Inevitably, language could be rough and ready. In 1876, the same observer at the United North v United South game at Huddersfield who had bemoaned the poor refreshment facilities also regretted that:

> bad language – nay, not bad only, but nasty language prevails to a pitiful extent, and it is not confined to the 'sixpenny' lot by any means. I observed men with good clothes on their backs, men, fathers of families, probably men with grown-up daughters who used language which would disgrace a Birmingham rough. The policeman all the while stood quietly by or joined in the 'chaff' and enjoyed the fun.[1448]

The reaction of players to the noise of the Yorkshire crowd varied. Some enjoyed the experience. Fred Grace said that he would rather field on the boundary at Sheffield than anywhere in England, 'as he revelled in the original comments of the Sheffield grinders, who were a racy, if not a Rabelaisian, folk.'[1449] Others took exception to such behaviour. In 1889, at the request of his team, J.A.Dixon, the Nottinghamshire captain, complained to his county committee about the treatment they had received at Bramall Lane. The team 'were very sore' at being jeered and derided, and objected to any further matches at Sheffield, asking instead for future fixtures to take place at Huddersfield or Bradford.[1450]

Although it was mainly towards the end of the century that Yorkshire crowds really grew in size, on regular occasions, cricket matches of all kind were watched by many thousands from the 1820s onwards. From the start, the Yorkshire crowd was known for its knowledge, irreverence, partisanship and enthusiasm. In general, spectators responded increasingly positively to tough, competitive cricket, whilst novelty varieties of the game died through lack of support, and because what they offered was poor in comparison to the excitement generated by hard-fought contests.

CHAPTER NINE

SPREADING THE WORD

Just as cricket was dependent on spectators to pay to watch the players, so the press also played a crucial role in generating interest and informing a wide audience on the game. As Huggins has put it, 'The media's importance in constructing the Victorian sporting world cannot be overestimated. Many first came across sport not by playing or watching but through media coverage, a combination of factual reportage, viewpoint and promotion.'[1451] This chapter examines how the press in Yorkshire covered cricket at local and county level and what role it played in shaping the game.

The development of newspapers

The mid-Victorian period saw a dramatic development in the spread of newspapers, with the quantity and type of publication printed, bought and read changing profoundly after the 1850s. There appears to have been no single cause, but instead a series of contributory factors. There were two important political developments. In 1855, newspaper Stamp Duty was abolished, followed in 1861 by excise duty on paper, both of which helped to reduce the final cost of newspapers. The reduction in working hours for many gave greater opportunity for self-improvement and, in general, the economic circumstances in the 1860s and early 1870s were favourable to the expansion of reading. In turn, this encouraged newspaper owners and writers to go beyond the dull content of most early newspapers, which lacked appeal to a mass audience. Also fuelling the changes were the development of the telegraph, the express train and news agencies, as well as the growth of provincial and urban pride.[1452] The creation of a larger market for cheap newspapers and other literature was particularly rapid in the provinces. Until the 1850s, there were no daily newspapers outside London, but they expanded in number in the 1870s and 1880s.

As newspapers developed over the period from the 1840s to the 1890s, so the amount of space devoted to sport and the range of sports covered grew, and Mason has argued that, by the 1890s, no newspaper aiming at popular readership could neglect sport.[1453] Brown, in her book, 'Victorian News and Newspapers', came to a similar conclusion, observing that sports reporting grew substantially in the late 19th century, particularly in provincial papers, where it occupied a more central place than those in London. Evening papers established in the 1870s 'gained immediately from the fact that they could offer a results service the same day.'[1454] Brown also notes that the changes in technology allowed for the collection of different types of information. In particular, the newspaper agencies 'made it commercially practicable to collect by telegraph the results of a large number of race meetings and football matches, tabulate the results and transmit them to many small circulation papers across the country.'[1455] Cricket scores could also be handled in the same way. A close relationship grew up. As newspapers became more widely read, an increasing number of organisations felt the need to provide them with information. Cricket clubs were amongst those bodies which tried to draw attention to their existence, communicate their progress and attract new members and patrons through the press.

Coverage of cricket

From an early point, many Yorkshire newspapers took seriously the challenge of providing accurate and comprehensive information about cricket matches. In 1826, for example, the *Sheffield Independent* mused in an editorial that readers' tastes were so varied that it would only be disappointed if it tried to satisfy everyone. Whilst some were interested in reading about government papers or parliamentary debates, others wanted 'nothing but a light and flimsy story, a cricket match, a pugilistic contest, or a sporting anecdote. Our best plan, therefore, is to provide all these things.'[1456] Others took a bit more time to be sure about the merits of sport. The *Leeds Mercury* informed readers in August 1826 that it 'really cannot find room for any long details on the subject of Cricket Matches, which, however interesting to the parties engaged, are not of any very high importance to the public.'[1457]

Nevertheless, cricket scores and reports appeared in the columns of Yorkshire papers on a growing scale in the 1830s. The *Yorkshire Gazette*, for example, printed a long report of the game between York and Husthwaite in 1834, describing the developments in detail and providing the full score.[1458] The *York Herald* had a column headed 'Cricket Playing' in the 1830s where it collected together reports and scores of local games. It included lengthy reports on games involving York and Bedale, amongst others, as well as short notes in response to correspondents.[1459] The *Yorkshire Gazette* also had a column headed 'Cricket', containing scores and reports, and, for example in 1834, provided full details of changes to the laws of cricket under a heading 'Important to Cricketers.'[1460] The *Sheffield Independent* was particularly strong on cricket, and included almost a whole column on contests such as the Yorkshire v Norfolk match in 1836.[1461]

As well as giving cricket more space, we also see changes in the nature of the reporting, with an expansion of the coverage from small snippets of news to longer, more detailed reports, as well as a slower shift to more insightful and analytical reporting. In the 1820s, for example, references tended to be short notices, detailing the results of a small number of teams. Scores were generally just the team total, although on occasions more detail was given; the *Leeds Mercury* in 1826, for example, gave a full breakdown on the scores of each player with the mode of dismissal, also recording the number of byes for the game between Wakefield and Leeds.[1462] Only the most significant matches were covered in any detail; for example, each day's play in the All-England v Twenty-Two of Yorkshire game in 1825. The game in 1828 between Sheffield and Nottingham took up more than a column of the *Sheffield Independent*, with quite detailed descriptions of the main developments and ending with an analysis of the performances of individual players. The match soon after between All-England and York, Leicester and Nottingham had progress of play broken down into quarter or half-hour descriptions, with summary remarks throughout. [1463]

A review of references to cricket in the pages of the *Bradford Observer* in the early 1840s provides further evidence of the focus of early coverage. In 1840, for example, the paper reported on significant local matches, described the nature of the play, and commented on wider features such as the number of spectators or the state of the pitch and weather.[1464] There were sizable reports of the big games between Leeds, Bradford, Dalton and a number of other clubs or touring sides, with full scores. Smaller matches were covered in short reports, with brief reference to the scores and main performers.[1465] In the 1850s, cricket coverage in the *Bradford Observer* was regular, but not often extensive in terms of a written summary of play. Only the most significant matches merited a full score with cause of dismissal, and in general scores were not accompanied by a report. The geographical coverage was generally limited to Bradford but some scores of major games in Leeds and Otley appeared. On occasions, the paper explained that it did not have space to go into more detail, but at other times it was able to find room for matches between warehouse and factory teams.

Over the course of the 1860s, however, *Observer* coverage changed in a number of ways. By the end of the decade there was simply more space devoted to cricket than at the start, with scores of games of all kinds and some discussion of the game in different forms. The number of local matches covered varied but at times filled an entire column of the paper. County games, especially involving Yorkshire, were reported at length, and increasingly this broadened out to include the scores and reports of other major county fixtures. By the end of the decade there were also reports of games held at Lord's or The Oval, or involving teams such as MCC, Lords and Commons, I Zingari and the universities. The coverage of significant local matches widened to include teams outside Bradford such as Dewsbury Savile, Hull, Malton and Gentlemen of Yorkshire, and these games increasingly had reports. Part of the explanation for this expansion must be that towards the end of the decade the paper began to be published daily and so there was simply more space to cover cricket. The cricket column also listed the matches of the day or week, and included advertisements for sporting equipment. There was clearly a desire to give the game fuller coverage, and a weekly 'Cricket Notes' column started – signed by 'Butterfly' – with discussion of the week's events, including performances across the country. The coverage continued to grow in the 1870s and 1880s.

The *Sheffield Independent* had a long history of reporting cricket. In 1828, a correspondent commented, 'As your Paper is read by many cricketers, and is the only one in which I have found matches fully reported, I send you for publication a comparative table of the merits of a number of provincial and metropolitan cricketers...during a few past seasons.' [1466] Its reports of the major matches were long and detailed, with full scores and reports of the great games of the 1820s and 1830s such as the 1829 contest between Sheffield and Nottingham.[1467] Coverage of cricket grew considerably in the late 1840s. The town's most important games received extensive space in the paper, for example, the XX of Sheffield v All-England game in 1846, when two whole columns were used for the report and scores, some parts of it in smaller print to allow for even more extensive description.[1468] Similarly, the edition of 24 June 1848 had a two-column report on the match with Burton-upon-Trent, and almost a column on All-England's game with Birmingham.[1469] Despite the limited space, quite considerable coverage was also given to small-scale matches between works teams, including the full details of each innings and a short report of the main developments. In the 1850s, the game often had one or more columns of coverage in an edition, with long descriptions of major matches played in the area, as well as shorter reports of those involving MCC or All-England.

Developments continued in the coverage of cricket in the Sheffield papers as the town continued to dominate Yorkshire cricket in the 1860s. The establishment of the county club and its early struggle was reported in detail, with much support for the investment at Bramall Lane. Further developments were later made in cricket reporting in the 1870s. In 1875, the *Sheffield Daily Telegraph* styled itself 'the best Cricket Journal of South Yorkshire and Derbyshire' and advised its readers that it had long been regarded as the best authority on the game. It promised important changes for the coming season, in particular:

> Special reports, by qualified cricket reporters, will be published of all the chief matches of the season, due prominence being given to the performances of the county eleven, and of local players in other great matches.....Attention will also be devoted to local club matches, which will always as heretofore be given as fairly and as fully as the demands on our space will permit....[and] we shall be favoured with early and reliable information of all new movements and matters of importance transpiring in the cricketing world.[1470]

Providing more space was not the only sign of a desire to provide good cricket coverage, and in the 1880s, extra editions were printed for the cricket follower. In 1887, the *Sheffield Daily Telegraph* reported that considerable satisfaction had been expressed at the news that it was bringing out an evening paper. As a result, someone with an interest in the game no longer needed to buy five separate editions of an evening paper to find out what had happened.[1471] The same year, the *Independent* announced that, during the cricket season, the sixth edition of the *Sheffield Evening Star* ('for the best and most reliable Cricket News') would contain full reports of all county matches and other matches of general interest, appearing at 7.15pm every night but Saturday.[1472] The *Sheffield Independent* also attempted to develop links with cricket clubs by offering to undertake printing of every description including fixture cards and membership tickets.[1473]

The *Huddersfield Chronicle* provided regular coverage of the main games of the Huddersfield club, as well as Lockwood, Armley and Holmfirth, and some smaller works and club matches. It went beyond match descriptions and in November 1852, for example, published batting and bowling averages for the Huddersfield club.[1474] During the 1860s, the paper maintained a column of local scores, which included club averages but, in comparison with others, gave relatively limited attention to fixtures beyond the area. Important local matches such as Lockwood's game with All-England in 1865 or the visits of the Mancunian Wanderers side were given long and detailed reports, but the paper offered limited coverage of the development of the county game, although it did report the Yorkshire matches (without much commentary) when they started. One cricket-related matter it did cover in detail was the dispute between Sir John Ramsden and the Huddersfield Cricket Club (mentioned in Chapter 5), to which it accorded blow-by-blow accounts of the discussions in court and subsequent correspondence.[1475]

Coverage of cricket grew in the 1870s, partly helped by the paper appearing several times a week, which provided more space. Results of matches could take up two columns of the paper in the early 1870s, and more scores were in full tabulated format with expanded description. This continued, and a Saturday edition of the paper later in the decade at times included four full columns of local scores.[1476] The doings of numerous local clubs were recorded in some detail, especially the annual meetings of clubs like Lascelles Hall, St John's, Dalton and Batley, which by the mid-1870s could take up much of a whole column.[1477] Their financial state was covered and discussion of the performance over the season was recorded. In the 1870s, the paper's reports on important games became longer and better informed. The paper also included some more reflective pieces, such as a long critique of arrangements for the United North v United South game in 1876, plus more information and analysis of the Yorkshire county side.[1478]

Leeds was also well served for cricket, with the *Leeds Times* offering more coverage over time. In the 1860s it had a column entitled 'Cricket Notices', which incorporated advertisements for cricket equipment supplied both locally as well as from the south of England. It also published the batting and bowling averages of the county side.[1479] In the 1880s it contained extensive 'Cricket Weekly Notes', commenting on the county game and local matches. The *Yorkshire Post and Leeds Intelligencer* also gave the game very good coverage, much of it focused on Leeds clubs. In 1882, for example, the edition of 16 May included the scores of 97 matches of different standards, as well as advertisements and a Notes column, commenting on features of the games. The issue of 13 June 1885 included scores of 160 matches. The most significant were presented in full scorecard format, itemising each dismissal, while lesser games were simply shown in summary form.[1480]

A sign of how much this coverage was followed came in August 1885 when, because of pressures on space, it dropped discussion of local cricket for a week. The paper responded to complaints of this move by saying that 'we can only say that we devote far more space to sport than most papers, but are compelled at times to give preference in this column to county matches of the greatest importance only.'[1481] Its coverage throughout the summer was extensive as fixture lists grew in the 1880s. In 1887, for example, it noted 'matches seem to have been more numerous than ever, a fact made apparent in the columns of The *Yorkshire Post*, which during the past day or two has chronicled events without end.'[1482]

Type of coverage

While the scale of coverage of cricket grew over time, so the nature of the coverage also changed and diversified. Reporting the results of games was at the heart of the service provided by newspapers, and in terms of space dominated throughout the century. The writing style was usually a long description of every twist and turn in the game in chronological sequence, with the innings of every player mentioned and aspects of the bowling and fielding described. Reports might include interesting features of the match such as the size of the crowd (frequently including whether influential individuals were present), starting times, the weather and the nature and scale of any betting. For weekly papers, the timing of games could be a problem, and three-day games which started at particular points in the week were often carried over and reported in two separate editions, sometimes several days apart. Together the scores could take up long columns of an edition, particularly as papers added short reports, and moved to tabulate the scores. Such was the pressure on space that, in 1881, the *Sheffield Independent* announced that in future full scores of local matches could only be inserted on payment of a fee of 2s 6d per match, whilst condensed reports would continue to be inserted free of charge where space allowed.[1483]

A second role played by the newspapers was that of an information exchange for clubs. The press took to announcing that teams were available for matches, confirmed challenges that had been made, and advertised the existence of agreed fixtures. The *York Herald* in the 1840s was full of such notices. Papers also reported the disputes and differences between players arising from these challenges. In September 1844, for example, the *York Herald* explained that friends of a David Halton had waited in Burn's Coffee House from eight until 10 o'clock to make arrangements with a Thomas Weatherill. Unfortunately, as 'neither Weatherill or any of his friends made their appearance, Halton begs leave to state that he shall take leave of him as not being worthy of notice.'[1484]

Other papers contained similar information. In March 1829, Tom Marsden advertised in the Sheffield press to inform potential backers that he was holding a meeting at his house to consider proposals for a single-wicket match with Fuller Pilch.[1485] In 1839, the *Bradford Observer* included an advert placed by the Bradford Cricket Club headed 'Challenge!' which responded to comments in the *Halifax Guardian* 'containing bragging expressions and insinuations (from the Secretary of the Halifax Clarence Cricket Club).' The item said that the club 'hereby CHALLENGE THEM TO PLAY (the same Eleven on each side that played in the last match) ONE GAME, for the Sum of TWENTY-FIVE POUNDS A SIDE, 10 pounds of the Winnings to be given to the BRADFORD INFIRMARY, if the Bradford Players win, or to the HALIFAX INFIRMARY, if the Halifax Players win.'[1486] In the 1850s, the *Leeds Times* started a column entitled 'Matches to be Played and Challenges', advising readers that it would be glad to announce coming matches and challenges if secretaries passed them on. The column became a clearing-house for teams seeking matches and, in time, this turned into a regular list of fixtures for the coming week.

There were some limits to the use of the papers for these purposes. The *York Herald* was keen not to fall foul of regulations governing the press, and advised in 1829 that a challenge of the Knaresboro Cricket Club would be charged at the Stamp Office as an advertisement and so declined to include it.[1487] In 1864, the *Leeds Times* (presumably spotting a revenue-generating opportunity) announced that it would be charging 1s for four lines for 'cricket challenges' (changed to 3d a line in 1868).[1488] The following year, perhaps as a sign that clubs were getting better organised, the challenges started to appear in January and February, rather than in-season, when there was a risk of not finding opponents for every summer weekend. Some set time limits within which they would entertain responses to arrange matches ('between 10 February and 10 March') in order that they could start the season with some clarity around their programme.[1489]

Newspapers also became the recipients of letters on cricketing subjects, often relating to incidents in matches, but also on more general topics, which staff attempted to answer. In 1865, the editor of the *Bradford Observer* stated that he had received so much correspondence over the winter that a cricket column would appear earlier than planned in order to respond to them. One man had sent in 14 questions, and the editor pointed him to *Wisden's Cricketers Almanack* in each case.[1490] At other times, editors chose to print interesting correspondence. In 1883, the *Sheffield Independent* included a long letter from a gentlemen musing on the meaning of the expression 'a thorough Tyke', which he had seen used in Billy Whittham's 'new work on modern cricket.' The correspondent commented that, 'When I see that name applied to Yorkshiremen, as I have done in the Sheffield and other newspapers, I always feel a sense of pain.' He quoted various dictionaries which defined it in many negative ways including 'a lousy, dirty, vulgar fellow' or someone as 'contemptible and vile as a dog.' Given all this, the letter asked for assurance that it was not just 'an offensive epithet.'[1491]

On other occasions editors refused to publish letters, arguing that they could be libellous. In 1829, the *Yorkshire Gazette* advised readers that it had received correspondence from Husthwaite Cricket Club complaining about the umpires in their game with Hovingham. The paper declined to publish the letter 'as it can answer no good purpose.'[1492] At other times, they refused to get drawn into disputes. In 1850, the *York Herald* stated it declined 'interfering in the squabbles of Cricket Clubs. If the Barmby Moor players are dissatisfied with the manners of the Thornton men, their best course is to hold no further communication with them.' In 1856, the *Leeds Times* commented piously that the Waterloo Cricket Club had sent in:

> a frightfully long letter in reference to some disputed decision of some umpire, in some match, which match we know nothing at all about. To us – although we must confess to not being able to struggle through it – the effusion appears nearly as interesting as one of Old Moore's old almanacks or Walker's Dictionary.

The paper assumed that its readers would feel the same way, so 'we must really decline to insert the letter, leaving the members of the WCC to settle their quarrel.'[1493] It later noted that it could not possibly find space for a letter from the Birstall club severely censuring the conduct of the Earlsheaton cricketers.[1494]

Inevitably, at times papers were accused of being unfair to a particular club or getting on the wrong side of disputes. On one occasion, the secretary of the Ripon club wrote to a rival paper complaining about a paragraph in the *Yorkshire Gazette* 'which had a tendency to injure the Ripon club.' The *Gazette* stated firmly this had not been its intention and blamed the secretary for not sharing information on the match with all the York papers.[1495] In 1868, the *Leeds Times* reported that the Chairman at the Dudley Hill's annual meeting had 'warmly deprecated the abusive language of the cricketing editor of a certain local journal', who, in relation to a match dispute, had written 'Can no one teach these stupid men cricket?' He said they considered the stupidity was on the side of their opponents, who had led the reporter astray, and thus made him appear more stupid than themselves.[1496]

Some clubs and individuals also used papers to complain about perceived slights from others or what they considered was misreporting. In 1827, for example, an item complained about an 'ungenerous' announcement which said that the Leeds New Club would receive assistance from two outside players, when in fact they belonged to the club.[1497] On the other hand, the *Bradford Observer* was happy to stir things up in 1843, and commented on a report in the *Leeds Times* of games involving officers of the 32nd Regiment and members of the Leeds cricket club, and the Bradford club. Having outlined the dispute, the paper commented that 'a more vain tissue of self-exaltation, jealousy, and misrepresentation, has but seldom appeared — at least, under the shade of the manly game of cricket.' It assured its readers that the officers of the 32nd Regiment were totally unconnected with the matter. [1498]

Papers liked to present themselves as concerned with accuracy and sought to make corrections where necessary. In 1826, having reported that a match took place between Huddersfield and Dewsbury, the *Leeds Mercury* subsequently included a paragraph explaining that there had been no match, only practice, to be followed shortly after by a statement that the original story was in fact correct. Frustrated, the paper ended by stating that having 'told the story for both sides, we hope we shall be excused from any further notice on the subject.'[1499] Editors were of course dependent on people being honest, and correspondence pages could sometimes be the subject of forgeries and jokes. The *York Herald* included a letter in 1849 which promised a game between Yarm and Stockton to decide which town would host the October Cheese Fair the following year. The next week, the real secretary of the Yarm club wrote in, pointing out that there was absolutely no truth in the matter, which had been generated from the 'senseless cranium of some petty scoundrel.'[1500]

Another important feature of cricket coverage was the reporting of the wider activities of local clubs. The advertisement pages contained notices for club meetings, particularly AGMs or social events, aimed at members, or, on occasions, included details of the letting of contracts for bars and refreshments on the larger grounds. The news columns increasingly reported on club on- and off-field activities, and from the early 1870s, more organisations provided details of their annual dinners and end-of-season meetings and AGMs.[1501] The *Huddersfield Chronicle*, for example, published descriptions of club activities at the end of each season, noted which players had received awards, and sometimes reported the main points of speeches given by club officials and patrons. Over the winter, reports of concerts and events were included, which were an opportunity to list the successes (or otherwise) of the season, print summarised averages, and set out the details of the financial state of the club. More detailed discussion of the annual accounts of larger clubs was not uncommon. Pre-season reviews also appeared; in 1874, for example, the *Huddersfield Daily Examiner* included three columns considering the prospects of major local sides.[1502]

Yorkshire papers reported on developments in the wider game, for example, the rise of W.G.Grace in the 1860s and the visits of the Australian teams from the 1870s onwards. Overseas tours to Australia, the United States and Canada attracted much coverage from the early 1860s, particularly since the touring parties often included members of the Yorkshire county side. Inevitably, there was a time delay, so that, for example, the *Leeds Times* reported on the match between Richard Daft's team in Toronto on 27 September 1879, the game having been played nearly three weeks earlier.[1503]

Newspapers also published club averages and statistical analysis. We saw earlier that the *Sheffield Independent* had published a comparative table of performances of players in 1828. Such information became increasingly common. In the 1840s, for example, the *Doncaster Gazette* printed averages for the local side, and the *Sheffield Independent* published Sheffield cricketers' averages in 1849.[1504] There were occasional discussions of the averages of the top players in the country; in 1855, the *Sheffield Independent* printed an analysis, but it was really the 1860s when more space was given to such material at club level, in some cases in considerable detail.[1505] The 1870s saw a further expansion, including data for the All-England Eleven, the Yorkshire county side, and nationally.[1506] The *Leeds Times* included the averages and analysis of scores for the tour of America in 1872, and discussed the performances of the counties and their batting and bowling averages. In October 1877, the national batting averages for all batsmen who had played three innings or more were included in alphabetical order.[1507] In 1879, the same paper extended the averages to include more counties, as well as games between the MCC and the counties, and placed them in performance order, adding that 'the averages take a much wider range than has been thought necessary in previous years.'[1508] The *Yorkshire Post* included full batting and bowling averages for many major clubs in Yorkshire during the 1880s.

Some papers reprinted articles on cricket which had appeared elsewhere. The *Hull Packet* included the story 'Lost and Won' by Mary Russell Mitford in November 1828, based around a cricket match[1509], while the following year an article, previously published in the *Leeds Patriot*, but actually written by a reporter at the *Sheffield Independent*, appeared on the 'Origin of Cricketing.'[1510] Reprinting such material was a common feature of papers in the 1860s as the game became more popular, including on the key cricketing issues of the day. In 1863, the *Sheffield Independent* featured an article from *Bell's Life* on expectations of cricketers[1511], and the same year, the *Leeds Times* published a piece critical of single-wicket matches from *London Society*, followed shortly afterwards by an article from *Sporting Life* on 'Willsher and the Great Bowling Question.'[1512] In October 1865, the *Leeds Times* published a piece across almost two columns on 'The Game of Cricket and the essential qualifications of a good cricketer', and shortly after, a feature entitled 'What is Fair Bowling? Grace v Jupp.'[1513] In 1867, a long, reflective discussion entitled 'The Siege of the Wicket – An Article on Old Cricketers' appeared in the *Leeds Times*. This contrasted the 1839 match between Kent and England with Kent and Surrey from the July of 1867.[1514]

A further development which emerged in the 1870s was the inclusion of cricketing news and gossip columns. Snippets about cricketers such as Tom Marsden had appeared many years earlier, but they were limited and occasional. In the late 1860s, however, a column of 'Cricket Notes' was included in the *Sheffield Daily Telegraph*, signed by 'Wicket'. The equivalent in the *Bradford Observer* was signed by 'Butterfly'. In the 1880s several Yorkshire papers had a long 'Cricket Notes' column.[1515] In the 1890s an even more detailed and informative 'Cricket Gossip' feature appeared in a number of papers such as the *Yorkshire Evening Post* and the *Sheffield Evening Telegraph*. These columns took a step back from describing individual games and summarised the main developments of the week on the field or conjectured on trends in the game around the country at all levels. They were clearly prepared by writers with knowledge of the game and its history, and incorporated statistical analysis and comparisons. They also offered strong opinions on local and national cricket ('Disaster follows disaster in quick succession, and still are Yorkshiremen intensely disappointed, discontented, and disgusted at finding their county in the unenviable position of last in the list.').[1516]

Such columns became a fixture in Yorkshire papers, and the authors clearly saw themselves as providing a service to a regular readership ('I have at least to hope that my endeavours to please have been satisfactorily realised.')[1517] A column, 'Gossip in the pavilion', appeared in the *Leeds Mercury* written by 'Long-On.' At the end of the season, he commented that:

> In the letters week by week we have dealt with features of the game which, as they presented themselves, we considered required comment, and occasionally raised a warning note against incongruities as they arose. In the present letter, and as a farewell for the season, we desire to call serious attention to a few matters which we incline to believe require attention.

These points included whether there should be a widening of the range of players chosen for Yorkshire; and whether there should be a better authority than MCC to make decisions on 'scientific points and definitions' about the game.[1518] A regular 'Cricket Notes' feature was included in later years in the same paper, summarising recent events on the field and commenting on developments and controversies ('I question the wisdom of allowing Ulyett to bowl without a long stop' and 'The institution of the gauge in order to check the use of unlawfully wide bats was a feature of the match noticed which will be remembered.'[1519]).

Finally, the press featured considerable advertising relevant to cricket, showing what equipment was available for purchase, and also drawing attention to major or local cricket publications. In April 1833, a number of newspapers including the *Hull Packet* advertised prominently the appearance of *The Young Cricketer's Tutor* by John Nyren, available at 2s 6d and bound in cloth with *The Cricketers of my time*.[1520] Reviews in the *York Herald* and the *Leeds Mercury* reinforced that this was a book worth purchasing.[1521] In 1845, the *Northern Star* advertised

Clark's Cricketers' Handbook, which contained the history of the game, an account of celebrated players, instructions to young players and the new laws of the game.[1522]

Role of the press in the development of cricket

Given the variety of coverage, it is worth considering what role all this attention to the game played in its development in Yorkshire. Papers gave cricket prominence and generally emphasised that the game was something of importance, which should be played seriously, and which had real meaning for the prestige of individuals and communities. It gave it respectability and standing, and associated it with patriotism and English traditions. This visibility within many newspapers during the months from April to October (and earlier, for example, in reporting on matches on ice, overseas tours or requests from teams to fix games for the summer) was a sign that the paper felt it was a worthy pastime and one which it believed its readers found interesting. Increasingly, the papers provided evidence that a lot of cricket was played, and that it was enjoyed by large and 'respectable' audiences. Reporters regularly left readers in no doubt that health, and frequently moral, benefits could be derived from playing it at a time of anxiety in society about the effects of urbanisation and industrialisation. In an editorial critical of those who puritanically opposed sports and pastimes, the *Sheffield Independent* commented as early as 1829 that 'It seems to be the practice of some over-righteous persons, to prevent all relaxation among the poorer classes. They may not play at cricket, or sing, or hear music, or indulge in any merriment, if it can be prevented.'[1523]

The game was also supported as a civilising influence. In 1868, the *Bradford Observer* commented that it was within 'the recollection of men now living, when the chief attractions at our village feasts were cock-fighting and bull- and bear-baiting. Thanks however, to the great improvement that has taken place in the social, moral and intellectual condition of the people in the last half-century, these brutal sports have given place to cricket matches and similar athletic games.'[1524] As well as publicising the merits of cricket as a game, the coverage also indicated to the reader that it provided an enjoyable and supportive social life, with many clubs clearly offering companionship and fun, regular physical exercise and, potentially, local notoriety.

The press also did much to champion particular ways of playing and was very clear about the manner in which teams should conduct themselves. In 1847, the *Hull Packet* bemoaned the behaviour of a local side who had:

> nothing but their own unconquerable idleness to blame for their want of success...If their object is, as it appears to be, to get through a match with the least possible physical exertion, we would

> suggest that they should leave a number of easy chairs scattered about the field in which they might recline until the ball is thrown into their hands.[1525]

After efforts were made by one side to avoid losing a local game in 1865, the *Bradford Observer* commented, 'Both sides can't win, but the losers have always the next greatest pleasure to that of winning – we mean the pleasure of congratulating their friends (they are opponents only during the game) on their victory.'[1526]

The press frequently encouraged competition and took the view that cricket was a serious game to be played properly, which meant in determined fashion and following extensive practice. In August 1845, when York were again badly beaten by Dalton, the *York Herald* hoped the experience would induce the York cricketers to practise more because otherwise 'it would certainly be advisable for them to withdraw from the club altogether, and make room for those individuals who entertain different views to theirs as to the requisites of a cricketer.'[1527] Reporting in 1849 on Knaresborough v York, the *York Herald* highlighted the poor fielding of the former side, arguing that this was due to a lack of practice, especially amongst the junior players.[1528]

Certain forms of the game were also deemed better than others by the press. In 1869, at a time when the touring elevens were very prominent and 'clown cricket' was seen for the first time, the *Leeds Times*, commenting on the Yorkshire v Cambridgeshire game at Hunslet, stated that those who arranged county cricket 'deserve our warmest thanks, for in a tolerably well-balanced county match we undoubtedly see cricket in all its glory.'[1529] Linked to this was approval for a Yorkshire-only policy. In 1864, the *Bradford Observer* commented favourably on the selection of only Yorkshire-born players by the Bradford committee for the county game with Nottinghamshire, which it contrasted with the side that the Sheffield-based committee had selected for the Surrey game.[1530]

Coverage in newspapers also helped to make individual cricketers local, and sometimes, national, heroes. These included working men who took up cricket as professionals and became famous – in ways impossible to most of their contemporaries – as a result of their prowess on the field. The *Huddersfield Chronicle* was very proud of the efforts of the Lascelles Hall side, commenting in September 1876 that there was something 'exceedingly pleasant in the thought that the picturesque hamlet of Lascelles Hall is the nursery of celebrated cricketers who carry the fame of their county far and wide.' Supporters should 'feel highly proud of, and indebted to, the homely professionals, who hold their own so gallantly against the best gentlemen players of the day. Where would the county be in the cricketing world but for Lascelles Hall?'[1531]

Unsurprisingly, local papers could be very biased in favour of their local teams and players. Although some saw themselves as a paper of record, at times they could display a complete lack of objectivity. Commenting on the defeat of Leeds by Dalton in 1841, the *Bradford Observer* reported that Leeds had scored just 14 in the second innings:

> *Fourteen !* what a splendid, unexampled, but never-to-be forgotten score ! and that, too, by men who have had such a name (but 'What's in a name?') for superiority and science, and who wished it to be understood that they wore the belt in this neighbourhood ! O, how are these 'little great men' humiliated ![1532]

Gathering the news

Much of the information about early cricket that was contained in the press came from clubs and players themselves. Secretaries of clubs provided scores of local matches, although getting them to send information in promptly and in a suitable format was a constant challenge for editors. In 1845, the *Bradford Observer* complained that it was 'always anxious to oblige our cricketing friends, but statements of games which came off so long ago as the 8th instant, are scarcely suited to a *news* – paper.'[1533] Twenty years later, the same complaint was still being made, with the editor of the *Bradford Observer* explaining that, because they were delivered late, a number of match reports 'are comfortably reposing in the editor's waste basket.'[1534] Papers also felt the need to filter out some reports on the grounds of significance. In September 1846, the *Sheffield Independent* drew the line, stating sternly that it had been sent the score of a school match played at Hyde Park, but did not think it was sufficiently important to include.[1535]

Papers also often refused to include reports without them being signed or else were very specific about format.[1536] In 1858, the *York Herald* stated its requirement that reports should be written on one side of the paper only, with the first and second innings set out '*in the same order of going in*, and in all cases, the utmost brevity and condensation must be practised, to ensure insertion.'[1537] The *Leeds Times* was also frustrated, noting it had received the score of one game, 'but where the match was played and on what day our correspondent does not inform us. If secretaries of clubs will not take the trouble to send us intelligible accounts we cannot attend to their communications.'[1538]

Similar sentiments were expressed in Huddersfield papers, and the *Chronicle* later provided scoresheets for teams to fill in, presumably to help ensure they provided complete and consistent information. Initially free, the paper started charging 2d for a dozen from 1876 because of the 'improper use' which had been made of them.[1539] The *York Herald* was happy to provide scoring sheets to clubs free from the 1870s, but only on the understanding that reports were sent direct by railway parcel on the day of the match.[1540]

As well as relying on clubs themselves, some papers made use of reports sent in by those who had attended the game as spectators. In 1847, the *Bradford Observer* noted that 'Through the kindness of a gentleman who was present during the progress of this contest, and who arrived at a late hour last evening, we are enabled to present our readers with a correct score of the game [between All-England and the 18 of Yorkshire].'[1541] This could lead to problems, however. In 1865, the same paper, apparently keen to make use of an independent observer for its reports, commented that it had been let down by a man 'well known in the cricketing circles of Bradford', who had promised to provide a report of the Bradford v Middlesbrough match. The paper saw this approach as a model for its future reporting but, having not received it, accepted an alternative description from the Bradford club itself.[1542]

As time went on, arrangements became better organised and newspapers began to engage specialist cricket reporters. Mason suggests that it is doubtful if many newspapers employed specialist sports reporters before 1870.[1543] One exception appears to be the *Bradford Observer*, which in the mid-1860s appointed a Cricket Editor, referred to as 'Philip Henry'. He was in fact David Goodman Dixon (c1813-1868), who acted as the paper's cricket writer. Dixon expanded the paper's coverage of the game and his columns were notable for strongly-held views on how cricket should be played and clubs organised. On his death, his paper reported that:

> His devotion to the literature of the game, in which in his younger days he was a practised and able hand, and upon which he was one of the best authorities, was well known to our readers.....Suffice it to say, that few who stepped into the little shop and talked over the counter to the thin, finely-featured man in spectacles, whose hair was changing silvery and grey, were aware that he was an *alumnus* of Cambridge University, had been a private tutor of a baronet, and had drifted into the place he will be carried from, chiefly because of a marriage from no other motive than love.[1544]

In the late 1860s, Dixon made use of what the paper described as 'special commissioners', who attended games incognito, filing more independent reports than those derived from participants or representatives of the clubs involved. In 1867, the *Bradford Observer* (probably Dixon) wrote caustically under a published letter from the Honorary Secretary of the Keighley Cricket Club that 'the Secretary knows well that we make a point of rejecting all remarks about their own playing which are made by any club.'[1545] Efforts were made by the paper to make sure its reporters were not known to the teams. On one occasion, a match report identified the individual by stating that he loved to smoke a pipe and subsequently, 'our special took care to be on the ground in good time, and, keeping his pipe in his pocket, smoked a cigar or two instead.'[1546]

Other papers also took steps to provide an improved service by engaging writers with specialist knowledge. In 1875, the *Sheffield Daily Telegraph* announced it had recruited 'one of the ablest writers on cricket, whose position renders his opinions authoritative, and who enjoys special facilities for obtaining the earliest and most reliable information, to write exclusively for this journal an interesting weekly letter (or notes) on 'The Cricket of the Week.'[1547] The same year, the Sheffield paper boasted that, in addition to giving 'full, graphic and reliable reports, from specially retained and experienced correspondents, of all the great cricket matches', it would continue to devote a considerable portion of its space to local cricket.[1548] The *Sheffield Independent* also had its own cricket correspondent in the 1870s and 1880s known as 'Point', as well as the 'Cricket Editor.' At times, there was rivalry between the journalists. In July 1882, the compiler of the regular 'Cricket of the Week' column in the *Sheffield Daily Telegraph* fired off a tirade against another paper which had accused him of plagiarism. He denied the charges, saying the other paper never had anything worth stealing, if he borrowed material he always acknowledged it, and in any case, his reports were written before the other paper was printed.[1549]

The nature of coverage expanded. In the late 1880s and early 1890s, the Sheffield papers occasionally took to sending an additional reporter to roam the ground to describe what he found. One from the *Sheffield Evening Telegraph* in 1887 commented from the crowd, suggesting that whilst the 'pit' or outer circle enjoyed a reputation for being sound judges of the game, many spectators did not seem that well informed and were happy for any distraction, including scuffles between others, dogs wandering on the field and a visit from the scorecard seller. A man styled 'One in the Crowd' wrote on the Yorkshire v the Australians game in 1890 in a separate column alongside the main match description on the debate and arguments amongst the spectators.[1550] He did the same three weeks later for the match with Nottinghamshire, seating himself near the score box 'for the purpose of obtaining a little amusement.'[1551]

As coverage of sports increased in scale, local sports reporters were sufficiently important that the death and funeral of a John Rodgers, 'respected football and cricket reporter' on the staff of the *Sheffield Independent* and *Evening Star*, was included in the Sheffield papers in 1876, and many well-known cricketers and football players attended his funeral.[1552] Another noted correspondent was T.J.Anderson, brother of George, who wrote for the *Sheffield Daily Telegraph* for 20 years until his death in 1888, being described as a local cricket reporter 'whose fidelity and impartiality were and are so highly esteemed.' He suffered a stroke, aged 56, while watching Yorkshire against a Twenty-Two of Rotherham for the *Telegraph* and was unable to work.[1553] Anderson provided the *Sheffield Daily Telegraph* with detailed reports and short pieces, and a private subscription with trustees was opened to raise money for him at the start of 1887.[1554]

The most significant journalist who covered Yorkshire cricket in the 19th century was A.W.Pullin (or 'Old Ebor' as he styled himself), whose work has been drawn on in this book. Pullin (1860-1934) – who also reported rugby and football – travelled with the Yorkshire XI, acting as a 'permanent non-playing member' in Lord Hawke's words. The *Yorkshire Evening Post* commented that Pullin, 'probably more than any other journalist of his time, created a public interest in Yorkshire cricket and football which they had never enjoyed before.' He began as a reporter on local newspapers in Wakefield, Cleckheaton and Bradford, later contributing to *Athletic News* from around 1885 under his pen name. He became the cricket and football writer of the *Yorkshire Post* and *Yorkshire Evening Post* in 1893, for whom he wrote until 1931. Lord Hawke also described him as 'one of the best-informed and finest writers on cricket in this country' who did a great deal through his writing to encourage Yorkshire cricket.[1555]

Specialist publications

Most information about cricket was provided through general newspapers but alongside them were specific sporting publications available in Yorkshire. In 1862, Richard Thorp, a noted supporter of cricket in Huddersfield, who appeared in the game between XX of Yorkshire and All-England Eleven in 1862, produced a publication which included scores of the 'great matches', the rules of the game and a list of Yorkshire professional bowlers. It was widely advertised at the start of the 1863 season and described as 'a useful little book which cannot fail to be prized by cricketers as a work of reference.'[1556] The *Bradford Cricketers' Journal* made a short-lived appearance, for the first time in April 1874, published by James Hanson and Son.[1557]

In 1877, '*The Leeds Cricketers' Guide*' was published, costing 4d. It contained 1,200 engagements of the 'adult clubs of the borough', stating when and where the matches would be played. The *Leeds Times* described it as 'well got up and pretty complete, and no doubt it will be found very useful for reference purposes.'[1558] The following year, W.Duthoit's *Yorkshire Cricketers' Guide* appeared. Duthoit sold cricket goods from his shop in Boar Lane in Leeds and clearly used the *Guide* to help advertise his business. It included 'a well-written sketch of the cricketing career of Ephraim Lockwood, captain of the Yorkshire county team (with portrait); the Marylebone laws of cricket; hints to umpires, batters, bowlers and fielders; a comprehensive review of Yorkshire county cricket; the averages of district clubs; and many other items of interesting information, including an alphabetical list of past and present Yorkshire cricketers.'[1559]

The 1880s saw the further development of specialist publications. *The Yorkshire Cricketers' Handbook* appeared at a price of 2d, and contained the fixtures of the principal clubs in Yorkshire, the counties, Australians and the Philadelphians.[1560] This had previously been *The West Riding Cricketers' Guide*, which had included the engagement list for over 60 clubs. In 1887, it contained principal fixtures for the year, batting and bowling performances from the previous season, laws relating to the various challenge cups and other information.[1561] In the 1880s, newspapers also carried adverts for *Cricket – A weekly record of the game*, which the *Sheffield Telegraph* described as containing 'smartly written notes, articles interesting to the lovers of the game, scores of the principal matches, and many scraps of interesting gossip.'[1562] *Lillywhite's Cricketers' Annual* and *Wisden Cricketers' Almanack* were also highlighted in the press. The *Yorkshire Post* brought out its own 'Cricket Record' for each month at 2d, containing scores and information.[1563]

For those wanting regular information, *Athletic News*, established in 1875 in Manchester, carried detailed coverage of Yorkshire cricket, while in 1887, the *Athletic Journal*, another Manchester weekly publication, appeared, including an interview with George Ulyett in its first edition.[1564] And for those who wanted to keep a permanent record, in 1892, the *Sheffield Independent* advertised a 'Cricketers' Diary and Companion', small enough to fit in a waistcoat pocket, but with all the scores and averages from the past season, and fixtures for the coming one.[1565] By the end of our period, there was no shortage of material for those who wanted more on cricket than even the expanding daily and weekly general papers could offer.

Facilities for the press

Early cricket coverage did not require any facilities for journalists since, as we have seen, clubs usually provided the information. Once newspapers began to send a reporter to the bigger games, however, expectations increased that they would have an uninterrupted view of the game. Despite this, the conditions in which journalists often had to work were basic in the 19th century. As Mason notes, 'reporters often found themselves sitting at a table just in front of the spectators with no cover, exposed both to the vagaries of both crowd and weather.'[1566] Several journalists used their columns to point out the inadequacies of facilities. A *Morley Reporter* writer, for example, who attended a game at Savile Town in 1870, described the scene there in some detail. He complained that:

> The committee provided a long desk and seats which were placed in front of their tent, but they failed to take efficient means of preventing people passing and re-passing and standing between the press and the players, and the reporters were compelled almost perpetually to request spectators of the game to stand out of the way.

They were also placed very close to the bars and noisy spectators made 'various stupid comments on the game, mixed up with squabbles about bets of a trifling amount.'[1567]

Facilities were also poor in June 1873 for Bradford v United South of England Eleven, and the *Observer* commented sarcastically that 'we may suggest to the committee that it is just possible that the arrangements for enabling the representatives of the press to discharge their duties might, on careful consideration, be found capable of some trifling improvement.'[1568] At Sheffield, things were better. In 1872, a small room was fitted out for journalists, and the reporter of the *Sheffield Independent* started his description of the play between Yorkshire and Surrey in June by commenting that 'our thanks are due to the management for the very superior accommodation afforded for the members of the press, which is another addition to the excellent arrangements to be found at 'The Lane'.[1569] Journalists were also more in the Dewsbury club's mind in 1878 and, when the Players of the North took on the Gentlemen of England, a reporter thanked the executive 'who on it being mentioned to them that there was no accommodation for the Press, set to work at once and erected a suitable table for its representatives.'[1570]

Facilities improved in the 1880s as Yorkshire grounds were modernised, and by the start of the decade reporters generally had their own room to work in, although even then some complained of cramped conditions hampering them. In 1881, the Sheffield authorities arranged with the Postal Telegraph authorities for the extension of a wire so that the press could communicate from the ground with any telegraph station in the United Kingdom. A portion of the reporters' room was set apart for a telegraph office, and the collection and delivery of messages was also made in the refreshment room in the pavilion and at the turnstile at the top gates, where telegraph officials were situated.[1571] Even so, Bramall Lane could not cope with all the journalists requiring accommodation by the 1890s, and in 1894 the *Sheffield Daily Telegraph* reported complaints that it was not right that 'a dozen knights of the pen should be cooped up within space scarcely sufficient for half that number.' Poor conditions at Dewsbury – a couple of desks and chairs in the pavilion – could be excused, but the paper argued that Bramall Lane ought to be better. A month later, the same paper reported that London press men had complained about the 'absurdly scant accommodation' at Bramall Lane. Only about half of those who wanted to could get into the box for the match with Warwickshire, and many of those had not been able to work in comfort. Others had had to write in the enclosure.[1572]

There was a different issue at Leeds, where the size of the ground was deemed a problem. In 1893, 'Old Ebor' wrote that the view for scorers and the press was 'simply execrable', so that twice during one game the scorers had to ask the players what had happened as they could not tell themselves. It was suggested that the press, scoring, and telegraph departments should be transferred to the space between the members and the general pavilion.[1573] Things were better at Bradford. When the new ground was opened in July 1880, the pavilion had a room set apart for representatives of the press, and in 1883 permission was sought from the Post Office to lay a wire to the telegraph office in the town to allow for the dispatch of reports of games.[1574]

Technical developments improved the lot of the journalist in the late 1880s and 1890s. During the match with Nottinghamshire in 1889, 1,800 telegrams were sent out, and 28,000 press words signalled – a record at the time. The *Sheffield Daily Telegraph* boasted proudly that:

> We in Sheffield are happily fixed with regard to telegraphy, having skilled operators, whilst from the esteemed chief Mr Gibbons down to the lowest, one meets with nothing but courtesy and urbanity, whilst red tapeism seems at a discount, and in many instances requirements are anticipated. It has been my lot to have to send thousands of words to newspapers from many grounds, but give me the Sheffield arrangements in preference to any I have yet met with.[1575]

There was also considerable interest in the Yorkshire v Australians match in 1890 at Sheffield, and on the Monday, 758 press messages were sent, running to 23,000 words, as well as numerous private telegrams.[1576]

The press played a crucial role in the development of cricket in Yorkshire. Newspapers included growing coverage of the game, which communicated very clearly that it was an important part of local life and a worthwhile activity. Editors gave increasing space to scores and cricket news, and clubs used the press to publicise their activities and build up their visibility, particularly from the 1860s onwards. Theirs was a close and mutually beneficial relationship.

CHAPTER TEN

RISE OF THE COUNTY CLUB

Although Yorkshire County Cricket Club celebrated its 150th anniversary in 2013 it is clear that the opening three decades of the club's history were characterised by uncertainty and disagreement among representatives of different parts of the county, much of it centred on animosity towards the domination of the game by the committee based in Sheffield. This feeling helped to shape the development of county cricket in Yorkshire in the 19th century, and was not sufficiently overcome for a fully representative club to be established until the 1890s. This chapter examines the different stages in the disputes over the county club, which focused around three key questions – who should run county cricket; which players should represent the county; and where should the most significant matches be held?

Regional and local pride

Chapter 2 described the strong sense of pride in their county felt by a group of Yorkshiremen living in London in the 1840s. Unusual at the time in having relocated so far, their identification with home was a very natural human feeling. In the past, most people did not travel very far from their birthplace, but developments in the mid-Victorian period allowed greater movement, and industrialisation drew people into towns and cities from outlying areas to live and work. Such change was highly unsettling for those involved and for those who looked on as many of the certainties of the past appeared to be cast aside.

As towns and cities grew up, piecemeal efforts were made from the middle of the century to develop amenities for the health, wellbeing and pleasure of residents (and counter the feared risk of popular unrest). Associated with these changes was the emergence of a growing sense of affinity for, and pride in, the new centres of population.[1577] Such sentiments had a direct influence on leisure and the creation of sporting traditions. In his history of the development of rugby league, Collins suggests that rivalry at football between towns and counties 'mirrored precisely the great growth in civic and commercial rivalry in the decades immediately following 1850.' Sport became closely identified with these rivalries and 'clubs were, on the whole, no longer formed to be private recreational associations for young gentlemen but were created to represent towns and districts.'[1578]

A number of writers have seen the development of Yorkshire cricket as closely linked to the industrialisation of the West Riding and the local rivalry which came with it. In his study of cricket and the construction of regional identity in 19th century Yorkshire, Light concluded:

> Cricket's formative growth in the century took place in a distinctive and particularly dynamic environment in which a wide range of meanings came to find expression through the sport. As the West Riding, in particular, experienced its own definitive period of urban industrial growth, the game developed a vigorous popular following which became focused upon a powerful sense of local and civic identity. These dynamics helped numerous rapidly changing communities to define themselves and found their fullest expression through major commercial matches between rival neighbouring towns in which professional players predominantly took part. It was within this context that teams claiming to represent the county first began to appear.[1579]

The West Riding – Light's main focus – experienced a particularly fast and intense form of economic development, but it is important to recognise (as we saw in Chapter 3) that this was not matched elsewhere in Yorkshire. As a result, it seems likely that these economic and social changes are only part of the picture of the development of cricket in the county as a whole.

Local rivalries and local identities were also present or built up in the cricket played in the rest of Yorkshire, and were felt strongly by followers of the game well away from the West Riding. As we saw earlier, the North Riding did not have the same intense economic growth, but also developed a vigorous cricketing culture from the start of the 19th century (and especially from the 1820s), based around a small number of prosperous towns and villages such as Thirsk, Bedale, Husthwaite, Ripon (just over the boundary in the West Riding) and Helmsley. Each had its own cricketing traditions and successes, a strong pride in the ability to resource its teams from local men, and some experience of taking on higher-quality opponents. Because of its geography, the game in the North Riding was different to that in the West Riding, and also more influenced by the aristocracy, who showed interest in the game and supported a number of clubs.

In contrast again, as we saw earlier, the East Riding had very different economic and social features and very limited industrial development outside Hull. Although there were town and village sides, the game evolved more slowly and without the same scale of fixtures at close proximity to generate quality cricket. As a result, to Holmes, in his history of cricket in Yorkshire in the 19th century, the East and (to some extent) North Ridings 'never loomed big in public notice', and, for example, the clubs which competed for the cup offered by the North and East Ridings County Cricket Club in the mid-1880s were 'not of first-rank importance.'[1580]

Thus, the development of the game in the three Ridings set off on different trajectories and it was not just industrialisation and urbanisation, but also the lack of it, that helped determine the pace and nature of developments around Yorkshire, and subsequently influenced the speed at which it was possible to create a representative county club. Different levels of economic development across the county affected the amount and quality of cricket played, and helped to ensure that the game was of varying standards in specific areas. Differences in the pace of change also meant that men in particular parts of Yorkshire saw the idea of a unified and representative county club differently, and this helped to create obstacles to cooperation, which took several decades to resolve. Put simply, a county club offered much more to some parts of Yorkshire than to others.

The idea of a team representing 'Yorkshire' was around in the 1820s, and thus predates the take-off in economic growth in the county. At the same time, it is clear that the powerful sense of local and civic identity which manifested itself in, amongst other things, support for local cricket, was an obstacle to the creation of a genuinely unified county cricket club. Instead it encouraged a parochialism which worked against efforts to develop a broader structure, which was hard enough anyway given the distances involved in such a large county. The domination of Yorkshire cricket from the 1820s by cricketers playing in Sheffield created conditions in which other West Riding towns – with their own sense of pride and tradition – were inevitably dissatisfied with their position in relation to Sheffield, and from the 1860s were reluctant to accept what they saw as 'scraps from the table' in the form of being able to host lower profile (and hence less profitable) county games.

In parallel, the faster development of cricket in the West Riding created conditions in which other parts of the county, in particular, the North Riding, with its own cluster of successful clubs, felt excluded. This situation fits with Sissons' view that 'the creation of county cricket clubs and hence a programme of county fixtures could only happen as fast as the counties emerged as unified social, political and economic entities. That entailed overcoming the rivalries between town and country, between different towns and cities within the same county, and between the county aristocracy and the rising urban bourgeoisie.'[1581] From the outset, it was clear that the development of stable county cricket in Yorkshire was never going to be easy.

Yorkshire county cricket before 1863

Although Yorkshire County Cricket Club first played in 1863, teams labelled as representing Yorkshire had by then taken the field for more than 30 years. It is generally accepted that the first county match by a team styled as 'Yorkshire' was against Norfolk at the Hyde Park Ground in Sheffield between the 2nd and 5th September 1833.[1582] On the day that the *Sheffield Independent* reported on the outcome of the famous Tom Marsden-Fuller Pilch single-wicket match at Hyde Park, it also announced that:

> Two Cricket Matches, home and home, are made between the County of Norfolk and the County of York, for £50 each match. The first is to take place at Hyde Park, Sheffield, in the first week in September. This match will be the crack match for the season, in which all the best players will be engaged; the three Pilches will play on the Norfolk side. Betting even.[1583]

The two-innings-a-side match resulted in a Yorkshire win by 120 runs, with Marsden and Dearman making significant contributions with both bat and ball.[1584] Wondering why the county's first game was against Norfolk, Holmes concluded that, not only was it closer than the southern counties at a time when transport was not easy, but it also possessed the greatest batsman of the day, Fuller Pilch, who had Sheffield connections.[1585] Just as likely, however, was that, given the summer had been spent in anticipation of the single-wicket contest between Marsden and Pilch, which had been such a success at Hyde Park in August (albeit not for Marsden, who lost), the organisers wanted to generate yet more interest and thus money from the involvement of these two great players.

The *Sheffield Independent* was in no doubt about the significance of the Norfolk match. It commented:

> Nothing can exceed the interest this match excites in Sheffield and its neighbourhood, and many hundreds are betted upon the event; Norfolk for choice, in consequences of the three Pilches, who are reckoned first raters, playing on that side. The Yorkshire players, likewise, have got a tower of strength in their eleven, the best perhaps, that ever turned out upon the field.

Such was its importance, men from the north of Yorkshire travelled down to witness the game, as well as to get a sight of some of the players they were due to play the following month when Bedale took on Sheffield.[1586] The match was affected by rain, with only an hour played on the second day, but Yorkshire still proved victorious.

Further games against Norfolk took place in 1834 and 1836, with the first of these advertised as 'The Return Match between Yorkshire and Norfolk.' The papers commented that the:

> best players in Yorkshire, we hope, will be engaged in this match, for the honour of the county; and if the Norfolk men do win, let it be said, that the whole of the strength of Yorkshire was brought into the field, and that nothing but superior playing on the part of Norfolk, was the cause of the defeat of Yorkshire.[1587]

The 1836 home-and-away matches proved to be financially problematic, and in September of that year, Woolhouse advertised that, whilst grateful to those who had contributed, the receipts did not cover the expenses. Consequently:

> WHW begs respectfully to assure his Friends and the Public generally, that no effort on his part shall be wanting to arrange such Matches as will deserve their patronage; but experience has taught him that first-rate talent cannot be procured, unless he is indemnified to a certain extent from the great risk of such heavy Expenses.[1588]

The financial risks involved may have helped to limit the number of representative games in the following years. Yorkshire sides played Sussex in 1835 and 1855, as well as Manchester in 1844 and 1845, Lancashire in 1849 and 1851, Kent in 1849, Surrey in 1851, and Sheffield in 1849 and 1850. Yorkshire XIs also played against All-England Elevens between 1846 and 1862, with varying numbers of players on the county side. They also took on the United All England Eleven.[1589] By the middle of the century, however, there were signs that the press at least considered there was a representative side for the county during this period. In 1851, for example, the *Sheffield Independent* reported that the team playing against Surrey was a strong one and added:

> Nor was Yorkshire, to all appearance, at all behind their compeers; for knowing the force which the Southrons were able to muster, the greatest care was manifested in the selection of the men to take part in the contest. Indeed, a choicer set than those forming the respective sides, it would be difficult to select.[1590]

Examination of developments in the game up to the 1850s indicates a number of themes which run through the entire period. Firstly, it seems that from an early point, many cricketers in Yorkshire thought about their club and its status in the wider context of their Riding or the whole county, helped by the local press which made some effort to draw comparisons and 'puff up' the claims to prominence of certain teams. Reports of matches commented favourably on particular clubs, suggesting, for example, that Tadcaster was on the way to surpassing any club in Yorkshire in 1820, while the players of Scruton were becoming the 'best in the north-riding' the same year.[1591] Holmes's view was that Ripon was 'almost the strongest club in Yorkshire' in the period from the mid-1810s, a view likely to have been shared by many at the time.[1592] In 1828, the *Yorkshire Gazette* referred to the Husthwaite club as the best players in the North Riding.[1593]

Rivalries and reputations built up. In 1821, for example, three games between Harewood and Tadcaster were referred to as the 'Grand Rubber.'[1594] In September 1822, the *Leeds Mercury* summarised the results of 'the summer's campaign' – three matches in August and September – between the Harewood and Wighill Cricket Clubs. It stated that 'The Wetherby Club consists of the gentlemen from Leeds and Harewood, and the Wighill of those from Wetherby and Tadcaster, and their reputation as cricket players stand higher than any other clubs in the county, Sheffield perhaps excepted.'[1595] Such claims did not go unchallenged. Shortly after, a correspondent commented that such a statement 'must naturally be expected to excite the envy of their Yorkshire inferiors.....In the sporting world Wighill must now be considered classic ground, to be visited by every amateur of the science possessing taste enough to appreciate excellence, and anxious to show respect for it.' However, he argued that the Wighill players actually had little to do with the Club, and the side was in fact a far broader selection from Wetherby, Tadcaster, Nun-Appleton and Selby. The correspondent ended by making a challenge on behalf of the Leeds Players to any 12 players in any township in Yorkshire, East, West or North of Leeds.[1596] This prompted a further, equally caustic, response denying the accusation and emphasising that players from just the two towns were united in the name of Wighill as it was situated between them. The author mocked the challenge, given it was made after the season was over. A reposte came the following week, offering to play the following spring if it could not be fitted in during 1822.[1597]

As we saw earlier, there were other hints of a strong sense of competition between the best clubs in the county such as in the early 1840s, when Sheffield, Dalton, Bradford and Harewood clubs competed 'for a final settlement of the palm of victory.'[1598] The *Sheffield Independent* referred to these matches as for the 'Championship of Yorkshire', as was the game between Dalton and Sheffield Wednesday in 1844.[1599] In 1855, the match between Bedale and Stockton-upon-Tees was described as being for the 'championship of the North.'[1600]

Secondly, notwithstanding that some of the premier clubs vied for prominence in the county from an early point, there was little doubt that Sheffield was the pre-eminent cricketing town from the 1820s onwards, and widely recognised as such. The cricketers of the town were the most effective (or, in the language of the time, 'the most scientific') and successful. They took on some of the strongest teams from outside the county such as Nottingham and Leicester, and they needed to make concessions in terms of the number of opposing players when they contested with other clubs in Yorkshire. The high standing of the Sheffield Cricket Club appears, for example, in the challenge they gave the Leeds Club in 1832 to produce 22 men to play their eleven for £22 a side. The *Sheffield Independent*, which referred to it later as 'The great Yorkshire Cricket Match', commented, 'When it is considered that the Leeds Club is to have the privilege of choosing its players throughout the county, that they will be two to one against Sheffield, it must be inferred that our townsmen feel very confident in their own strength to give such a challenge.'[1601]

The supremacy of Sheffield was well recognised by many in cricketing circles, and for some this was seen to boost the reputation of all Yorkshire cricketers. When the Darnall ground was sold in 1829, the *Sheffield Independent* observed that the game would continue to be played in the coming season 'under the management which has already raised the reputation of the Yorkshire clubs.'[1602] As a result of the town's strength, however, challenges sent out to all Yorkshire clubs often excluded Sheffield in order to avoid the contest being meaningless. At the same time, the dominance could be double-edged and, while Sheffield was proud of its reputation, some in the town complained that other parts of the county were not contributing enough. In July 1851, for example, all but two of the Yorkshire side who appeared against 16 of Nottingham Commercial Club were Sheffield men, other players having dropped out to play elsewhere. In their absence, the *Sheffield Independent* commented, 'the brunt of the battle fell upon Sheffield, which supplied the whole of the eleven, with the exception of Berry and Baldwinson.'[1603]

In other parts of the county, Sheffield domination could also lead to some feelings of envy and irritation. In 1852, a speaker at a heated special meeting of York Cricket Club commented that 'they could never hope to flourish like Sheffield and other towns, which possessed greater advantages than York for cricket.'[1604] In August 1855, when Yorkshire played Sussex at Sheffield, the *Leeds Times* reporter commented that the side, made up of 'about the choice of Yorkshire', might 'have been made much stronger....if fewer Sheffield men had been put in the eleven'.[1605]

One consequence of Sheffield's pre-eminence was that for many years there was ambiguity around the terms 'Sheffield' and 'Yorkshire', labels which were often used interchangeably. In May 1825, Darnall hosted a major match between what was described as 'twenty-two of the county of York, with Sparks (from London) on the side of the Yorkshire players' against the eleven of All-England.[1606] Reports talked of 'All Yorkshire' or 'Yorkshire' interchangeably with 'the Sheffield players' or 'Sheffield'.[1607] In 1830, a match was advertised as between Eleven Members of the Wednesday Club and Eleven Picked Players from the County of York. The latter players were listed, but only Ibbotson and Gatenby (Ripon) and Ward (Doncaster) were not from Sheffield.[1608] In August 1851, the *Leeds Mercury* commented that a match styled as Yorkshire against Surrey was in fact 'Sheffield v Surrey, eight of the Yorkshire players being Sheffield, and only three from the county.'[1609]

Thirdly, despite the dominance of Sheffield cricketers, the concept of a more broadly-based Yorkshire team, involving players from around the county, was voiced early on. In August 1828, an article in the *Sheffield Independent* discussed the idea in terms which were still being put forward in the same way over 60 years later. Referring to the great matches that Woolhouse had brought to Sheffield, it argued:

> We put the proposition to the patrons of the game throughout the Riding, that if they are desirous Yorkshire should retain its reputation for practising in perfection the most elegant athletic amusement in Europe, they should form a common club for the county. This measure would make the best players known to each other; it would enable them to concentrate their strength, and by the collection of a small contribution, produce an adequate fund to pay certain players (whose circumstances render it necessary) for practising, make up stake money, travelling expenses, etc. At present, we merely hint at the expediency of forming a county club; but if those Noblemen and Gentlemen of fortune who patronise the game should think favourably of the proposition, we will, at another opportunity, enter into further detail.'[1610]

Subsequent games give a sense of where the best players outside Sheffield were to be found. In 1832, a game advertised as between 'Eleven scientific Players of Sheffield and Twenty-two chosen Men of all Yorkshire' took place, with the Yorkshire players advertised as being chiefly selected from the Leeds, Thirsk, Ripon, Bedale, Harewood and Yarm cricket clubs.[1611] As it turned out, however, the team was made up of seven players from Leeds, two from Hunslet, four from Harewood, two from Armley, two from Knaresborough, four from Wetherby, and one from Bradford.[1612] A further game was held in September, again against a team 'of the chosen men of all Yorkshire.'[1613] Ten years later, a game involving 'the whole strength of Yorkshire' was organised between the North Riding and West Riding, a further sign that the East Riding was considered unimportant in cricketing matters.[1614]

The value of drawing together the strength of the whole county was also recognised in 1850. Reporting on the game between the Gentlemen (with Anderson and Letby) and Players of Yorkshire, the *Sheffield Independent* commented that when the gentlemen of Yorkshire met the gentlemen of the Manchester club, the game had significance not only in that it was attractive to the public, but would also 'bring together again several gentlemen, patrons of the game, in various districts of the county, and from which might result that unity of action necessary to the advancement of the noble game in Yorkshire, which bids fair to rival the famous cricketing counties of the south.'[1615] It would, however, be some time before this happened.

The first steps

As we saw, in the late 1840s and early 1850s, county cricket became a little more common, and although Yorkshire was defeated at The Oval in August 1851, there remained a belief that things would improve. Despite observing that the Yorkshire side disappointed on this occasion, the *Sheffield Independent* commented that 'Yorkshire is not dismayed, but will gladly hail the opportunity next season, of again meeting the champions of Surrey in the field of friendly warfare.'[1616] Some outside observers were actually very positive about the quality of Yorkshire cricketers. William Caffyn, for example, commented that in 1851, 'Yorkshire had undoubtedly a good team now, and it is strange that they did not at this time come more to the front in the cricket world. They had good and experienced batsmen in Tom Hunt, Harry Wright, Sam Baldwinson, Harry Sampson, George Anderson, and others, and good bowlers in Ellis and Armitage; still they played very few matches at this period.'[1617]

Despite the perceived high-quality players in Yorkshire, the next steps to create a properly constituted county club were not taken until the early 1860s. Exactly why this should have been is hard to say with certainty. Holmes puts it down to 'a lack of public spirit, and so of the necessary funds',[1618] but it seems clear that the creation of the county club required Yorkshire cricketers to overcome the parochialism and the strong local pride which we have seen was present in Leeds, Bradford and many other towns in their own clubs. This local focus was reinforced by the considerable effort that towns put into organising games with touring elevens in the late 1840s and early 1850s, which for many years carried a strong cachet, as well as not inconsiderable financial risk, and therefore needed to be taken seriously.

Added to this, mistrust towards Sheffield and its domination of cricket in the region remained a factor throughout the period. The town had several well-established clubs in the 1850s – including Sheffield United, Wednesday, Hallam and Shrewsbury – capable of organising games with the major touring teams, but ironically, it was probably that cricket in Sheffield was in something of a decline in the late 1840s (as we saw in Chapter 3) and did not have a high-quality ground until Bramall Lane opened in 1855, that slowed down this stage of development of county cricket. There could be no Yorkshire county club without Sheffield but, for a while, the town and its cricketers were not in a sufficiently buoyant state to be able to offer the leadership needed. Creating the Bramall Lane ground provided the stability and facilities required, and gave the town the solid base it needed to take the lead in the county. At the same time, however, the demands of the financial arrangements for Bramall Lane (also discussed in Chapter 3) made it necessary for Sheffield to host the most significant – and most profitable – matches. These circumstances reinforced the tensions which had existed since the 1820s between Sheffield and other parts of Yorkshire.

The early 1860s saw significant developments. On 7 March 1861, a special general meeting of the proprietors of the Sheffield United cricket ground was held at the Adelphi Hotel 'for the purpose of considering and determining whether the Funds of the Ground shall be appropriated towards Defraying the Expenses of County or other Public Matches.'[1619] Holmes states that it was resolved that:

> the Match Committee should consist of the Committee of Management of the Bramall Lane Cricket Ground, and of one representative of each club contributing any sum of not less than twenty shillings to the Fund. Mr M.J.Ellison was elected President and Treasurer, Mr W.Whittles Secretary. The Pitsmoor, Sheffield Wednesday and Hallam clubs at once forwarded a subscription, and Scarborough [the Sheffield club, not the coastal town] followed their example the year after. But that was all the public support given to the appeal.[1620]

A match was arranged between a first eleven and the next sixteen for the benefit of the Match Fund, along with home-and-away games between Yorkshire and Surrey. The committee also resolved to prepare two dozen canvassing books with which to solicit financial support from local noblemen and gentlemen.[1621] Subsequently, Ellison wrote to a number of these people for assistance.[1622] The first Surrey game was preceded by a match between Hallam and Yorkshire for £100 between 15 and 17 July, although this provoked some disquiet and apparently 'resuscitated the unpleasant feeling which has existed between the Hallam and the principal Sheffield clubs ever since the dispute on the match between the Hallam and Wednesday clubs several years ago.' Sheffield players who had appeared for Hallam (in this 'money match') were consequently not included in the Yorkshire side against Surrey as the committee organising that match saw the earlier one as a rival fixture which threatened the profitability of its 'long announced' county game in aid of the Fund. John Berry and Rowbotham absented themselves from the Hallam game and were therefore included in the Yorkshire side, but William Slinn was 'too important' to Hallam to be allowed to withdraw and, as a result, did not play for the county.[1623]

In July, Sheffield and Bradford also played in aid of the public match fund.[1624] However, the initiative was not a great success. In November 1861, the Sheffield United accounts showed that the club had lost £27 on matches played for the match-fund committee.[1625] Despite this, negotiations began for fixtures for the 1862 season against Kent and Surrey.[1626] However, the Committee decided, in view of the other games, to decline a request from the Manchester Club to play Lancashire, and also turned down a request from Bradford.[1627] Over the winter, the Sheffield authorities built a new pavilion at Bramall Lane which was very positively received at the match against Kent in June 1862, and described as 'decidedly one of the best cricketing grounds in the kingdom.'[1628] Significant efforts were made to attract crowds to the county games. Boards were placed at the railway stations announcing the Kent match, as well as all round Sheffield. Some 500 one shilling and 1,000 6d tickets were printed, along with 1,000 handbills and 150 larger posters. The proprietors of the omnibus company were asked to carry placards announcing the games, and a military band was engaged.[1629] Helped by this activity, at the end of the year, the finances of the Sheffield club were generally fine but with some areas for concern. The number of clubs which paid to use the Bramall Lane ground had declined in 1862, perhaps because many were developing their own facilities. In addition, changes to the licensing laws added considerably to the expenses because of the need for regular applications for occasional licences. Although the balance in the hands of the treasurer was £355, the authorities in Sheffield still had to be mindful of their finances.[1630]

The driving force behind the Public Match Fund – and Yorkshire cricket for the coming decades – was Michael Ellison (1817-1898). The eldest son of the longstanding local agent for the Duke of Norfolk, Ellison took over this role from his father. From 1838 to 1853 he appeared for Sheffield, played for Yorkshire before the county club was formally established, and opened the innings for England against the MCC at Lord's in 1853. Between 1863 and 1893 he was Treasurer of Yorkshire, and between 1864 and 1897, the President, acting with Wostinholm as one of 'a jolly old pair of autocrats', in the words of Lord Hawke, who also called him 'the founder of modern Yorkshire county cricket.'[1631] On Ellison's death, the *Yorkshire Evening Post* observed that he did:

> probably more than any other individual to keep county cricket going in the days when the risks were many and funds were few. This fact had always been cordially recognised by Yorkshiremen outside Sheffield amid all the controversies that have existed in recent years.[1632]

Years later, Holmes speculated as to why the Public Match Fund had not been a success, suggesting 'doubtless it was thought that a Match Committee was lacking in the weight of an executive constituted on the broadest lines. It was not sufficiently representative of the county as a whole.'[1633] On this, he was almost certainly correct. It was clearly a Sheffield-led affair and this fact rankled with those running cricket elsewhere, particularly in Bradford. There was a strong sense of pride in that town's ability to hold its own in games with Sheffield over the previous decade, including a win by 54 runs in 1855 and a 10-wicket win on equal terms in 1859. In 1863, the club's overall record was one defeat in 11 matches.[1634] The town also had a good reputation for hosting big games. In 1861, Bradford had overwhelmed the United England Eleven by an innings and six runs, and beaten the All-England Eleven by 17 runs. In 1862, there was another very successful contest with the All-England Eleven, with interest added because the local side was reduced to 18 men.[1635] Increasingly, therefore, Bradford wanted to host attractive fixtures and needed to do so to satisfy its members and patrons that they were getting value for money for their fees.

Despite the failure of the Public Match Fund, the Sheffield authorities did not let things rest, and were backed by the press and other supporters of the game. Many saw that other counties were better organised and were irritated that some influential figures clearly looked down on cricket in Yorkshire. In 1860, George Parr had made disparaging comments about a lack of bowlers in Yorkshire (although the *Leeds Times* pointed out that Hodgson had recently been very effective against the United England Eleven at Bradford).[1636] Two years later, the Chairman of the Surrey County Cricket Club, expressed the view that Yorkshire cricket was weak, which also rankled, particularly after the county's win over the southern side in July by three wickets.[1637] Such slights were not forgotten. In 1863, the *Leeds Times* referred back to it, and suggested that now, despite not being able to practise together, Yorkshire's recent performances entitled them to be called 'the champion eleven.'[1638]

Some outsiders urged greater efforts in the county. In 1861, a London journalist called on Yorkshire cricketers to raise their game, stating:

> Yorkshire, you are wanted, that is, the leading men and cricketers of Yorkshire are wanted to bestir themselves, beat up the wealth, rank and influential men of their shire, and establish a County Cricket Club. Good cricket grounds you have already in various parts of the county. Cricketers are ready at hand of that metal and ability that even under the present disorganised – or rather NO – state of things, were found an eleven that could beat Surrey....To let a county droop in the cricket world that has found an eleven which can beat Surrey, appears to us a burning shame.[1639]

Responding to such calls, others in Yorkshire showed an interest in the quality of cricket played in the county and sought to give it the push it needed. In September 1862, a match was organised between All-England and XX of Yorkshire, arranged by R.C.Thorp, one of the 'most liberal supporters of cricket in the Huddersfield area', deliberately organised in order 'to bring out the young players of the county.'[1640]

Against this background, a meeting was held at the Adelphi Hotel on 8 January 1863 where it was resolved, 'That this Committee undertake to get up a home and home match between Surrey and Yorkshire to be played at the Oval on the 4th June and then on the 27th July in accordance with the proposition received from Mr Burrup.' It was also agreed 'That a County Club be formed, the Annual Subscription to be not less than 10/6 per member', and that a sub-committee be established to carry out this resolution.[1641] Subsequently, on 22 April 1863, another meeting was held, chaired by M.J.Ellison, which agreed 'to form a

County Cricket Club, its object being to provide funds for the playing of first-class county matches, either in Sheffield or in other towns of the county, according as arrangements may be made. A president, vice-president, treasurer, secretary, and committee were appointed, to collect subscriptions, draw up rules, and make all other preliminary arrangements.'[1642] The meeting adjourned until 28 April, when the rules proposed by the subcommittee were unanimously approved. [1643]

The Committee consisted entirely of Sheffield men, although many of the rules, at least in principle, sounded more inclusive. In particular, the purpose of the county club was 'to develop the cricketing power of the County and promote the game generally.' The rules stated there would be no interference with local clubs and invited 'recommendations from all local clubs of any young players who may be considered likely to add to the strength of the County in any department of the game.' It also said the Managing Committee would consider 'propositions from any part of the County for the choice of its particular neighbourhood as the locality for one county match in any year.' This was dependent on the club 'having a cricket ground in first-rate playing condition.' Where such a match took place, the Managing Committee would accept a sum of money from the club or district or have the ground surrendered to it 'absolutely and unconditionally' for the match days.[1644]

By the time of these announcements, games for the 1863 season had been arranged for Sheffield. In early February, however, the *Bradford Observer* announced that Yorkshire would play Nottinghamshire in Bradford in June and in Nottingham in July, matches to be arranged by the Bradford Cricket Club. The paper added that its subscribers could expect to get better value for their money this season than many felt had been the case in the previous one.[1645] The Sheffield press was less impressed and the fact that such a big game was to be played in Bradford caused some anxiety. The *Independent* reported that this development was owing to the lack of the necessary support in Sheffield which was:

> much to be regretted, as the facilities for playing such an important match at Bradford cannot be compared with those to be found here. But the Bradford gentlemen have handsomely subscribed the funds, and they have provided for their townspeople a cricketing treat of rare excellence. This circumstance has given rise to a good deal of comment and we are glad to learn that a club is being formed, under the auspices of the Sheffield United Cricket Club, solely for the purposes of getting up first class county matches to be played here.[1646]

The game at Bradford against Nottinghamshire in June 1863 – advertised as the 'Grand County Match' – was the highlight of the Bradford club's season, attracting the highest attendance ever seen in the town. The ground was in excellent condition, and the Nottinghamshire side so well entertained that John Jackson, the county Secretary, expressed himself 'highly gratified' at his team's reception. Despite his side's eight-wicket defeat, he hoped it would be an annual event.[1647]

The 1863 season went well on the field and after the win over Surrey in July the *Leeds Times* stated that Yorkshire 'occupies a truly proud position in the cricketing world.'[1648] At this time, it appears that attempts were made to reach some form of rapprochement between Sheffield and Bradford. A correspondent to the *Yorkshire Post* many years later commented that, 'in 1863 Sheffield asked Bradford for its co-operation in the task and risk of playing county cricket and was refused it.'[1649] There is also some evidence that the Sheffield committee accepted that they still had to sell the new arrangements to others. On 11 June, George Padley, the club's first Secretary, wrote to H.S.Hirst, the Bradford Cricket Club Secretary, promising to forward copies of the Yorkshire County Club Rules which he hoped would meet with the approval of local cricketers. And he added, 'Some of our people will (I expect) get over to see the Nottingham match and will then talk the matter over with you. In the hope that your co-operation will be secured, I am, &c.'[1650] However, the Bradford club had by now clearly demonstrated it was capable of organising not just local but county matches, and had no desire to allow Sheffield to dominate Yorkshire county cricket. The development of county cricket was thus clearly being driven by local pride in Sheffield and Bradford, and also by financial necessity on the part of both clubs, and by the honest desire of the respective club authorities to put on the best cricket for people in their towns.

It is therefore possible to see the creation of Yorkshire County Cricket Club in 1863 less as a breakpoint in the history of the game in the county, and more in terms of continuity. The picture is far from straightforward. Firstly, it is important to recognise that games immediately after 1863 were essentially no different from those before. Certain players turned out in the 1860s who had appeared for Yorkshire sides in the late 1840s (John Berry, Jonathan Joy) and 1850s (Roger Iddison, George Anderson, and Isaac Hodgson), and a number of others had featured in games in the early 1860s. Reports of the Yorkshire-Surrey game, played in July 1863, also suggest that contemporary opinion was not convinced that anything new had been created, and instead the games that season were continuing an established tradition. *The Sheffield Independent*, for example, commented that games between the counties 'have been so numerous, the strife for superiority has been so keen, and the results so evenly balanced that the present match has excited unusual interest.'[1651]

Secondly, it is clear that Holmes' depiction of the matches outside Sheffield 'for which the County Committee were not responsible' as only possibly possessing 'a passing interest' is misleading and lacking in objectivity.[1652] In the context of the time, the matches arranged by Bradford and elsewhere were of equal standing to those of Sheffield, and were organised legitimately by the Bradford committee with the (very willing) county authorities in Nottinghamshire. In 1863, the Sheffield-based committee was not regarded by all cricketers in Yorkshire as the centre for county cricket and, as one Leeds paper put it, 'What is termed a "Yorkshire Cricket Club" has been formed in Sheffield, but as its officers (president, secretary, committee, &c.), are all Sheffield men, the project is not likely to meet with much encouragement out of that town.'[1653] In the 1860s, other club committees felt perfectly entitled to organise matches in the name of Yorkshire, and other county authorities were content to make arrangements with them. The scores count in the county records, and there was nothing particularly lower status about the arrangements. Thus, in 1863, the Yorkshire game against Nottinghamshire was arranged thanks to 'the spirit of a few Bradford gentlemen, headed by Lieut-Col. Hirst', while the Kent match at Middlesbrough in 1864 was arranged by Messrs Dickens, Coates and Vaughan, notable patrons of the sport in that town.[1654]

Thirdly, contemporaries were well aware of the divisions between the towns, but still considered Yorkshire cricket could only get better if someone – but not necessarily the committee in Sheffield – took the lead. Aware that efforts were being made in York to organise a second county club (which will be examined shortly), in December 1863, the *London Evening Standard* reflected that the county ranked second to none and could put out a second eleven which was almost as strong as its first. There was 'hearty support' for cricket, especially in the large towns, and it had some of the best players of the day. As a result:

> Yorkshire ought to, and might, have a good county club, and that instead of some two out and home matches in the year (supplemented, however, by a very large number of "odds" matches), Yorkshire might meet all the cricketing counties on one or other of its town grounds. And the very influential representative committee appointed last week, whilst wisely making a central ground for their gentlemen's matches at York, has avoided the grave — nay, fatal, error which was talked of at first, of playing their county matches there, by placing as a chief object before themselves the giving the opportunity to all their cricketing localities of seeing their county strength pitted against the best players of the north and south.[1655]

Around the same time, the editor of *Sporting Life*, reporting on the same alternative initiative, stated that it wished 'the spirited Yorkshiremen who have taken the initiative every success, and shall be happy to aid the movement in any way in our power.'[1656] Thus, Yorkshire cricket was seen in many parts of the country as having great potential which still needed to be nurtured.

'Gentlemanly' disquiet

The challenge to the Sheffield-based committee began at the end of the summer of 1863. On 30 September, a meeting took place at Harker's Hotel in York, at which representatives from most parts of the county were present. The *York Herald* reported that:

> for several years it has past been the desire of many gentlemen in Yorkshire to establish a cricket club, open to the whole county, with a committee composed of gentlemen selected from every part of it, who should undertake the arrangement of both gentlemen's and professional county matches, to be played on *any* ground deemed by the committee sufficiently good for the purpose.[1657]

Under a heading 'Formation of a County Cricket Club', details were given of a number of resolutions passed, namely that a cricket club should be established for the county of Yorkshire; a provisional committee be appointed to make the necessary preliminary arrangements; a special fund be set up to procure a ground near York; and that the committee consist of Lord Wenlock, Hon. G.Lascelles, Major Coates, Rev. H.M.Clifford, B.W.Waud and C.J.Key, with Clifford appointed as Secretary. After discussions, the meeting was adjourned until 4 November 1863, and Clifford was asked to send out circulars to the promoters of cricket in the county, and to advertise the meeting in the county papers. These duly appeared in late October, and read: 'Yorkshire County Cricket Club. A General Meeting of the Yorkshire County Cricket Club will be held at Harker's Hotel, York on Wednesday 4th November at half-past THREE o'clock in the Afternoon.'[1658] The minutes of the (Sheffield-based) Yorkshire County Cricket Club committee meeting in late October indicate that Ellison and Prest were deputed to attend the York gathering.[1659]

There was a good response, with 26 men present, including some who had attended the first meeting. Hon.G.Lascelles was in the chair and explained the objects of the club. After initial discussions, Colonel Hurst of Bradford – apparently ignoring the arrangements made in Sheffield – proposed forming a cricket club for Yorkshire, and this was passed unanimously. A committee was established with representatives from York, Bradford, Leeds, Wakefield, Halifax, Huddersfield, Middlesbrough, Doncaster, Sheffield, Hull, the Yale of Derwent, Harewood, Boroughbridge, Bedale and Redcar. Committee members were appointed for most of the towns, with others to be made later. Not all those nominated were present, and although Sheffield was represented by Messrs. Prest and Sale, who were appointed to the committee. M.J.Ellison, who was also chosen, was not there. The purpose of the club was described as 'promoting the game of cricket in Yorkshire', and it was reported that when 'duly organised and got into working operation, the society will have matches at cricket played under its auspices' at a number of venues.[1660] Despite the apparent challenge to the existing club, the *Sheffield Independent* simply reported the details uncritically, noting that Sheffield would be represented by Prest, Ellison and Sale.[1661]

The 4 November meeting next considered the establishment of a separate gentlemen's cricket club. The Chairman stated that, with similar arrangements being made in Lincolnshire and Nottinghamshire:

> it was desirable that steps should be promptly taken to form a gentlemen's cricket club at York for the whole county....[with York] the headquarters, on account of its central and favourable position. Already nearly 100 gentlemen had given in their names as members, and Lords Feversham, Wenlock, and Londesborough had signified their intention of joining the club.

It was then reported that a ground had been secured behind Bootham Asylum in York.[1662] The Yorkshire Gentlemen's Cricket Club was established and by early 1864 had over 150 members, including many of the 'leading names' of the North Riding. The first games were played in Ireland in June 1864.[1663]

Following the November meeting, the members of the second Yorkshire county club gathered again in York on 18 December 1863. Further resolutions were carried that:

> 10s. 6d. be the "minimum" subscription to the County Cricket Club; that five members of the committee shall constitute a quoram; that Major Coates be the honorary secretary of the club and R.Swann, Esq., the treasurer; that the secretary be requested to solicit the various noblemen of the county and county members to become members and patrons of the club; and that Earl Fitzwilliam be requested to act as president for the first year.[1664]

The meeting also agreed to seek county matches with Surrey, Nottinghamshire, and Kent or Cambridgeshire. Despite this, other evidence of developments is hard to come by, although in late November 1863, the *Huddersfield Chronicle* included an advert which stated 'Yorkshire County Cricket Club. Huddersfield District. Notice is hereby given that a meeting will be held at the house of Mr Benjamin Hutchinson, the Commercial Inn, Huddersfield, on Wednesday evening, the 2nd December, at Seven o'clock, for the purpose of Nominating a person to act on the County Club Committee.[1665]

The Sheffield committee kept a close eye on developments and for a while it seems it might have been prepared to go along with the York-based arrangements – described in the Yorkshire club minutes as 'the General County Committee.' On 4 January 1864, Prest reported back from the December meeting that he and Sale had been asked to convey the wish of the York gathering for the co-operation of the Sheffield committee. Following this, the Committee called a meeting of Sheffield subscribers to the Yorkshire County Cricket Club to consider the desirability of joining the York club. On 15 January 1864, those attending agreed to the proposal and it was resolved that 'the Provisional Committee be empowered to enter into arrangements with a view to join the General County Committee and that they report the result to the Annual meeting or to a Special meeting on an earlier day if necessary.'[1666]

Word got out that discussions were taking place. *Sporting Life* reported in January that, since the original meeting in November:

> circumstances have occurred to endanger the unanimity which ought to prevail in all undertakings of this kind, but we trust these minor difficulties will now be overcome, as we are pleased to learn that Sheffield (hitherto the head-quarters of cricket in Yorkshire) committee has resolved to send a deputation to confer with the committee at York, with a view to join the General County Club.[1667]

This was confirmed in February, and in March the matter was again discussed by the Sheffield committee, when a replacement had to be found for Ellison, who could not attend. A replacement was also lined up in case anyone else could not make it, suggesting that the committee thought the meeting was important.[1668] However, there was no agreement on plans for this second Yorkshire County Cricket Club, and it seems the sticking point was that Sheffield would not support York's desire for a general fund into which all clubs would subscribe.

The York-based club appears to have been a dead end for those pushing for a broadly-based Yorkshire County Cricket Club, and it disappeared without ever playing a match. During the disputes in 1882 about the running of the county club, to be covered later, one correspondent to the *Yorkshire Post* stated, 'In 1863 and 1864 meetings of delegates from the principal clubs and towns were held at York for the purpose of forming a Yorkshire County Cricket Club, but the scheme failed utterly on account of financial difficulties.'[1669] The efforts of many of those who met in York were instead channeled into the Yorkshire Gentlemen club.[1670]

Continuing split

The divided arrangements for the organisation of county cricket matches in Yorkshire continued in the mid-1860s as a normal state of affairs, and there is no doubt that the county club was in a quite fragile state. The minutes for the July 1864 committee meeting include discussion about a possible postponement of the Yorkshire v Cambridgeshire game, apparently because of a clash with an All-England match. And it was resolved to pay a Mr Riley for the cost of the refreshments provided at the Surrey game, but to advise that nothing be supplied on the committee's account in future without a direct order, an indication perhaps of vulnerable finances.[1671] The appearance of the second county club committee also seemed to create confusion elsewhere. In April 1864, a letter from Kent County Cricket Club was read to the county committee expressing doubt as to which was the proper authority for organising Yorkshire matches. Members agreed to respond forcefully, questioning why there should be any doubts given that the Sheffield-based committee had handled the 1862 game. Shortly afterwards, however, Kent declined to play at Bramall Lane.[1672]

In contrast, Bradford maintained an important place in Yorkshire county cricket. In February 1864, whilst the *Sheffield Daily Telegraph* announced that Sheffield would host the 'annual match' with Surrey in June[1673], the *Independent,* reflecting on the competition to host games, commented that:

> Some disappointment was felt when we announced that the county match between Yorkshire and Nottinghamshire would take place at Bradford; but the county club are not without hope that an arrangement can be made for a match on Bramall lane ground, at a time when it will not interfere with or detract from the interest of the match at Bradford.[1674]

Bradford opinion was less conciliatory, and the local press picked on selection and fixture issues in order to criticise Sheffield. There was also a clear sense that the Bradford authorities felt a responsibility to try and bring on new players for the county. In June 1864, the *Bradford Observer* provided the names of the Yorkshire team to play at Nottingham. It then queried the arrangements for Sheffield's Yorkshire v Cambridgeshire match in July, suggesting that Cambridgeshire already appeared to be committed elsewhere on those days.[1675]

That season Bradford hosted the Nottinghamshire game in August, and Middlesbrough – rather than Sheffield – put on the match with Kent in mid-September, while Sheffield was the venue for the Surrey and Cambridgeshire fixtures. The uncertainty continued into 1865 and began to get worse. In January, the county committee received unfavourable replies from Cambridgeshire, Nottinghamshire and Sussex to invitations to play that summer. As a result, on 10 January, it decided to write to Kent, as well as to George Parr and Edgar Willsher, suggesting games with their teams, and to George Anderson, asking him to arrange a North v South match at Sheffield.[1676] On 14 January, Anderson responded, commenting that there was 'a good deal of misunderstanding and unpleasantness between the North and the South players', and adding that, 'I should think that there would be some little difficulty in getting the sides up from the best players.' He suggested writing to Parr and Willsher to enquire.[1677]

In contrast, there again seemed to be more confidence in Bradford. In February 1865, the *Bradford Observer* reported that Yorkshire would be playing Cambridgeshire at Bradford in May. When asked later by a correspondent who would be playing for Yorkshire against Surrey in June, the Bradford paper caustically commented that 'we are not in the secrets of the Sheffield Committee, who alone have the selection of the players.' At the same time, it reported that the Bradford committee had been 'indefatigable' in its efforts over the winter in having the ground enlarged and got into proper condition for the coming season, as well as arranging a series of first-class matches.[1678] The Bradford club also arranged a game between XI of Bradford and XI Colts of the County to test the merits of the players with a view to them playing for the county.[1679] Bradford's confidence was later boosted by the success of the game with Nottinghamshire in July 1865, and by an eight-wicket victory in June over Sheffield in the annual match to determine the club which could call itself 'first among the town clubs in the shire.'[1680]

Events elsewhere began to deteriorate. Unrest among the leading players had simmered for some time and was known about in the early months of 1865. West comments that the secession of southern professionals from the AEE and UAEE, leading to the formation of the United South of England Eleven was interpreted by northern players as a deliberate attempt to destroy the original sides, 'the source of the lion's share of their summer wages.'[1681] The *Bradford Observer* noted in March that it had heard that 'several of the celebrities of the county' had decided not to play against Surrey this season, adding that whilst 'we regret differences amongst cricketers or any other men, we are not surprised at this. The Surrey players have lately done everything in their powers to separate themselves from those of the North.'[1682]

The county committee fixed games with the All-England Eleven and Kent, and in April wrote to George Anderson offering him the county captaincy and asking for any suggestions he had for the approaching season. At the end of the month, Anderson wrote back, outlining his opposition to the behaviour of the southern players and their 'feeling of hostility to the North.' He stated that he would not play against them, but advised that, with the exception of Iddison and Atkinson (who he thought agreed with him), he did not know how the others felt. He added that he was sure that it would be very annoying to the county committee to find there is such 'bad spirit amongst us', but no right-thinking person would blame him for sticking to his views where he was not to blame.

The committee minutes stated that up to this time they had not heard of any disinclination on the part of the Yorkshire players to play against southern players, and in early May the club wrote to Anderson again. The letter regretted that he would be prevented from taking up the captaincy, and commented that without getting into the merits of the dispute ('if indeed any merit can be found in it'), they felt it necessary to state that every professional player stood bound to play for his county when called upon to do so, and they did not expect any differences to be allowed to interfere with county matches. The letter added that the club was committed to playing six county games and would do so with whatever talent was available, even though this would probably be disastrous for the club and the players who refused to appear. Subsequently, Yorkshire committee members met with representatives of Surrey County Cricket Club, who denied that there was any hostility towards the North amongst their players. To back this up, they said the list of players in the North v South game included seven Surrey men. They added that if any Surrey men had misbehaved as Anderson claimed, they would be made to apologise, and that matters should be resolved by means of friendly arbitration.[1683]

On 4 May, Wostinholm was asked to write to all the players who had appeared against Surrey in 1864, with the exception of Anderson and Luke Greenwood (who had apparently already been engaged), asking them to play against Surrey, Kent and Parr's Eleven, home and away, with replies wanted by return. Stephenson and Rowbotham agreed to play in all, but on 15 May Iddison responded that, while he would appear against Kent and All-England, he could not think of playing against 'those Surrey men who sent in their resignations to the Secretary of the United Eleven' and had publicised this development through the papers. He added that by trying to break up the United Eleven they are 'taking the bread out of our mouths.' On 27 May, Stephenson then wrote to the committee to say he too would not play. He apologised and said he hoped it would not be interpreted as hostility to the committee as he would rather play at Bramall Lane than anywhere else in England. Further efforts to bring the problems to a close were made by Surrey County Cricket Club's Honorary Secretary, who suggested that if any Yorkshire cricketers wanted to drop by during the game with Sussex at The Oval (played 8-10 June), they could have any questions answered by his players.

The Yorkshire committee then decided to make one last effort to induce the players to change their minds and a member went to Manchester to talk to them. The five were advised that refusal to play against Surrey would be regarded as a refusal to play any games. The unnamed committee member gave Anderson a copy of the letter from Surrey's Burrup and read it out. According to the minutes, all were reluctant to discuss, and Anderson said the letter was untrue. He said once he had made up his mind, he was not likely to change it, and Stephenson, Atkinson and Iddison agreed. Rowbotham stated he would like to play but could not agree until he had spoken with George Parr, with whom he was due to appear on the following Monday.

The players apologised and said that they assumed that as a result of their refusal the match could not go ahead. The committee member advised them that the club was determined it would take place but added that if they agreed to play, as soon as the game was over, the committee would look into their grievances. If they found they were in the right, the club would not play Surrey again. The players refused to change their position. In June, Rowbotham wrote to the committee, advising that he too could not play. He said he was sorry he had not advised them earlier, but he had hoped the matter would have been resolved. It grieved him to refuse to play, but as his 'townsman' [presumably Stephenson] had declined, 'I know what would be the consequences' of playing, suggesting that pressure was being applied. The committee felt it had done all it could and decided to go ahead and accept the almost certain defeat and financial loss.[1684]

Thus, Anderson, Atkinson, Iddison, Rowbotham and Stephenson declined to play against Surrey in 1865. As Anderson put it, 'I uphold the North and will not play against those who have combined to sweep us from the cricket field altogether if they could.'[1685] The five were then excluded from county games for the season by the Sheffield committee, including that against the All-England Eleven (on which a loss of £70 was made).[1686] Ellison wrote to a number of other cricketers asking whether they could play against All-England, including A.J.Wilkinson, C.Appleton and Ashley Walker.[1687] Wilkinson was not available but the others appeared. In August, Slinn was also unable to play in the matches in the south and, owing to a misdirected letter, Luke Greenwood's unavailability due to illness was not known until late on.[1688]

Despite others apparently being aware of the problems in March, the official Yorkshire County Cricket Club view, set out in June when Wostinholm wrote to the *Sheffield Daily Telegraph,* was one of surprise, stating that the Committee of the County Club were in 'entire ignorance' of any problems until they wrote to Anderson, offering him the usual engagement in April.[1689] Other places saw no reason to stand with Sheffield, and although excluded from Sheffield-organised county matches, the players appeared for Yorkshire in other fixtures. To West, 'Jealousy, resentment of the dictatorial attitude emanating from Sheffield, and sympathy for the victims resulted in the issue of invitations to Anderson and the others to appear in home-and-away matches with Nottinghamshire and Cambridgeshire, which came under the management of other authorities, such as the Bradford committee.'[1690]

Just before Christmas 1865, a special meeting of the Yorkshire committee was held which approved a detailed report of what had gone on during the year. It was resolved to publish the paper and send a copy to the five players, who were asked to submit their grievances to the MCC.[1691] Over the following winter, Bradford organised games with Nottinghamshire and Cambridgeshire, as well as another Colts game (although this did not eventually take place). Four of the five 'secessionists' assisted Yorkshire in all these games, and Atkinson was only missing against Nottinghamshire because his employer required him in Middlesbrough.[1692]

This proved to be a high-water mark for Bradford, however, reinforced by the fact that the Sheffield committee did not host a county match in 1866. On

28 February 1866, the committee minutes state that Rowbotham, Stephenson, Atkinson and Anderson (Iddison was not mentioned) were to be excluded from any game, and it was resolved unanimously that it was left to the committee to determine whether any, and if so, what matches should be played during the ensuing season.[1693] None took place and one local paper reflected that, 'The prospects of the cricketing season in this locality are sombre...notwithstanding the unrivalled facilities afforded by the ground, and the love of good cricket which is so widely diffused in Sheffield.'[1694]

Things improved the following year, 1867. The county committee decided that 'the choice of players in the coming season be left in the hands of the Committee, and they are empowered (if they think well) to play those cricketers who refused to play in the past season, on their expressing their regret for what has occurred.'[1695] In June 1867, Roger Iddison and Joe Rowbotham played home and away against Surrey. Atkinson and Stephenson then appeared in 1868, although in fact the latter wrote in 1867 expressing regret for his conduct and the committee tried to engage him in that season. [1696]

If matters in Sheffield were improving by the end of the 1860s, cricket in Bradford was in something of a decline. In April 1868, there were complaints about the small number of quality matches in the town, and regrets that however much the people of Bradford loved outdoor sports, 'they love their pockets much better' and did not like to spend their money on things that did not interest them.[1697] The club's funds were in a bad state and a concert was held in March 1868 to try to raise revenue.[1698] Another article in the *Observer* the following year analysed the situation further. It argued that the club had gone into decline in recent years. Not so long ago it had been the best in Yorkshire but since then, some of the heroes of those days had died, some had left the town, and others were too old for the game.

In addition, there had also been a draining away of influential 'gentlemenly' support – Captain Bankhart and Colonel Hirst were mentioned – who had turned to other things, and the article suggested that the 'decadence of the club' contrasted with the growth of the volunteer movement in Bradford. Finally, the commentator, while not wanting to criticise current players, argued that the club had become too much of a 'gentlemen's' association. As a result, 'that lower order of society, that undeniably contains the best material for cricketers, seems to be absent from the club.' As a solution, the article called for fresh enthusiasm and public spirit. It noted that the Horton ground was only held on an annual tenancy and there was a risk of it being lost for housing. It suggested that if possible the ground be bought and the club put on a more democratic basis.[1699]

As Bradford's position waned, other towns aspired to host county games, with varying degrees of success. Dewsbury held the match with Cambridgeshire in July 1867 during the local Feast, which attracted good crowds – 4,000 on the first day and 6,000 on the second – and more than exceeded the committee's expectations. Some of the sporting press assumed this game was a replacement for the Sheffield-organised game which did not take place in early July when Cambridgeshire advised very late on that four of its players could not make it, but the *Bradford Observer* said, 'This is all bosh'. The match had in fact been organised by the Savile club over the winter and was nothing to do with Sheffield.[1700] The same summer, Middlesbrough hosted Yorkshire v Lancashire, but the match proved a financial disaster. The visitors put out a weak side, the weather was poor, and the game lasted only two days. For all these reasons, the club had to pay £37 out of its own funds for the game, and because of the state of the local economy some of the guarantors were unable to provide the promised support. So damaging was this experience that the Middlesbrough club reined back its programme of local games the following year.[1701]

County fixtures were also played at both Holbeck and Dewsbury. The *Leeds Times* praised the 'enterprising committee' of the Holbeck Recreation Society for arranging first-class matches for the 1868 season, with the Lancashire fixture the first county match played there.[1702] Less well received elsewhere, however, were the efforts made by Dewsbury. The *Bradford Observer* commented that 'no-one but the Dewsbury committee had anything to do with the selection of this team....We have no hesitation in telling the Dewsbury committee that they have failed to satisfy the rest of Yorkshire in their selection.'[1703] Added to this, the wicket played very badly according to a report of the game against Nottinghamshire in July.[1704] On the other hand, the Dewsbury committee hosted the All-England v United England match, which was considered a great success with more than £400 being taken.[1705] Cricket was also played on the Woodhouse Hill Ground in Hunslet, which held games with the United All-England XI and the Australian Aboriginals in 1868, and then a match between Yorkshire and Cambridgeshire in July 1869, but it was not popular, being considered small and well outside the town. [1706]

Yorkshire county cricket was thus in a very confusing and uncertain state in the second half of the 1860s. Reflecting on the 1867 season, the *Sporting Life* commented that progress in Yorkshire cricket 'has not of late years gone smoothly.' It suggested that this was down to the lack of unity as to where games should be played. York, Bradford, and Sheffield had all argued the case that its ground should be *the* Yorkshire ground, and if this was not sufficiently confusing, a game had been played in Dewsbury. It then proceeded to report Yorkshire's results, although ignoring what it described as the 'gate-money affair' at Whalley against Lancashire.[1707]

Efforts to arrange matches at Sheffield with Cambridgeshire, Nottinghamshire and Sussex failed in 1868, and the only games at Bramall Lane were against Middlesex and Surrey, while Nottinghamshire appeared at Dewsbury and Lancashire at Holbeck.[1708] This situation provoked strong feelings. When

Sporting Life listed the Nottinghamshire fixture at Dewsbury separately from the other county games in February 1868, the Honorary Secretary of the Savile club wrote that the distinction:

> may lead some to suppose that the match arranged by us is not a *bona-fide* county match. We are not aware of the existence of a county committee for Yorkshire, though we admit the desirability of one, and have had some talk with the Sheffield secretary on the subject....Such a club, with representatives on the committee from the principal towns in the county, and under an able secretary (say George Anderson, who I think well deserving of the post, and in every way fit to fill it) would command a very large patronage, and be the means of establishing the Yorkshire cricket county as second to none.[1709]

In response, someone signing himself as 'Subscriber to the Sheffield Cricket Club' commented that it was entirely right that they should be shown as under separate management. Efforts had been made in the past to form a county committee with representatives of all parts of the county, but it had failed 'for want of support.' He also noted that Dewsbury had wished to have the match during feast week as any other time would lead to a serious loss. This clashed with the Yorkshire v Surrey game but Sheffield had asked the Surrey authorities if they could change the dates in order to help Dewsbury. Finally, he commented that the secretary's post required a 'gentleman cricketer above professional bias'.[1710]

The difficult situation was saved by two factors, both of which strengthened Sheffield's position. First was the willingness of the authorities at Bramall Lane to allow Yorkshire County Cricket Club to use its ground free of charge in the early years. The proprietors did this on the basis that in better times the money outstanding would be repaid in annual grants. Prior to 1871, nothing was paid out for use of the ground and facilities or for wages of the men who worked on it. The proprietors spent money on improving the ground, and by 1881 had invested nearly £8,000, and were £2,200 in debt. In addition, it was reported in 1882 that Sheffield had lost £1,800 since 1870 by allowing players to have benefit matches – usually the best paying games - at the ground, and more than £600 by holding Colts games. In 1875 alone, the Colts match lost £115.[1711]

Eventually, money began to be repaid. In 1871, with the county funds showing a balance of £300, the sum of £50 ('a gift') was handed over to the Bramall Lane Ground Commitee towards repairing and improving the seats on the Bramall Lane side of the ground and for accommodation of visitors.[1712] In December 1873, £50 from the funds of the county club was paid over to the Ground Committee 'towards the improvements effected during the past season.'[1713] The following December, it was reported that every county match in the 1874 season had led to a profit for the club and crowds had been in excess of previous years.

The committee of the Sheffield United Cricket Club had invested large sums in enlarging and improving the accommodation, mainly for the comfort of spectators at county games and, as a result, the Sheffield committee applied for a grant to cover the cost. A grant of £350 was paid by Yorkshire (along with a loan of £100 at 5% interest), which still left the county club with a balance of around £500.[1714] In 1876, the county club was again in a good financial position, with receipts £130 up on the previous year and expenditure £33 down, and as a result £250 was paid to Sheffield United and £200 loaned at 2.5% interest.[1715] This continued in the 1880s with grants and loans; for example, a loan of £600 in 1884 and a grant of £700 in 1886 towards the cost of improvements. The finances of the two clubs were closely intertwined.

The second factor was the drive and enthusiasm of J.B.Wostinholm, who paid his own travelling and hotel expenses until 1876 and accepted a very low salary of between £3 10s and £10 a year (and 10% commission on all subscriptions[1716]) in his capacity as Secretary of the county club. In 1862, Wostinholm became Secretary of Sheffield United Cricket Club and 'immediately set about effecting the liquidation of a heavy debt which vested upon the club' and improving Bramall Lane because he saw that developing it would be commercially successful. He was given considerable discretion by his employers, the proprietors of Bramall Lane, who were 'men, smart in business, but knew little about the sports of the country', and as an accountant, he was trusted with the handling of the finances. Thus, when he became secretary in 1864, the Bramall Lane owners were prepared to allow Yorkshire to use the ground free of charge because they believed that, with Wostinholm in a position of influence, they were certain to be repaid.[1717] Wostinholm took this responsibility seriously and, to an important extent, the financial position explains the tenacity with which he clung on to Sheffield's control of the major, money-making fixtures. He had a vested interest in maintaining as many Yorkshire matches as possible at Sheffield, and ensuring that the best opponents came there. He was devoted to the cause of Sheffield United and the town, but just as importantly had to ensure that a considerable sum of money was repaid to the club.

Disquiet in the north and east - Yorkshire United

If the 1860s were characterised by differences between Sheffield, York and Bradford about the running of Yorkshire cricket and the hosting of major games, the early 1870s saw discord elsewhere, focused around the perceived lack of representativeness of the county side. In the North and East Ridings, feelings ran high about the virtual exclusion of their men from the county team. In 1873, steps were taken to try to rectify the situation. Following a single-wicket match for £100 at Malton in early September between Alfred Brown of Malton and John Hicks of York, a meeting was held at which representatives of town clubs including Hull, York, Bedale, Scarborough, Middlesbrough, Malton and Thirsk discussed the state of Yorkshire cricket. They entrusted Roger Iddison, the first

Yorkshire county captain (who some considered was involved as revenge for being kept out of the county team[1718]), and Tom Smith of York Cricket Club, with the job of considering how changes could be effected, and of organising a more formal gathering of those dissatisfied with the state of Yorkshire cricket.[1719]

The result was a meeting on 5 December 1873 in the Talbot Hotel, Malton. About 30 men from York, Scarborough, Middlesbrough, Malton and Hull attended what was described as 'a large and influential gathering.' Tom Smith from York dominated the meeting, calling for a cricket club for the two Ridings and denouncing the scant attention paid to those outside Sheffield. He said he believed North and East Yorkshire 'to be labouring under a disadvantage in regard to its cricketing talent.' Smith and others stated that, while they had no wish to fight Sheffield, they wanted to give their professionals a chance to earn a living, which was not possible at present. Captain Middleton from Hull, who seconded Smith's motion to form the club, said that the East Riding had been 'cut off and shut out in the cold.' His aim was to establish a good county club and 'if the Sheffield club chose to approach them, or they approached the Sheffield club and united it would be all the better for the county.'[1720]

The meeting heard letters of support from Lord Londesborough and MPs from the North and East Ridings, all of whom promised money to help in the early stages of the club. He suggested that they should be looking for £500 in subscriptions to put them on a par with any club in the country. Smith also recommended that the club be called by the rather cumbersome name of the North and East Ridings and County Cricket Club, and for a month the name stuck. Iddison and Smith were appointed secretaries and a subscription was opened to defray expenses.[1721] A meeting of the provisional committee was held on 3 January 1874 in York to agree the rules.[1722] According to the *Sheffield Daily Telegraph*, the choice of name was then deferred in case some of the West Riding towns wanted to join. An annual meeting was fixed for November, subscriptions were set at half a guinea, and it was recommended that a committee of 25 men be chosen.[1723]

The first general meeting of the club was held a week later and the question of the name was raised again. There were demands for the title 'Yorkshire County Club', a further sign of the confidence amongst the organisers, but, as a compromise, Yorkshire United County Cricket Club was decided upon. Vice-presidents would represent each Riding, and Lord Londesborough was elected as President, subject to his approval.[1724] The committee met for the first time on 30 January 1874, with Captain Middleton of Hull in the chair. Lord Londesborough accepted the office of President and remarked that he would spare no effort to make the new county club successful. Finally, a circular setting out the objects of the club and soliciting annual subscriptions from cricket clubs was issued. It was agreed that riding matches be played at Hull, Middlesbrough and Dewsbury.[1725]

By the end of February 1874, letters had been received from Durham County

Cricket Club and Derbyshire County Cricket Club agreeing to play the United side. The club's financial position was developing; £113 10s had been promised, donations were £45 and annual subscriptions £78, and there were other offers of support. Teams were selected for the opening game under the auspices of the club, to be held in Hull to mark the opening of the Argyle Street ground pavilion.[1726] The 1874 season, although the best organised and the only one in which Yorkshire United side faced senior opponents, was not particularly successful. They played both Derbyshire and Durham twice, and Lancashire and Harrow Wanderers once each. In the latter game, against a side including A.N.Hornby, United won by seven wickets, thanks largely to 98 by the Rev H.M.Sims, but four other games ended in fairly uninspiring draws. In the match at Holbeck in August, United were comprehensively beaten by Durham, being dismissed for 88 and 24, despite having no weaker a side than usual.[1727]

The following season saw a change of arrangements for the club, and it appears that pretensions to senior status were over. There were no 'county' games, and the fixture list appearing in the papers indicated that matches would henceforth be played against twenty-twos of local districts.[1728] Years later, Holmes commented that, in 1875, Yorkshire United became an 'itinerant eleven' in much the same way as the All-England Eleven.[1729] They continued to perform for fairly small attendances, although the prospect of seeing such quality players brought out the crowds in Boston Spa in June 1875. The same year they travelled to Northampton, Malton, Sheffield, Wakefield, Nunhead in London, Leek and Harrogate.[1730]

The uncertain nature of the club can be seen in September 1875, when its appearance caused some confusion in Derbyshire. According to the *York Herald*, a match was arranged against an Eighteen or Twenty-Two of Chesterfield and District, with Charlwood, but was then changed 'to what might virtually be termed Yorkshire v Derbyshire'. The Derbyshire committee objected to it being designated as a county match and in the end, the contest was called United North v Chesterfield and District, although the visitors were all Yorkshiremen.[1731] This question of identity was certainly one of Yorkshire United's many problems. Newspaper reports often failed to distinguish between the official county and United matches, or even reported a match using both names on different days. The game at Prince's between Yorkshire and Middlesex in May 1874 was described as a United game in its original list of fixtures[1732], but was reported as the 'first *bona-fide* county match of the season' by several papers.[1733] To a large extent, rather than bringing on new talent, the club was providing more matches for the same established professionals.

Holmes suggests that by 1877 'the club ceased to be', but really its demise started following the 1875 season. The matches that were played in 1876 were indistinguishable from those played by teams of Yorkshire players across the country (and, on one occasion, in Dublin) and, when they did play, as in Crewe in July, the response was not impressive. Despite the local paper's description of Yorkshire United as the 'celebrated' club, the hosts made a big loss and had to beg donations from local supporters to recoup. Holmes argued that it proved there was no room for a second county side even in an area as large as Yorkshire.[1734] Perhaps this was because there was a lot of cricket played in the North and East Ridings at the time. Touring teams appeared regularly and, in 1875, Hull hosted the important North v South match. In 1876, Lord Londesborough's other initiative, the Scarborough 'cricket carnival', provided several days of play, while the standard in towns like Hull, Malton and Scarborough was high. Compared to the industrialised West Riding, the rural regions of east and north Yorkshire simply did not have the population to maintain a separate side.

Yorkshire County Cricket Club in the 1870s

In parallel with these developments, the performance of the official county club generated concern. In June 1873, the *Leeds Times* commented, 'There is a screw loose somewhere', and questioned whether proper judgement was being used to select representative players, calling for a Colts match to identify new blood.[1735] Things improved the following year, and in the September the same paper reflected that with new management and 'by liberal rewards for won matches, our players have succeeded in placing the county of broad acres very near the head of the cricketing world.' Hill and Emmett were proving fine bowlers, Pinder was an excellent wicketkeeper, and Lockwood and Greenwood were two of the finest bats of the day. The veterans Rowbotham and Thewlis continued to perform and Ulyett was a most promising player.[1736] The *Huddersfield Chronicle* too praised the county committee, suggesting, 'The rewards they offer for all matches won, stimulate the players to increased efforts – and the results have been most satisfactory.'[1737]

However, renewed complaints were made at the end of the summer of 1875. The *York Herald* wrote at length on the disquiet in Yorkshire, noting that 'partisans of county cricket in Yorkshire are busy talking of a change of quarters, the monopoly of the Sheffield committee not being at all relished in some nurseries of the game.' The writer avoided siding with the 'discontents', arguing that things would be the same if another Yorkshire town was the headquarters, and in fact there would 'shortly be an outcry for further change, as the exchequer would in all probability soon be in a languishing condition.'[1738] A couple of years later, at the end of the 1877 season, the *Leeds Times* also spoke of 'a sad falling-off' which it interpreted as indicative of bad management since it was hard to believe there were fewer first-class cricketers in the county than in the past.[1739]

The following season, Emmett took over as captain and some new names were expected amongst the likely team.[1740] Not everyone was impressed. One correspondent to The *Yorkshire Post* approved of the change of captaincy but said that the omission of some names 'are calculated to destroy the confidence (already weak) felt in the wisdom of the Sheffield committee.' For some time, he argued, Yorkshire might as well have been 'The Sheffield and Lascelles Hall United C.C.', for very few players outside these areas got in the team, and concluded by suggesting the selection of the county team be done by a representative body chosen from all parts of the county. In these circumstances, 'Fairness and impartial treatment would be dealt to all, and no suspicion of money matters entering into the question would be entertained.'[1741]

Despite the gloom, the *Leeds Times* was able to report at the end of 1878 that those who were selected 'thoroughly maintained the high reputation of our county.'[1742] The paper reproduced an article from *The Sportsman* which felt there was 'a general air of prosperity about county cricket...Yorkshire is so far fortunate that it is not forced by any considerations of finance to reduce its programme.'[1743] The following year, however, the strain was again showing in the available resources, and there was talk of the need to look to the colts.[1744] Things did improve and Yorkshire embarked on a period of success in the early 1880s. Nevertheless, concern at the fragility of arrangements and the belief that the committee was not tapping into the full resources of the county were not far from the surface.

Huddersfield and Bradford (again)

The North and East Ridings were not the only parts of the county which felt left out of Yorkshire cricket in the 1870s, in particular, around the allocation of first-class matches. The Bradford press gloomily mused in 1873 that the prospect of seeing a county match in the town was remote as long as Yorkshire affairs were 'mismanaged' by the Sheffield Committee. It hoped that 'the day is not very distant when by the organisation of a second team – for which there is plenty of material – or some other revolutionary measure, the present monopoly will be overthrown.'[1745] In Huddersfield at the end of the same season, the St John's club was in confident mood after the success of its county game with Nottinghamshire, at which Richard Daft, Roger Iddison and others were very impressed at what Huddersfield could offer on and off the field.[1746] During the winter, St John's made strenuous efforts to get a further county game against Nottinghamshire, but had to make do with Yorkshire against the All-England Eleven.[1747] Daft and the Graces were not available, but the match was still a great success, and the committee soon announced that it had already made arrangements for a game in July 1875 between the North and South, with W.G. and G.F. Grace appearing.[1748]

Dissatisfaction with its status grew as sport developed in the Huddersfield area. According to later interviews with those involved, the 1870 match created a lot of ill feeling between Lascelles Hall and Sheffield, although it strengthened the view in Lascelles Hall that its players ought to be included routinely in the county team. Despite this, and the success of the club in getting many more players into the county side, Walter Haigh, President of the Lascelles Hall club, still complained that in 35 years as President he was never once consulted on what his men might do for county cricket and he was even refused permission to enter the pavilion at Bramall Lane to speak to his players, and to convey a message to Ephraim Lockwood. To Haigh, the Sheffield authorities 'certainly did not go out of their way to promote good feeling between our cricket fraternity and themselves.'[1749]

Developments in the town added to local confidence. The Huddersfield Athletic Club and St John's Cricket Club merged in March 1876 to make Huddersfield Cricket and Athletic Club.[1750] That summer, the club hosted another United North v United South game, involving some of the best players in the country. The local paper said the arrangements for the game were 'admirably devised and equally well carried out.' Some 3,000 turned up on the first day and 4,000 on the second, while after lunch on the final afternoon there were reported to be 5,000-6,000 people present.[1751] As a result, some questioned why Huddersfield did not host county games. In early November 1876, a deputation from the club attended a committee meeting of the Yorkshire County Cricket Club to ask whether one or two county matches could be played in the town, and committee members resolved 'that an effort be made to comply with their request.'[1752] Local opinion was strongly in favour. At the Lockwood Cricket Club AGM in 1877, for example, the committee urged members to develop their club so they were prepared to have a quota of men in a reformed Yorkshire County Club.[1753]

The pressure did seem to have some effect and in December 1878, the Yorkshire committee agreed 'to assist County Cricket in the towns of Yorkshire where they consider it desirable.'[1754] Just before Christmas, another deputation from Huddersfield went to Sheffield to request a county match, and the county committee agreed they could have the Middlesex game in 1879.[1755] The Huddersfield club President, John Marsden JP, later reported that county officials had not inspired him with much awe, a comment that was greeted with laughter. Looking to the future, Marsden hoped Huddersfield would be a centre for Yorkshire cricket and, in pursuit of this, encouraged the club to build a new pavilion.[1756]

A flavour of the dissatisfaction across Yorkshire was also given in the *Leeds Mercury* at the close of the 1879 season. The paper's columnist 'Long-On' wrote at length at the oddity that 'the body calling itself the County Club should be centred in some fifteen or sixteen individuals in the border town of Sheffield.' He complained that the game was played throughout the county now and thousands never had the chance to watch a county match. The author said there were strong feelings on this in the county and asked what could be done to open up the team to players from elsewhere. He suggested that professionals were not in a position to challenge the situation, being too much controlled by the present executive. Instead, it would have to be amateurs, who were more independent and not so bothered if the committee did not invite them to play again. Failing this, he argued that the county's leading amateur club ought to bring the matter to a crisis, or there ought to be more than one county team, with each riding represented.[1757]

At the start of the 1880s, matters were improving in Leeds. In April 1880, the *Leeds Times* expressed pleasure that both the Australians and the Canadians would play in the town given that Leeds was not often favoured with a county game.[1758] However, it was Bradford that reignited the debate about the county club in the autumn of 1881. On the 8 October, Jennings, the Bradford Treasurer, wrote to J.B.Wostinholm, asking when his club would be invited to Sheffield to discuss arrangements for the next county season, as they had in 1880. On 10 November, Wostinholm informed Jennings that Yorkshire had decided not to play a county match at Bradford in 1882 and, therefore, no deputation would be received. Unsurprisingly, Jennings was not impressed and wrote back expressing astonishment and regret, and again requesting a meeting. Wostinholm replied unequivocally 'that your ground is not fit to play a county match upon. I beg to remind you that when the Derbyshire match was played at Bradford such was the state of your ground that an arrangement had to be made between the captains of the contending counties for a different wicket to be pitched at the commencement of each innings...[which] was very discreditable to Yorkshire cricket.' And, he emphasised, the decision was final.

The Bradford club had been aware of the inadequacies of its wicket, and when Jennings heard that this was the problem, he telegrammed and then wrote to Wostinholm to reassure him that this was being dealt with. The letter presumed that the telegram would have changed the Secretary's mind, and he asked for confirmation of the time and place of the meeting with the Yorkshire committee. So confident was Bradford that the club suggested that a competent person examine the wicket a fortnight before a proposed county match to ensure it was of a suitable standard. Wostinholm replied to Jennings' telegram with a one-line refusal to receive a deputation. In mid-December, the Honorary Secretary of the Bradford Cricket Club, W.A.Dawson, repeated the Bradford view that they had been promised two county matches, which Wostinholm rejected, saying only 1881 had been discussed.[1759] Christmas led to a break in the correspondence with Sheffield, but Bradford took the opportunity to sound out other towns on the subject.[1760]

Some sense of the financial issues at stake can be gleaned from correspondence in the *Yorkshire Post* in February 1882. Someone calling himself 'A County Club Subscriber' and stating that the figures were taken from his private memoranda, noted that between 1861 and 1881 the total sum paid by the Yorkshire County Cricket Club to the 'proprietary of Bramall Lane' for using the ground had been £2,550, or just over £120 a year. He added that as the Bramall Lane committee usually 'do not let the ground at a less sum than £25 for the day, for festivals or sports, I take it that each county match of three days is worth not less than £50. At that reckoning it is pretty certain the YCCC have not paid more than two-thirds of what is due. Ample accommodation is provided for players, excellent seating for many thousands of spectators, and the whole expense of keeping the turf in order is borne by the Bramall Lane proprietary.'[1761] Thus, Sheffield supported Yorkshire cricket financially to a very significant degree.

Emotions built up in Bradford. On 24 January, the Bradford Cricket, Athletic and Football club held its Annual General Meeting, where the chairman, J.H.Mitchell JP said that, whilst a lack of county fixtures was understandable in the past, now Bradford had a ground which was second to none. The balance in favour of the club was £203, but there remained a debt of between £3,000 and £4,000 on the sports facilities. Officials were keen to clear the debt off quickly to safeguard the club and enable them to provide sport at a lower cost than at present.[1762] County cricket against the best teams was thus vital for the Bradford club, and announcing that a meeting of secretaries of the leading clubs in Yorkshire had been called, Mitchell demanded that the organisation of Yorkshire County Cricket Club be reformed, insisting 'all unjust monopolies must be broken down.'[1763]

A meeting was held in Leeds on 11 March 1882 for the purpose of discussing a more thoroughly representative county committee. Thirty-nine clubs sent members and another 24 were invited but did not attend. Sheffield and a few other towns in the south of the county did not send anyone, but the north, east and west of Yorkshire were fully represented.[1764] Mitchell, the Bradford chairman, was elected to the chair, and did his best to discourage animosity towards Sheffield. He explained that there was no doubt that Sheffield had done a great deal for Yorkshire cricket, but many people could neither afford the time nor the money to go there to see county cricket.[1765] He suggested that if necessary more fixtures should be arranged to enable Sheffield to continue with all the games it wanted and still allow a fairer distribution.

Charles Lonsdale, representing Bradford, read a series of letters of support from distinguished supporters. This seemed to indicate that a broad alliance was building between representatives of those towns in the West Riding that felt excluded, and a number of aristocratic supporters of cricket in the North and East Ridings, who had their own reasons for disliking the current arrangements. The first, from Lord Londesborough commented:

> it is most undesirable that the management of county cricket should rest entirely in the hands of a local committee. I should like every club to have a voice in the selection of the committee, which should consist principally, if not entirely, of well-known cricketers.

A letter from W.H.A.Worsley of Hovingham Hall also spoke of the:

> widespread and growing feeling in the North Riding that the riding

> was much neglected by the county committee in two respects – 1. That no county matches are played in the North Riding, 2. That very few cricketers, amateur or professional, living in the North Riding are selected to play for the county.

He pointed to Scarborough and York as two more than adequate grounds, and suggested that many of the Yorkshire Gentlemen were suitable for inclusion in the county XI. Following these letters, the meeting voted for a motion which stated, rather unadventurously, that 'the present system of controlling county cricket in Yorkshire is unsatisfactory.' Although anxious to give Sheffield credit for their work, there was a call for a broader-based committee, and a common fund for all gate money. In addition, it was argued that the club should make more use of amateurs, as in Lancashire, Gloucestershire, Middlesex and elsewhere. The meeting resolved to discuss this matter with Sheffield.[1766]

At this point, Wostinholm agreed to see a delegation. The Bradford committee tried to elicit ideas for the way forward, but the response was very disappointing and suggested that some towns were having second thoughts about pursuing the campaign. Barnsley and Halifax did not reply, while Wakefield and Scarborough declined to take any further action. The interview was set for 13 April at Bramall Lane, but the deputation that arrived was even smaller than expected. At the last minute, Lamplough Wallgate from Hull was unable to attend, and even a Bradford delegate failed to appear, along with Rev. E.S.Carter, despite having been seen arriving in Sheffield the previous day. Proposals were prepared by Bradford and sent to the various delegates in advance, but were not approved, and the delegation decided not to lay them before the Sheffield committee. Meeting up just two hours prior to the interview, they had nothing else ready and so had no clear idea of what they wanted.

Lonsdale began the discussions and emphasised they were willing to acknowledge all that had been done by the Sheffield committee for Yorkshire cricket. The sole intention of his deputation was, he said, to extend the committee. Ellison asked if the deputation had prepared any scheme for consideration. Lonsdale replied that they had not, but would first like to know whether the Sheffield men thought it desirable to add members from other districts. Ellison expressed surprise at the lack of ideas and questioned whether it was really for the committee to make suggestions. If, as they said, there was no criticism to be made, he could not see the point of Bradford's agitation, which was, in his opinion, ill-advised.[1767]

The next speaker, Nicholson, suggested that additional committee members around the county would help to bring new talent to light. Ellison replied that he had never missed an opportunity to find new men, and said that Wostinholm regularly wrote to clubs all over the county. But, he complained, clubs had not been prepared to fund the expenses of colts, and Sheffield had always had to pay.

Nicholson denied that this was true, saying his club, Hunslet, had contributed. The question of the choice of grounds for county matches was then raised, and the Secretary emphasised that his committee would like to be able to take county games all over. However, several counties had specifically refused to play anywhere but Sheffield. Certain members of the deputation were surprised at this, but Ellison added that after their two-day innings defeat at Bradford in 1881, Kent had refused to play outside Sheffield and Lord Harris had called the wicket a 'disgrace'.

Discussions returned to the question of places on the committee, and Ellison said he did not think there would be objections to five gentlemen from different parts of Yorkshire being added 'to deliberate as to the choice of grounds, clubs and management of matches', but he did not think the committee would ever consent to the receipts from matches at Sheffield being put into a common fund. T.G.Sharpe of Huddersfield said that the delegates did not want this. Ellison asked for a suggestion as to the number of members, but Lonsdale and Sharpe countered by asking how many the Sheffield men would allow. Ellison said no town could be represented without having a fit ground, and suggested that they adjourn to discuss this matter between themselves and decide where the representatives were to come from. He emphasised 'that in all the arrangements there was to be no interference whatever with the financial affairs of any particular district. The finances of county cricket, as regards Sheffield, were to remain exactly as at present, and with regard to other places, of course, it would be the same.' The town or club taking on a county match would be responsible for the profit or loss. Ellison said he thought five new representatives would be sufficient, but did not see why the Yorkshire Gentlemen should be represented since two of its members were already on the committee. The interview ended with the delegates satisfied that they had made substantial gains.[1768]

Just over two weeks later, representatives of town clubs around the county assembled at Bradford Park Avenue to hear the report of the deputation, and to consider the offer of committee places. Only two of the six delegates – Lonsdale and Sharpe – were present, and the former expressed his disappointment at the failure of others to attend. He suggested that although five places had been offered in the end he felt that they could get seven out of the committee. T.G.Sharpe expressed surprise at Lonsdale's description and said Huddersfield was satisfied with five, and was not prepared to fight what he called 'the battle of Bradford.' He added that it was not fair for them to start trying to tell Sheffield how to run Yorkshire cricket after so many years, and accepted that Middlesex probably was unwilling to come to Huddersfield, due to the wicket and financial loss. Some disagreed, however, and found a vocal champion in Rev E.S.Carter, whose suggestion that they insist on seven new members was passed by a small majority, the only proviso being that if seven was rejected, Keighley and Middlesbrough be dropped.[1769]

Correspondence from Lord Londesborough was read out in which he observed that he was not surprised that no real concessions had been made when the delegates had not had any definite proposals. He argued that they now needed to identify influential clubs, and develop some rules which had popular support so that Sheffield 'would be forced to come to terms.' If there was insufficient support, an alternative was to use the proposed North and East Ridings Cricket Club as the nucleus of a county club. Londesborough suggested that because the interests of different towns clashed so frequently, a 'club governed like the MCC would be most suited to them', and in a second letter added that 'the more he thought the matter over the more certain he was that a properly organised Yorkshire cricket club would be an enormous success.' He offered to subscribe £25 annually for three years.[1770]

Poor performances by the county side fuelled the case for change which was argued out in the correspondence pages of the papers throughout the summer. This was added to by criticism of the failure to use amateur players. As the *Yorkshire Post* put it, until the time comes when the county is properly represented, including with amateurs, very little improvement could be expected.[1771] Reflecting on developments in July 1882, it criticised the Dewsbury club for failing to support the pressure for change, noting:

> there is very little chance of Dewsbury taking up the matter [of amateur players] since it may be remembered when asked to aid in the present agitation at the outset they declined, although subsequently they actually did send in a claim to the Sheffield executive to be represented on the board.

And it praised Charles Lonsdale for his part, since it was through Bradford's efforts that 'at least three gentlemen have been chosen to represent the county.'[1772] In August, the same paper commented further on the continuing dispute, approving of the position that Leeds had taken of not accepting a seat on the committee and standing with the other towns until they were given seven places.[1773] At the same time, however, the *Yorkshire Post* expressed concern at the 'apparent indifference shown by the Yorkshire clubs about the agitation' and feared that, with the autumn general meeting of the county club close, the protesters would again be unprepared.[1774]

On 11 October 1882, a special general meeting of the Yorkshire County Cricket Club was held, at which consideration was given to widening the committee and a new set of rules was adopted. Sheffield's control of the club was still very clear, with Rule 2 stating, 'The affairs of the Yorkshire County Cricket Club shall be under the management of a president, vice-president, treasurer and twelve other members, to be elected at a general annual meeting, to be held in Sheffield (seven of what shall be the Ground Committee of the Sheffield United Cricket Club), and of one representative from each of the following districts viz. [to be completed].' Proprietors of Sheffield United Cricket Club were assured lower subscriptions.[1775]

There remained confusion about what had happened, however, and without journalists in attendance, reports of the meeting were unclear. Later in the month, Lonsdale sent correspondence to the press between himself and W.R.Wake, one of the Sheffield committee members, which he said underlined that the 'late agitation (so much condemned by many) was after all not so unnecessary.' Lonsdale asked Wake about the rule that stated that the county club was to consist of an unlimited number of members, and whether, supposing he was a member, he could question financial matters. On the latter point, he added, 'The County Club can't expect people out of Sheffield to subscribe 21s, and not receive any account of what is done with it.' Lonsdale said he had written to Wake because 'you are inclined to take a more liberal view of these matters.' Wake responded by sending back his rough notes of the meeting, stating that he too had not understood the meaning of the rules, and did not think those who framed them did either. He said he hoped some members would try and establish a representative club to take the place of what was effectively 'Sheffield Yorkshire County Club.' If no-one moved, he said, he would do so, 'although I am aware that by so doing I should get into pretty hot water here.'[1776]

Whatever the confusion, after all the debate, on 28 December, the matter came to a head at the annual meeting of the Yorkshire County Cricket Club and, as well as the announcement of a loss of £118, W.J.Dewhurst (Bradford), P.G.Beaumont (Dewsbury), Alderman Riley (Halifax), J.G.Sharpe (Huddersfield), B.Naylor (Leeds) and Rev.E.S.Carter (York) were chosen to represent other towns on the committee.[1777] Progress towards a more representative county cricket club had been made.

Leeds and Dewsbury

In the 1883 season, Yorkshire played only half of its eight home games in Sheffield, with the others at Dewsbury (Kent), Bradford (Gloucestershire), Holbeck (Surrey) and Huddersfield (Middlesex). The *Leeds Mercury* thought this was a step in the right direction, and would have 'a beneficial effect in consolidating cricket throughout the vast area of Yorkshire.'[1778] There remained disquiet, however, as the county side struggled on the field and the newspapers were full of suggestions for new players.[1779] The idea of a second eleven was raised by some to try and rectify matters. The following season, Leeds was not given a county game, which caused considerable annoyance in the town. This followed complaints about the accommodation at Holbeck for the match in 1883, which had reportedly been poor both in the pavilion and luncheon-room, where the players could find little to eat. As a result, a game was unlikely in Leeds until it had a larger ground and better facilities.[1780]

Not satisfied with its allocation in 1884 (although it did secure the Surrey match), the Dewsbury committee entered into negotiations for additional games. In April, they corresponded with the management of the Australian touring side about filling a vacancy in its itinerary with a game against a North of England XI or perhaps an England XI. There proved to be competition, however, and the Australians said they would come if they could not find somewhere more profitable. The *Dewsbury Reporter* deplored the way in which Sheffield allocated so many county games to itself, stating that sooner or later 'matters will come to a crisis on this point; indeed, if Dewsbury had helped Bradford and other towns who agitated for an alteration two years ago, larger concessions would have been obtained. But Dewsbury had a match promised by the County Committee, and therefore were content to rest and be thankful.'[1781]

Dewsbury was not alone in seeking first-class games. Batley and Leeds also attempted to attract the Australians, but in the end the Huddersfield executive was successful. As a result, Dewsbury only hosted the Surrey game in 1884 (resulting in receipts of £167), and when the 1885 fixtures were announced, the town was not included, the reason given being that the town had inadequate hotel accommodation for gentlemen players. The local committee was indignant, particularly since new seating had been put in and there was now considered to be adequate accommodation within the ground. The response was to begin negotiations for another important match in lieu of a county game.[1782] In 1886, Yorkshire played Lancashire at Dewsbury and the ground hosted a game most seasons for several decades thereafter.

North Riding Cricket Club

At the end of September 1884, further moves were made to improve matters in the north of the county and a new North Riding club was formed at a meeting at Hovingham Hall, near Malton. The initiative on the part of W.H.A.Worsley, honorary secretary of the Hovingham Hall Cricket Club, was not intended to be 'anti-Sheffield' and in fact Wostinholm and another county committee member were present. Instead, the club stated that it was established to provide a service by bringing on talented players from the area, and put them in a position to compete for a place in the county side. The club required two years' residence in the North Riding as qualification, rather than being born in the county. Eventually, it hoped to compete in first-class matches, but initially aimed to play on local grounds with a central committee taking the gate money. Sir William Worsley proposed that they did not involve the East Riding. At the meeting, representatives of 12 of the 22 clubs contacted attended, seven others wrote expressing their support, while three – Yorkshire Gentlemen, Flaxton and Leyburn – disapproved.[1783]

The club's committee met for the first time in October 1884 to draw up rules, arrange matches and carry out other business. Games were arranged for

Scarborough, Middlesbrough and Hovingham Hall, with returns.[1784] The club's first match was against Northumberland in June 1885, and proved a big disappointment as a result of a poor attendance and 'simply execrable' fielding.[1785] Later that month, they played at Middlesbrough against a Yorkshire XI, which made 530, with Peel scoring 213 and Hall 166. In 1888, it was renamed the North and East Ridings County Cricket Club and continued until 1900. The officials were all from aristocratic families, but the club struggled and was described as in 'a poor way' at the end of 1889.[1786] The *Leeds Mercury* said that if the intention was to popularise cricket, then the club should reduce its one-guinea membership fee, and reported that 27 men had been approached for one match before they could get together a team.[1787]

The pressure builds up

The 1880s saw Nottinghamshire dominate county cricket, although Yorkshire finished second or third in each of the seasons from 1881 to 1885. Woodhouse notes that 1883 was Yorkshire's best season since 1870 and, with Harrison added to a bowling attack as strong as any in the country, the future looked bright.[1788] At the club annual general meeting in January 1884 there was much positive feeling. There was a balance in hand of £536, and it was resolved to refund Mr Ellison for expenses incurred from his own pocket in supporting county cricket since 1863.[1789] In comparison, the following season was disappointing despite Louis Hall's best-ever showing. Edward Lumb was also unable to play when most needed, whilst the failure of Harrison was an 'added disappointment.'[1790] The 1885 season saw an improvement in form, with Yorkshire second to Nottinghamshire. Nevertheless, there were complaints at the way in which the county eleven played in some of the final games of the season, having looked as though they might be champions at one stage. Off the field, developments at Bramall Lane in 1884 and 1885 were popular with spectators, helping to ensure the continued financial success which allowed the authorities at Sheffield to be reimbursed on a regular basis.

Others were less happy. Over the winter of 1885/86, officials at Bradford expressed disappointment at their relationship with the county club, the Chairman stating that the county committee 'seemed inclined to humiliate the Bradford representative on the committee.'[1791] Charles Lonsdale, the Bradford secretary (and the man later described by the *Yorkshire Post* as mainly responsible for ensuring that county matches were more distributed than they had been[1792]), was even more outspoken in a letter to the *Yorkshire Post* in January 1886. He argued that the county committee had systematically tried to hamper efforts to have first-class cricket at Bradford by forcing weak counties upon the club, stifling its efforts to introduce amateur talent to the county eleven and 'damning with faint praise' its wicket. Bradford had offered to pay for professionals to stand aside so as to let amateurs such as Forbes, Landon, Roper and Leatham show what they could do, but this gesture had not been taken up.

Finally, he regretted 'there is so much division and jealousy among the various representatives that the Sheffield executive can play off one against another.'[1793]

In 1886, the performances on the field declined, with only five out of 21 first-class matches ending in victories. According to Woodhouse, the fielding was poor, Joe Hunter's wicketkeeping so weak that he was dropped, and reliance on the 44-year-old Tom Emmett an indication that new players were not coming through as hoped.[1794] As early as the end of May, the press noted that everybody seemed to be grumbling that the Yorkshire side was not meeting expectations, especially in batting.[1795] By August, there had only been one win and complaints continued at the failure to try promising Colts.[1796] Part of the explanation was considered to be what was referred to as 'over-indulgence', and ominously one reporter commented that the man 'who turns night into day is a person upon whom county honours should not be showered, as he not only sets a bad example, but entirely destroys the *morale* of the whole eleven.'[1797]

Many of the same themes returned with the next season, 1887. Reporters urged county players to pay greater attention to what they described as their 'condition' and early-season advice was to avoid 'everything alcoholic'.[1798] The environment at Bramall Lane also came in for criticism during the season, the poor performance on the second day against Surrey being put down to the bad light and clouds of smoke which blew from the factories and affected the Yorkshire batsmen.[1799] Established players yet again failed to perform and new talent did not make the strides hoped for.

Improvements in the second half of the 1887 season were not carried into the following one, and the *Leeds Times* commented, 'I ought to most reverently doff my *chapeau* to the Yorkshire County Eleven, for the apparent indifference they are manifesting towards such trifling things as wins in the cricket field.'[1800] The team scored under 60 three times in the first three matches, and did not reach 200 in an innings until the last week of June. Under pressure, the county committee invited clubs in the neighbourhood of Sheffield to send promising men under 24 for practice, to be viewed by Luke Reaney, who was engaged as coach.[1801] Things looked up in the last 12 days of July with wins against Lancashire (against whom Peel took 12-62), Nottinghamshire (who scored 24 and 58, with Peel taking 14-33) and Gloucestershire (Peel 13-84), and eventually the county ended up second to Surrey.[1802]

Nevertheless, only 13 out of the 40 games played in 1887 and 1888 ended in victory, and off the field, there were also financial concerns, caused in part by bad weather. At the AGM in January 1889, the committee lamented the 'wretched' season of 1888.[1803] The following season was what Holmes called the 'low-water mark of Yorkshire cricket', with the county side winning only three matches, and losing 11, and Woodhouse described the summer as 'one of the worst for cricket followers in Yorkshire.[1804] In July, the *Leeds Times* joked that 'unalterable fame awaits the man who can invent some new and comprehensive 'cuss' words, which shall express adequately the sentiments of Yorkshiremen over the staggering defeat Lancashire administered to the cricket representatives of the Tykes, at Huddersfield.'[1805] Overall, it was a very poor year, not helped by dropped catches and a weaker bowling attack than in 1888.

Yorkshire cricket was reaching a crisis point. In Coldham's view, for a long time 'the cracks had been papered over, the genius of individuals had rescued countless lost causes.' Now, however, it was clear to Hawke that the problems he had inherited from Emmett had not been resolved and it was for the committee to let him 'act as he thought fit in the interests of his county side...Yorkshire cricket was at a crossroads; drastic action was required and Hawke was prepared to take it.'[1806] Subsequently, Wade, Preston, Grimshaw and Lee played their last games as Hawke sought to change the behaviour of the team.

Unhappiness continued off the field. In 1887, a request from the Heavy Woollen District Challenge Cup Council for representation on the county committee was turned down, the committee stating it 'was undesirable to increase the number of the members of the Committee at present.'[1807] Wakefield was also refused representation in 1889. The position was slightly eased when Barnsley was admitted in 1888 and Wakefield in 1890. In 1892, the Committee therefore consisted of 13 men from Sheffield and one each from nine other towns.[1808] The financial consequences of hosting lower-quality games also remained a cause of controversy. In 1887, Dewsbury was the venue for the Leicestershire fixture and lost £40. As it was a two-day game, each player received £4, umpires £5 each and the scorer 50s, which the *Yorkshire Post* suggested was 'sufficient to cause even the most favoured of club executives to think twice before accepting a second-rate fixture.' Thankfully, they made up for it with the game against Gloucestershire, which raised £120, leaving them £80 ahead from the two matches.[1809] In 1891, the Halifax club stated it had lost £700 through county matches, which had included playing against Cheshire and Warwickshire.[1810]

Financial problems were also in evidence at the county club when, at the start of January 1890, it held its annual general meeting at Bramall Lane. The position was set out in a report, with a favourable balance of £139 16s 9d at the start of the year falling to £7 9s 10d at the end, a loss of £132 and a significant decline on previous years. The causes were given as the experimental colts matches, on which a loss of over £203 had been made, as well as deficits incurred in games with Warwickshire, Derbyshire and Kent. No Colts match was arranged for the coming year and Ellison described the 1889 season as a 'lamentable failure.'[1811] He then went on to accuse spectators of contributing to the poor performances of the team, criticising those 'who could not see a professional cricketer without wanting to give him a glass of drink.'[1812] Not everyone agreed with these accusations, which were taken badly by some people. Later in the month, a columnist in the *Sheffield Daily Telegraph* commented that Ellison's remarks were still causing 'a great deal of excitement in cricket circles.'[1813] In Coldham's view, Ellison's comments were 'arrant nonsense' and showed the club 'had no answers.' The Sheffield committee had, he argued, 'backed itself in a corner from which there was no escape. It could no longer put forward a coherent case for its own continuation; instead it looked for scapegoats.'[1814]

In fact, the club's performance in the 1890 season, when they won half of their games and lost only four out of 20, helped to postpone the calls for change, and at the following AGM, on 2 February 1891, the committee was also able to report an improved financial position, the balance in favour of the club increasing from £7 9s 10d to £258 13s 4d.[1815] The following summer of 1891, however, highlighted again how fragile things were. The performance that season was appalling by any standards. The team also suffered some ill-luck. Lord Hawke broke a finger batting against Gloucestershire, and missed a number of matches in August. R.W.Frank had his right forefinger broken by Sammy Woods in August and had to retire from the match. Yorkshire lost the toss on a regular basis, and were put into bat on very unfavourable wickets on a number of occasions.

Yet, overall the malaise was more serious than these problems, and rumours of reform appeared in the press in the summer of 1891. The *Huddersfield Chronicle* reported that the county committee had appointed a sub-committee 'consisting of the Sheffield members of the committee and Lord Hawke, with a special view of devising the best means of retaining the services of young Yorkshire professional players.'[1816] In the *Leeds Times*, Lord Hawke was described as taking the matter 'very coolly' and his only suggestion was that the county executive should receive all the gate money at county fixtures, less a percentage to the host club. In this way a fund for keeping professionals at certain grounds such as Bradford, Leeds, Huddersfield or Sheffield could be provided. He also argued that 'it would be advantageous to confine the playing of county matches to a limited number of grounds.'[1817]

The issues were widely debated. The *Yorkshire Post* expressed suspicion of the composition of the sub-committee and questioned whether it was really interested in reform. It described the Sheffield monopoly as 'one of the greatest of the present evils', but noted there was widespread division within cricket circles. In its opinion, 'Bradford is jealous of Leeds, Leeds is jealous of Bradford, Huddersfield is envious of both, whilst Halifax and Dewsbury call out for their own particular interests, to say nothing of Hull, whose persistent cry is that the West Riding can see nothing good in the East Riding.'[1818]

The pressure for change built up throughout the summer of 1891 as Yorkshire suffered defeat after defeat – 11 in 17 first-class matches. At luncheons and matches committeemen and senior players heard persistent demands for reform. At the Yorkshire-Derbyshire game at Leeds in June 1891, W.B.Nicholson, one of the directors of the Leeds Cricket, Football and Athletic Club, welcomed the teams, but expressed the hope that in the future they would be able to welcome others, including Nottinghamshire, Surrey, Gloucestershire, and Lancashire. These sentiments were greeted with applause. In response, Louis Hall commented that the players did not mind where they played as long it was a good ground, and loyally added that had it not been for Sheffield, Yorkshire cricket might not exist.[1819] At the annual dinner of the committee of the Heavy Woollen District Cricket Challenge Cup in Dewsbury, Hall again tactfully parried fierce criticism of the committee.[1820]

In November, the Yorkshire County Cricket Club report for the season 1891 was published and detailed many of the difficulties. Only Hall's benefit match against Surrey, and the Nottinghamshire fixture, had been a financial success. As a result, the Club's balance, which in 1890 had stood at £258, had dropped to £153, receipts being £909 and payments £756. In these circumstances, given the results and with subscriptions totalling only £120, the committee announced that it had 'seen fit to yield to some degree to the agitation.' The old system of management had been adopted, it was explained:

> in the first instance, because no other town or district, except Bradford, would support Sheffield (in the risk which was undertaken by the supporters of cricket in that town) in the establishment of County Cricket; and although Bradford assisted in the earlier stages of the endeavour, it was eventually left to Sheffield to support the entire burden of the work; of the weight of this burden the present generation of Cricketers can form no idea; and finding County Cricket established on a sure foundation, they are now clamorous to have a share in the profit and gratification which it affords. Sheffield, in its love of the Game, can afford to be generous; and it is hoped that the concessions which have been made by the Founders of County Cricket in Yorkshire will be appreciated and received in the same spirit in which they were accorded.

The Committee regretted the performances of 1890 and 1891, which they could not believe reflected the county's true position. Despite all the criticism they had received in the press, they did not think 'that any neglect on their part in the selection of players has contributed to this, and they will hail with great pleasure any improvement which may result from the proposed alteration.'[1821]

On 17 November 1891, the Yorkshire County Cricket Club committee discussed a new constitution. The sub-committee's report was presented at the meeting, where it was recommended that in future first-class matches would only be played at Bradford, Leeds and Sheffield, the proportion being four to Sheffield, and three each to the other two. Huddersfield, Halifax, Dewsbury and other venues used in the past were deemed no longer suitable because of their 'unsatisfactory' grounds, their poor accommodation and low gates. In addition, the composition of the county committee was to be radically altered. It was reported that it would henceforth consist of a President, two Vice-Presidents, a Secretary, a Treasurer, five representatives from Sheffield, three each from Bradford and Leeds, and one each from Huddersfield, Dewsbury, Halifax, Wakefield, and Hull. The President would be a Sheffield man. Town clubs could be affiliated to the committee by paying one guinea per annum, entitling them to vote for a delegate in their district. It was also announced that committee members would attend open meetings at which the implications of the changes would be explained.[1822]

Bradford held its meeting on 23 November and gave the scheme 'general acceptance', with only 'minor amendments' suggested to the rules.[1823] Leeds waited until 10 December for its meeting. J.W.Bannister, the town's committee member, said that Sheffield had been prepared to make concessions, although there were others who were far more critical, and several amendments were put forward. Some felt that the North Riding was still inadequately represented, and considered that Keighley or Skipton, Northallerton, York and Scarborough all ought to be given a member. A representative from York suggested that a West Riding monopoly was replacing a Sheffield one. [1824]

There was considerably disatisfaction elsewhere and a strong feeling of injustice, articulated, for example, by Sam Shaw, Dewsbury's representative on the county committee in the *Yorkshire Post*.[1825] Huddersfield also felt aggrieved by the proposed changes. Local committee member Arthur Crosland commented that 'the new rules have been drafted by a sub-committee composed of Sheffield men and Lord Hawke, and were consequently sprung on the other members of the committee rather suddenly.' Unsurprisingly, Rule 22, allocating county games only to the three main towns, was described as the 'greatest mistake.' The Huddersfield area, Crosland remarked, had between 30-40 clubs in it, and had probably done more than anywhere else to provide Yorkshire with players. They had also spent a considerable amount of money on their ground on the understanding, given by Mr Ellison, they would get county cricket.[1826]

Outside the West Riding, there was acceptance of their lower status, which influenced how they saw the changes. At the annual meeting of the North and East Ridings County Cricket Club at Thirsk on 15 December, Mr A.Worsley remarked that the power of their club compared with the West Riding was 'slight'. Prior to 1884 there had been discontent in the North and East Ridings with the Yorkshire County Cricket Club, which had been seen as a 'far-away and inaccessible institution, of little practical use to them.' Since then, relations had improved and their players who were good enough 'had not only been asked to take part in county matches, but had been pressed to do so'. Some had even been asked whom they had not dared to recommend. Worsley did not think they could reasonably ask for county matches because of the limited population, railway facilities and public interest, and they did not want second-class matches. Therefore, they did not see any benefit to the changes, which he suggested, were 'likely to end in ignominious failure' because of the rivalry and jealously between the West Riding towns. Added to this, he commented that because of the distance involved in going to committee meetings in Sheffield, it would be hard to get North Riding men involved. Worsley ended by reporting that Lord Londesborough had said that he did not think it was possible 'to devise anything more disastrous to Yorkshire cricket than this proposal.' The meeting decided to adopt a motion expressing satisfaction with the county committee as presently constituted and describing the reforms as 'all rubbish.'[1827]

On 16 February 1892, at the Corn Exchange, Sheffield, the county committee discussed the rules at length, presided over by M.J.Ellison. Although a few amendments had been tabled, the rules were unanimously accepted. The existing committee was to remain in office for the 1892 season, but a new committee would be elected for 1893. Unallocated matches against Essex, Durham and Staffordshire were given to Dewsbury, Halifax and Hull respectively. It was also stated 'that the privileges now enjoyed by the proprietors of the Sheffield United Cricket Club shall be recognised and maintained by the committee of the Yorkshire County Cricket Club on all occasions, so far as the arrangements of the latter affect the Bramall Lane cricket ground.'[1828]

Some people continued to be unhappy. Reflecting on the announcements, the *Leeds Mercury* commented that if the changes were acceptable:

> then Yorkshiremen have lost their hard-headed, practical common sense which has so universally been regarded as one of their characteristics. The scheme is a sham, a delusion, and a snare in which Sheffield retains the solid substance, while to the rest of Yorkshire is given the larger but unsubstantial shadow which it casts.

It argued that Rule 27 made it necessary that three-quarters of those present at an AGM or special general meeting were in favour of rule changes before they could be passed. Given that Sheffield had seven representatives and the president was a Sheffield man, there seemed little chance of others securing this proportion, even if they could get all those from outside Sheffield involved and to agree. As a result, the change leaves Sheffield 'practically undisturbed in the possession of the reins of government.'[1829] The paper went to some lengths to canvas opinions on the reforms, suggesting that overall observers had not 'excited any great degree of enthusiasm.' Nevertheless, it considered supporters of the game were 'on the whole vaguely hopeful rather than enthusiastically sanguine.'[1830]

The new beginning

Having been eighth in the county rankings in 1891, Yorkshire moved up two places in 1892, winning and losing six out of 19 first-class matches. As Woodhouse put it, sixth 'was probably a fair reflection of their form but bitterly disappointing after leading the table up to the middle of June.' The first report of the county club under the new constitution regretted that the side 'did not fulfil the promise held out by its commencement' and suggested that it needed some 'considerable addition to the bowling strength of the team.'[1831]

As agreed under the reform arrangements, in the early weeks of 1893, meetings of the districts of Yorkshire County Cricket Club were held to elect the members of the county committee. Club representatives and members who had paid a subscription of 21s for the 1893 season before 23 January were entitled to attend a meeting and vote.[1832] On 27 January, the Bradford meeting elected three members. Wostinholm urged any club which had a good player to draw them to the county's attention. Where they could not afford to keep a good player, they must not let them go to another county, and instead should appeal for financial assistance.[1833] In Sheffield, seven members were elected to represent the district on the Yorkshire committee. There was also discussion about what should be done about the balance currently in the hands of the Sheffield section of the county club – £600 loaned to the Sheffield United Cricket Club and £156 in hands of the Treasurer. A decision was made to transfer the money permanently to the United club.[1834]

There was a lively meeting in Leeds on 31 January 1893, where three representatives were to be elected rather than just one in the past. More than a dozen men burst in late, objecting to what they saw as the poor arrangements and lack of notice. A number complained that Wostinholm – as a paid official – should have been there and after discussion the meeting was adjourned until he could be present.[1835] On that occasion, the club secretary attended, although he insisted it was only as a courtesy. There were some complaints about the payment of money to Sheffield United, which it was argued should have been shared around the districts. Wostinholm explained the money 'properly belonged to Sheffield, many of the gentlemen there having helped to maintain the ground, and had never received any interest for their money.' The sum of £700 represented profit made on matches played at Sheffield.[1836] In Dewsbury, there were still strong objections that the town had been excluded from first-class matches.[1837]

Thus, Yorkshire County Cricket Club started the 1893 season with agreement on a new structure and an expanded committee of men from around Yorkshire. In accordance with Rules 4 and 5, the Committee for the years 1893, 1894 and 1895 was elected. The committee was made up of members for Barnsley, Bradford (3 members), Craven, Dewsbury, Halifax, Huddersfield, Hull, Leeds (3 members), Scarborough, Sheffield (7 members) and Wakefield and York. Two representatives were accorded to the North and East Ridings Cricket Club. [1838] On the field Yorkshire triumphed and the following year, the Committee expressed delight 'on the distinguished success which, throughout the Season of 1893, attended the efforts of the County team, and has once more placed Yorkshire in the premier position amongst the County Clubs.' The financial position did not match this exactly, with expenditure up and receipts down on 1892, but the committee felt the county 'has room to congratulate itself upon having a team which is thoroughly reliable at all points, and whose performance and behaviour in the field afforded to those who had the pleasure to see them, the greatest gratification.'[1839] Looking back in his history of the club, Tony Woodhouse wrote that after all the struggles of recent years, 'A new dawn appeared to be on the horizon.'[1840] So it proved.

CHAPTER ELEVEN

CONCLUSIONS

The decades that followed 1893 saw several glorious periods of success for Yorkshire County Cricket Club – the late 1890s and early 1900s when both Hirst and Rhodes completed the 'double' of more than 1,000 runs and 100 wickets regularly; the 1920s, the era of Holmes and Sutcliffe; the 1930s, when the side of Verity, Bowes and Leyland only failed to win the county title three times in the decade before war; and the 1960s, the era of Close, Illingworth, Boycott and Trueman, when first-class success was matched by triumphs in the newly-established one-day game. Although they did not know it, the Yorkshire team in 1893 was bringing to an end several decades of under-achievement and false dawns, and setting out on the road to a long period of cricketing greatness. Between that season and 1910, the county was only outside the top three places on one occasion. Records created in the next few fruitful seasons have lived on to this day – the highest first-class total by any English county – 887 in 1896, and the county's fifth- and eighth-wicket partnership records. Brown and Tunnicliffe's 554 for the first wicket in 1898 has only been beaten twice in first-class cricket.

As well being more successful than in the past, from the mid-1890s Yorkshire County Cricket Club had a different feel in other ways. As we have seen, there was broader representation on the county committee from around the county, and less domination by one place – Sheffield – than had been the case since the 1820s. It was only a coincidence, but it seems appropriate that the new era should have been ushered in with a boundary scored by an East Riding man, J.T.Brown, perhaps the most significant Yorkshire player ever from an area that had been at the margins of the county's cricket history. On occasions in the 1890s, he was joined in the team by another player from that side of the county, Frank Mitchell, who was also part of another marked shift - the greater contribution made by a more talented breed of amateur player who turned out for Yorkshire in the late 1890s. Another university-educated amateur, F.S.Jackson, who had made a number of appearances since 1890, also became a significant part of the team, playing over 200 times up to 1907. Such men – and others like Ernest Smith and Frank Milligan – were blended with the extraordinary talents of George Hirst and Wilfred Rhodes, two of the greatest Yorkshire players ever and, for contrast, the rough-speaking Ted Wainwright from Sheffield, and Pudsey's Methodist lay preacher, John Tunnicliffe. Together they made up a side that looked markedly different, a richer mix, than those put out in the 1870s and 1880s. All were led by Lord Hawke, whose career lasted until 1911, helping to establish Yorkshire as the premier club in the country through his 'determination and unquestioned authority'.[1841]

The level of success these players achieved did not just happen, however, but was the product of the decades of development described in this book. Yorkshire County Cricket Club was established in 1863, but it took thirty years for it to be a fully representative club. The momentum that started with the 1893 championship triumph was the product of the resolution of the internal differences and also the development of strongly competitive cricket which had its roots in the early decades of the 19th century. It was also the result of reforms imposed on the field by Lord Hawke, and off it through decisions of the committee, which altered Yorkshire county cricket for good, but only after periods of turmoil. Together these changes started to harness more fully the huge talent that was generated by the town and village clubs of the county.

As we have seen, it was a long and involved story. The inspiration provided by the All-England Eleven and other touring sides which visited Yorkshire from the 1840s built on the existing (if, in places, patchy) interest in cricket in the county, and stimulated a significant change in the popularity of the game. A further surge of interest in the 1860s and early 1870s, generated in part by the unprecedented performances of W.G.Grace and the gradual shift away from the domination of the game by the ball, led to a significant increase in investment in cricket clubs in Yorkshire. Greater expectations of what was required for a high-performing cricket club – in particular, a well-tended ground with a flat playing surface, a strong fixture list and skilled paid assistance – allied to the increasingly competitive spirit in which cricket was played, created the demand for professionals, and increased the opportunities for better players to make a living from the game. This, in turn, provided many men with the incentives to refine their skills, and the existence of a strong professional cadre helped to raise standards of club cricket in the county. In general, the cost of running an organisation with such facilities and professional assistance exceeded the amount of money that could be raised solely from those who played and a club's immediate supporters. Officials therefore sought other ways of generating income such as through galas and athletic sports festivals, or by attracting wealthier patrons. This valuably raised the profile of a cricket club in the community, but also ensured such clubs needed to protect their reputation by eradicating some of the more turbulent behaviour which had characterised the game since its earliest days, often associated with disputed or biased umpiring decisions, and with the prospect of losing a game and its associated stakes and bets.

This desire to purge the game of its more disorderly aspects is entirely in keeping with developments elsewhere in Victorian society to cultivate a sense of 'respectability'. The need to generate more interest in the game at a time when other activities were finding audiences in the 1870s, led to the creation of better organised and more competitive forms of cricket – in particular, cups and leagues. This also helped to kill off the 'exhibition cricket' – single-wicket matches or unequal games between the professional touring sides and district teams – which was increasingly found wanting by the paying public and which was heavily associated with betting. While not necessarily welcomed by traditionalists as being in keeping with the spirit of the game, the leagues that first emerged in Yorkshire in the early 1890s provided the discipline and structure within which higher-quality cricket could be played, timekeeping improved, poor umpiring reduced and unruly behaviour controlled, and began to produce generations of fine players, schooled in seeing hard-fought games through to a conclusion.

Yet if these developments did eventually work their way through towards the end of the 19th century, they raise the question – why did it take until the 1890s for such forces to come together? Yorkshire cricket – and especially cricketers from Sheffield – was an acknowledged force from the 1820s, with players admired around the country. Once the railway network expanded from the 1830s onwards, there were fewer reasons why the best Yorkshire players could not play in games at some distance from home or come together to represent the whole county, a concept that was not unknown in the 1820s. Nevertheless, it took most of the century for the potential to be fulfilled. The reason for the delay has its roots in the way in which the cricket developed in the different Ridings of Yorkshire, which, in part, was influenced by the very different trajectories of social and economic development around the county.

The West Riding became increasingly industrialised and urbanised in the first half of the century, bringing hundreds of thousands of people into large towns and cities where they lived, worked and played games and sports together. These conditions provided intensely fertile ground in which large amounts of cricket could be played regularly in increasingly competitive style. However, Sheffield's dominance within cricket in Yorkshire – which was evident from the 1820s – created tensions with other major towns, which had their own cricket traditions, and for periods the facilities and finances to host important games successfully. The strong local pride which grew up in towns like Leeds, Bradford, Huddersfield and Dewsbury, and manifested itself in civic architecture, public parks and other amenities, also showed itself in pride in their ability to host significant cricket matches, which each had demonstrated they could do at various times from the 1840s onwards. The financial reality of cricket meant that such clubs also wanted and needed to host major, profit-making county games and not be saddled with loss-making contests against lesser county sides, which for some time was all the Sheffield-based committee would offer. Thus, a combination of civic pride and financial necessity encouraged the leaders of cricket in a number of towns in the West Riding to resist efforts by Sheffield to entirely monopolise county cricket, and to press, with varying degrees of strength, for 30 years for changes in the arrangements which had developed.

At the same time, the pace and intensity of modernisation which created the climate in the West Riding in which a strongly competitive, high-quality, cricketing scene developed, was almost entirely lacking in the North and East Ridings. Yet the north of the county, in particular, also had its own strong tradition of cricket going back to the turn of the 19th century, which had ebbed and flowed, and was based around York and a small number of prosperous towns. Places like Thirsk and Bedale (and Ripon just over the riding boundary) had at times some of the strongest teams in the county. Dissatisfaction here – and to a lesser extent, in the East Riding, where development was restricted by a small and more dispersed rural population – at the exclusion of their cricketers from the county team and the lack of county matches, meant that there also existed resistance to the pretensions of a county club that was always likely to ignore or downplay their interests. Backed by a number of aristocrats, in particular, Lord Londesborough, with an interest in cricket and with social reasons for not wishing to be subordinate to the middle-class decision-makers in Sheffield, there developed at times a loose 'alliance' of opposition to the county club. This alliance came together at the time of the birth of Yorkshire County Cricket Club in 1863, with a failed attempt to form an alternative, York-based county club; was revived in the form of Yorkshire United, which spluttered on briefly and ineffectively during the mid-1870s, found further voice in the 1880s, with the pressure on the committee in 1882 which led to some concessions on representation and fixtures; and stimulated the creation of the feeble North Riding County Cricket Club in the middle of the decade. None of these were particularly effective, but they were signs of on-going and strongly felt dissatisfaction. Such sentiments worked against a united and representative county club.

Ultimately, however, all the efforts of those advocating reform were undermined by a lack of quality when alternative county sides took to the field, and by divisions and disagreements between representatives off it when they came to press the arguments for change. Many appeared unwilling or unable to put their case effectively, often falling back on the line that they simply wanted to help find new players for the county side. The intermittent on-field success of the Yorkshire XI in the 1870s and particularly in the early 1880s, albeit mixed with periods of depressing failure, meant that the county committee was never under consistent pressure to reform for many years. The demonstrably poorer standards of the grounds away from Sheffield, at least until the early 1880s in the case of Bradford, and the early 1890s in the case of Leeds, meant defenders of the *status quo* always had a credible case that arrangements in other towns were simply not good enough to avoid embarrassing the county club.

In the end, though, it was not the building of better venues, or the persistence of the voices of protest that led to the changes agreed in 1892 and introduced the following year. Instead, the woeful performances on the field in the late 1880s and early 1890s meant that the existing county arrangements could no longer be defended as likely to lead to a successful Yorkshire County Cricket Club at any time soon. While protecting its predominance and financial position – as had always been the case – Sheffield agreed to reforms which made the club more representative of the county as a whole. This finally helped to unleash the resources of the county and channelled them more effectively towards sporting success.

Against this background, in the late 1880s, Lord Hawke removed those deemed to be undermining the discipline of the team, and tapped into, and further developed, a strong cricketing culture that was competitive, professional and fiercely proud of the ability of the club to rely on local resources, traits which we can see in the cricket played since the 1820s in Yorkshire. Less reliant on amateur cricketers than some other county clubs, and with a strong pipeline of new professional talent generated by the growing league structure, Yorkshire County Cricket Club became a powerful force in the English game, and was synonymous with a hard-nosed and effective approach to winning matches. Such cricket had widespread appeal in the county amongst people increasingly schooled in (or observers of) competitive local cricket, and its heroes, myths and traditions were built up and celebrated by a press which had devoted considerable attention to it for decades, and which derived considerable commercial benefits from reporting on a game that was - in the truest sense - taken seriously.

ACKNOWLEDGEMENTS

I would like to acknowledge the support of the Association of Cricket Statisticians and Historians in publishing this book.

I would also like to thank the many people who have helped to bring this book to fruition. In particular, Mick Pope for his considerable advice and very helpful comments and corrections on earlier versions of the manuscript, and for very generously allowing me to make use of many pictures from his collection. His support has been invaluable.

I am grateful to Roger Moulton, who acted as editor, for his wise advice which, amongst other things, ensured that the manuscript was kept to a sensible length. And to Jenny Moulton, for painstakingly preparing the index, and to Ric Finlay and John Ward for their careful proof reading. Any remaining errors are entirely mine.

I am grateful to Ron Deaton who read an early manuscript and provided many important comments and corrections.

David Hall, the former Director of the Yorkshire County Cricket Club Museum at Headingley, kindly arranged for me to consult the county's early minute books, which provided some hugely important insights into the early days of the club. I am grateful to Yorkshire County Cricket Club for allowing me to use this material.

I am grateful to the staff of various libraries: the British Library Newspaper Library, at the start of my research when consulting newspapers involved long trips from Kent to Colindale, North London, to get covered in brown dust from the crumbling volumes of original papers; the West Riding Archive Service at Morley, where I consulted the Yorkshire CCC minute book for 1883-93; the West Yorkshire Archive Service in Huddersfield; the Hull History Centre; and the East Riding Archive and Local Studies Service in Beverley.

I would like to emphasise and acknowledge the essential contribution made by the online British Newspaper Archive (www.britishnewspaperarchive.co.uk) and the digitisation project which has transformed the availability of early newspapers – 16 million pages and counting. A marvellous resource.

I would also like to acknowledge the assistance of Roger Mann, who identified a number of suitable pictures from his extensive collection.

I would like to thank Sir William Worsley of Hovingham Hall for generously allowing me to use two pictures from his collection of photographs of Hovingham.

I am also grateful to the Castle Howard Archive for the use of a picture of the 7th

Earl Morpeth, which is reproduced by kind permission of the Howard family.

I would like to acknowledge the Sheffield Galleries and Museums Trust for the picture of the Darnall token and the 1824 handbill; Hull History Centre for the Scarborough Cricket Club membership card for 1876; and the East Riding Archive and Local Studies Service for the Beverley Westwood picture (ERALS:PH/4/7 (127).

Finally, I would like to thank my father, who took me to see Yorkshire in August 1971, which sparked my love 'for a game taken seriously'.

BIBLIOGRAPHY

Newspapers

The main sources of information are the following newspapers: *Bradford Observer, Dewsbury Reporter, Driffield Times, Hull Daily Mail, Hull News*, Hull Packet, Huddersfield Chronicle, Huddersfield Daily Examiner*, Leeds Intelligencer, Leeds Mercury, Leeds Times, Sheffield Daily Telegraph, Sheffield Evening Telegraph, Sheffield Independent, Whitby Gazette, York Herald, Yorkshire Evening Post, Yorkshire Gazette, Yorkshire Post* and *Leeds Intelligencer.* In addition, I have also made use of *Athletic News* and *Bell's Life*. All but those marked * are available on the British Newspaper Archive website.

Yorkshire County Cricket Club minute books

A number of parts of this book benefited considerably from information gained from reviewing the minute books of the Yorkshire County Cricket Club. I am very grateful to David Hall, the former Director of the Yorkshire Cricket Museum at Headingley, for giving me access to the minute books for the period from 1861 to 1878. I am also grateful to the staff at the West Yorkshire Archive Service at Morley for access to the minute book for 1883-1893. Unfortunately, that covering the intervening period is not currently available.

Books and articles

Allen, D, *Early Books on Cricket*, Europa Publications, 1987

Association of Cricket Statisticians, *First-Class Cricket Matches*, volumes for each of the years from 1863-1893, Association of Cricket Statisticians, 1980 onwards

Baker, R , *Iron and Willow: A History of Middlesbrough Cricket Club, Volume One 1855 to 1911*, Ray Baker, 1989

Baker, R (ed), *In the Big League: 100 Years of Cricket in the North Yorkshire and South Durham League, Part 1*, 1992

Beachill, J, *See the Conquering Hero Comes*, J Beachill, 1986

Brookes, C, *English Cricket: The Game and its Players through the Ages*, Weidenfield and Nicolson, 1978

Brown L , *Victorian News and Newspapers*, Oxford University Press, 1985

Butler, M, *From Batley to Barnsley: A History of the Heavy Woollen District Cricket Challenge Cup 1883-2005*, Mike Butler and Cricket Heritage Publications, 2006

Catton, J A H, 'Famous Cricket Grounds' in T.Moult (ed) *Bat and Ball – A New Book of Cricket*, Arthur Barker, 1935

Cobley, F, *Black Hats v White Hats or Ilkley Tradesmen at the Wickets, and Around the Festive Board*, William Walker and Sons, Otley, 1895

Coldham, J P, *Lord Hawke: A Cricketing Legend*, Tauris Parke Paperbacks, 1990

Collins, T, *Rugby's Great Split: Class, Culture and the Origins of Rugby League Football*, Routledge, London, 2006

Collins, T, *Sport in Capitalist Society: A Short History*, Routledge, London, 2013

Davies, P with Light, R, *Cricket and community in England: 1800 to the present day*, Manchester University Press, 2012

Dewar, W (ed), *The Cricket Annual*, Driffield, 1892

Dickinson, J, *The Origins of Sheffield Wednesday*, Amberley, 2015

Dixon, R, and Muthesius, S, *Victorian Architecture*, Oxford University Press, Oxford, 1978

Draper, S, 'Pre-1770 References to Cricket in Leeds and Sheffield.' In The Cricket Statistician, Issue 84, 1993 pp12-14

Draper, S, *Cricket Grounds of Yorkshire*, The Association of Cricket Statisticians and Historians, West Bridgford, 1995

Farnsworth, K, *Before and After Bramall Lane: Sheffield United CC and Yorkshire Cricket in Sheffield*, published by the author, 1988

Gent, D, '*Aristocratic Whig Politics in Early-Victorian Yorkshire: Lord Morpeth and his World*', PhD thesis, University of York, 2010 at http://etheses.whiterose.ac.uk/876/1/Gent_-_Aristocratic_Whig_Thesis.pdf

Greaves, G, *Over the Summers Again: A History of Harrogate Cricket Club*, Harrogate Cricket Club, 1976

Griffin, E, *Liberty's Dawn: A People's History of the Industrial Revolution*, Yale University Press, 2013

Heywood, F, M and B, *Cloth Caps and Cricket Crazy: Todmorden and Cricket 1835-1896*, Upper Calder Valley Publications, 2004

Hall, I with Found J, *Cricket at Scarborough: A Social History of the Club and its Festival*, Breedon Books, 1992

Hawke, Lord, *Recollections and Reminiscences*, Williams and Norgate, London, 1924

Hignell, A, *A 'Favourit' Game: Cricket in south Wales before 1914*, University of Wales Press, Cardiff, 1992

Hodgson, D, *The Official History of Yorkshire County Cricket Club*, The Crowood Press, 1989

Holmes, R S, *The History of Yorkshire County Cricket*, Archibald Constable and Co, London, 1904

Holt, R, 'Football and the Urban Way of Life in Nineteenth-Century Britain' in *Pleasure, Profit and Proselytism: British Culture and Sport at Home and Abroad 1700-1914*, Frank Cass, 1988

Holt, R, 'The Amateur Body and the Middle-Class Man: Work, Health and Style in Victorian Britain' in *Sport in History*, Volume 26, Number 3, December 2006, pp352-369

Howarth, P, *East Yorkshire Cricket 1778-1914*, Lowndes Publications, Driffield, 1995

Huggins, M, *The Victorians and Sport*, Hambledon Continuum, London, 2004

James, C L R, *Beyond a Boundary*, Yellow Jersey Press, London, 1963

Kelly's Directory of West Riding of Yorkshire, 1881, available at http://specialcollections.le.ac.uk/cdm/compoundobject/collection/p16445coll4/id/278523/rec/4

Kelly's Directory of the North and East Ridings, 1893, available at http://specialcollections.le.ac.uk/cdm/compoundobject/collection/p16445coll4/id/278530/rec/46

Kilburn, J M, *The Scarborough Cricket Festival*, The Scarborough Cricket Club, 1948

Light, R, 'Cricket's Forgotten Past: A Social and Cultural History of the Game in the West Riding of Yorkshire 1820-1870', PhD thesis, De Montfort University, 2008

Light, R, 'In a Yorkshire Like Way: Cricket and the Construction of Regional Identity in Nineteenth Century Yorkshire' in *Sport in History*, 29(3), 2009, pp500-518

Lillywhite, F, *Frederick Lillywhite's Cricket Scores and Biographies of Celebrated Cricketers from 1827 to 1840*, Volume II, Frederick Lillywhite, 1862

Lillywhite, J, *James Lillywhite's Cricketers' Annual,* James Lillywhite, Frowd and Co, *1892*

Lillywhite, J, *James Lillywhite's Cricketers' Annual,* James Lillywhite, Frowd and Co, *1894*

Lodge, H, *Lascelles Hall Cricket Club Centenary 1825-1925,* 1925

Lonsdale, J, 'Charles Edward Ullathorne' in *The Cricket Statistician*, Issue 42, 1983, pp5-6

Lonsdale, J, 'When the Australians came to Scarborough...Joe Frank and Spofforth's Fingers' in *White Rose*, Yorkshire County Cricket Club, November 1985, pp23-24

Lonsdale, J, 'John Briggs – English Cricket's Youngest Professional?' in *The Cricket Statistician*,Issue 65, 1989, pp10-11

Lonsdale, J, in R Richtering *Cricket in Hornsea 1859 to 2006*, Hornsea Cricket Club, 2006

Major, J, *More than a Game: The Story of Cricket's Early Years*, Harper Press, 2007

Malcolmson, R, *Popular Recreations in English Society 1700-1850*, Cambridge University Press, 1973

Marshall, J, *Headingley*, Pelham Books, 1970

Mason, T, 'Sporting News, 1860-1914,' in Michael Harris and Alan Lee (eds), *The Press in English Society from the Seventeenth to Nineteenth Centuries*, Associated University Presses,1986

Maude, D, *A Century of Yorkshire County Cricket at Park Avenue, 1881-1981*, 1981

Moriarty, B and Cooper, J, *A Brief History of the Golcar Cricket and Athletic Club*, 1971

O'Keefe, D, *Start of Play: The Foundation and Progress of Illingworth St Mary's Cricket Club c 1884-1920, A Social History*

'Old Ebor', *Talks with Old Yorkshire Cricketers*, Yorkshire Evening Post, 1898

'Old Ebor', 'Interview with Charlie Ullathorne', reprinted in *The Cricket Statistician*, Issue 166, 2014, pp9-22

Pope, M, *Headingley Ghosts: A Collection of Yorkshire Cricket Tragedies*, Scratching Shed Publishing, 2013

Programme and Souvenir of the Grand Bazaar in aid of the Manningham Cricket Club, February 25-27 1892 at Local Studies Library, Bradford

Russell, D, 'The Pursuit of Leisure' in Victorian Bradford, (eds) D.G.Wright and J.A.Jowitt, *Victorian Bradford*, City of Bradford Metropolitan Council, 1982, pp199-221

Russell, D, 'Sport and Identity: The Case of Yorkshire County Cricket Club, 1890-1939' in *Twentieth Century British History*, Vol 7, No 2, 1996, pp 206-230

Sandiford, K A P, *Cricket and the Victorians*, Scolar Press, 1994

Scowcroft, P, *Cricket in Doncaster and District: an outline history*, Doncaster Library Services, 1985

Sissons, R, *The Players: A Social History of the Professional Cricketer*, The Kingswood Press, London, 1988

Swain, P, 'The Origins of Football Debate: The 'Grander Design and the Involvement of the Lower Classes', 1818-1840 in *Sport in History*, Volume 34, Number 4, December 2014, pp519-543

Teal, R, *Beverley Town Cricket Club 1862 to 2012: 150 years of club cricket*, Ray Teal, 2013

Thomas, P, *Yorkshire Cricketers 1839-1939*, Derek Hodgson Publisher, Manchester, 1973

Thompson, F M L, *The Rise of Respectable Society: A Social History of Victorian Britain, 1830-1900*, Fontana Press, 1988

Thomson, A A, *Hirst and Rhodes*, The Epworth Press, 1959

Ulyatt, M, *Hull Railway Clerks Cricket Club Centenary 1873-1973,* 1973

Ulyatt, M *See you down at The Circle*, Mike Ulyatt Enterprises, 2004

Underdown, D, *Start of Play: Cricket and Culture in Eighteenth-Century England*, Allen Lane, London, 2000

Vamplew, W, *Pay Up and play the game: Professional sport in Britain, 1875-1914*, Cambridge University Press, Cambridge, 1988

West, G D, *The Elevens of England*, Darf Publishers Limited, 1988

West, G D, *Six More Days of Grace*, Darf Publishers Limited, 1992

Woodhouse, A, *The History of Yorkshire County Cricket Club*, Christopher Helm, 1989

Woodhouse, A, *A Who's Who of Yorkshire County Cricket Club*, Breedon Books, 1992

Yorkshire County Cricket Club Yearbooks, various

Also consulted:

A Cricket Archive for Nidderdale and District: From the newspapers of the day at http://www.nidderdalecricketarchive.co.uk/

Cricket Archive at http://cricketarchive.com/ for scorecards.

REFERENCES

1 `The Guardian, 13 August 2012

2 Russell, D (1996), 'Sport and Identity: The Case of Yorkshire County Cricket Club, 1890-1939' in Twentieth Century British History, Vol 7, No 2, 1996, pp216-217

3 Underdown, D (2000), Start of Play: Cricket and Culture in Eighteenth Century Cricket, Allen Lane, London, pxviii

4 Quoted in Russell, D (1996), p211

5 See Swain, P (2014), 'The Origins of Football Debate: The 'Grander Design and the Involvement of the Lower Classes', 1818-1840 in *Sport in History*, Volume 34, Number 4, December, pp519-543

6 Thomson, A (1959), Hirst and Rhodes, p102

7 Sheffield Daily Telegraph, 24 August 1893

8 Sheffield Daily Telegraph, 28 August 1893

9 Leeds Mercury, 5 June 1893

10 James Lillywhite's Cricketers' Annual 1894, p5

11 Coldham, J P (1990), Lord Hawke: A Cricketing Legend, p92; Sheffield Independent, 10 March 1893

12 The Cricket Annual 1892, p123

13 Leeds Mercury, 22 May 1893

14 Holmes, RS (1904) The History of Yorkshire County Cricket Club 1833-1903 p67

15 James Lillywhite's Cricketers' Annual 1894, p132

16 Manchester Courier and Lancashire General Advertiser, 10 March 1893

17 Leeds Mercury, 24 August 1893

18 Leeds Mercury, 1 September 1893

19 Yorkshire Evening Post, 1 May 1893

20 Leeds Mercury, 1 February 1893, Sheffield Independent, 1 February 1893

21 Sheffield Independent, 1 February 1893, 10 February 1893

22 Sheffield Daily Telegraph, 28 August 1893

23 James Lillywhite's Cricketers' Annual 1894, p5

24 Sheffield Independent, 1 September 1893, James Lillywhite's Cricketers' Annual 1894, pp132-133

25 Quoted in Leeds Mercury, 24 August 1893

26 Leeds Mercury, 1 September 1893

27 Sheffield Independent, 2 September 1893

28 James Lillywhite's Cricketers' Annual 1894, p7

29 Leeds Mercury, 1 September 1893

30 Leeds Times, 26 August 1893

31 Coldham, p97

32 Sheffield Evening Telegraph, 22 August 1893

33 Sheffield Daily Telegraph, 28 August 1893

34 Coldham, p95

35 Yorkshire Evening Post, 12 June 1893

36 Sheffield Evening Telegraph, 22 August 1893

37 Coldham, p102

38 Hull Daily Mail, 5 June 1893

39 Sheffield Daily Telegraph, 8 August 1893

40 Sheffield Daily Telegraph, 18 August 1893

41 Yorkshire Evening Post, 28 August 1893

42 Holmes, p67

43 Yorkshire County Cricket Club Yearbook 2013, pp265-266

44 The Cricket Field quoted in Sheffield Independent, 4 January 1893

45 James Lillywhite's Cricketers' Annual 1892, pp 9, 81

46 The Yorkshire County Cricket Club Yearbook 2013, p267

47 Yorkshire County Cricket Club Yearbook, 115th edition, 2013, pp368-389

48 Quoted in Sheffield Evening Telegraph, 3 April 1893

49 Coldham, pp87-88

50 Sheffield Evening Telegraph, 29 August 1893, Leeds Mercury, 1 September 1893

51 Yorkshire Evening Post, 25 March 1893

52 Sheffield Evening Telegraph, 22 August 1893

53 Yorkshire Evening Post, 1 May 1893

54 Leeds Mercury, 3 June 1893, Yorkshire Evening Post, 5 June 1893

55 Quoted in the Sheffield Evening Telegraph, 22 June 1893

56 Hull Daily Mail, 16 June 1893

57 Sheffield Evening Telegraph, 29 August 1893

58 Holmes, p66

59 Leeds Mercury, 17 April 1893

60 Baker, R (ed) (1992), 'In the Big League: 100 Years of Cricket in North Yorkshire and South Durham League' p11

61 York Herald, 14 January 1893

62 York Herald, 24 January 1893

63 Drakes Huddersfield Cricket League, Centenary 1891-1991, Official Souvenir, p13

64 Holmes, p174
65 Leeds Mercury, 22 April 1893
66 Leeds Mercury, 24 April 1893
67 Leeds Mercury, 13 May 1893
68 Leeds Mercury, 1 May 1893
69 Hull Daily Mail, 4 May 1893
70 Huddersfield Chronicle, 6 May 1893
71 Yorkshire Evening Post, 15 May 1893
72 Hull Daily Mail, 20 January 1893
73 Leeds Mercury, 24 April 1893
74 Yorkshire Evening Post, 8 May 1893
75 Yorkshire Evening Post, 20 May 1893
76 Daily Gazette for Middlesbrough, 11 May 1893
77 Hull Daily Mail, 8 May 1893, Daily Gazette for Middlesbrough, 11 May 1893, Yorkshire Evening Post, 8 May 1893
78 Leeds Mercury, 8 May 1893
79 Drakes Huddersfield Cricket League, Centenary 1891-1991, Official Souvenir, p13-14
80 Yorkshire Evening Post, 16 January 1893
81 Yorkshire Evening Post, 7 April 1893
82 Yorkshire Post and Leeds Intelligencer, 18 April 1887
83 Woodhouse, A (1989), The History of Yorkshire County Cricket Club, Helm; Hodgson, D (1989) The Official History of Yorkshire County Cricket Club, Crowood.
84 James, CLR (1963), Beyond a Boundary, preface
85 Davies, P with Light, R (2012), Cricket and community in England, Manchester University Press, p55
86 Huggins, M (2004), The Victorians and Sport, Hambledon Continuum, p111
87 Yorkshire Gazette, 23 November 1861
88 York Herald, 29 June 1893
89 Holmes, p1
90 York Herald, 22 April 1843
91 York Herald, 29 March 1845
92 York Herald, 8 December 1849
93 Sheffield Daily Telegraph, 15 May 1893
94 Sheffield Daily Telegraph, 27 May 1890
95 Sheffield Independent, 4 January 1893
96 Brookes, C (1978), English Cricket: The game and its players through the ages; Underdown (2000); Major, J (2007), More than a Game: The Story of Cricket's Early Years
97 Davies, P, p29
98 Holmes, p10
99 Draper, S (1993), 'Pre-1770 References to Cricket in Leeds and Sheffield.' In The Cricket Statistician, Winter, No 84, pp12-14
100 Leeds Intelligencer, 20 May 1760
101 Leeds Intelligencer, 7 July 1761, 27 August 1765, Leeds Intelligencer, 8 July 1777, Holmes p11
102 Leeds Intelligencer, 25 August 1778, Holmes, p11
103 Leeds Intelligencer, 17 August 1784, Holmes, p11, Leeds Intelligencer, 8 July 1788, 25 July 1796, 5 September 1796, 14 November 1796
104 Leeds Intelligencer, 6 August 1798.
105 Holmes, pp 19, 13
106 Leeds Mercury, 2 September 1809
107 York Herald, 10 November 1810, 17 November 1810
108 Leeds Intelligencer, 13 September 1813, York Herald, 9 October 1813, 23 July 1814, 3 September 1814
109 Leeds Mercury, 23 September 1815
110 Hull Packet, 23 July 1816
111 Leeds Mercury, 2 September 1809, Hull Packet, 23 July 1816, Leeds Mercury, 15 September 1821
112 Malcolmson,R, (1973), Popular Recreations in English Society 1700-1850, Cambridge University Press, pp118-157
113 York Herald, 11 August 1827
114 Sheffield Independent, 4 September 1830
115 Sheffield Independent, 12 July 1834
116 Bradford Observer, 24 June 1841
117 York Herald, 20 November 1858
118 Bradford Observer, 14 February 1861, Leeds Times, 24 July 1869, Whitby Gazette, 27 September 1862
119 Leeds Times, 14 October 1865
120 Yorkshire Post and Leeds Intelligencer, 20 April 1885, 4 May 1885
121 Yorkshire Post and Leeds Intelligencer, 21 June 1886,
122 Leeds Times, 23 July 1881
123 Leeds Mercury, 15 September 1860
124 Sheffield Independent, 30 August 1862, 2 September 1862
125 Huddersfield Chronicle, 21 May 1873
126 Yorkshire Gazette, 18 September 1886
127 Yorkshire Post and Leeds Intelligencer, 29 June 1885
128 A traditional game played in the north of England in which the object is to hit the small knurr as far as possible.
129 Yorkshire Post and Leeds Intelligencer, 22 September 1885
130 Leeds Times, 9 May 1835, Leeds Intelligencer, 9 May 1835
131 Sheffield Independent, 28 June 1845, 25 July 1846

132 Bradford Observer, 4 May 1848
133 Leeds Times, 28 May 1881
134 Leeds Times, 18 March 1882
135 Malcolmson, R, pp16-20
136 Sheffield Independent, 24 August 1850, 21 August 1858
137 Leeds Times, 19 August 1865
138 Leeds Times, 18 September 1880
139 Bradford Observer, 9 September 1869
140 Sheffield Independent, 2 June 1832
141 Leeds Intelligencer, 30 June 1838
142 Hull Packet, 23 May 1856
143 Beverley Guardian, 29 September 1860
144 Huddersfield Chronicle, 18 May 1867
145 Yorkshire Post and Leeds Intelligencer, 4 August 1885
146 Scowcroft, P (1985), Cricket in Doncaster and District: an outline history, p7
147 Hull Packet, 12 June 1835, 8 April 1836
148 Leeds Times, 4 July 1863
149 Sheffield Independent, 13 May 1862, Leeds Times, 26 July 1873
150 Hull Packet, 21 August 1835, Leeds Times, 29 July 1854
151 York Herald, 20 October 1849
152 Bradford Observer, 18 June 1857
153 Hull Packet, 9 July 1841, Leeds Mercury, 6 April 1861, Yorkshire Post and Leeds Intelligencer, 27 March 1885
154 Sheffield Independent, 15 June 1850, Box was the Sussex wicketkeeper. Bernard Wake was an amateur who played for Yorkshire between 1849 and 1851
155 Yorkshire Post and Leeds Intelligencer, 20 June 1887
156 West, G (1988) The Elevens of England, p21
157 Leeds Intelligencer, 28 September 1826
158 Leeds Times, 29 April 1854
159 Leeds Times, 3 May 1856, Bell's Life in London first appeared in 1822, coming out every Sunday until the 1860s and surviving until the 1880s. For many years it was the premier sporting paper in the country.
160 Yorkshire Post and Leeds Intelligencer, 19 September 1882
161 Leeds Times, 17 May 1879
162 Sheffield Independent, 14 September 1844
163 Sheffield Independent,10 May 1845
164 Huddersfield Chronicle, 26 July 1851
165 Sheffield Independent, 7 June 1851
166 Sheffield Independent, 30 July 1859
167 Leeds Times, 8 July 1882
168 Leeds Times, 29 July 1882, 5 August 1882
169 Leeds Times, 24 November 1883
170 York Herald, 26 March 1859
171 York Herald, 9 July 1859
172 York Herald, 10 September 1859
173 Sheffield Independent, 16 October 1830
174 Yorkshire Gazette, 20 June 1835
175 York Herald, 4 June 1853
176 Huddersfield Chronicle, 13 July 1861
177 Huddersfield Chronicle, 19 October 1861
178 Leeds Times, 12 September 1863
179 Leeds Times, 23 December 1876
180 Leeds Times, 30 December 1876
181 Leeds Times, 6 January 1877, 20 January 1877, 27 January 1877
182 Sheffield Independent, 5 February 1859
183 For example, Huddersfield Chronicle, 11 July 1863
184 Yorkshire Post and Leeds Intelligencer, 24 August 1882, Leeds Mercury, 4 May 1883
185 Leeds Times, 25 August 1883, 1 September 1883, Pope, M (2013) Headingley Ghosts: A Collection of Yorkshire Cricket Tragedies, pp 231-232
186 Huddersfield Chronicle, 9 September 1865
187 Yorkshire Gazette, 8 September 1838
188 Sheffield Independent, 6 September 1851
189 Leeds Intelligencer, 26 October 1826
190 Sheffield Independent, 4 September 1830
191 Sheffield Independent, 6 June 1835
192 Leeds Times, 2 July 1836
193 York Herald, 15 March 1845, Leeds Mercury, 11 August 1849
194 Leeds Times, 23 August 1856
195 Leeds Times, 22 August 1857
196 Leeds Mercury, 26 April 1883
197 York Herald, 28 July 1838
198 Leeds Times, 10 August 1839
199 Sheffield Daily Telegraph, 18 April 1868
200 Hull Packet, 12 September 1879, Leeds Times, 22 November 1879
201 Sheffield Independent, 7 September 1850
202 Leeds Times, 10 August 1889
203 Sandiford, K A P (1994) Cricket and the Victorians, Scholar Press, p2
204 Leeds Intelligencer, 7 April 1825, Leeds Mercury, 9 April 1825
205 Sheffield Independent, 21 October 1837
206 York Herald, 17 September 1842
207 Leeds Mercury, 23 December 1843
208 Leeds Times, 11 April 1874
209 Huddersfield Chronicle, 13 April 1874
210 Driffield Times, 21 July 1900
211 Hull News, 9 May 1868

212 Bradford Observer, 5 August 1858
213 Bradford Observer, 28 June 1849
214 'Old Ebor' Talks with Old Yorkshire Cricketers, Yorkshire Evening Post, p25
215 Yorkshire Gazette, 6 December 1828, Yorkshire Gazette, 22 November 1834, 20 December 1834
216 Sheffield Independent, 27 November 1841
217 Leeds Mercury, 30 December 1843, Sheffield Independent, 23 November 1844
218 York Herald, 19 November 1842
219 York Herald, 30 November 1844
220 York Herald, 14 January 1843
221 Sheffield Independent, 1 November 1851
222 Sheffield Independent, 7 January 1837
223 Leeds Mercury, 3 February 1838
224 Farnsworth K (1988) Before and After Bramall Lane: Sheffield United CC and Yorkshire Cricket in Sheffield, p6
225 Malcolmson, p85
226 Yorkshire Post and Leeds Intelligencer, 2 May 1887
227 Malcolmson, p84
228 Ulyatt, M (1973) Hull Railway Clerks Cricket Club: Centenary 1873-1973, p11
229 Leeds Times, 24 September 1853
230 Leeds Times, 21 June 1856
231 Sheffield Independent, 19 May 1855
232 Huddersfield Chronicle, 23 May 1873
233 York Herald, 23 August 1845, 27 September 1845
234 York Herald, 30 August 1845
235 Sheffield Independent, 7 July 1855
236 Leeds Times, 15 June 1878
237 York Herald, 20 September 1834
238 Sheffield Independent, 25 September 1847
239 Huddersfield Chronicle, 29 January 1870
240 Bradford Observer, 28 May 1857
241 York Herald, 13 December 1845
242 Sheffield Independent, 5 September 1846
243 Sheffield Independent, 7 June 1856
244 Sheffield Independent, 25 September 1858
245 Bradford Observer, 19 August 1869, 26 August 1869, Driffield Times, 15 August 1874
246 Yorkshire Gazette, 21 June 1834
247 Leeds Intelligencer, 31 August 1826, Greaves, G (1976) Over the Summers Again: A History of Harrogate Cricket Club, p14
248 Bradford Observer, 3 September 1846
249 Beverley Guardian, 5 September 1857
250 Bradford Observer, 6 August 1840
251 Leeds Times, 2 July 1881
252 Bradford Observer, 6 October 1842
253 York Herald, 6 October 1855
254 Sheffield Independent, 23 September 1843
255 Bradford Observer, 21 September 1854
256 Bradford Observer, 19 October 1843
257 Bradford Observer, 16 June 1842
258 Bradford Observer, 12 August 1841, Mason, T (1986) 'Sporting News, 1860-1914' in The Press in English Society from the Seventeenth to Nineteenth Centuries, Associated University Presses, p169
259 Bradford Observer, 19 August 1841
260 Bradford Observer, 19 August 1847
261 Bradford Observer, 3 September 1846
262 Huddersfield Chronicle, 11 May 1850
263 Huddersfield Chronicle, 20 July 1850
264 Farnsworth, pp1-2
265 Leeds Intelligencer, 11 October 1834, Bradford Observer, 10 September 1846
266 York Herald, 9 June 1866, 11 August 1866
267 Leeds Times, 2 July 1881
268 Sheffield Independent, 8 June 1833, York Herald, 8 June 1833
269 Yorkshire Gazette, 22 August 1835, 2 April 1836
270 Leeds Times, 12 May 1877
271 Yorkshire Gazette, 10 January 1835
272 York Herald, 11 December 1852
273 Bradford Observer, 30 September 1847
274 Sheffield Independent, 25 March 1843
275 Huddersfield Chronicle, 18 January 1868
276 Leeds Times, 19 May 1888
277 Sheffield Independent, 16 September 1848
278 Leeds Mercury, 16 August, 1851
279 York Herald, 6 December 1856
280 Bradford Observer, 6 August 1840
281 Leeds Times, 10 September 1853
282 Leeds Times, 25 April 1846
283 Sheffield Independent, 19 October 1844
284 Leeds Times, 25 January 1845
285 York Herald, 8 May 1852
286 Bradford Observer, 22 July 1858
287 Leeds Times, 30 August 1856
288 Leeds Times, 31 March 1883
289 Malcolmson, pp100-105
290 York Herald, 19 April 1834
291 York Herald, 22 October 1842
292 York Herald, 15 October 1842
293 York Herald, 5 April 1851
294 York Herald, 16 February 1856
295 Huddersfield Chronicle, 8 May 1869

296 Huddersfield Chronicle, 6 July 1861
297 Huddersfield Chronicle, 23 May 1863
298 Yorkshire Post and Leeds Intelligencer, 24 August 1887
299 Underdown(2000); Hignell, A (1992) A 'Favourit' Game: Cricket in south Wales before 1914, University of Wales Press, Cardiff
300 Information drawn from Kelly's Directory of West Riding of Yorkshire, 1881 and Kelly's Directory of the North and East Ridings of Yorkshire, 1893 available at http://specialcollections.le.ac.uk/cdm/compoundobject/collection/p16445coll4/id/278523/rec/4 http://specialcollections.le.ac.uk/cdm/compoundobject/collection/p16445coll4/id/278530/rec/46
301 Gerrard, D, Victorian and Edwardian North Riding, p5
302 Sheffield Independent, 26 September 1829
303 Holmes, p19
304 Farnsworth, p2
305 Sheffield Independent, 29 March 1851
306 Farnsworth, p2
307 Dickinson, J (2015), The Origins of Sheffield Wednesday, Amberley, p10
308 Leeds Mercury, 31 August 1822
309 Farnsworth, p4
310 York Herald, 4 June 1825
311 Quoted in Holmes, p35
312 Farnsworth, p7
313 Davies, p30
314 Frederick Lillywhite's Cricket Scores and Biographies of Celebrated Cricketers from 1827 to 1840, Vol II, p68
315 Sheffield Independent, 13 September 1828
316 Sheffield Independent, 8 November 1828
317 Sheffield Independent, 14 May 1831
318 Draper,S, Cricket Grounds of Yorkshire, pp10-11, Sheffield Independent, 20 April 1833, 9 August 1834
319 Sheffield Independent, 19 October 1833, 14 May 1836
320 Leeds Mercury, 12 January 1839
321 Sheffield Independent, 10 August 1833
322 Sheffield Independent, 3 July 1847
323 Sheffield Independent, 14 June 1845
324 Sheffield Independent, 22 June 1844
325 Sheffield Independent, 29 March 1851
326 Sheffield Independent, 8 August 1846
327 Sheffield Independent, 29 April 1848
328 Sheffield Independent, 15 April 1848
329 Sheffield Independent, 11 October 1851
330 Sheffield Independent, 24 July 1852
331 Farnsworth, p15
332 Sheffield Independent, 28 January 1854
333 Sheffield Independent, 4 February 1854
334 Sheffield Independent, 4 February 1854
335 Sheffield Independent, 16 September 1854
336 Sheffield Independent, 21 April 1855
337 Sheffield Independent, 5 May 1855
338 Sheffield Independent, 16 June 1855
339 Sheffield Independent, 27 October 1855
340 Sheffield Independent, 26 May 1855
341 Sheffield Independent, 11 October 1856
342 Sheffield Independent, 22 April 1854
343 Sheffield Independent, 6 May 1854
344 Draper, p16
345 Sporting Life, 25 January 1868
346 Sheffield Daily Telegraph, 19 July 1873
347 Sheffield Independent, 21 October 1870
348 Sheffield Daily Telegraph, 1 June 1875
349 Sheffield Daily Telegraph, 2 July 1873
350 Leeds Times, 2 November 1878
351 Sheffield Independent, 2 February 1881, 11 May 1881, 16 May 1881, 26 May 1881
352 Yorkshire Post and Leeds Intelligencer, 13 April 1885
353 Huddersfield Chronicle, 2 May 1874, Holmes, pp 15-16, 92
354 Yorkshire Gazette, 3 August 1839
355 Lodge, H, p2, Holmes, p91
356 Sheffield Independent, 17 August 1844
357 Huddersfield Chronicle, 19 October 1850
358 Leeds Times, 10 September 1842
359 Leeds Times, 13 August 1842, 10 September 1842, 17 September 1842, 15 October 1842, 2 September 1848,
360 Leeds Times, 30 August 1845
361 Huddersfield Chronicle, 4 October 1851
362 Draper, p29
363 Huddersfield Chronicle, 16 June 1860
364 Huddersfield Chronicle, 6 September 1862
365 Huddersfield Chronicle, 20 April 1861
366 Huddersfield Chronicle, 4 May 1861
367 Huddersfield Chronicle, 31 August 1861, 22 August 1863
368 Huddersfield Chronicle, 28 May 1864, 4 June 1864
369 Huddersfield Chronicle, 13 May 1865, 14 April 1866
370 Huddersfield Chronicle, 9 June 1866, 30 June 1866, 7 July 1866, 13 October 1866
371 Huddersfield Chronicle, 18 November 1871

372 Huddersfield Chronicle, 28 March 1868
373 Huddersfield Chronicle, 18 June 1870
374 Huddersfield Daily Examiner, 23 October 1878
375 Yorkshire Post and Leeds Intelligencer, 22 April 1884
376 Yorkshire Post and Leeds Intelligencer, 20 April 1885
377 Huddersfield Chronicle, 29 May 1886
378 Yorkshire Post and Leeds Intelligencer, 18 April 1887
379 Huddersfield Chronicle, 26 January 1889
380 Holmes, p89
381 Lodge,H, pp5-6
382 'Old Ebor', pp228-229
383 Holmes, p90
384 Huddersfield Chronicle, 24 September 1864
385 'Old Ebor', p235
386 Holmes, p11, Leeds Intelligencer, 20 May 1760, Draper, p12
387 Leeds Times, 7 September 1833
388 Leeds Times, 4 May 1839
389 Leeds Times, 16 June 1838
390 Leeds Times, 15 June 1839, 22 June 1839, 8 November 1834
391 Leeds Times, 17 July 1847
392 Draper, p25
393 LeedsTimes, 9 April 1853
394 Leeds Times, 25 June 1853,
395 Leeds Times, 27 March 1858, 22 May 1858
396 Leeds Times, 15 June 1861
397 Leeds Mercury, 22 August 1861
398 Leeds Mercury, 26 October 1861
399 Leeds Mercury, 23 May 1862
400 Leeds Mercury, 18 June 1863
401 Leeds Mercury, 17 August, 20 August, 22 August, 24 August, 28 October, 10 November 1863
402 Yorkshire Gazette, 7 November 1863
403 Leeds Intelligencer, 26 March 1864
404 Leeds Intelligencer, 2 April 1864
405 Leeds Times, 20 August 1864, 15 October 1864
406 Draper, p25-28
407 Leeds Times, 22 August 1874
408 Yorkshire Post and Leeds Intelligencer, 24 April 1882
409 Leeds Times, 9 November 1878, 16 November 1878
410 Leeds Times, 17 April 1880
411 Leeds Times, 18 November 1882
412 Leeds Times, 7 April 1883
413 Draper, p28
414 Leeds Times, 13 January 1883
415 Leeds Times, 11 November 1882
416 Leeds Mercury, 13 February 1883
417 Yorkshire Post and Leeds Intelligencer, 22 April 1884
418 Yorkshire Post and Leeds Intelligencer, 12 August 1884
419 Yorkshire Post and Leeds Intelligencer, 13 January 1885
420 Yorkshire Post and Leeds Intelligencer, 19 April 1886
421 Draper, p52-53
422 Leeds Times, 2 March 1889
423 Draper, p53
424 Bradford Daily Telegraph, 19 June 1893
425 Yorkshire Evening Post, 26 June 1893
426 Marshall, J, Headlingley, Pelham Books, 1970, p3
427 Bradford Bystander (1965), 'A History of the Bradford Cricket Club', Volume 12, Number 10, June
428 Bradford Observer, 18 September 1875, Maude, D (1981), A Century of Yorkshire County Cricket at Park Avenue 1881-1981 p7
429 Bradford Observer, 18 September 1875, 25 July 1839
430 Bradford Observer,18 September 1875
431 Bradford Observer, 23 July 1840, 28 November 1844
432 Bradford Observer, 1 June 1843
433 Bradford Observer, 24 June 1847
434 www.cricketarchive.com
435 Draper, p21
436 Bradford Observer, 6 May 1852
437 Bradford Observer, 17 July 1856, 28 May 1863
438 Bradford Observer, 26 April 1877
439 Bradford Observer, 30 May 1861
440 Leeds Times, 25 May 1867
441 Leeds Times, 17 April 1869
442 Leeds Times, 19 June 1869
443 Bradford Observer, 4 November 1874
444 Leeds Times, 18 April 1874
445 Bradford Observer, 30 April 1874
446 Leeds Times, 13 March 1875
447 Leeds Times, 11 September 1875
448 Draper, p21,
449 Leeds Times, 26 April 1879, Draper, p41
450 Leeds Times, 23 August 1879
451 Leeds Times, 13 March 1880
452 Leeds Times, 6 September 1879
453 Leeds Times, 13 March 1880
454 Draper, p41
455 Leeds Times, 5 February 1881

456 Leeds Times, 12 February 1881
457 Leeds Times, 27 August 1881
458 Leeds Times, 17 June 1882
459 Yorkshire Post and Leeds Intelligencer, 10 June 1884
460 Leeds Times, 15 September 1883
461 Yorkshire Post and Leeds Intelligencer, 27 January 1885
462 Draper, p38
463 Draper, p49
464 Leeds Mercury, 29 April 1837
465 Leeds Times, 4 May 1839
466 Draper, p49-50
467 Bradford Observer, 18 September 1834, Draper, p23
468 Draper, pp24-25
469 Leeds Mercury, 2 June 1868
470 Yorkshire Post and Leeds Intelligencer, 3 May 1886, Draper, p24
471 Butler, M, (2006), From Batley to Barnsley: A History of Heavy Woollen District Cricket Challenge Cup 1883-2005, pp 4-10
472 Scowcroft, pp5-12
473 Leeds Intelligencer, 14 November 1796
474 York Herald, 21 May 1814, York Herald, 9 November 1816
475 Greaves, p14
476 Greaves, pp 14-17, Draper, p45-46
477 Many of these references to Ripon cricket have been found with the help of the excellent Nidderdale Cricket Archive site at www.nidderdalecricketarchive.co.uk
478 York Herald, 17 November 1810
479 Holmes, p14, York Herald, 18 September 1813, 25 September 1813, 9 October 1813, Leeds Intelligencer, 20 September 1813, Leeds Mercury, 23 September 1815, York Herald, 4 May 1816, 20 July 1816
480 York Herald, 6 August 1814, Holmes, p14
481 Sheffield Independent, 22 August 1829
482 Bell's Life, 11 October 1829
483 York Herald, 10 August 1833
484 Holmes, p14
485 York Herald, 5 June 1841
486 York Herald, 31 July 1841
487 York Herald, 23 April 1842
488 Quoted on nidderdalecricketarchive.co.uk, 6 May 1847
489 www.cricketarchive.com
490 Holmes, p9
491 Howarth, P (1995) East Yorkshire Cricket 1778-1914, Lowndes Publications, p9, Leeds Intelligencer, 25 August 1778
492 Howarth, p20, p95
493 Howarth, p11
494 Hull Packet, 30 April 1852
495 Beverley Guardian, 19 April 1856
496 Teal, R (2012), Beverley Town Cricket Club 1862 to 2012, p12
497 Howarth, p20
498 Howarth, p45
499 Howarth, p95
500 Lonsdale, J in Richtering, R (2006), Cricket in Hornsea 1859 to 2006
501 Howarth, p9, Leeds Intelligencer, 6 August 1798, Ulyatt, M, (2004), See you down at The Circle, p6
502 Hull Packet, 27 May 1828
503 Hull Packet, 10 July 1832
504 Hull Packet, 17 May 1833, 30 August 1833
505 Sheffield Independent, 11 July 1835, Hull Packet, 18 September 1835
506 York Herald, 2 September 1837
507 Hull Packet, 24 March 1848
508 Hull Packet, 9 March 1849
509 Hull Packet 16 August 1844
510 Hull Packet 14 May 1847
511 Hull Packet, 26 May 1848
512 Hull Packet, 20 July 1849
513 Ulyatt (2004), p6
514 Draper, p37, Ulyatt (2004), p6
515 Hull News 12 September 1863
516 Hull Packet, 11 September 1863, Hull News, 9 May 1868
517 Hull News, 7 November 1874
518 Howarth, pp63, 66
519 Draper, p37
520 Hull Packet, 8 March 1878
521 Howarth, p70,
522 Draper, p37, Howarth, p71
523 Holmes, p10
524 Leeds Intelligencer, 9 October 1797
525 York Herald, 24 October 1829, Leeds Times, 23 June 1838
526 York Herald, 19 April 1834
527 York Herald, 3 September 1831
528 Yorkshire Gazette, 3 September 1831
529 Leeds Intelligencer, 27 September 1832
530 Sheffield Independent, 28 September 1833
531 Leeds Times, 24 July 1858
532 Hall, I (1992), Cricket at Scarborough: A Social History of the Club and its Festival, pp24-25
533 Hall, pp25, 30
534 Draper, p33
535 Kilburn, J M (1948), The Scarborough

Cricket Festival, p53
536 Hall, p44
537 Draper, p33-34
538 Hall, p44
539 York Herald, 5 November 1879
540 Yorkshire Post and Leeds Intelligencer, 27 October 1886
541 Yorkshire Gazette, 7 July 1838
542 Whitby Gazette, 28 March 1863, 11 April 1863
543 Yorkshire Gazette, 13 July 1833
544 York Herald, 26 October 1839, 7 May 1842
545 York Herald, 25 May 1844
546 York Herald, 29 January 1848
547 York Herald, 25 September 1852
548 York Herald, 17 May 1862
549 Yorkshire Gazette, 19 October 1833
550 Yorkshire Gazette, 28 September 1833
551 Leeds Times, 30 August 1834, York Herald, 15 November 1845
552 York Herald, 30 May 1835
553 York Herald, 25 May 1833, Yorkshire Gazette, 1 June 1833
554 Yorkshire Gazette, 16 November 1833, 29 March 1834
555 Yorkshire Gazette, 23 May 1835
556 Yorkshire Gazette, 6 September 1834
557 York Herald, 25 October 1834, Yorkshire Gazette, 11 June 1836
558 Yorkshire Gazette, 6 May 1837, York Herald, 10 June 1837, 17 June 1837
559 Yorkshire Gazette, 7 October 1837
560 York Herald, 22 May 1847
561 York Herald, 8 December 1849
562 Sheffield Independent, 4 October 1861, 8 October 1861, Yorkshire Gazette, 4 May 1861
563 Yorkshire Gazette, 31 October 1863
564 Draper, S, pp51-52
565 York Herald, 14 September 1844
566 York Herald, 2 August 1845
567 York Herald, 5 April 1845
568 Whitby Gazette, 9 October 1869
569 York Herald, 2 August 1845
570 Drawn from Baker, R (1989), 'Iron and Willow: A History of Middlesbrough Cricket Club volume one 1855 to 1911.
571 Howarth, p13
572 Old Ebor, p228
573 Hull Packet, 20 July 1849
574 Davies, P p14
575 Griffin, E, Liberty's Dawn: A People's History of the Industrial Revolution, p55
576 Howarth, p13
577 Griffin, p 245
578 Leeds Mercury, 2 August 1879
579 Davies, P, pp14-15
580 Light R, 'Cricket's Forgotten Past: A Social and Cultural History of the Game in the West Riding of Yorkshire, 1820-1870,' pp 85-86, 100-104
581 Holmes, p91
582 'Old Ebor', pp 232-233, 235
583 Sheffield Independent, 29 April 1848
584 Russell, D (1981) 'The Pursuit of Leisure' in (eds) D.G Wright and J.A Jowitt, Victorian Bradford, City of Bradford Metropolitan Council, Libraries Division, p201
585 Thompson, FML, (1988), The Rise of Respectable Society: A Social History of Victorian Britain, 1830-1900, p276
586 Russell (1981), p201
587 Thompson, p275
588 Bradford Observer, 16 September 1852, 30 September 1852
589 Bradford Observer, 24 June 1858
590 Leeds Mercury, 10 June 1862
591 Leeds Mercury, 26 August 1862
592 Huddersfield Chronicle, 7 October 1871
593 Russell (1981), p201
594 Leeds Times, 9 August 1879
595 Russell (1981), p202
596 Leeds Times, 14 September 1867
597 Morning Post quoted in Huddersfield Chronicle, 24 May 1876
598 West, p1
599 Leeds Times, 16 September 1876
600 Holmes, pp104-105
601 York Herald, 24 January 1893
602 Sheffield Independent, 9 May 1862
603 Bradford Observer, 14 April 1869
604 Yorkshire Post and Leeds Intelligencer, 2 June 1885
605 Yorkshire Post and Leeds Intelligencer, 20 July 1885
606 Yorkshire Post and Leeds Intelligencer, 10 August 1886
607 Sandiford, pp128-143
608 Howarth, p14
609 Sheffield Independent, 8 June 1844
610 Howarth, p30
611 Heywood, F, M and B (2004), Cloth Caps and Cricket Crazy, p 48
612 Leeds Times, 2 June 1888
613 Bradford Observer, 2 September 1841
614 Leeds Mercury, 8 July 1863
615 Sandiford, p73
616 Bell's Life, 18 October 1840
617 Leeds Intelligencer, 21 June 1845

618 Huddersfield Chronicle, 29 May 1858
619 Sheffield Independent, 13 September 1856
620 Leeds Mercury, 14 August 1841
621 Bell's Life, 15 August 1841
622 Bradford Observer, 19 August 1841
623 Bradford Observer, 11 November 1841
624 Sheffield Independent, 16 October 1847
625 York Herald, 30 June 1866
626 York Herald, 23 September 1865
627 Yorkshire Post and Leeds Intelligencer, 27 June 1887
628 Sandiford, p141
629 Thomas, P, Yorkshire Cricketers 1839-1939, pp 57, 62
630 Thomas, pp 5,7, 67
631 Leeds Times, 20 June 1833
632 Sheffield Independent, 16 October 1847, Leeds Times, 17 July 1847
633 Sheffield Independent, 7 August 1847,
634 Yorkshire Post and Leeds Intelligencer, 27 June 1887
635 Holmes, pp23-24
636 Howarth, p39
637 Scores taken from the Leeds Times for these years.
638 Howarth, pp40-41
639 Yorkshire Post and Leeds Intelligencer, 18 April 1887
640 Yorkshire Post and Leeds Intelligencer, 23 August 1886
641 York Herald, 17 June 1837
642 Sheffield Independent, 31 August 1844
643 Leeds Mercury, 31 August 1844
644 Bradford Observer, 12 June 1845
645 Sheffield Independent, 16 June 1855
646 Sheffield Independent, 30 June 1855
647 Sheffield Independent, 5 July 1856
648 Sheffield Independent, 20 June 1857
649 Leeds Intelligencer, 17 October 1857
650 York Herald, 30 August 1828
651 Yorkshire Gazette, 20 July 1833
652 York Herald, 30 August 1845
653 Leeds Times, 10 September 1864
654 Sheffield Independent, 10 August 1833
655 Leeds Times, 10 September 1864
656 Sheffield Independent, 7 October 1843
657 Bradford Observer, 3 August 1848
658 Sheffield Independent, 22 May 1841
659 Bradford Observer, 30 September 1841
660 Leeds Times, 14 November 1857, 2 November 1861
661 Leeds Times, 13 September 1873
662 Sheffield Independent, 27 July 1833
663 Leeds Intelligencer, 17 October 1857
664 Leeds Times, 28 September 1861, 5 October 1861
665 Leeds Mercury, 23 September 1862
666 'Old Ebor', pp 18-19
667 Sheffield Independent, 5 October 1861
668 Bradford Observer, 26 February 1863
669 Huddersfield Chronicle, 6 October 1866
670 'Old Ebor', p 19
671 Leeds Times, 17 October 1857, 24 October 1857
672 Leeds Times, 6 September 1873
673 Huddersfield Chronicle, 6 September 1873
674 Huddersfield Chronicle, 6 September 1873
675 Huddersfield Chronicle, 1 July 1876
676 Howarth, p29
677 West (1988), p21
678 Sheffield Independent, 11 September 1858
679 Leeds Times, 23 September 1848
680 York Herald, 13 August 1853
681 Leeds Times, 19 September 1857
682 West, p27
683 Quoted in West, p30
684 York Herald, 14 August 1847
685 York Herald, 2 October 1858
686 Sheffield Independent, 29 July 1854
687 Sheffield Independent, 22 September 1855
688 Leeds Mercury, 12 August 1863
689 Sheffield Independent, 3 May 1856
690 Scowcroft, p15
691 Sheffield Independent, 29 October 1862
692 Leeds Times, 20 September 1862
693 Lonsdale in Richtering (2006), p5-6
694 Sheffield Independent, 12 May 1863, Leeds Mercury, 5 May 1863
695 York Herald, 22 July 1854
696 York Herald, 11 August 1855, 13 September 1856
697 Leeds Times, 3 July 1858
698 Leeds Times, 10 July 1858
699 Leeds Times, 29 August 1863
700 Leeds Times, 2 June 1866
701 Leeds Times, 19 September 1868
702 Howarth, p64
703 Yorkshire Post and Leeds Intelligencer, 24 August 1885
704 Leeds Times, 1 May 1869
705 Huddersfield Chronicle, 17 June 1871
706 Huddersfield Chronicle, 22 July 1873, Scowcroft, p17
707 Leeds Times, 10 June 1876
708 Thomas, p140

709 Huddersfield Daily Examiner, 11 July 1871, 12 July 1871
710 Driffield Times, 27 September 1879
711 Leeds Times, 22 November 1873
712 Yorkshire Post and Leeds Intelligencer, 7 October 1884
713 Holmes, p175
714 Leeds Times, 17 January 1880
715 Leeds Times, 6 March 1880
716 Leeds Times, 9 October 1880
717 Yorkshire Post and Leeds Intelligencer, 9 September 1882
718 Leeds Times, 13 October 1883
719 Beachill, J (1986), See the Conquering Hero Comes, p12
720 Beachill, p16
721 Leeds Times, 17 July 1880
722 Yorkshire Post and Leeds Intelligencer, 6 June 1882
723 Yorkshire Post and Leeds Intelligencer, 7 October 1882, Butler, p4
724 Butler, pp5-8
725 Yorkshire Post and Leeds Intelligencer, 22 August 1887
726 Leeds Times, 10 November 1883
727 Yorkshire Post and Leeds Intelligencer, 23 January 1885
728 Yorkshire Post and Leeds Intelligencer, 11 March 1885
729 Yorkshire Post and Leeds Intelligencer, 12 January 1886
730 Holmes, p175
731 Yorkshire Post and Leeds Intelligencer, 14 April 1885, 17 April 1885
732 Drakes Huddersfield Cricket League Centenary 1891-1991 Official Souvenir, pp 7, 13-14
733 Leeds Mercury, 17 April 1893
734 Leeds Times, 29 April 1893
735 Yorkshire Evening Post, 18 February 1893
736 Leeds Times, 4 March 1893
737 Yorkshire Evening Post, 11 May 1893
738 Leeds Mercury, 7 April 1893, 17 April 1893
739 Yorkshire Evening Post, 28 April 1893
740 Leeds Mercury, 8 May 1893
741 Baker (1992), 'p11
742 Sheffield Daily Telegraph, 8 May 1893
743 Leeds Mercury, 13 May 1893
744 Drakes Huddersfield Cricket League, Centenary 1891-1991, Official Souvenir, p13-14
745 Sheffield Independent, 26 April 1893
746 Hull Daily Mail, 5 May 1893
747 Yorkshire Evening Post, 15 May 1893
748 Yorkshire Evening Post, 8 March 1893, Leeds Mercury, 1 July 1893
749 Holmes, p174
750 Sandiford, p53
751 Sheffield Independent, 29 January 1831
752 Howarth, p45
753 Davies, p40-53
754 Leeds Times, 10 November 1838
755 Leeds Times, 14 October 1854
756 Leeds Times, 25 April 1857
757 Yorkshire Gazette, 10 May 1862
758 Leeds Mercury, 21 September 1811
759 Howarth, p21
760 Yorkshire Gazette, 15 January 1831
761 Sheffield Independent, 21 January 1863
762 Leeds Times, 18 October 1856
763 Sheffield Independent, 23 September 1854
764 Leeds Times, 22 August 1857
765 Beverley Guardian, 8 March 1862, quoted in Teal, R p11
766 Davies, p41
767 Huddersfield Chronicle, 22 November 1851
768 Leeds Times, 18 November 1871
769 Bradford Observer, 5 December 1844, 12 December 1844
770 Huddersfield Chronicle, 8 August 1874
771 Leeds Times, 4 August 1877
772 Leeds Times, 21 October 1871
773 Leeds Times, 11 November 1871
774 Leeds Times, 13 October 1883, 10 November 1883
775 York Herald, 4 August 1849
776 Leeds Times, 21 June 1873
777 Sheffield Daily Telegraph, 25 April 1887
778 Leeds Times, 11 January 1879
779 Huddersfield Daily Examiner, 1 November 1871
780 Leeds Times, 1 October 1870
781 Butler, p14
782 Dewsbury Reporter, 6 September 1884
783 York Herald, 10 September 1859
784 Hull News, 3 November 1877
785 Moriarty, B and Cooper, J (1971), A Brief History of the Golcar Cricket and Athletic Club, p5
786 Huddersfield Daily Examiner, 31 January 1879
787 Holmes, p21
788 Hull News, 27 June 1863
789 Maude, p6
790 Lodge, H, p22
791 Baker, R (1989), p1

792 Bradford Observer, 1 August 1850
793 York Herald, 18 April 1846
794 York Herald, 26 September 1857
795 Bradford Observer, 2 July 1840
796 Huddersfield Chronicle, 5 September 1874
797 Draper, pp27, 49, Scowcroft, p6
798 York Herald, 3 October 1829
799 Yorkshire Gazette, 2 August 1834
800 York Herald, 30 September 1843, 7 October 1843
801 Sheffield Independent, 2 August 1851
802 Leeds Times, 25 June 1853
803 York Herald, 13 August 1859
804 Howarth, p23
805 Leeds Times, 3 September 1864
806 Leeds Times, 3 August 1878
807 York Herald, 10 May 1834
808 Yorkshire Gazette, 24 June 1837
809 Howarth, p57
810 'Old Ebor', p230
811 Bradford Observer, 26 April 1877
812 Bradford Observer, 18 September 1875
813 York Herald, 10 December 1853
814 York Herald, 20 November 1858
815 York Herald, 4 September 1852
816 York Herald, 10 December 1853
817 Thomas, p9
818 Huddersfield Chronicle, 12 November 1873, 11 October 1873, 22 November 1879, 13 November 1884
819 Huddersfield Chronicle, 1 February 1879
820 Huddersfield Chronicle, 24 January 1890
821 Huddersfield Chronicle, 20 November 1874
822 Baker (1989), p30
823 Heywood, pp43, 74
824 Huddersfield Chronicle, 24 November 1874
825 York Herald, 8 December 1849
826 Hull Packet, 19 July 1850, Bradford Cricketers' Journal, 25 April 1874
827 Hull Packet, 29 April 1853
828 Bradford Observer, 18 September 1875
829 Huddersfield Daily Examiner,15 July 1878
830 Scowcroft, pp 9, 17
831 Heywood, p20
832 Beverley Guardian, 15 March 1862
833 Baker (1989), p18
834 York Herald, 21 May 1836, Yorkshire Gazette, 11 June 1836
835 York Herald, 13 June 1863
836 Ulyatt, M (1973), Hull Railway Clerks Cricket Club Centenary 1873-1973, p11
837 Huddersfield Chronicle, 11 October 1873
838 Huddersfield Daily Examiner, 14 November 1877
839 Huddersfield Daily Examiner, 19 October 1874
840 Huddersfield Chronicle, 19 November 1877
841 York Herald, 13 December 1851,
842 York Herald, 27 December 1851,
843 York Herald, 24 January 1852, 6 March 1852
844 Howarth, p74
845 Baker (1989), pp49-55
846 Leeds Times, 5 October 1872
847 Leeds Times, 28 November 1874
848 York Herald, 10 December 1853
849 York Herald, 6 December 1856
850 Leeds Mercury, 14 September 1850
851 York Herald, 29 May 1858
852 Baker (1989), pp30, 45
853 Howarth, p46
854 Morning Post, 20 April 1900, Hampshire Advertiser, 21 April 1900
855 Hall, p79
856 Hall, p80
857 Sheffield Daily Telegraph, 8 September 1869
858 Yorkshire Post and Leeds Intelligencer, 13 March 1882
859 Gent, D (2010), 'Aristocratic Whig Politics in Early-Victorian Yorkshire: Lord Morpeth and his World', PhD thesis, University of York
860 Leeds Mercury, 16 February 1850
861 Sheffield Independent, 4 September 1858
862 Leeds Times, 2 October 1869
863 Davies, pp44-48
864 O'Keefe, D (2007), Start of Play: The Foundation and Progress of Illingworth St Mary's Cricket Club c1884-c1920, A Social History, pp10-20
865 Holt, R (1988), 'Football and the Urban Way of Life in Nineteenth-Century Britain' in Pleasure, Profit and Proselytism: British Culture and Sport at Home and Abroad 1700-1914, p76
866 Hull Packet, 16 August 1850
867 Bradford Observer, 28 September 1865
868 Huddersfield Chronicle, 29 December 1866
869 Thomas, p169, Holmes, p37
870 Thomas, p40
871 Thomas, p166
872 Sheffield Independent, 13 May 1848
873 Hull Packet, 2 August 1850

874 Lodge, H, pp2-3, Old Ebor, pp228-229
875 Huddersfield Chronicle, 30 October 1852, 4 June 1864
876 Yorkshire Gazette, 27 September 1828
877 Yorkshire Gazette, 7 June 1828
878 Sheffield Independent, 19 June 1830
879 Sheffield Independent, 25 June 1831
880 Sheffield Independent, 4 August 1832
881 'Old Ebor', p231
882 Scowcroft, p7
883 York Herald, 12 August 1843
884 York Herald, 4 May 1816
885 York Herald, 3 August 1844
886 York Herald, 6 September 1845
887 Yorkshire Gazette, 13 November 1830
888 York Herald,16 June 1849
889 York Herald, 25 August 1855
890 Leeds Times, 4 July 1857
891 Yorkshire Gazette, 5 July 1834
892 Leeds Times, 30 July 1859
893 Sheffield Independent, 22 May 1830
894 York Herald, 7 July 1849
895 Sheffield Independent, 28 August 1852, 4 September 1852
896 York Herald, 21 August 1847
897 Yorkshire Gazette, 17 May 1834, 7 June 1834
898 York Herald, 6 June 1846
899 Leeds Times, 22 March 1862
900 York Herald, 2 December 1826
901 Leeds Times, 30 August 1834
902 Leeds Times, 11 October 1856
903 Leeds Times, 18 October 1856
904 Yorkshire Gazette, 23 June 1838, York Herald, 30 June 1838
905 Bell's Life, 13 September 1840
906 Leeds Times, 29 October 1870, 5 November 1870
907 Leeds Times, 1 November 1873
908 Heywood, p166
909 Leeds Times, 14 April 1877
910 Yorkshire Post and Leeds Intelligencer, 15 June 1885, 20 June 1885, 24 July 1885, 13 August 1885, Athletic News, 30 August 1887
911 York Herald, 31 October 1846
912 Leeds Times, 15 May 1880
913 Bradford Cricketers' Journal, 9 May 1874
914 Huddersfield Chronicle, 11 October 1873
915 Huddersfield Daily Examiner, 24 June 1875
916 Huddersfield Daily Examiner, 17 August 1875
917 Sheffield Independent, 24 July 1874, 25 July 1874
918 Heywood, p98
919 Huddersfield Daily Examiner, 17 June 1871, 4 April 1874
920 Yorkshire Post and Leeds Intelligencer, 3 May 1886, 25 April 1887
921 Yorkshire Post and Leeds Intelligencer, 5 July 1886, 23 August 1886
922 Sheffield Independent, 24 April 1890
923 Hull Packet, 26 May 1848
924 Howarth, p48
925 Huddersfield Chronicle, 22 May 1879
926 Programme and Souvenir of the Grand Bazaar in aid of the Manningham Cricket Club, 25-27 February 1892
927 Leeds Mercury, 4 October 1862
928 Huddersfield Chronicle, 4 November 1865
929 Sheffield Independent, 4 June 1859
930 Yorkshire Gazette, 28 February 1863
931 York Herald, 17 May 1862
932 Cobley, F (1895), Black Hats v White Hats or Ilkley Tradesmen at the Wickets and Around the Festive Board, William Walker and Sons, Otley
933 Bradford Observer, 4 April 1844,
934 Leeds Times,3 January 1857
935 Hull News, 30 April 1870
936 Leeds Times, 31 July 1869
937 Leeds Times, 27 July 1872
938 Huddersfield Chronicle, 18 August 1873
939 Leeds Times, 12 May 1888
940 Leeds Times, 15 July 1871
941 West, p84
942 York Herald, 1 September 1827
943 York Herald, 27 August 1842
944 York Herald, 22 October 1842
945 Bradford Observer, 24 July 1856
946 Bradford Observer, 31 July 1856
947 Bradford Observer, 14 August 1856, Leeds Times, 11 October 1856
948 Leeds Times, 5 August 1854
949 Bradford Observer, 19 July 1866
950 Huddersfield Daily Examiner, 8 May 1875
951 Sheffield Independent, 29 May 1858
952 Yorkshire Gazette, 9 November 1833
953 Huddersfield Chronicle, 26 September 1868
954 Huddersfield Chronicle, 8 September 1860
955 Huddersfield Chronicle, 4 October 1862
956 Huddersfield Chronicle, 7 September 1867
957 Huddersfield Daily Examiner, 8 May 1875
958 Huddersfield Daily Examiner, 22 May 1875

959 Yorkshire Post and Leeds Intelligencer, 6 June 1882, 13 June 1882
960 Yorkshire Post and Leeds Intelligencer, 25 July 1882
961 Leeds Times, 9 September 1882
962 Yorkshire Post and Leeds Intelligencer, 6 June 1887, 20 June 1887
963 Yorkshire Post and Leeds Intelligencer, 27 May 1884
964 Baker (1992), p11
965 Sheffield Daily Telegraph, 14 January 1885
966 Huddersfield Chronicle, 8 November 1886
967 Athletic News, 20 April 1886, p1
968 Hull Packet, 10 July 1832
969 Hull Packet, 16 August 1844
970 Bradford Observer, 1 June 1843
971 York Herald, 11 April 1846
972 York Herald, 6 December 1856
973 York Herald, 3 January 1852, 14 August 1852
974 York Gazette, 23 June 1860
975 York Herald, 6 March 1852
976 York Herald, 20 November 1858
977 Sheffield Independent, 21 November 1857
978 Sheffield Independent, 20 November 1858
979 Sheffield Independent, 15 April 1848
980 York Herald, 14 August 1852
981 Teal, p13
982 Huddersfield Chronicle, 4 May 1850
983 Davies, p69
984 Leeds Times, 25 November 1871 for example
985 Leeds Times, 14 November 1874
986 Huddersfield Chronicle, 5 February 1870
987 Leeds Times, 26 November 1870
988 Leeds Times, 11 May 1872
989 Leeds Times, 7 June 1873
990 Leeds Times, 18 October 1873
991 Leeds Times, 13 November 1875
992 Leeds Times, 13 July 1872
993 Leeds Times, 3 May 1873
994 Leeds Times, 2 November 1872
995 Huddersfield Chronicle, 1 January 1876
996 Leeds Times, 29 November 1873
997 Hull Packet, 21 February 1868, 20 February 1874
998 Huddersfield Daily Examiner, 16 October 1871
999 Bradford Observer, 8 September 1875
1000 Huddersfield Chronicle, 21 November 1877
1001 Huddersfield Chronicle, 24 October 1874
1002 Huddersfield Daily Examiner, 7 June1880
1003 Huddersfield Daily Examiner, 4 April 1874
1004 Hull Packet, 2 August 1878
1005 Leeds Mercury, 26 December 1870, Dewsbury Reporter, 24 December 1870
1006 Hull News, 21 February 1874, 21 March 1874, 7 November 1874
1007 Huddersfield Daily Examiner, 22 January 1872
1008 Yorkshire Post and Leeds Intelligencer, 15 July 1884
1009 Howarth, p17
1010 Teal, p11
1011 Howarth, p46
1012 Teal, p13
1013 Sheffield Independent, 9 May 1857
1014 Huddersfield Chronicle, 9 November 1874
1015 Huddersfield Chronicle, 21 November 1877, 24 October 1874, Huddersfield Daily Examiner, 19 October 1874
1016 Huddersfield Chronicle, 8 October 1873
1017 Huddersfield Chronicle, 14 October 1871
1018 Bradford Observer, 20 May 1869
1019 Huddersfield Chronicle, 8 October 1873
1020 Howarth, pp98-99
1021 Yorkshire Post and Leeds Intelligencer, 3 April 1867
1022 Huddersfield Chronicle, 20 November 1874
1023 Yorkshire Post and Leeds Intelligencer, 16 April 1886
1024 Teal, p19
1025 Huddersfield Chronicle, 12 November 1873
1026 Huddersfield Chronicle, 14 November 1877
1027 Leeds Times, 29 November 1879
1028 Hull News, 11 May 1878
1029 Yorkshire Post and Leeds Intelligencer, 27 January 1885
1030 Huddersfield Chronicle, 22 October 1870
1031 Huddersfield Daily Examiner, 6 November 1878
1032 Huddersfield Chronicle, 31 January 1879,
1033 Huddersfield Chronicle, 13 November 1880, 25 January 1881
1034 Huddersfield Chronicle, 29 January 1881

1035 Dewsbury Reporter, 15 November 1873
1036 Huddersfield Chronicle, 12 December 1876
1037 Huddersfield Chronicle, 17 November 1877, 20 November 1880
1038 Huddersfield Chronicle, 8 December 1883
1039 Huddersfield Chronicle, 3 February 1885
1040 Leeds Times, 18 March 1882
1041 Huddersfield Chronicle, 18 November 1876
1042 Huddersfield Chroncile, 21 November 1867
1043 Huddersfield Chronicle, 10 August 1867
1044 Huddersfield Chronicle, 11 February 1871
1045 Leeds Times, 23 February 1884
1046 Yorkshire Post and Leeds Intelligencer, 23 April 1886, 26 April 1886
1047 Cobley, pp17-23
1048 Dewsbury Reporter, 16 November 1872
1049 Dewsbury Reporter, 15 November 1873
1050 Thompson, pp 277-284
1051 Hull News, 30 April 1870
1052 Huddersfield Chronicle, 24 October 1874
1053 Huddersfield Chronicle, 5 November 1877
1054 Butler, p10
1055 Yorkshire County Cricket Book Yearbook, 2014, pp361-382
1056 Sissons, R (1988), The Players: A Social History of the Professional Cricketer, The Kingswood Press, London, pp5-6
1057 Sissons, p10
1058 Yorkshire Post and Leeds Intelligencer, 1 April 1882
1059 Howarth, p42
1060 Hull Daily Mail, 21 June 1893
1061 Holmes, pp126-127
1062 Thomas, pp 33, 67
1063 Teal, p13
1064 Bradford Observer, 4 July 1867
1065 Huddersfield Chronicle, 26 November 1864
1066 Huddersfield Chronicle, 13 October 1876
1067 Huddersfield Chronicle, 12 November 1873
1068 Lonsdale, J (1989), 'John Briggs – English Cricket's Youngest Professional?' in The Cricket Statistician Spring, p11
1069 Howarth, p42
1070 Yorkshire Post and Leeds Intelligencer, 19 September 1882
1071 Yorkshire Post and Leeds Intelligencer, 14 September 1885
1072 'Old Ebor', p16
1073 Huddersfield Chronicle, 2 October 1869
1074 Huddersfield Chronicle, 11 October 1873
1075 Huddersfield Chronicle, 8 October 1873
1076 Sheffield Independent, quoted in Leeds Times, 22 July 1882
1077 Leeds Mercury, 28 August 1883
1078 Yorkshire CCC Minute Book, 7 February 1878, 16 April 1878
1079 Sheffield Independent, 2 September 1848
1080 Leeds Times, 16 September 1876
1081 Leeds Times, 24 November 1877
1082 Hull News, 19 October 1878
1083 Yorkshire Post and Leeds Intelligencer, 5 August 1882
1084 Sheffield Independent, 29 April 1879, Huddersfield Chronicle, 8 April 1879
1085 'Old Ebor', p16
1086 Bell's Life in London, 28 April 1861
1087 Thomas, p190
1088 Thomas, p186; Huddersfield Chronicle, 9 April 1870
1089 Sheffield Independent, 9 November 1877
1090 Thomas, p102
1091 Huddersfield Chronicle, 26 July 1876
1092 Leeds Times, 18 September 1869
1093 Old Ebor, p235
1094 Huddersfield Chronicle, 20 November 1874
1095 'Old Ebor', pp39-40
1096 'Old Ebor', pp 75-76
1097 West, p46
1098 Sheffield Daily Telegraph, 2 September 1870, Old Ebor, p6
1099 Holmes, p171, Yorkshire CCC Minute Book, 23 February 1877
1100 Sheffield Independent, 23 January 1877
1101 Yorkshire Post and Leeds Intelligencer, 16 May 1887
1102 Sheffield Independent, 8 May 1877, Huddersfield Chronicle, 10 May 1877, 28 March 1879
1103 Yorkshire Post and Leeds Intelligencer, 18 July 1887
1104 Sheffield Independent,15 May 1888
1105 Leeds Times, 9 June 1888
1106 Sheffield Daily Telegraph, 27 May 1889
1107 Sheffield Independent, 18 June 1891
1108 York Herald, 28 January 1893

1109 Yorkshire County Cricket Club Yearbook 1894, pp66-73
1110 Athletic News, 5 January 1881
1111 Thomas, p74
1112 Sheffield Independent, 11 June 1881
1113 Sheffield Daily Telegraph, 24 May 1881
1114 York Herald, 11 June 1881,Sheffield Daily Telegraph, 26 August 1881, York Herald, 2 September 1882, 9 September 1882
1115 Woodhouse (1992), p75
1116 Sheffield Daily Telegraph, 26 June 1883
1117 Sheffield Daily Telegraph, 28 May 1878
1118 Woodhouse (1992), p211
1119 Baker (1989), pp4,12
1120 Bradford Observer, 16 July 1863
1121 Leeds Times, 18 July 1863
1122 Bradford Observer, 27 June 1867
1123 Yorkshire County Cricket Club Yearbook 1992, p5
1124 Thomas, p99
1125 Thomas, p54
1126 Bell's Life, 18 June 1864
1127 Thomas, p154
1128 Leeds Times, 17 November 1883, Yorkshire Post and Leeds Intelligencer, 1 February 1884
1129 Yorkshire CCC Minute Book, 12 September 1872
1130 Sissons, pp85-86
1131 Bradford Observer, 31 March 1881
1132 Yorkshire Post and Leeds Intelligencer, 11 July 1882
1133 Sheffield Independent, 28 April 1884
1134 Yorkshire Post and Leeds Intelligencer, 15 September 1884,16 September 1884
1135 Yorkshire Post and Leeds Intelligencer, 29 April 1887
1136 Yorkshire Post and Leeds Intelligencer, 2 May 1887
1137 Yorkshire Post and Leeds Intelligencer, 28 April 1890, Northern Echo, 7 May 1890
1138 Yorkshire Evening Post, 24 August 1893
1139 London Life, 1863, p239
1140 Yorkshire CCC Minute Book, 21 April 1871, 26 May 1871
1141 Yorkshire CCC Minute Book, 7 February 1878
1142 Sheffield Independent, 26 March 1883
1143 Yorkshire Post and Leeds Intelligencer, 22 April, 1884, 3 June 1884
1144 Sissions, p99, Yorkshire CCC Minute Book, 21 August 1877
1145 Sissons, p100
1146 Sissons, p100, 'Old Ebor', p8
1147 'Old Ebor', 22
1148 'Old Ebor', pp55-56
1149 Yorkshire CCC Minute Book, 17 April 1862
1150 Yorkshire CCC Minute Book, 21 May 1862
1151 Yorkshire CCC Minute Book, 12 May 1863
1152 Yorkshire CCC Minute Book, 14 July 1863
1153 Huddersfield Chronicle, 8 June 1872
1154 Sheffield Independent, 17 August 1871
1155 Sheffield Independent, 26 June 1878, 13 August 1879
1156 Huddersfield Chronicle, 11 November 1882
1157 Yorkshire CCC Minute Book, 19 June 1863
1158 Yorkshire CCC Minute Book, 27 July 1864
1159 Yorkshire CCC Minute Book, 29 June 1876
1160 Sissons, p102
1161 Leeds Times, 14 August 1869
1162 Leeds Times, 26 August 1871
1163 'Old Ebor', p12
1164 Leeds Times, 23 September 1876
1165 Leeds Times, 24 September 1881
1166 Sissons, p117
1167 'Old Ebor', 'Interview with Charlie Ullathorne, reprinted in The Cricket Statistician, Summer 2014, p9
1168 'Old Ebor', Interview with Charlie Ullathorne, p20
1169 Yorkshire Evening Post, 22 June 1898, Hull Daily Mail, 23 August, 31 August, 12 September 1898
1170 Lonsdale, J (1983), Charles Edward Ullathorne in The Cricket Statistician, Issue 42, June p5
1171 Correspondence with the author from Graham Ullathorne, 22 November 1983
1172 Sheffield Independent, 23 November 1867, 10 January 1868
1173 Leeds Times, 12 February 1870, Huddersfield Chronicle, 12 February 1870, 19 March 1870, 16 April 1870
1174 Thomas P, p106
1175 Yorkshire Post and Leeds Intelligencer, 13 March 1884, 29 March 1884
1176 Yorkshire Post and Leeds Intelligencer, 17 April 1886
1177 Sheffield Daily Telegraph, 26 August 1875

1178 Sheffield DailyTelegraph, 2 June 1890
1179 London Society, abridged in Leeds Times, 7 October 1876
1180 Sheffield Independent, 9 June 1879
1181 Yorkshire Post and Leeds Intelligencer, 25 August 1880
1182 Leeds Times, 28 August 1880
1183 Yorkshire Post and Leeds Intelligencer, 28 September 1882, 30 September 1882
1184 Thomas, p78
1185 Hawke, Lord, Recollections and Reminiscences, pp79-80
1186 Yorkshire Post and Leeds Intelligencer, 8 January 1890, Holmes, p63
1187 Yorkshire Evening Post, 19 January 1893
1188 'Old Ebor', p 8
1189 'Old Ebor', p34
1190 Sissons, p115
1191 Scores and Biographies Vol II, pp221, 224, 225, 231
1192 Sheffield Independent, 10 August 1833
1193 Yorkshire Gazette, 3 September 1836
1194 Bradford Observer, 3 May 1866
1195 'Old Ebor', pp 7-8, 21-22
1196 Sporting Life, 25 May 1861
1197 Yorkshire Post and Leeds Intelligencer, 22 August 1882
1198 Sheffield Daily Telegraph, 29 July, 30 July 1887
1199 Leeds Times, 30 August 1834
1200 York Herald, 2 October 1858, Thomas p93, Pope pp134-138
1201 Sheffield Independent, 6 August 1868, Huddersfield Chronicle, 8 August 1868
1202 Sheffield Independent, 4 September 1830
1203 Sheffield Independent, 11 September 1830, 30 April 1831, 14 May 1831
1204 Sheffield Independent, 16 July 1831, 23 July 1831
1205 Sheffield Independent, 29 April 1854
1206 York Herald, 9 April 1859, Leeds Mercury, 24 June 1882
1207 York Herald, 12 January 1850, 3 August 1850
1208 York Herald, 5 February 1859
1209 York Herald, 2 April 1859
1210 Yorkshire Post and Leeds Intelligencer, 2 March 1878
1211 Sheffield Daily Telegraph, 25 September 1883
1212 Leeds Mercury, 1 July 1904,
1213 See Thomas, pp57-58
1214 Leeds Times, 23 September 1876
1215 Sheffield Independent,15 November 1879
1216 Leeds Times, 8 November 1879
1217 Sheffield Independent, 4 July 1884
1218 Thomas, p143
1219 Thomas, p146
1220 York Herald, 29 June 1878, Yorkshire CCC Minute Book, 4 July 1878
1221 Sheffield Independent, 12 August 1867, Leeds Times, 5 June 1869
1222 Sheffield Daily Telegraph, 3 February 1885, York Herald, 9 February 1885
1223 Thomas, p15, West, G Derek (1992), Six More Day of Grace pp152-155
1224 'Old Ebor', p79
1225 'Old Ebor', interview with Charlie Ullathorne, reprinted in The Cricket Statistician, Summer 2014, p18
1226 Sandford, p99-102
1227 Thomas, p 83
1228 Leeds Times, 31 August 1867
1229 Bradford Observer, 4 April 1867
1230 Leeds Times, 13 July 1867, 24 August 1867, 31 August 1867, Sheffield Independent, 28 November 1867
1231 Bradford Observer, 6 October 1864
1232 Leeds Times, 7 October 1882
1233 Yorkshire CCC Minute Book, 17 December 1869
1234 Sheffield Independent, 8 June 1850
1235 Leeds Times, 31 January 1857
1236 York Herald, 2 October 1858, 16 October 1858, Yorkshire Evening Post, 8 April 1899
1237 York Herald, 5 February 1859
1238 Sheffield Independent, 5 February 1859
1239 Bradford Observer, 6 December 1866
1240 Sheffield Iris, 13 December 1836
1241 Leeds Times, 22 May 1869
1242 Leeds Times, 10 September 1870
1243 Huddersfield Chronicle, 25 August 1866
1244 'Old Ebor', p 13, Yorkshire Post and Leeds Intelligencer, 10 May 1895, Northern Echo, 19 June 1895
1245 Yorkshire CCC Minute Book, 24 September 1869
1246 Huddersfield Chronicle, 5 September 1873
1247 Yorkshire CCC Minute Book, 19 March 1873, 23 February 1877
1248 Yorkshire CCC Minute Book, 2 November 1876, Leeds Times, 3 August 1878
1249 Leeds Times, 17 May 1879
1250 Sheffield Daily Telegraph, 2 May 1887,

Sheffield Independent, 7 July 1887, 23 May 1888
1251 Yorkshire Post and Leeds Intelligencer, 3 July 1890
1252 Yorkshire Post and Leeds Intelligencer, 11 July 1890
1253 Yorkshire CCC Yearbook 1909, p116
1254 Thomas, pp 67,73, 76
1255 Thomas, p146
1256 Thomas, p210
1257 'Old Ebor', pp35-36
1258 'Old Ebor' p34
1259 Thomas, p39
1260 Pope, pp 114,117, 122
1261 Thomas, p58, Pope, pp241-244
1262 Thomas, p7
1263 Batley Reporter, 19 November 1915
1264 Holmes, pp4-5
1265 Thomas, p77, Holmes, p5
1266 Sandiford, p80
1267 Holt, R (2006), 'The Amateur Body and the Middle-Class Man: Work, Health and Style in Victorian Britain' in Sport in History, Volume 26, Number 3, December, pp352-369
1268 Sandiford, p83
1269 Sheffield Independent, 14 May 1879
1270 Sheffield Independent, 12 September 1887
1271 Yorkshire County Cricket Club Yearbook 2014, pp361-382
1272 Thomas, pp 4,110
1273 Thomas, p199
1274 Yorkshire Post and Leeds Intelligencer, 1 July 1884
1275 Yorkshire Post and Leeds Intelligencer, 13 March 1882
1276 Yorkshire Post and Leeds Intelligencer, 23 May 1882
1277 Yorkshire Post and Leeds Intelligencer, 4 July 1882, 15 August 1882
1278 Yorkshire Post, quoted in Huddersfield Chronicle, 4 September 1876
1279 Yorkshire Post and Leeds Intelligencer, 22 July 1884
1280 Sheffield Daily Telegraph, 20 August 1881
1281 Yorkshire Post and Leeds Intelligencer, 18 April 1882
1282 Leeds Times, 19 April 1884
1283 Yorkshire Post and Leeds Intelligencer, 7 April 1891
1284 Yorkshire Post and Leeds Intelligencer, 20 August 1890, Huddersfield Chronicle, 15 August 1890, Sheffield Daily Telegraph, 15 August 1890, 20 August 1890
1285 Yorkshire Post and Leeds Intelligencer, 28 August 1882
1286 Sheffield Independent, 15 July 1882
1287 Yorkshire Post and Leeds Intelligencer, 25 July 1893
1288 Sheffield Daily Telegraph, 12 August 1887, 22 August 1887
1289 Thomas, p62
1290 Yorkshire Post and Leeds Intelligencer, 17June 1882
1291 Yorkshire Post and Leeds Intelligencer, 2 July 1889
1292 Lonsdale, J (1985), 'When the Australians came to Scarborough...Joe Frank and Spofforth's Fingers' in The White Rose, November, pp23-24; Thomas, pp 61-62
1293 Vamplew, W (1988), Pay Up and play the game: Professional sport in Britain, 1875-1914, p58
1294 Collins, T (2013), Sport in Capitalist Society, p50
1295 Sheffield Independent, 28 May 1825
1296 York Herald, 30 September 1843
1297 Bradford Observer, 29 July 1841, 5 August 1841
1298 Bradford Observer, 27 September 1855
1299 Morley Reporter, 24 September 1870
1300 Leeds Times, 4 June 1870
1301 Sheffield Independent, 31 July 1879, Sheffield Daily Telegraph, 31 July 1879,
1302 York Herald, 28 September 1850
1303 Sheffield Independent, 2 August 1851
1304 Bradford Observer, 22 June 1865, Leeds Times, 24 June 1865
1305 Leeds Intelligencer, 17 October 1857
1306 Leeds Times, 15 September 1860
1307 Huddersfield Daily Examiner, 30 May 1878
1308 Leeds Mercury, 30 June 1863
1309 Leeds Times, 5 September 1868
1310 Leeds Times, 15 August 1868
1311 Baker (1989), pp 26-27
1312 Bradford Observer, 29 June 1843
1313 Leeds Times, 8 September 1883
1314 Leeds Times, 29 September 1855
1315 Leeds Mercury, 6 December 1860
1316 Yorkshire Post and Leeds Intelligencer, 7 September 1885
1317 York Herald, 18 September 1819
1318 Yorkshire Gazette, 14 June 1828, 12 July 1828
1319 Leeds Intelligencer, 20 August 1829

1320 Sheffield Independent, 10 August 1833
1321 Bradford Observer, 15 October 1840
1322 York Herald, 6 August 1842, 22 July 1843
1323 Sheffield Independent, 6 August 1842
1324 Leeds Mercury, 7 July 1863, Leeds Intelligencer, 13 September 1862
1325 Huddersfield Chronicle, 17 August 1867
1326 Leeds Times, 5 July 1879
1327 Leeds Times, 9 September 1882, Yorkshire Post and Leeds Intelligencer, 5 September 1882
1328 Butler, pp5,8
1329 Sheffield Independent, 5 September 1846
1330 Leeds Mercury, 5 August 1863, York Herald, 11 July 1877, Leeds Times, 27 September 1873
1331 Leeds Times, 28 June 1873
1332 Sheffield Independent, 29 July 1873
1333 Huddersfield Daily Examiner, 19 July 1875, Sheffield Daily Telegraph, 19 July 1875
1334 Leeds Mercury, 11 August 1880
1335 Leeds Times, 10 June 1882, 24 June 1882, Yorkshire Post and Leeds Intelligencer, 22 June 1882
1336 Sheffield Daily Telegraph, 27 May 1890
1337 ACS First Class Cricket Matches, 1884, p80
1338 Leeds Times, 9 July 1881
1339 Yorkshire Post and Leeds Intelligencer, 5 July 1887
1340 Sheffield Independent, 10 August 1833
1341 Bradford Observer, 27 September 1855
1342 Sheffield Independent, 2 September 1848
1343 Leeds Times, 5 September 1863
1344 Sheffield Daily Telegraph, 27 May 1890
1345 Sheffield Daily Telegraph, 24 July 1889
1346 Sheffield Daily Telegraph, 23 May 1893
1347 Sheffield Independent, 2 July 1884
1348 Yorkshire Gazette, 7 June 1834
1349 Huddersfield Chronicle, 29 August 1863
1350 Sheffield Independent, 1 July 1884
1351 Manchester Guardian, quoted in Sheffield Evening Telegraph, 19 June 1893
1352 Farnsworth, p6, Leeds Intelligencer, 2 June 1825
1353 Sheffield Independent, 5 September 1846
1354 Sheffield Independent, 5 March 1864
1355 Sheffield Independent, 5 September 1846
1356 Leeds Times, 23 July 1864
1357 Yorkshire Post and Leeds Intelligencer, 18 May 1869
1358 Leeds Times, 28 August 1875
1359 Leeds Times, 6 November 1880, 18 June 1881
1360 Leeds Mercury, 8 April 1893
1361 Huddersfield Daily Examiner, 19 July 1875
1362 Sheffield Daily Telegraph, 12 June 1894
1363 Sheffield Independent, 2 October 1830, 17 August 1839
1364 Leeds Times, 3 June 1848
1365 Sheffield Independent, 30 May 1862, 23 September 1862
1366 Sheffield Independent, 6 August 1853
1367 Yorkshire CCC Minute Book, 12 June 1872, Sheffield Daily Telegraph, 18 June 1872, Sheffield Independent, 18 June 1872
1368 Huddersfield Chronicle, 14 July 1876, Yorkshire Post and Leeds Intelligencer, 10 September 1878
1369 Kilburn, p53
1370 Sheffield Independent, 20 June 1882
1371 Leeds Times, 13 June 1863, Tadcaster Post, 9 July 1863
1372 Sheffield Independent, 3 May 1845
1373 Sheffield Independent, 7 July 1884
1374 Leeds Mercury, 22 June 1833
1375 York Herald, 24 August 1833
1376 Bradford Observer, 13 August 1846
1377 York Herald, 12 September 1846
1378 Leeds Times, 25 August 1838
1379 Sheffield Independent, 9 August 1851
1380 Sheffield Independent, 23 August 1828
1381 Sheffield Independent, 12 October 1833
1382 Sheffield Independent, 25 September 1830
1383 Leeds Times, 16 May 1868, Sheffield Independent, 3 September 1862, Yorkshire Post and Leeds Intelligencer, 22 June 1872
1384 Sheffield Independent, 3 October 1829
1385 Sheffield Independent, 1 July 1884
1386 Howarth, p23
1387 Sheffield Independent, 1 July 1884
1388 Sheffield Daily Telegraph, 23 May 1893
1389 Leeds Times, 27 September 1856
1390 Yorkshire Post and Leeds Intelligencer, 6 September 1869
1391 York Herald, 30 June 1860
1392 Yorkshire Post and Leeds Intelligencer, 13 July 1882
1393 Sheffield Daily Telegraph, 1 June 1875

1394 'Old Ebor', Interview with Charlie Ullathorne, p12
1395 Sheffield Independent, 25 August 1832
1396 Huddersfield Chronicle, 30 June 1874, 2 July 1874
1397 Sheffield Independent, 24 September 1862
1398 Sheffield Daily Telegraph, 23 May 1893
1399 Sheffield Daily Telegraph, 23 May 1893
1400 Sheffield Independent, 20 May 1873
1401 Sheffield Telegraph, 28 August 1873
1402 Sheffield Daily Telegraph, 11 July 1876
1403 Sheffield Independent, 29 July 1876
1404 Sheffield Daily Telegraph, 7 August 1894
1405 Huddersfield Chronicle, 26 July 1876
1406 Huddersfield Daily Examiner, 24 August 1883
1407 Leeds Times, 25 September 1880
1408 Sheffield Daily Telegraph, 28 May 1890
1409 Yorkshire Post and Leeds Intelligencer, 24 July 1886
1410 Huddersfield Daily Examiner, 27 July 1875
1411 Sheffield Independent, 5 June 1862
1412 Sheffield Daily Telegraph, 27 May 1890
1413 Sheffield Independent, 1 July 1884
1414 Sheffield Daily Telegraph, 16 June 1874
1415 Sheffield Independent, 31 August 187
1416 Huddersfield Daily Examiner, 23 October 1878
1417 Leeds Times, 2 November 1878
1418 Sheffield Daily Telegraph, 23 July 1889
1419 Thomas, p229, Holmes, p35
1420 Sheffield Daily Telegraph, 23 July 1889
1421 Sheffield Daily Telegraph, 17 June 1890
1422 'Old Ebor', p33
1423 Sheffield Daily Telegraph, 18 June 1890
1424 Sheffield Daily Telegraph, 18 June 1890
1425 Yorkshire CCC Minute Book, 7 June 1864, 5 July 1864
1426 Bradford Observer, 4 September 1834
1427 Sheffield Independent, 1 July 1837
1428 Bradford Observer, 6 October 1842
1429 Bradford Observer, 6 July 1843
1430 Bradford Observer, 3 August 1843
1431 Bradford Observer, 27 August 1846
1432 Bradford Observer, 10 September 1846
1433 Thomas, pp147-148, Sheffield Independent, 27 July 1861
1434 Huddersfield Daily Examiner, 11 August 1875
1435 Sheffield Daily Telegraph, 15 June 1886
1436 Huddersfield Daily Examiner, 2 June 1875
1437 Leeds Times, 18 June 1881
1438 Leeds Intelligencer, 16 August 1832
1439 Yorkshire Post and Leeds Intelligencer, 30 October 1878
1440 Huddersfield Daily Examiner, 28 July 1874, 14 July 1876
1441 Sheffield Independent, 18 June 1884
1442 Sheffield Daily Telegraph, 16 August 1893
1443 Sheffield Daily Telegraph, 14 June 1893
1444 Thomas, p112
1445 Sheffield Independent, 4 January 1893, quoting The Cricket Field, interview with Tom Emmett
1446 Sheffield Daily Telegraph, 27 July 1876
1447 Sheffield Daily Telegraph, 17 August 1876
1448 Huddersfield Chronicle, 26 July 1876
1449 Catton, J A H (1935), 'Famous Cricket Grounds' in Bat and Ball – A New Book of Cricket, (ed) Thomas Moult
1450 Sheffield Daily Telegraph, 6 August 1889
1451 Huggins, p141
1452 Huggins, pp142-144, Brown, L (1985) Victorian News and Newspapers, Clarendon Press
1453 Mason, T, p174
1454 Brown, pp244-245
1455 Brown, p124
1456 Sheffield Independent, 7 January 1826
1457 Leeds Mercury, 19 August 1826
1458 Yorkshire Gazette, 10 May 1834
1459 eg York Herald, 16 August 1834
1460 Yorkshire Gazette, 4 October 1834
1461 Sheffield Independent, 3 September 1836
1462 Leeds Mercury, 2 September 1826
1463 Sheffield Independent, 6 September 1828, 13 September 1828
1464 For example, Bradford Observer, 9 July 1840
1465 Bradford Observer, 7 September 1848
1466 Sheffield Independent, 4 October 1828
1467 Sheffield Independent, 29 August 1829
1468 Sheffield Independent, 5 September 1846
1469 Sheffield Independent, 24 June 1848
1470 Sheffield Daily Telegraph, 4 May 1875
1471 Sheffield Daily Telegraph, 30 May 1887
1472 Sheffield Independent, 4 May 1887
1473 Sheffield Independent, 30 May 1879
1474 Huddersfield Chronicle, 27 November 1852
1475 For example, Huddersfield Chroni-

cle, 13 September 1862, 12 December 1863, 4 November 1865
1476 Huddersfield Chronicle, 27 May 1876
1477 For example, Huddersfield Chronicle, 23 April 1870, 20 November 1874
1478 Huddersfield Chronicle, 26 July 1876, 4 September 1876
1479 Leeds Times, 4 September 1869
1480 Yorkshire Post and Leeds Intelligencer, 16 May 1882, 13 June 1885
1481 Yorkshire Post and Leeds Intelligencer, 3 August 1885
1482 Yorkshire Post and Leeds Intelligencer, 6 June 1887
1483 Sheffield Independent, 10 May 1881
1484 York Herald, 21 September 1844
1485 Sheffield Independent, 28 March 1829
1486 Bradford Observer, 29 August 1839
1487 York Herald, 23 May 1829
1488 Leeds Times, 16 April 1864, 15 February 1868
1489 Leeds Times, 11 February 1865, 10 February 1866
1490 Bradford Observer, 9 March 1865
1491 Sheffield Independent, 13 August 1883
1492 Yorkshire Gazette, 1 August 1829, 8 August 1829
1493 York Herald, 7 December 1850, Leeds Times, 5 July 1856
1494 Leeds Times, 19 July 1856
1495 Yorkshire Gazette, 10 September 1836
1496 Leeds Times, 10 October 1868
1497 Leeds Intelligencer, 13 September 1827
1498 Bradford Observer, 27 July 1843
1499 Leeds Mercury, 19 August 1826
1500 York Herald, 20 October 1849, 27 October 1849
1501 Leeds Times, 4 November 1871
1502 Huddersfield Daily Examiner, 4 April 1874
1503 Leeds Times, 27 September 1879
1504 Scrowcroft, p7, Sheffield Independent, 13 October 1849
1505 Sheffield Independent, 1 December 1855, Yorkshire Gazette, 21 December 1867
1506 Sheffield Independent, 12 September 1871, Leeds Mercury, 10 September 1878, Sheffield Independent, 13 September 1879
1507 Leeds Times, 19 October 1872, 13 October 1877
1508 Leeds Times, 13 September 1879
1509 Hull Packet, 4 November 1828
1510 Sheffield Independent, 26 September 1829
1511 Sheffield Independent, 16 February 1863
1512 Leeds Times, 28 February 1863, Leeds Times, 7 March 1863
1513 Leeds Times, 21 October 1865
1514 Leeds Times, 14 September 1867
1515 See for example, Leeds Mercury, 20 May 1884 and Yorkshire Gazette, 4 August 1883
1516 Sheffield Independent, 23 July 1889, Sheffield Daily Telegraph,13 July 1886
1517 Sheffield Daily Telegraph, 4 October 1869
1518 Leeds Mercury, 26 September 1879
1519 Leeds Mercury, 23 May 1882, 20 May 1884
1520 Hull Packet, 26 April 1833
1521 York Herald, 11 May 1833, Leeds Mercury, 18 May 1833
1522 Northern Star, 19 July 1845
1523 Sheffield Independent, 21 November 1829
1524 Bradford Observer, 20 August 1868
1525 Hull Packet, 9 July 1847
1526 Bradford Observer, 10 August 1865
1527 York Herald, 6 September 1845
1528 York Herald, 21 July 1849
1529 Leeds Times, 10 July 1869
1530 Bradford Observer, 30 June 1864
1531 Huddersfield Chronicle, 5 September 1876
1532 Bradford Observer, 26 August 1841
1533 Bradford Observer, 25 September 1845
1534 Bradford Observer, 15 June 1865
1535 Sheffield Independent, 12 September 1846
1536 York Herald, 14 December 1844
1537 York Herald, 14 August 1858
1538 Leeds Times, 14 August 1858
1539 Huddersfield Chronicle, 22 April 1876
1540 York Herald, 8 April 1876
1541 Bradford Observer, 26 August 1847
1542 Bradford Observer, 10 August 1865
1543 Mason, p179
1544 Bradford Observer 29 October 1868
1545 Bradford Observer, 4 July 1867
1546 Bradford Observer, 13 August 1868
1547 Sheffield Daily Telegraph, 25 May 1875
1548 Sheffield Daily Telegraph, 10 August 1875
1549 Sheffield Daily Telegraph, 18 July 1882
1550 Sheffield Evening Telegraph, 7 September 1887, Sheffield Daily Telegraph, 28 May 1890

1551 Sheffield Daily Telegraph, 17 June 1890
1552 Sheffield Daily Telegraph, 26 December 1876, Sheffield Independent, 30 December 1876
1553 Sheffield Daily Telegraph, 25 June 1888
1554 Sheffield Daily Telegraph, 8 February 1887
1555 Yorkshire Evening Post, 23 June 1934
1556 Leeds Times, 28 February 1863, Allen, D (1987), Early Books on Cricket, p97
1557 Bradford Observer, 21 April 1874
1558 Leeds Times, 14 April 1877
1559 Leeds Times, 9 March 1878
1560 Yorkshire Post and Leeds Intelligencer, 11 March 1884, 8 April 1884
1561 Yorkshire Post and Leeds Intelligencer, 28 March 1887
1562 Yorkshire Post and Leeds Intelligencer, 28 July 1882
1563 Yorkshire Post and Leeds Intelligencer, 28 July 1886
1564 Yorkshire Post and Leeds Intelligencer, 12 May 1887
1565 Sheffield Independent, 20 January 1892
1566 Mason, p179
1567 Morley Reporter, 11 June 1870
1568 Bradford Observer, 24 June 1873
1569 Sheffield Independent, 18 June 1872
1570 Sheffield Daily Telegraph, 20 May 1878
1571 Sheffield Daily Telegraph, 2 July 1881
1572 Sheffield Daily Telegraph, 14 June 1894, 17 July 1894
1573 Yorkshire Evening Post, 26 June 1893
1574 Leeds Times, 24 July 1880, 18 August 1883
1575 Sheffield Daily Telegraph, 29 July 1889
1576 Sheffield Daily Telegraph, 28 May 1890
1577 Dixon, R and Muthesius, S (1978), Victorian Architechture, p144
1578 Collins, T (2006), Rugby's Great Split: Class, Culture and the Origins of Rugby League Football, pp14-15
1579 Light, R (2009), 'In a Yorkshire Like Way: Cricket and the Construction of Regional Identity in Nineteenth Century Yorkshire' in Sport in History, 29(3), pp500-518
1580 Holmes, p175
1581 Sissons, pp-73-74
1582 Hodgson, D, p11, Woodhouse (1989), p7
1583 Sheffield Independent, 10 August 1833
1584 Scores and Biographies, vol II, p240-1
1585 Holmes, p29
1586 Sheffield Independent, 31 August 1833
1587 Sheffield Independent, 12 July 1834
1588 Sheffield Independent, 3 September 1836
1589 Holmes, pp31-32
1590 Sheffield Independent, 26 July 1851
1591 Yorkshire Gazette, 7 October 1820,York Herald, 21 October 1820
1592 Holmes, p14
1593 Yorkshire Gazette, 14 June 1828
1594 Leeds Mercury, 15 September 1821
1595 Leeds Mercury, 28 September 1822
1596 Leeds Mercury, 5 October 1822
1597 Leeds Mercury, 12 October 1822, 19 October 1822
1598 Bradford Observer, 6 October 1842
1599 Sheffield Independent, 1 October 1842, 17 August 1844
1600 York Herald, 6 October 1855
1601 Sheffield Independent, 11 August 1832
1602 Sheffield Independent, 28 February 1829
1603 Sheffield Independent, 5 July 1851
1604 York Herald, 24 January 1852
1605 Leeds Times, 1 September 1855
1606 Yorkshire Gazette, 21 May 1825
1607 York Herald, 4 June 1825
1608 Sheffield Independent, 2 October 1830
1609 Leeds Mercury, 9 August 1851
1610 Sheffield Independent, 23 August 1828
1611 Leeds Intelligencer, 16 August 1832
1612 Leeds Intelligencer, 23 August 1832
1613 Yorkshire Gazette, 15 September 1832
1614 Leeds Mercury, 7 October 1843
1615 Sheffield Independent, 10 August 1850
1616 Sheffield Independent, 9 August 1851
1617 Caffyn, quoted in Holmes p 33
1618 Holmes, p21
1619 Sheffield Independent, 2 March 1861
1620 Holmes, p39
1621 Holmes, p39, Sheffield Public Match Fund Committee Minute Book, 7 June 1861
1622 Yorkshire CCC Minute Book, 15 July 1861
1623 Sheffield Independent, 20 July 1861
1624 Sheffield Independent, 13 July 1861
1625 Sheffield Independent, 30 November 1861
1626 Sheffield Independent, 25 January 1862
1627 Holmes, p39, Yorkshire CCC Minute Book, 4 November 1861, 21 May 1862
1628 Sheffield Independent, 3 June 1862
1629 Yorkshire CCC Minute Book, 14 June 1862, 27 June 1862, 4 July 1862
1630 Sheffield Independent, 15 November 1862

1631 Hawke p58, Woodhouse (1992), p 71
1632 Yorkshire Evening Post, 12 July 1898
1633 Holmes, p39
1634 Bradford Observer, 22 October 1863
1635 Bradford Observer, 4 September 1862
1636 Leeds Times, 29 September 1860
1637 Bradford Observer, 10 July 1862
1638 Leeds Times, 27 June 1863
1639 Holmes,pp39-40
1640 Thomas, p199, Huddersfield Chronicle, 13 September 1862
1641 Yorkshire CCC Yearbook 1963, plate
1642 Sheffield Independent, 23 April 1863
1643 Yorkshire CCC Minute Book, 28 April 1863
1644 Holmes, p41
1645 Bradford Observer, 12 February 1863, 19 February 1863
1646 Sheffield Independent, 4 April 1863
1647 Bradford Observer, 25 June 1863, Leeds Times, 27 June 1863
1648 Leeds Times, 1 August 1863
1649 Yorkshire Post and Leeds Intelligencer, 7 March 1882
1650 Bradford Observer, 23 February 1882
1651 Sheffield Independent, 28 July 1863
1652 Holmes, p45
1653 Leeds Times, 2 May 1863
1654 Leeds Times, 27 June 1863, First-Class Cricket Matches 1864-1866, p50
1655 London Evening Standard, 4 December 1863
1656 Sporting Life, 7 October 1863
1657 York Herald, 3 October 1863
1658 York Herald, 3 October 1863, Yorkshire Gazette, 31 October 1863
1659 Yorkshire CCC Minute Book, 28 October 1863
1660 Sheffield Independent, 7 November 1863, Leeds Mercury, 5 November 1863, York Herald, 7 November 1863
1661 Sheffield Independent, 5 November 1863
1662 Yorkshire Gazette, 7 November 1863
1663 York Herald, 8 October 1864, Yorkshire Gazette, 26 March 1864
1664 Yorkshire Gazette, 26 December 1863
1665 Huddersfield Chronicle, 28 November 1863
1666 Yorkshire CCC Minute Book, 4 January 1864, 15 January 1864
1667 Sporting Life, 20 January 1864
1668 Yorkshire CCC Minute Book, 1 March 1864
1669 Yorkshire Post and Leeds Intelligencer, 7 March 1882
1670 www.ygcc.co.uk
1671 Yorkshire CCC Minute Book, 5 July 1864
1672 Yorkshire CCC Minute Book, 5 April 1864, 3 May 1864
1673 Sheffield Daily Telegraph, 6 February 1864
1674 Sheffield Independent, 5 March 1864
1675 Bradford Observer, 30 June 1864
1676 Yorkshire CCC Minute Book, 10 January 1865
1677 Yorkshire CCC Minute Book, 21 December 1865
1678 Bradford Observer, 16 February 1865, 9 March 1865
1679 Bradford Observer, 30 March 1865
1680 Bradford Observer, 29 June 1865
1681 West, p103
1682 Bradford Observer, 9 March 1865
1683 Yorkshire CCC Minute Book, 21 December 1865
1684 Yorkshire CCC Minute Book, 21 December 1865
1685 West, p104
1686 Yorkshire CCC Minute Book, 21 December 1865, 3 August 1865
1687 Yorkshire CCC Minute Book, 28 June 1865, 6 July 1865, 3 August 1865
1688 Yorkshire CCC Minute Book, 21 August 1865
1689 Sheffield Daily Telegraph, 21 June 1865
1690 West, p104
1691 Minute Book, 21 December 1865
1692 West, p106
1693 Minute Book, 28 February 1866
1694 Sheffield Independent, 29 May 1866
1695 Holmes, p44
1696 West, pp108-109
1697 Bradford Observer, 30 April 1868
1698 Leeds Times, 21 March 1868
1699 Bradford Observer, 27 August 1869
1700 Huddersfield Chronicle, 27 July 1867, Bradford Observer, 18 July 1867
1701 Baker (1989), pp21-25
1702 Leeds Times, 29 February 1868
1703 Bradford Observer, 2 July 1868
1704 Huddersfield Chronicle, 1 August 1868
1705 Leeds Times, 5 June 1868
1706 Leeds Times, 12 June 1869, Draper, pp27-28, Bradford Observer, 13 July 1869
1707 Sporting Life, 25 January 1868
1708 Minute Book, 19 March 1868, First Class Cricket Matches 1868
1709 Sporting Life, 29 February 1868
1710 Sporting Life, 4 March 1868

1711 Minute Book,14 December 1875
1712 Minute Book, 18 January 1871
1713 Minute Book, 18 December 1873
1714 Minute Book, 8 December 1874
1715 Holmes, p55, Minute Book, 21 December 1876, 28 October 1877, 14 December 1877, Minute Book 1883-93
1716 Minute Book, 18 October 1864
1717 Sheffield Independent, 24 April 1909
1718 Huddersfield Daily Examiner, 4 April 1874
1719 York Herald, 6 September 1873,
1720 York Herald, 13 December 1873, Hull Packet, 12 December 1873
1721 York Herald, 13 December 1873
1722 York Herald, 3 January 1874
1723 Sheffield Daily Telegraph, 3 January 1874
1724 Yorkshire Post and Leeds Intelligencer, 10 January 1874
1725 Yorkshire Post and Leeds Intelligencer, 2 February 1874
1726 York Herald, 2 March 1874
1727 York Herald, 21 November 1874, Thomas, p22
1728 York Herald, 14 May 1875
1729 Holmes, p170
1730 www.cricketarchive.com
1731 York Herald, 3 September 1875
1732 York Herald, 18 May 1874
1733 Huddersfield Chronicle, 30 May 1874, Bradford Observer, 29 May 1874, Sheffield Independent, 29 May 1874
1734 Holmes, p171
1735 Leeds Times, 21 June 1873
1736 Leeds Times, 19 September 1874
1737 Huddersfield Chronicle, 16 September 1874
1738 York Herald, 24 September 1875
1739 Leeds Times, 8 September 1877
1740 Leeds Times, 23 February 1878
1741 Yorkshire Post and Leeds Intelligencer, 21 February 1878
1742 Leeds Times, 31 August 1878
1743 Leeds Times, 28 December 1878
1744 Leeds Times, 30 August 1879
1745 Bradford Observer, 24 June 1873
1746 Huddersfield Chronicle, 11 October 1873
1747 Huddersfield Daily Examiner, 4 April 1874
1748 Huddersfield Chronicle, 24 October 1874
1749 Old Ebor, pp237-238
1750 Huddersfield Chronicle, 29 January 1876, 1 April 1876
1751 Huddersfield Chronicle, 14 July 1876, 15 July 1876, 17 July 1876
1752 Yorkshire CCC Minute Book, 2 November 1876
1753 Huddersfield Daily Examiner, 14 November 1877
1754 Yorkshire CCC Minute Book, 11 December 1878
1755 Yorkshire CCC Minute Book, 20 December 1878
1756 Huddersfield Daily Examiner, 31 January 1879
1757 Leeds Mercury, 26 September 1879
1758 Leeds Times, 10 April 1880
1759 Yorkshire Post and Leeds Intelligencer, 10 January 1882
1760 Sheffield Independent, 26 January 1882
1761 Yorkshire Post and Leeds Intelligencer, 11 February 1882
1762 Yorkshire Post and Leeds Intelligencer, 26 January 1882
1763 Sheffield Independent, 26 January 1882
1764 Yorkshire Post and Leeds Intelligencer, 13 March 1882
1765 Yorkshire Post and Leeds Intelligencer, 13 March 1882
1766 Yorkshire Post and Leeds Intelligencer, 13 March 1882
1767 Leeds Mercury, 14 April 1882
1768 Yorkshire Post and Leeds Intelligencer, 14 April 1882, Leeds Mercury, 14 April 1882
1769 Yorkshire Post and Leeds Intelligencer, 2 May 1882
1770 Yorkshire Post and Leeds Intelligencer, 2 May 1882
1771 Yorkshire Post and Leeds Intelligencer, 27 June 1882
1772 Yorkshire Post and Leeds Intelligencer, 4 July 1882
1773 Yorkshire Post and Leeds Intelligencer, 22 August 1882
1774 Yorkshire Post and Leeds Intelligencer, 29 August 1882
1775 Yorkshire Post and Leeds Intelligencer, 12 October 1882
1776 Yorkshire Post and Leeds Intelligence, 24 October 1882
1777 Leeds Mercury, 30 December 1882
1778 Leeds Mercury, 2 April 1883
1779 Leeds Times, 7 July 1883
1780 Yorkshire Post and Leeds Intelligencer, 18 April 1884
1781 Dewsbury Reporter, 26 April 1884

1782 Dewsbury Reporter, 18 April 1885, 25 April 1885

1783 The twelve were Duncombe Park, Pickering, Kirkbymoorside, Hovingham Hall, Scarborough, Northallerton, 'Ironopolis', Whitby, Grosmont, Thirsk, Hovingham and Middlesbrough. Yorkshire Post and Leeds Intelligencer, 29 September 1884

1784 Yorkshire Post and Leeds Intelligencer, 13 October 1884

1785 Yorkshire Post and Leeds Intelligencer, 2 June 1885, 8 June 1885

1786 York Herald, 28 October 1889

1787 Leeds Mercury, 30 June 1890

1788 Woodhouse (1989), p84

1789 Yorkshire County Cricket Club Minute Book 1883-1893 (WYL2053/1/1/1/3, held at the West Yorkshire Archive Service, Morley), 10 January 1884

1790 Minute Book 1883-1893, 8 January 1885

1791 Yorkshire Post and Leeds Intelligencer, 23 January 1886

1792 Yorkshire Post and Leeds Intelligencer, 10 May 1886

1793 Yorkshire Post and Leeds Intelligencer, 25 January 1886

1794 Woodhouse (1989), p101

1795 Yorkshire Post and Leeds Intelligencer, 31 May 1886

1796 Yorkshire Post and Leeds Intelligencer, 16 August 1886, 30 August 1886

1797 Yorkshire Post and Leeds Intelligencer, 6 September 1886

1798 Yorkshire Post and Leeds Intelligencer, 9 May 1887, 11 May 1887

1799 Yorkshire Post and Leeds Intelligencer, 7 July 1887

1800 Leeds Times, 2 June 1888

1801 Leeds Times, 9 June 1888

1802 First-Class Cricket Matches 1888

1803 Yorkshire CCC Minute Book 1883-1893, 18 January 1889

1804 Holmes, p62, Woodhouse (1989), p121

1805 Leeds Times, 20 July 1889, 27 July 1889, 7 September 1889

1806 Coldham, p71

1807 Woodhouse (1989) pp107-108, Holmes, p65

1808 Holmes, p65

1809 Yorkshire Post and Leeds Intelligencer, 13 June 1887, 1 August 1887

1810 Yorkshire Evening Post, 18 December 1891

1811 Yorkshire CCC Minute Book 1883-1893, 7 January 1890, Sheffield Daily Telegraph, 8 January 1890

1812 Sheffield Daily Telegraph, 8 January 1890

1813 Sheffield Daily Telegraph, 20 January 1890

1814 Coldham, pp77-78

1815 Yorkshire CCC Minute Book 1883-1893, 2 February 1891, Sheffield Independent, 4 February 1891

1816 Huddersfield Chronicle, 27 June 1891

1817 Leeds Times, 20 June 1891

1818 Yorkshire Post and Leeds Intelligencer, 27 June 1891

1819 Yorkshire Evening Post, 8 June 1891

1820 Yorkshire Post and Leeds Intelligencer, 26 September 1891

1821 Minute Book 1883-1893, 14 January 1892

1822 Leeds Mercury, 19 November 1891

1823 Yorkshire Post and Leeds Intelligencer, 24 November 1891

1824 Sheffield Evening Telegraph, 11 December 1891

1825 Yorkshire Post and Leeds Intelligencer, 14 December 1891

1826 Yorkshire Post and Leeds Intelligencer, 24 November 1891

1827 Sheffield Evening Telegraph, 16 December 1891, Leeds Mercury, 18 April 1892

1828 Yorkshire Post and Leeds Intelligencer, 17 February 1892

1829 Leeds Mercury, 18 February 1892

1830 Leeds Mercury, 27 February 1892

1831 Woodhouse (1989), p142, Yorkshire Cricket Club Yearbook 1893, p18

1832 Leeds Mercury, 16 January 1893

1833 Sheffield Independent, 28 January 1893

1834 Sheffield Independent, 31 January 1893

1835 Sheffield Independent, 1 February 1893

1836 Sheffield Independent, 10 February 1893

1837 Sheffield Independent 1 February 1893

1838 Yorkshire County Cricket Club Yearbook 1893, pp 6,19.

1839 Yorkshire County Cricket Club Yearbook 1894, pp18-19

1840 Woodhouse (1989), p142

1841 Thomas, p78

INDEX

A page number in bold indicates an illustration